Sydney

Sally O'Brien

LONELY PLANET PUBLICATIONS
Melbourne • Oakland • London • Paris

Sydney
5th edition – January 2002
First published – November 1985

Published by
Lonely Planet Publications Pty Ltd ABN 36 005 607 983
90 Maribyrnong St, Footscray, Victoria 3011, Australia

Lonely Planet offices
Australia Locked Bag 1, Footscray, Victoria 3011
USA 150 Linden St, Oakland, CA 94607
UK 10a Spring Place, London NW5 3BH
France 1 rue du Dahomey, 75011 Paris

Photographs
Many of the images in this guide are available for licensing from
Lonely Planet Images.
email: lpi@lonelyplanet.com.au
Web site: www.lonelyplanetimages.com

Front cover photograph
Sydney's monorail zips past in Darling Harbour (Gillianne Tedder)

Sydney map section title page
Traffic passes the pedestrian walkway on the Sydney Harbour Bridge
(Gillianne Tedder)

ISBN 1 74059 062 7

Printed by The Bookmaker International Ltd
Printed in China

Although the authors and Lonely Planet try to make the information as accurate as possible, we accept no responsibility for any loss, injury or inconvenience sustained by anyone using this book.

Contents – Text

Contents – Maps

The Author

SALLY O'BRIEN

Born in Melbourne, raised in Seoul and Sydney, and almost lost in countries too numerous to mention here, Sally moved back to her home town to edit South-East Asian titles in Lonely Planet's Melbourne office. She jumped the fence in 2001 to author the 5th edition of *Sydney*. Despite loving almost everything about travelling, she still calls Australia home (just not reverse-charges).

FROM THE AUTHOR

There are many people to thank in regard to the production of this book. First, gratitude is due to Kristin Odijk for helping me as an editor and as a budding author. Others in the Fuji unit who were of great help during this book's research and production are Kim Hutchins, Mary Neighbour, Corie Waddell, Meredith Mail, Chris Love and Jane Thompson. Special thanks to Chris Thomas for coordinating the book's design and Gina Tsarouhas for coordinating the editing with such ease and professionalism. LP's Out to Eat unit were a great help with restaurant review tips and lists. In Sydney, thank you to my parents Barbara and Peter for lending me the old tank and the shack – they made things so much easier. Thanks to Helen for letting me stay with her in the Blue Mountains and for all her help. Thanks to all my old friends in Sydney and the staff at numerous offices, tourist information centres, national parks and hotels for all the help and information. Thanks to Sam Benson for tips and text relating to the Lower Hunter Valley. In Melbourne, thanks to Lara, Jodie and Matt for looking after things both vegetable and mineral.

This Book

The 1st edition of *Sydney* was written by Barbara Whiter, drawing on the Sydney section of Lonely Planet's *Australia*. The 2nd edition was thoroughly revised by Jon Murray. The 3rd edition was updated by Tom Smallman and the 4th edition was updated by Meg Mundell. This 5th edition was researched and revised by Sally O'Brien.

FROM THE PUBLISHER

This 5th edition of *Sydney* was produced in the Melbourne office. The book was edited by Gina Tsarouhas with assistance from Helen Yeates, and proofread by Lara Morcombe, Jane Thompson and Gina; Joanne Newell assisted with the index.

The mapping and design of the book were coordinated by Chris Thomas with support from Corinne Waddell, Kieran Grogan and Chris Love. Simon Bracken designed the stunning cover and Matt King commissioned the outstanding illustrations, which were done by Mick Weldon and Kate Nolan. Lonely Planet Images provided more photographs than could possibly be used. Thanks to Critical Mass for allowing us to reproduce its logo.

We salute Rachael Antony for the fantastic blurb. Thanks go to the Out to Eat team for providing restaurant advice, to Paul Clifton for invaluable assistance with the gay and lesbian entries, and to Jane Thompson, senior editor, who oversaw the editorial coordination with guidance and support throughout.

ACKNOWLEDGMENTS

Grateful acknowledgment is made for reproduction permission:
CityRail: Sydney Suburban Network Map © August 2000
State Transit: Sydney Ferries Map © 2000

THANKS
Many thanks to the travellers who used the last edition and wrote to us with helpful hints, advice and interesting anecdotes. Your names appear in the back of this book.

Foreword

ABOUT LONELY PLANET GUIDEBOOKS

The story begins with a classic travel adventure: Tony and Maureen Wheeler's 1972 journey across Europe and Asia to Australia. Useful information about the overland trail did not exist at that time, so Tony and Maureen published the first Lonely Planet guidebook to meet a growing need.

From a kitchen table, then from a tiny office in Melbourne (Australia), Lonely Planet has become the largest independent travel publisher in the world, an international company with offices in Melbourne, Oakland (USA), London (UK) and Paris (France).

Today Lonely Planet guidebooks cover the globe. There is an ever-growing list of books and there's information in a variety of forms and media. Some things haven't changed. The main aim is still to help make it possible for adventurous travellers to get out there – to explore and better understand the world.

At Lonely Planet we believe travellers can make a positive contribution to the countries they visit – if they respect their host communities and spend their money wisely. Since 1986 a percentage of the income from each book has been donated to aid projects and human rights campaigns.

Updates Lonely Planet thoroughly updates each guidebook as often as possible. This usually means there are around two years between editions, although for more unusual or more stable destinations the gap can be longer. Check the imprint page (following the colour map at the beginning of the book) for publication dates.

Between editions up-to-date information is available in two free newsletters – the paper *Planet Talk* and email *Comet* (to subscribe, contact any Lonely Planet office) – and on our Web site at www.lonelyplanet.com. The *Upgrades* section of the Web site covers a number of important and volatile destinations and is regularly updated by Lonely Planet authors. *Scoop* covers news and current affairs relevant to travellers. And, lastly, the *Thorn Tree* bulletin board and *Postcards* section of the site carry unverified, but fascinating, reports from travellers.

Correspondence The process of creating new editions begins with the letters, postcards and emails received from travellers. This correspondence often includes suggestions, criticisms and comments about the current editions. Interesting excerpts are immediately passed on via newsletters and the Web site, and everything goes to our authors to be verified when they're researching on the road. We're keen to get more feedback from organisations or individuals who represent communities visited by travellers.

Lonely Planet gathers information for everyone who's curious about the planet – and especially for those who explore it first-hand. Through guidebooks, phrasebooks, activity guides, maps, literature, newsletters, image library, TV series and Web site we act as an information exchange for a worldwide community of travellers.

Research Authors aim to gather sufficient practical information to enable travellers to make informed choices and to make the mechanics of a journey run smoothly. They also research historical and cultural background to help enrich the travel experience and allow travellers to understand and respond appropriately to cultural and environmental issues.

Authors don't stay in every hotel because that would mean spending a couple of months in each medium-sized city and, no, they don't eat at every restaurant because that would mean stretching belts beyond capacity. They do visit hotels and restaurants to check standards and prices, but feedback based on readers' direct experiences can be very helpful.

Many of our authors work undercover, others aren't so secretive. None of them accept freebies in exchange for positive write-ups. And none of our guidebooks contain any advertising.

Production Authors submit their manuscripts and maps to offices in Australia, USA, UK or France. Editors and cartographers – all experienced travellers themselves – then begin the process of assembling the pieces. When the book finally hits the shops, some things are already out of date, we start getting feedback from readers and the process begins again ...

WARNING & REQUEST

Things change – prices go up, schedules change, good places go bad and bad places go bankrupt – nothing stays the same. So, if you find things better or worse, recently opened or long since closed, please tell us and help make the next edition even more accurate and useful. We genuinely value all the feedback we receive. A well-travelled team reads and acknowledges every letter, postcard and email and ensures that every morsel of information finds its way to the appropriate authors, editors and cartographers for verification.

Everyone who writes to us will find their name listed in the next edition of the appropriate guidebook. They will also receive the latest issue of *Planet Talk*, our quarterly printed newsletter, or *Comet*, our monthly email newsletter. Subscriptions to both newsletters are free. The very best contributions will be rewarded with a free guidebook.

We may edit, reproduce and incorporate your comments in all Lonely Planet products, such as guidebooks, Web sites and digital products, so let us know if you don't want your comments reproduced or your name acknowledged.

Send all correspondence to the Lonely Planet office closest to you:

Australia: Locked Bag 1, Footscray, Victoria 3011
USA: 150 Linden St, Oakland, CA 94607
UK: 10a Spring Place, London NW5 3BH

Or email us at: talk2us@lonelyplanet.com.au

For news, views and updates see our Web site: www.lonelyplanet.com

HOW TO USE A LONELY PLANET GUIDEBOOK

The best way to use a Lonely Planet guidebook is any way you choose. At Lonely Planet we believe the most memorable travel experiences are often those that are unexpected, and the finest discoveries are those you make yourself. Guidebooks are not intended to be used as if they provide a detailed set of infallible instructions!

Contents All Lonely Planet guidebooks follow roughly the same format. The Facts about the Destination chapters or sections give background information ranging from history to weather. Facts for the Visitor gives practical information on issues like visas and health. Getting There & Away gives a brief starting point for researching travel to and from the destination. Getting Around gives an overview of the transport options when you arrive.

The peculiar demands of each destination determine how subsequent chapters are broken up, but some things remain constant. We always start with background, then proceed to sights, places to stay, places to eat, entertainment, getting there and away, and getting around information – in that order.

Heading Hierarchy Lonely Planet headings are used in a strict hierarchical structure that can be visualised as a set of Russian dolls. Each heading (and its following text) is encompassed by any preceding heading that is higher on the hierarchical ladder.

Entry Points We do not assume guidebooks will be read from beginning to end, but that people will dip into them. The traditional entry points are the list of contents and the index. In addition, however, some books have a complete list of maps and an index map illustrating map coverage.

There may also be a colour map that shows highlights. These highlights are dealt with in greater detail in the Facts for the Visitor chapter, along with planning questions and suggested itineraries. Each chapter covering a geographical region usually begins with a locator map and another list of highlights. Once you find something of interest in a list of highlights, turn to the index.

Maps Maps play a crucial role in Lonely Planet guidebooks and include a huge amount of information. A legend is printed on the back page. We seek to have complete consistency between maps and text, and to have every important place in the text captured on a map. Map key numbers usually start in the top left corner.

Although inclusion in a guidebook usually implies a recommendation we cannot list every good place. Exclusion does not necessarily imply criticism. In fact there are a number of reasons why we might exclude a place – sometimes it is simply inappropriate to encourage an influx of travellers.

Introduction

Sydney, Australia's oldest and largest settlement, on arguably the most spectacular harbour in the world, is a vibrant, alluring city of many natural attractions, bold colours, skyscrapers and yachts.

Sydneysiders tend to be casual, forthright, irreverent and sybaritic. According to outsiders, they're also addicted to mobile phones and obsessed with the price of real estate. Despite the city's fixation with waterfront properties, its corporate culture has always been balanced by the knowledge that the best things about life in Sydney – the beaches, the mountains, the surf and the much-loved harbour – are free.

The majority of Australia's immigrants come to Sydney, and the city's mixture of pragmatic egalitarianism and natural indifference has made it a beacon of pluralism. It is ironic that a settlement that began life as a British Gulag has been transformed in just over 200 years into one of the world's most tolerant and diverse societies. A potpourri of ethnic groups contributes to the city's cultural life. Chinese newspapers, Lebanese restaurants and Greek Orthodox churches are as much a part of the city as its English and Irish traditions. Evidence of the region's original inhabitants survives in the Aboriginal stencils to be found in coastal caves, and in the indigenous names of many streets and suburbs.

Sydney has come a long way from its convict beginnings, but it still has a rough and ready energy that makes it an exciting place to visit. It offers an invigorating blend of the old and the new, the raw and the refined. You can explore the historic Rocks area in the morning, then ride the monorail to reborn Darling Harbour in the afternoon. While high culture attracts some to the Opera House, gaudy nightlife attracts others to Kings Cross.

Sydney is, above all, an outdoor city rich with natural assets. There are numerous options involving action and fresh air, whether it's yacht racing on the harbour, bushwalking in Sydney Harbour National Park or the Blue Mountains, or body-surfing at an iconic Sydney beach like Bondi.

The incredible success of the 2000 Olympic Games saw the city swell with pride (and visitors) and realise that all the inconvenient building and roadworks were worth the effort. Many predicted the mother of all hangovers for post-Olympic Sydney...but then again, a large part of Sydney life involves dealing with hangovers and the aftereffects of too much partying.

Facts about Sydney

HISTORY

Australia was the last great landmass to be 'discovered' by Europeans. However, the continent of Australia had been inhabited for tens of thousands of years before the First Fleet arrived.

Aboriginal Settlement

Australian Aboriginal (which literally means 'indigenous') society has the longest continuous cultural history in the world, its origins dating to at least the last ice age. Although mystery shrouds many aspects of Australian prehistory, it is thought that the first humans probably came here across the sea from South-East Asia, more than 50,000 years ago.

Archaeological evidence suggests that descendants of these first settlers colonised the continent within a few thousand years. They were the first people in the world to make polished, edge-ground, stone tools; to cremate their dead; and to engrave and paint representations of themselves and the animals they hunted.

Aborigines were traditionally tribal people, living in extended family groups. Knowledge and skills obtained over millennia enabled them to use their environment extensively, and in a sustainable manner. An intimate knowledge of animal behaviour and plant harvesting ensured that food shortages were rare.

The simplicity of the Aborigines' technology contrasted with their sophisticated cultural life. Religion, history, law and art were integrated in complex ceremonies, which not only depicted ancestral beings who created the land and its people, but also prescribed codes of behaviour. Aborigines continue to perform traditional ceremonies in many parts of Australia.

When the British arrived at Sydney Cove in 1788 there were somewhere between 500,000 and one million Aborigines in Australia, and more than 250 regional languages.

Around what is now Sydney, there were approximately 3000 Aborigines using three main languages to communicate, encompassing several dialects and subgroups. Although there was considerable overlap, Ku-ring-gai was generally spoken on the northern shore; Dharawal along the coast south of Botany Bay; and Dharug and its dialects were spoken on the plains at the foot of the Blue Mountains.

Because Aboriginal society was based on family groups with an egalitarian political structure, a coordinated response to the European colonisers wasn't possible. Without any legal right to the lands they once lived on, Aborigines became dispossessed. Some were driven away by force, some were killed, many were shifted onto government reserves and missions, and thousands succumbed to diseases brought by Europeans. Others voluntarily left tribal lands and travelled to the fringes of settled areas to obtain new commodities such as steel and cloth, and, once there, experienced hitherto unknown drugs such as alcohol, tea, tobacco and opium. See the section on the Australian Museum in the Things to See & Do chapter for more information on Aboriginal Settlement.

European Settlement

When the American War of Independence disrupted the transportation of convicts to North America, Britain's prisons became badly overcrowded. So when Joseph Banks suggested in 1779 that New South Wales (NSW) would be a fine site for criminals, he was taken seriously. Banks had been the scientific leader of Captain James Cook's expedition that sighted Botany Bay in April 1770.

The First Fleet landed at Botany Bay in January 1788. It comprised 11 ships carrying 730 male and female convicts, 400 sailors, four companies of marines, and enough livestock and supplies for two years. It was under the command of Captain Arthur Phillip, who was to be the colony's first governor. Disappointed with the land and the water supply at Botany Bay, the fleet weighed anchor after only a few days and sailed 25km north to the harbour Cook had named Port Jackson.

The settlers established themselves at Sydney Cove, named in honour of the British home secretary at the time, Thomas Townshend, the first viscount of Sydney. From this settlement, the town of Sydney grew, clustered around what is the centre of harbour shipping to this day.

The Second Fleet arrived in 1790 with more convicts and supplies, and a year later, following the landing of the Third Fleet, Sydney's population had swelled to around 4000. The early days of the colony were tough and the threat of starvation hung over the settlement for at least 16 years.

Convicts were put to work on farms, road construction and government building projects, but Governor Phillip was convinced that the colony wouldn't progress if it relied solely on convict labour. He believed prosperity depended on attracting free settlers, to whom convicts would be assigned as labourers, and on the granting of land to officers, soldiers and worthy emancipists (convicts who had served their time).

When Governor Phillip returned to England his second in command, Francis Grose, took over. Grose tipped the balance of power further in favour of the military by granting land to officers of the New South Wales Corps.

With money, land and cheap labour at their disposal, the so-called Rum Corps made huge profits at the expense of small farmers. They began paying for labour and local products in rum. Meeting little resistance, they managed to upset, defy, outmanoeuvre and outlast three governors, including William Bligh of the *Bounty* mutiny fame.

Bligh faced a second mutiny when the Rum Corps officers rebelled and ordered his arrest. The Rum Rebellion was the final straw for the British Government, which in 1809 dispatched Lieutenant Colonel Lachlan Macquarie with his own regiment and ordered the New South Wales Corps to return to London. Having broken the stranglehold of the Rum Corps, Governor Macquarie began laying the groundwork for social reforms.

Colonial Expansion

In 1800 there were still only two small settlements in the Australian colony – Sydney

**Panorama from the Garden Palace, Sydney International Exhibition Buildings, 1879
(photograph by Charles Bayliss, 1850–97)**

Cove, and Norfolk Island in the Pacific Ocean. The vast interior of the continent was explored in the ensuing 40 years.

In 1813 the explorers Gregory Blaxland, William Wentworth and Henry Lawson, found a route across the Blue Mountains, and a road was constructed that opened the western plains of NSW to settlers.

In 1851 the discovery of large gold deposits near Bathurst, 200km west of Sydney, caused an exodus of hopeful miners from the city, and forced the government to abandon the law of ownership of gold discoveries. Instead, it introduced a compulsory digger's-licence fee of 30 shillings a month. The fee was payable whether the miner found gold or not, to ensure the country earned revenue from the incredible wealth being unearthed.

Sydney, the capital of NSW, remained of secondary size and importance to Melbourne (the capital of the southern colony, Victoria) from the 1850s, due to Victoria's massive gold rush, until the economic depression of the 1890s.

The 20th Century

Federation took place on 1 January 1901, and NSW became a state of the new Australian nation. However, Australia's legal ties and its loyalty to Britain remained strong. When WWI broke out in Europe, Australian troops were sent to fight in the trenches of France, at Gallipoli in Turkey and in the Middle East.

Australia continued to grow in the 1920s until the Great Depression hit the country hard. By 1932, however, Australia's economy was starting to recover as a result of rises in wool prices and a revival of manufacturing. With the opening of the Harbour Bridge in the same year, Sydney's building industry revived.

Discontent continued to escalate in Aboriginal communities and in 1938 there was a national day of protest. The Day of Mourning protest was attended by Aborigines from NSW, Victoria and Queensland. In all, over 100 people attended the conference. However, it wasn't until 1967 that Aboriginal people were given the right to

vote, after a whopping 90.2% of voters supported changing the constitution in a national referendum on the issue.

In the years before WWII, Australia became increasingly fearful of the threat to national security posed by expansionist Japan. When war broke out, Australian troops again fought beside the British in Europe. Only after the Japanese bombed Pearl Harbor did Australia's own national security begin to take priority. A boom with a net barrage was stretched across the entrance channels of Sydney Harbour and gun emplacements were set up on the rocky headlands.

Sydney escaped WWII comparatively unscathed, although on 31 May 1942 several Japanese midget submarines were destroyed after becoming trapped in the harbour boom. A week later, another Japanese submarine entered the harbour, sank a small supply vessel and lobbed a few shells into the suburbs of Bondi and Rose Bay.

Ultimately, US victory in the Battle of the Coral Sea helped protect Australia from a Japanese invasion and marked the beginning of Australia's shift of allegiance from Britain towards the USA.

Postwar immigration programs brought new growth and prosperity to Australia, and Sydney spread west rapidly. Migrants at this time came predominantly from Britain, Ireland and Mediterranean countries.

Despite the influx of European immigrants and a strong trade-union movement, Australia came to accept the US view that communism threatened the increasingly Americanised Australian way of life. It was therefore no surprise that in 1965 the conservative government committed troops to serve in the Vietnam War.

During the Vietnam War years, the face of Sydney changed as American GIs flooded the city for R&R (rest and recreation). Kings Cross flaunted its sleaziness, providing entertainment for the US troops.

Civil unrest over the issue of conscription eventually contributed to the election of the Australian Labor Party (ALP) in 1972. This was the first time in 23 years that it had been in power. The government, under the leadership of Gough Whitlam, withdrew Australian troops from Vietnam and abolished national service.

A hostile Senate and rumours of mismanagement prompted Governor General John Kerr, the British monarch's representative in Australia, to dismiss the Whitlam government in November 1975. Until then, the position of governor general had been little more than ceremonial, and Kerr's act caused controversy. Kerr installed a caretaker government under the leader of the opposition, Malcolm Fraser.

The booming economy of the 1980s saw Sydney flush with new skyscrapers, although the subsequent bust left a number of holes in the city centre.

The Bicentennial celebrations in 1988 and the wildly successful 2000 Olympic Games have given Sydney a great deal of confidence and boosted the economy significantly – although there are still problems with unemployment.

Contemporary Aboriginal Issues

In 1992 the High Court ruled that Aborigines once owned Australia, and that where there was continuous association with the land they had the right to claim it back. This became known as the Mabo decision, after the indigenous activist Eddie Mabo. The decision was incorporated into subsequent federal government native title legislation.

Then, in 1996, the High Court handed down the Wik decision, which established that pastoral leases don't necessarily extinguish native title. This resulted in some fairly hysterical responses, which threatened to undermine the Reconciliation process between Aboriginal and non-Aboriginal Australians.

This Reconciliation was further undermined by the emergence of the right-wing conservative former independent federal MP Pauline Hanson. While Hanson's star has now faded, the divisive repercussions are still being felt.

Another issue that remains unresolved is that of the Stolen Generations. By the early 1900s legislation was designed to stop the development of an indigenous 'half-caste'

population and to assimilate them into Australian mainstream society. Children could be taken from Aboriginal families, placed in an institution, fostered or adopted, without the knowledge or consent of their parents. This practice continued until the early 1970s and those people who were taken from their families have become known as the Stolen Generations. It is now accepted that the trauma of this separation from family and culture has had wide-ranging impacts on Aboriginal society and been passed on down the generations. For more information see Lonely Planet's *Aboriginal Australia & the Torres Strait Islands*.

GEOGRAPHY

Sydney is on Australia's populous east coast, about 870km north of Melbourne by road, and almost 1000km south of Brisbane.

The city is centred on the harbour of Port Jackson, but Greater Sydney sprawls over 1800 sq km and has grown to encompass

Aborigines in Sydney

Although while Australia is at last recognising the complexities of traditional Aboriginal cultures, many nonindigenous Australians are still ignorant of the cultures of urban Aborigines, who maintain strong links with traditional ways. This causes frequent misunderstandings, and urban Aborigines are still often labelled as troublemakers because they don't conform to the norms of white Australia.

More Aboriginal people live in Sydney than in any other Australian city. The Sydney region is estimated to have around 30,800 indigenous inhabitants, most of whom are descended from migratory inland tribes. This figure includes a smaller number of Torres Strait Islanders, a people native to the group of islands just off the Australian coast, near Papua New Guinea. The suburb of Redfern has a large and vital Koori population (many Aborigines in south-eastern Australia describe themselves as Kooris).

Botany Bay in the south, the foothills of the Blue Mountains in the west and the fringes of the national parks to the north.

Sydney is hilly, and its layout is complicated by the harbour's numerous bays and headlands. It's built on a vast sandstone shelf, the rocky outcrops of which provide a dramatic backdrop to the harbour.

CLIMATE

Australian summer begins in December, autumn in March, winter in June and spring in September.

Sydney is blessed with a temperate climate. It rarely falls below 10°C (50°F), except overnight in the middle of winter. The average summer maximum is a pleasant 25°C (77°F), although temperatures can soar to 40°C (104°F) during hot spells. If it's hot and the humidity skyrockets, the climate can become quite oppressive.

The average monthly rainfall ranges from 75mm to 130mm (2.9 to 5 inches), and torrential downpours are quite common between October and March.

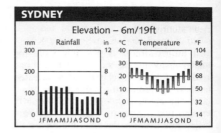

ECOLOGY & ENVIRONMENT

As Australians have become more environmentally aware, the conservation vote has become increasingly important. This, coupled with the recognition of the value of ecotourism, has resulted in many areas receiving greater, though varying, degrees of protection and management. However, problems remain.

In Sydney there's concern over pollution of the city's harbour and ocean beaches, especially after heavy rainfall, when rubbish and untreated effluent spew from overflow points. Millions of dollars have been spent

Flora & Fauna

You can see a wide range of Australian flora at Sydney's Royal Botanic Gardens and its outposts, Mt Annan Botanic Garden (between Camden and Campbelltown) and Mt Tomah Botanic Garden (between Bilpin and Bell). Several national parks are close to the city. Aside from many varieties of gum trees, other common natives include grevillea, hakea, banksia, waratah, bottlebrush, paperbark, tea, boronia and native pine.

The native animals you're most likely to see in the wild are wallabies, kangaroos, possums and koalas, but there's often a variety of small nocturnal animals going about their business unobserved. Parks and bushland in and around Sydney are home to several protected species of bat, notably the large flying foxes, which can often be seen heading for a comfortable tree around dusk. The sacred ibis struts its stuff around Hyde Park, while the mangrove swamps around Bicentennial Park are home to pelicans and other water birds.

Parrots, cockatoos and kookaburras are sometimes seen in the city and national parks, and you may be lucky enough to see lyrebirds at West Head. Colourful rainbow lorikeets can be spotted at Bradley's Head, while Middle Head and Obelisk Bay are home to fairy wrens and water dragons (a type of lizard). Botany Bay is a nesting and feeding site of the endangered little tern, a small migratory shore bird that divides its time between Australia and Japan.

There are many species of snake in NSW, all protected. Many are poisonous, some deadly, but they'll usually slither out of your way. Australian animals, birds and reptiles can also be seen at Taronga Zoo (see the Things to See & Do chapter) and at wildlife parks (see the Excursions chapter).

installing pollution traps and litter booms to clean stormwater.

Noise from aircraft at Sydney's Kingsford Smith airport is a major issue for nearby residents; the state government has tried to reduce the level in the worst-affected areas by 'spreading' the flight paths.

On the positive side, the use of public transport is increasing, and reduced car-usage should steady the air pollution levels, which are reported daily in newspaper weather sections.

If you'd like to find out more, the following agencies have offices in Sydney:

Australian Conservation Foundation (ACF; ☎ 9247 4285, **W** www.acfonline.org.au) 33 George St, The Rocks. The ACF is the largest nongovernmental organisation in NSW currently involved in protecting the environment.
Greenpeace Australia (☎ 9261 4666, **W** www.greenpeace.org.au) Level 4, 39 Liverpool St, Sydney. Greenpeace maintains a high profile in Australia, and handed out only a 'C' for the Sydney Olympics, which were supposed to be the 'Green Games'.
National Trust of Australia (Map 5; ☎ 9258 0123, **W** www.nsw.nationaltrust.org.au) Observatory Hill, Sydney. The Trust is dedicated to preserving historical buildings and Australia's cultural and environmental heritage.
Wilderness Society (☎ 9282 9553, **W** www.wilderness.org.au) Suite 203, 64 Kippax St, Surry Hills. It focuses on the protection of wilderness and the designation of wilderness areas.

GOVERNMENT & POLITICS
Sydney is the capital of NSW and the seat of the state government.

There are two main political groupings in NSW: the ALP, and a coalition of the Liberal and National Parties. At the time of writing, the Labor Party was in government and Bob Carr was premier.

At local government level, the various districts of Sydney are controlled by city councils, often operating out of Victorian-era town halls, such as Sydney Town Hall on the corner of George and Druitt Sts.

ECONOMY
Sydney is Australia's chief commercial, financial and industrial centre. It is also an important transport centre. It has two harbours – Sydney Harbour (also called Port Jackson) and, about 15km south, Botany Bay – plus Australia's busiest airport and a network of roads and rail. Most of Australia's foreign trade is conducted in Sydney and NSW.

About half the workforce is employed in manufacturing and the rest in services such as transport, finance, retailing, tourism etc. Oil refining is a major local industry.

POPULATION & PEOPLE
Sydney has a population of just over four million people, out of the Australian total of about 19 million. It's a multicultural city, although before WWII most Sydneysiders were predominantly of British and Irish descent. That changed dramatically in the aftermath of the war, with particularly large migrations from Italy and Greece, and significant influxes from Yugoslavia, Lebanon and Turkey.

Asian migration to Australia began in the 1850s when Chinese migrants were attracted by gold, but there were also large influxes of Vietnamese after the Vietnam War. More recently, the majority of Sydney's immigrants have come from China and New Zealand, with others arriving from Thailand, Cambodia and the Philippines. Almost a quarter of the citizens of the state of NSW were born overseas, and most of these recent arrivals live in Sydney.

ARTS
Aboriginal Art
Art has always been an integral part of Aboriginal life, a connection between past and present, the supernatural and the earthly, people and the land.

Earthly art is a reflection of the various peoples' ancestral Dreaming – the 'Creation', when the Earth's physical features were formed by the struggles between powerful supernatural ancestors. Although it is often considered to be a time in the past, or the 'Dreamtime', Aborigines believe that it is in the past, the present and the future. Ceremonies, rituals and sacred paintings are all based on the Dreaming.

Aboriginal art underwent a major revival in the last two decades of the 20th century. Artists throughout the country have found a means both to express and to preserve ancient Dreaming values, and a way to share this rich cultural heritage with the wider community in Australia.

While the dot paintings of the central deserts are the most readily identifiable and popular form of contemporary Aboriginal art, there's a huge range of material being produced – including bark paintings from Arnhem Land, wood carving and silkscreen printing from the Tiwi Islands north of Darwin, and batik printing and wood carving from central Australia.

A number of galleries specialise in Aboriginal and Torres Strait Islander art; see the Shopping chapter for details.

Dance

The Australian Ballet is the national ballet company and is considered one of the finest in the world. It tours Australia's major cities, with a mixed program of classical and modern ballets. It usually presents four ballets a year during its season at the Sydney Opera House.

Under the guidance of its artistic director, Graeme Murphy, the Sydney Dance Company (SDC) has become Australia's leading contemporary dance company. Like the Sydney Theatre Company (STC), it's based at Pier 4, Walsh Bay, and also performs at the Opera House.

One of the country's leading Aboriginal dance companies is the Bangarra Dance Theatre. (See the boxed text 'Aboriginal Performance' in the Entertainment chapter.)

Music

In Sydney you can hear everything from world-class opera to live electronic acts. The city has a vital music culture and attracts many international musicians.

Songs are an integral part of traditional Aboriginal culture. They function not only as musical forms but as creation myths, totems and maps, and as a system of land tenure. Hybrid Aboriginal music is popular in Australia, following the success of

Aboriginal group Yothu Yindi and Torres Strait Islander singer Christine Anu.

The first European settlers' bush ballads and bush songs comprise a uniquely Australian folklore, and mark the first attempt to adapt European cultural forms to the Australian environment. The ballads and songs evolved from convict songs, English, Scottish and Irish folk songs, and campfire yarns. Part poetry, part music-hall romp, they paint an evocative picture of life in the bush in the 19th century. You can hear bush songs at several venues in the Rocks area, although you're more likely to hear rock elsewhere.

Local performers of note include long-time favourites Midnight Oil, The Celibate Rifles, The Cruel Sea and The Whitlams, and newer acts like Frenzal Rhomb, Something for Kate and Skunkhour. Major international acts often kick-off Australian tours in Sydney.

Sydney has some good local DJs, and frequent appearances by international guests liven things up. There are clubs and dance parties catering to every subgenre, from hip-hop to drum and bass, funk, techno and house.

Sydney also has a healthy jazz scene, centred on city venues such as the Basement and the Harbourside Brasserie. Top Sydney performers include Mike Nock and hip acid-jazz group DIG.

Classical music is performed at the Sydney Opera House, universities, and at various city venues. Opera Australia is Australia's national opera company, and the third busiest opera company in the world. In a typical year it gives around 235 performances of some 18 operas. It's based at the Opera House for seven months of the year.

The diverse strands of Sydney's musical life are brought together each January in The Domain during the month-long Sydney Festival.

See the Sydney Opera House section in the Things to See & Do chapter, and the Entertainment chapter for information about other venues.

Literature

In the late 19th century, an Australian literary flavour began to develop with the

Harbour ferries and the Sydney Harbour Bridge viewed from Circular Quay

RICHARD I'ANSON

Body-surfers enjoy the water at Coogee Beach.

Reflecting over the water, Taylors Point Wharf

Aerial view of Bondi Beach

Taking a dip, Castle Rock Beach

Snorkelling, Camp Cove Beach

Bulletin School (named after the magazine of the same name), with authors such as Henry Lawson (1867–1922), AB 'Banjo' Patterson (1864–1941) and Miles Franklin (1879–1954), whose novel *My Brilliant Career* (1901) caused a sensation, especially when it was revealed that Miles was a woman.

The aftereffects of the Bulletin School's romantic vernacular tradition lasted many years and it wasn't until the 1970s (a time of renewed interest in Australian writing) that images of the bush, Australian ideas of mateship and the chauvinism of Australian culture were fully questioned by readers and writers.

Australian writers of international stature include: Patrick White (winner of the Nobel Prize in Literature 1973), Thomas Keneally (Booker Prize winner 1982 – *Schindler's Ark*) and Peter Carey (Booker Prize winner 1988 – *Oscar & Lucinda*). Other authors held in high regard include Thea Astley, David Malouf, Frank Moorhouse, Rodney Hall, Tim Winton, Helen Garner, Elizabeth Jolley and Robert Drewe.

A Sydney-centric reading list might include the following. *Seven Poor Men of Sydney* (1934) is a poetic account of a cross-section of Sydneysiders by expatriate author Christina Stead. *The Harp in the South* (1948) and *Poor Man's Orange* (1949) are New Zealand–born writer Ruth Park's accounts of life in Surry Hills. Patrick White's *Voss* (1957) contrasts the outback with colonial life in Sydney. David Ireland's *The Glass Canoe* explores Sydney's larrikin pub culture. *They're a Weird Mob* (1955) by Nino Culotta (the pseudonym of John O'Grady, who was born in NSW) is a humorous fictional tale of an Italian migrant in Sydney. Rosa Cappiello's *Oh Lucky Country* (1984) is a harrowing account of the modern migrant experience.

Offering a peek into the seamier side of Sydney are the works of prolific crime writer Peter Corris, such as *The Empty Beach* and *The Marvellous Boy*.

Kate Grenville's book *Lilian's Story,* loosely based on the life of Sydney eccentric Bea Miles, was made into a film. Also

The Miles Franklin Award is held every year to celebrate Australia's best literary fiction.

worth reading is poet Dorothy Porter's lesbian thriller *Monkey's Mask*. Janette Turner Hospital's *The Last Magician* is set in part around Newtown train station, and Amanda Lohrey's *Camille's Bread* is a postmodern love story set in Glebe, Leichhardt and Chinatown.

Architecture

Sydney is predominantly a Victorian-era city, although it also has some fine early colonial buildings. Grand Victorian structures include the Town Hall, the Queen Victoria Building (QVB) and the old post office on Martin Place. Many inner suburbs have row upon row of ornate Victorian terraces. Macquarie St in the city, Parramatta and the Windsor area are home to the most impressive early colonial architecture.

Although the Australian Dream supposedly involves a quarter-acre block and a three-bedroom house in the suburbs, most inner-city residents live in terrace houses, which often have elaborate lace ironwork and balconies. The best examples are in Paddington, where much of the iron used so effectively in the early terraces came from ballast on ships sailing to Australia from abroad.

Sydney flirted with post-Regency, Gothic and Renaissance styles in the second half of the 19th century, but at the turn of the 20th century Australia developed its own style of domestic architecture, known as Federation. Unlike Victorian houses, which are basically boxes with verandas tacked on, Federation houses have red-brick or weatherboard walls, tiled roofs, casement windows, turned-timber veranda posts and fretted woodwork. Examples of this style are in the next rank of suburbs out from the inner suburbs, such as Haberfield and Strathfield in the inner west.

California Bungalow became dominant in the 1920s, while the 1930s saw the flourishing of Art Deco; there are fine examples of Art Deco apartments in Potts Point, Elizabeth Bay and Edgecliff.

In the 1960s the Sydney School pioneered a distinctively Australian organic architecture that used over-burnt brick and native landscaping to blend into the local environment.

Since the 1960s, central Sydney has become a mini Manhattan of tall buildings vying for harbour views. Many modern buildings are striking, such as the Capita Centre on Castlereagh St, and Governors Phillip and Macquarie Towers on the corner of Young and Bent Sts, but only the Sydney Football Stadium, designed by Philip Cox, approaches the flair of the city's most famous modern building, the Opera House.

There's an encouraging trend in the city's development that is helping to retain some of Sydney's character. Old buildings like Daking House (near Central station), home to the Sydney YHA Hostel, are being restored and given a new lease of life. The old Customs House at Circular Quay has had a major facelift and now houses an arts and cultural centre.

Sympathetic modern extensions are being added to existing buildings; good examples include the Capitol Theatre complex, the Furama Hotel and Paddy's Markets in Chinatown. At the Museum of Sydney, the modern office tower perched atop the sandstone foundations of Australia's first Government House has won several architectural awards.

The controversial 'toaster' apartment blocks built near the Opera House on Circular Quay have attracted much criticism for their clunky design and view-blocking dimensions, but that hasn't stopped them from becoming some of the most expensive real estate in Australia.

Painting

The first European landscape painters' impressions of Australia feature colours that seem wrong and features that aren't what would now be regarded as typically Australian. However, some early painters, such as John Glover, made an effort to approach the Australian landscape on its own terms.

Colonial artists such as Conrad Martens painted Turneresque landscapes of Sydney Harbour in the 1850s that now startle Sydneysiders, who are used to seeing the foreshore dominated by exclusive housing instead of miles of bush.

Between 1885 and 1890 a distinctively Australian school of painting emerged. The painters of the Heidelberg School were the first to render Australian light and colour in a naturalistic fashion. Using impressionistic techniques and favouring plein-air painting, the school represented a major break with prevailing British and Germanic tastes.

Most major painters in the Heidelberg School were from Melbourne, although Tom Roberts and fellow Melburnian Arthur Streeton established an artists' camp at Little Sirius Cove in Mosman in 1891, which became a focal point for Sydney artists.

Roberts and Streeton depicted what are now considered typically Australian scenes of sheepshearers, pioneers and bushrangers. Their paintings were powerful stimulants to the development of an enduring national mythology.

At the beginning of the 20th century Australian painters began to flirt with Art Nouveau. Sydney Long painted bush scenes peopled with fairies in an attempt to mythologise and personify the landscape, something Aborigines had been doing successfully for thousands of years.

In the 1940s there began a flowering of predominantly expressionist art, which many considered to be the first authentically Australian art since the Heidelberg School. Again, the main practitioners were from Melbourne, but painters such as Sidney Nolan, Arthur Boyd, Albert Tucker and Russell Drysdale transcended locale to approach all Australians on the level of myth.

Mosman-based Margaret Preston's striking woodcuts and paintings of Australian flora and fauna combined elements of Aboriginal and French art and influences from her many travels throughout Asia, Africa and Europe.

Drawing on popular cultural images for much of his work, Martin Sharp first rose to prominence in the 1960s as cofounder of the satirical magazine *Oz*. In the 1970s he helped restore the 'face' at Luna Park and produced many famous posters for the productions of the Nimrod Theatre (these posters were incredibly eye-catching works of art by Martin Sharp, using the face of Roy Rene, or 'Mo', as he was known). Sydney artist Brett Whiteley, who died in 1992, was an internationally celebrated *enfant terrible* who painted bold, colourful canvases, often with distorted figures. His paintings of Sydney Harbour and Lavender Bay are famous; his studio, containing many of his works, has been preserved as a gallery in Surry Hills. (For more details see the section on Surry Hills in the Things to See & Do chapter.)

Other modern artists of note include Sandy Bruch, Ian Fairweather, Keith Looby and Judy Cassab.

Cinema

Australia's first cinema was opened in 1896, a year after the Lumiere brothers opened the world's first cinema in Paris. Maurice Sestier, one of the Lumieres' photographers, came to Australia and made the first films shot in the streets of Sydney and Melbourne.

One of the most successful of the early feature films was *The Sentimental Bloke*

(1919), with scenes shot in Manly, the Royal Botanical Gardens and Woolloomooloo.

Forty Thousand Horsemen (1940), directed by the great film maker Charles Chauvel, was a highlight of locally made and financed films of the 1930s to 1950s, which were often based on Australian history or literature. Chauvel is credited with giving Errol Flynn his first film role.

With the introduction of government subsidies during 1969 and 1970 and the creation of the Australian Film Commission in 1975, an ongoing renaissance of Australian cinema was established, and today Sydney is a major centre for film production.

Recent films such as *Strictly Ballroom* (Pyrmont, Marrickville), *Muriel's Wedding* (Parramatta, Oxford St, Darling Point, Ryde), *Priscilla – Queen of the Desert* (Erskineville), *The Matrix* (Sydney city) and *Mission Impossible 2* (Elizabeth Bay and Sydney Harbour) all feature recognisable parts of Sydney. *Moulin Rouge* was made at the Fox Studios at Moore Park, and the second and third prequels of *Star Wars* are to be made there.

See the Entertainment chapter for more information on films, festivals and cinemas.

Theatre

Sydney has something for all tastes, from imported blockbuster musicals at major venues like the State Theatre and Her Majesty's, to experimental productions in small theatres in the inner suburbs. The prestigious Sydney Theatre Company (STC) based at Pier 4, Hickson Rd, Millers Point, provides a balanced program of modern, classical, local and foreign drama. The National Institute of Dramatic Art (NIDA) in Kensington is a breeding ground for new talent and stages performances of students' work. There are also many smaller theatre companies, such as Griffin, which produce great local work, and companies like Pork Chop, Sidetrack and Cut Theatre. Look in the *White Pages* for details.

See the Theatre section in the Entertainment chapter for more information.

'The Best Games Ever'

The old adage about a poor dress rehearsal meaning a good show certainly proved true of the Sydney Olympics. In the run-up to the Games, newspaper stories told of alleged corruption and regular embarrassing stuff-ups by the Sydney Organising Committee for the Olympic Games. Many Australians predicted a fiasco: the spring weather would be shocking, the transport wouldn't cope with the hordes, and spectators would be lucky to get the right tickets.

But from 15 September–1 October 2000 the critics were proven wrong. The sun shone most days, the transport systems coped admirably with the 5.972 million people who travelled to the Olympic venues, and the Opening and Closing Ceremonies provided both a strong Reconciliation message and a party atmosphere. Some 87% of available tickets across Sydney and interstate venues were sold, breaking the previous Olympic record for sales (82%) set in Atlanta. Two hundred countries comprising 11,000 athletes (including independent athletes from East Timor) participated in Sydney. Two weeks after the Games, record numbers of athletes competed in the Paralympics: 3,824 athletes (including independent athletes from East Timor) from 123 countries. Sydney's reward for a hitch-free Olympics was having IOC president Juan Antonio Samaranch declare them 'the best Games ever' during the closing ceremony.

Not everything was perfect: The vault was set at the wrong height for the women's gymnastics all-around final, and the cross-country course at Horsley Park provided a shocking lack of shade for spectators. But these incidents were overshadowed by other events: the host country's 16 gold medals; the world records in the pool; and a host of spectacular Olympic performances, including Australian Cathy Freeman's 400m victory, British rower Steve Redgrave's fifth consecutive gold, the surprise triumphs of the Dutch swimmers, US athlete Marion Jones's five-medal haul (two of them gold)...

Even the obligatory Olympic drugs bust elicited sympathy rather than contempt for the victim. Andreea Raducan, a 17-year-old waif-like Romanian who won the all-around gymnastics gold, was stripped of her medal after testing positive for ephedrine after taking a cold cure.

However, staging the Olympics is about more than sport. Whether the $7.5 billion(ish) spent on the Games will be worthwhile, in terms of increased investment and tourism, is still not known. What *is* known is that the athletes' village will now provide much-needed housing in Sydney. So if you fancy spending your life in the place that once housed your Olympic hero, take a trip out to Homebush: a house will set you back around $600,000, an apartment up to $500,000.

One of Australia's finest athletes, Cathy Freeman took out the 400m gold medal at Sydney's Olympic Games

Liz Filleul

RELIGION

A shrinking majority of people in Australia are at least nominally Christian. Most Protestant churches merged to form the Uniting Church, although the Anglican Church of Australia remains separate. The Catholic Church is popular due to a large population with Irish or Mediterranean heritage.

Non-Christian minorities abound, the main ones being Buddhist, Jewish and Muslim. Islam is the second-largest religion in Australia and Buddhism is one of the fastest growing. About 13% of Australians have no stated religion.

LANGUAGE

English is the official and dominant language in Australia. However, about 15% of people in NSW speak a different language at home, and the proportion is probably much higher in Sydney. Italian, Turkish, Greek or Vietnamese, just to name a few, are often spoken as a first language.

For more information check out Lonely Planet's *Australian phrasebook*.

Facts for the Visitor

WHEN TO GO

Sydney is comfortable to visit at any time of the year. Autumn and spring are delightful, with clear, warm days and mild nights. Sydney gets its fair share of dismal days in winter and scorching days in summer, too!

The other major consideration is school and public holidays, when everything touristy gets decidedly more crowded and accommodation rates soar. Sydney students have a long summer break that includes Christmas and usually most of January. Other school holidays fall around March to April (Easter), late June to mid-July, and late September to early October.

ORIENTATION

Sydney wasn't a planned city and its layout is further complicated by its hills and by the numerous inlets of the harbour.

The harbour divides Sydney into northern and southern halves, which are connected by the Sydney Harbour Bridge and the Harbour Tunnel. Central Sydney and most places of interest are south of the harbour.

See Map 2 for an overview of central Sydney, and see Map 1 for the area surrounding Sydney.

City Centre

The central city area is relatively long and narrow, and George and Pitt Sts (the main thoroughfares) run 3km from Circular Quay south to Railway Square.

The historic Rocks and Circular Quay (Map 5), where you'll find the Sydney Opera House and the Harbour Bridge, mark the northern boundary of the city centre. Central station is on the southern edge; Darling Harbour forms the western boundary; and a string of pleasant parks border Elizabeth and Macquarie Sts on the east.

North of King St is the main financial and business district; south of King St is the main commercial area, with lots of shops, cafes, restaurants, cinemas and a number of hotels.

Inner Suburbs

Cafes, restaurants, interesting shops and good pubs are peppered throughout the inner suburbs.

East of the city centre are Kings Cross (Maps 6 & 7), Woolloomooloo, Potts Point and Elizabeth Bay. Further east are the exclusive suburbs of Double Bay and Vaucluse. South-east of the city centre are the interesting inner suburbs (Map 8) of Darlinghurst, Surry Hills and Paddington. At the city's eastern extreme are the ocean-front suburbs of Bondi Beach (Map 11) and Coogee (Map 10).

West of the centre is Pyrmont and south-west of there is bohemian Glebe (Map 9). West of Pyrmont across Johnstons and White Bays are Rozelle and the arty suburb of Balmain (Map 4).

Sydney's Kingsford Smith airport is in Mascot, 10km south of the city centre, jutting into Botany Bay.

North Shore

Suburbs north of the bridge are known collectively as the North Shore. Mainly middle-class enclaves, they lack the vibrancy and diversity of the areas south of the harbour, but there are some excellent views, beaches and pockets of bushland.

Across the Harbour Bridge from the city centre is North Sydney (Map 3), a continuation of the central business district (CBD). Military Rd runs east from North Sydney through the expensive harbourside suburbs of Neutral Bay, Cremorne and Mosman.

To the north-east, Manly (Map 12) sits on a narrow peninsula near the entrance to Sydney Harbour. It fronts both the ocean and the harbour. A string of ocean beaches runs north from Manly to Palm Beach, another of Sydney's wealthy suburbs. Palm Beach fronts the Pacific Ocean and backs onto Pittwater. Ku-ring-gai Chase National Park lies on the western side of Pittwater (see the Excursions chapter).

Greater Sydney

Westward, Sydney's suburbs stretch for more than 50km, encompassing Parramatta (once a country retreat for the colony's governor), and only coming to a halt at Penrith at the foot of the Blue Mountains. Southwest of the city there's a similar sprawl of housing developments, swamping old towns such as Campbelltown and Liverpool. This is where the majority of Sydneysiders live. Cabramatta, 30km south-west of Sydney, is a busy suburb with a large, active Vietnamese community.

North and south of the centre, suburbs stretch a good 20km, their extent limited by national parks.

MAPS

Lonely Planet's handy *Sydney City Map* is a comprehensive reference for the city centre and surrounding suburbs and the Blue Mountains. It also features a walking tour, transport map and a complete index of all streets and sights.

For driving, or exploration beyond the city centre, a street directory is indispensable. *UBD*, *Sydway* and *Gregory's* charge $25 to $40 for their full-sized directories, although there are smaller versions.

For maps of country areas, see the National Roads & Motorists Association (NRMA). See the Automobile Associations section in the Getting Around chapter for more details. For topographic maps, visit the Map Shop (☎ 9228 6111), at 23–33 Bridge St in the Lands Building.

Several bookshops specialise in maps and travel guides, including the Travel Bookshop (Map 5; ☎ 9261 8200), 175 Liverpool St, and Map World (☎ 9261 3601), 371 Pitt St.

TOURIST INFORMATION
Local Tourist Offices

There's a NSW Travel Centre (☎ 9667 6050) on the international arrivals level at Sydney airport; it's open from 6am to midnight daily. As well as being a travel agency, it sells hotel accommodation at discounted rates.

The travel centre often has the best deals, but if there's a queue you could try the nearby electronic bookings board for hotel accommodation. The useful Backpacker Board also lists hostels in Sydney, and allows you to phone them for free.

Helpful City Host tourist information kiosks are located at Circular Quay, Town Hall station and Martin Place. Opening hours are from 9am to 5pm March to November, and 10am to 6pm December to February.

There's a Tourist Information Service (☎ 9669 5111) answering phone inquiries from 8am to 6pm daily. In the Sydney Coach Terminal on Eddy Ave at Bay 14, the Travellers' Information Service (Map 8; ☎ 9281 9366) makes bus and accommodation bookings (not for hostels, but there's a hostel noticeboard) from 6am to 10.30pm daily.

The Countrylink Travel Centre at Shop W15, Station Concourse, Wynyard station (Map 5; ☎ 9224 4744) can book travel as well as hotel accommodation; it's open weekdays from 8.30am to 5pm.

The Sydney Visitors Centre (Map 5; ☎ 9255 1788, 1800 067 676) at 106 George St, The Rocks, is open from 9am to 6pm daily; it can book hotel accommodation, and there's a hostel noticeboard too. There's another visitors' centre (Map 5; ☎ 9286 0111) at Darling Harbour, next to the IMAX Theatre.

Tourist Offices Abroad
Australian Tourist Commission (ATC)

The ATC is the federal government body that provides information to potential visitors about the country. Its comprehensive Web site (W www.australia.com) is full of maps and information, and queries can be relayed to ATC staff through the site.

Tourism NSW This body operates along the same lines as the ATC, but at a state level. It has offices in the following countries:

Japan (☎ 03-5214 0777) Level 28, New Otani Garden Court Bldg, 4-1 Kioi-cho, Chiyoda-ku, Tokyo 102
New Zealand (☎ 09-379 9118) Level 13, 48 Emily Place, Auckland 1
Singapore (☎ 253 3888) Unit 13-04, United Square, 101 Thomson Rd, Singapore 1130

UK (☎ 020-7887 5003) Level 2, Australia Centre, The Strand, London WC2B 4LC
USA (☎ 310-301 1903) Suite C-10, 13737 Fiji Way, Marina Del Rey, CA 90292

Travel Agencies

Thomas Cook (Map 5; ☎ 9231 2877), 175 Pitt St, has a travel agency as well as a foreign exchange desk; it's open from 8.45am to 5.15pm weekdays, and from 10am to 2pm Saturday. American Express Travel Service (AmEx; Map 5; ☎ 9236 4200), Level 1, 130 Pitt St, opens 8.30am to 5pm weekdays. There are other branches of AmEx throughout the city.

Quite a few travel agents cater to budget travellers/backpackers. STA Travel (not to be confused with the State Transit Authority) has a number of branches around the city. These include its head office (Map 8; ☎ 9212 1255) at 855 George St, near Central station; and offices at 9 Oxford St, Paddington (☎ 9360 1822) and 127-39 Macleay St in Kings Cross (☎ 9368 1111), near the fountain.

Travellers Contact Point (Map 5; ☎ 9221 8744), 7th floor, 428 George St, is above Dymocks bookshop. You can have mail sent here, and there's information on finding work and accommodation, as well as a noticeboard for messages. It organises charter flights to the UK, but you need to book well in advance.

Free Publications

Several free magazines/booklets provide current listings. At the airport pick up a copy of the *Arrivals Guide* or *Sydney – The Harbour Connection* (one of the better ones, but aimed at visitors with a bit of money to spend). For budget travellers, *TNT Magazine* has heaps of information on accommodation, things to do, transport etc. Also useful are smaller publications *Aussie Backpacker* and *The Word*.

A blue leaflet, the *Guide and Map to Art Galleries*, covers the inner city and eastern suburbs and is available from antique shops, galleries, cafes and at the airport.

Sydney City Hub is an interesting weekly news, arts and entertainment paper available

from cafes. Music-lovers can check out news and gig guides in the weekly street papers *Drum Media* and *3D World* or the monthly dance music magazine *TRM*.

You'll find useful tourist tips, phone numbers and public transport information in the front of the A-K volume of the *Yellow Pages*.

Other Sources

Other excellent places to look for help and cheap travel tips are the hostel areas where most budget travellers stay – particularly Victoria St in Kings Cross and Potts Point, where there are countless posters and noticeboards offering everything from flat shares and backpacks to tours and unused air tickets. Several travel agents in Kings Cross cater to backpackers, which means they have all sorts of useful travel information.

DOCUMENTS
Visas

Visitors to Australia need a visa. Only New Zealand nationals are exempt, and even they receive a 'special category' visa on arrival. The type of visa you require depends on the reason for your visit.

Visa application forms are available from either Australian diplomatic missions overseas or travel agents; you can apply by mail or in person. Alternatively, many travel agents and airlines can now grant on-the-spot Australian visas, valid for three months, via the new Electronic Travel Authority (ETA).

Electronic Travel Authority (ETA) The ETA system allows participating airlines and travel agents to grant instant visas. This system is currently operational in around 30 countries, including Japan, the UK, the USA, Malaysia, Singapore, Germany and France. See travel agents, airlines, or the DIMA Web site at **W** www.dima.gov.au for further details. ETAs can be granted for both business and holiday trips, allowing a stay of three months.

Tourist Visas Issued by Australian consular offices abroad, Tourist Visas are the most common visa. They are generally valid for a stay of three or six months, and can be used to enter and leave Australia several times within that period. The Short-Stay Visa is valid for 12 months, with a maximum stay of three months for each entry; the Long-Stay Visa is valid for four years with a maximum of six months' stay for each entry.

When you apply for a visa, you need to present your passport and maybe a passport photo, as well as sign a statement that you have an onward or return ticket and 'sufficient funds' for your visit.

There is a $60 fee for visas applied for outside Australia, and a $150 fee for visas applied for within Australia.

Working Visas Visitors aged between 18 and 30 (without dependent children) from the UK, the Republic of Ireland, Canada, South Korea, the Netherlands, Malta, Germany and Japan may be eligible for a Working Holiday Visa.

A Working Holiday Visa allows for a stay of up to 12 months, but the emphasis is on casual, or incidental, employment rather than a full-time job, so working full time for longer than three months with any one employer is not allowed.

Conditions attached to the scheme include having a return ticket and sufficient funds. You cannot enrol in formal studies while in Australia. There is a fee of $150.

See the Work section later in this chapter for more information.

Visa Extensions The maximum stay is one year, including extensions.

Applications for visa extensions are made through Department of Immigration & Ethnic Affairs (DIMA) offices in Australia and, as the process takes some time, it's best to apply about a month before your visa expires. There's an application fee of $145 – and even if they turn down your application they can still keep your money! To qualify for an extension you must have sufficient funds and an onward ticket.

There's a DIMA office (☎ 9258 4599, 13 18 81) on the 4th floor, 88 Cumberland St, The Rocks.

Copies

All important documents (passport data page and visa page, credit cards, travel insurance policy, air/bus/train tickets, driving licence etc) should be photocopied before you leave home. Leave one copy with someone at home and keep another with you, separate from the originals.

Travel Insurance

A travel insurance policy to cover theft, loss and medical problems is a good idea. Some policies offer lower and higher medical-expense options; the higher ones are chiefly for countries such as the USA, which have extremely high medical costs. There is a wide variety of policies available, so check the small print.

Some policies specifically exclude 'dangerous activities', which can include scuba diving, motorcycling, even trekking. A locally acquired motorcycle licence is not valid under some policies.

You may prefer a policy that pays doctors or hospitals directly rather than you having to pay on the spot and claim later. If you have to claim later make sure you keep all documentation. Some policies ask you to call back (reverse charges) to a centre in your home country where an immediate assessment of your problem is made.

Check that the policy covers ambulances or an emergency flight home.

EMBASSIES & CONSULATES
Your Own Embassy

It's important to realise what your own embassy – the embassy of the country of which you are a citizen – can and can't do to help you if you get into trouble. Generally speaking, it won't be much help in emergencies if the trouble you're in is remotely your own fault. Remember that you are bound by the laws of the country you are in. Your embassy will not be sympathetic if you end up in jail after committing a crime locally, even if such actions are legal in your own country.

In genuine emergencies you might get some assistance, but only if other channels have been exhausted. For example, if you need to get home urgently, a free ticket home is exceedingly unlikely – the embassy would expect you to have insurance. If you have all your money and documents stolen, it might assist with getting a new passport, but a loan for onward travel is out of the question.

Some embassies used to keep letters for travellers or have a small reading room with home newspapers, but these days the mail holding service has usually been stopped and even newspapers tend to be out of date.

Australian Embassies & Consulates

Australian diplomatic representation abroad includes:

Canada *High Commission:* (☎ 613-783 7665) Suite 710, 50 O'Connor St, Ottawa, ON K1P 6L2

France *Embassy:* (☎ 01 40 59 33 00) 4 Rue Jean Rey, 75015 Paris

Germany *Embassy:* (☎ 30-880 0880) 6th floor, Philip Johnson House, Friedrichstrasse 200, 10117 Berlin

Hong Kong *Consulate-General:* (☎ 852-2827 8881) 24th floor, Harbour Centre, 25 Harbour Rd, Wanchai

Ireland *Embassy:* (☎ 01-676 1517) 2nd floor, Fitzwilton House, Wilton Terrace, Dublin 2

Japan *Embassy:* (☎ 03-5232 4111) 2-1-14 Mita, Minato-ku, Tokyo 108-8361

Malaysia *High Commission:* (☎ 03-246 5555) 6 Jalan Yap Kwan Seng, Kuala Lumpur 50450

New Zealand *Consulate-General:* (☎ 09-303 2429) 7th floor, Union House, 132–8 Quay St, Auckland

Singapore *High Commission:* (☎ 836 4100) 25 Napier Rd, Singapore 258507

Thailand *Embassy:* (☎ 02-287 2680) 37 South Sathorn Rd, Bangkok 10120

UK *High Commission:* (☎ 020-7379 4334) Australia House, The Strand, London WC2B 4LA

USA *Embassy:* (☎ 202-797 3000) 1601 Massachusetts Ave NW, Washington DC 20036-2273

Consulates in Sydney

Most foreign embassies are based in Canberra, but many countries also maintain a consulate in Sydney.

Canada (☎ 9364 3050) Level 5, Quay West, 111 Harrington St, Sydney

France (☎ 9261 5779) Level 26, St Martins Tower, 31 Market St, Sydney

Germany (☎ 9328 7733) 13 Trelawney St, Woollahra

Japan (☎ 9231 3455) 52 Martin Place, Sydney

Netherlands (☎ 9387 6644) 500 Oxford St, Bondi Junction

New Zealand (☎ 8256 2000) 55 Hunter St, Sydney

UK (☎ 9247 7521) Level 16, Gateway Bldg, 1 Macquarie Place, Sydney

USA (☎ 9373 9200) Level 59, 19–29 Martin Place, Sydney

For others see the *Yellow Pages* 'Consulates & Legations'.

CUSTOMS

When entering Australia you can bring most articles in free of duty, provided that customs is satisfied they're for personal use and that you'll be taking them with you when you leave. There's the usual duty-free quota per person of 1L of alcohol, 250 cigarettes and dutiable goods up to the value of $400.

Two issues need particular attention. Number one is illegal drugs – don't bring any in with you.

Number two is animal and plant quarantine – declare all goods of animal or vegetable origin and show them to an official. Authorities are naturally keen to prevent weeds, pests and diseases getting into the country. Fresh food and flowers are also unpopular, and if you've recently visited farmland or rural areas prior to entering Australia, it might pay to scrub your shoes before you get to the airport.

Weapons and firearms are either prohibited or require a permit and safety testing. Other restricted goods include products made from protected wildlife species, non-approved telecommunications devices and live animals.

When you leave, don't take any protected flora or fauna with you. Customs comes down hard on smugglers.

MONEY

Carry some Australian currency in cash – for small transactions and for places that don't accept credit cards (some of the cheaper hotels and places to eat).

Currency
The unit of currency is the Australian dollar, which is divided into 100 cents. There are $100, $50, $20, $10 and $5 notes and $2, $1, 50c, 20c, 10c and 5c coins. The 2c and 1c coins have been taken out of circulation, although prices can still be set in odd cents. Shops round prices up (or down) to the nearest 5c on your total bill.

There are few restrictions on importing or exporting currency or travellers cheques, but if you absolutely *must* enter or leave carrying more than $10,000 in cash, you're obliged to declare it.

Exchange Rates
The Australian dollar fluctuates markedly against the US dollar. At the time of research the Australian dollar was weak against the US dollar – a real bonus for overseas visitors. Approximate exchange values are:

country	unit		A$
Canada	C$1	=	1.23
Euro zone	€1	=	1.71
Hong Kong	HK$10	=	2.45
Ireland	IR£1	=	2.17
Japan	¥100	=	1.58
Malaysia	RM1	=	0.50
New Zealand	NZ$1	=	0.83
Singapore	S$1	=	1.09
Thailand	10B	=	0.43
UK	UK£	=	2.79
USA	US$	=	1.91

Exchanging Money
Changing foreign currency or travellers cheques is no problem at almost any bank or licensed moneychanger. The Commonwealth Bank, ANZ, St George, Westpac and National Australia Bank (NAB) all have numerous branches in the city centre and surrounding suburbs.

Thomas Cook has foreign exchange branches at 175 Pitt St (Map 5; ☎ 9231 2877), in the Queen Victoria Building (QVB; Map 5; ☎ 9264 1133) and at 210 George St

(☎ 9251 9063). The QVB branch is open from 9am to 6pm Monday to Wednesday and Friday, from 9am to 9pm Thursday, from 9am to 4pm Saturday and from 11am to 5pm Sunday; the other branches are open from Monday to Saturday. AmEx (Map 5; ☎ 9236 4200), Level 1, 130 Pitt St, opens from 8.30am to 5pm weekdays and 9am to noon on Saturday.

Travellers Cheques Travellers cheques generally attract a better exchange rate than foreign cash. AmEx, Thomas Cook and other well-known brands are widely used. A passport is usually adequate identification, but a driver's licence, credit card or plane ticket can also be useful in case of problems.

Buying Australian-dollar travellers cheques is a plan worth considering. These can be exchanged immediately at the cashier's window without being converted from a foreign currency or being subject to commissions, fees or fluctuations in exchange rates.

Fees for changing foreign-currency travellers cheques vary widely from bank to bank.

ATMs There are 24-hour automatic teller machines (ATMs) at the branches of most banks in Sydney. Most of the major banks have reciprocal arrangements: Westpac, Commonwealth Bank, National Australia Bank and ANZ Bank ATMs generally accept each other's cards – but charge you a small fee for the privilege.

Most banks will accept all debit cards that are linked to international network systems, such as Cirrus, Maestro, Barclays Connect and Solo.

Most banks place a $1000 limit on the amount you can withdraw daily.

Credit Cards Visa, MasterCard, Diners Club and AmEx are widely accepted. Cash advances from credit cards are available over the counter and from many ATMs.

A credit card makes renting a car much simpler; many agencies simply refuse to rent a vehicle to you if you don't have one.

Costs

Compared to other major world cities, Sydney is cheaper in some ways and more expensive in others. Manufactured goods like clothes tend to be more expensive, but food and wine are both high in quality and low in cost.

Many places to stay have high- and low-season prices, and special deals lower than the standard room-rate. Prices in this book are generally standard high-season ones.

At the budget end, a dormitory bed in a hostel costs about $18 to $24 a night and a cheap hotel room starts at $40/55 a single/double. A modest B&B costs around $55/75, and a mid-range hotel room with en suite starts at around $90/110. You can eat for as little as $5 at one of the city's food courts; dinner with a beer or wine in a reasonable restaurant or cafe costs about $18 to $40.

Tipping

Tipping isn't an entrenched practice in Australia. A tip of around 10% in restaurants is average, but feel free to vary the amount depending on your satisfaction with the service. Taxi drivers don't expect to be tipped, but rounding up the fare to the nearest dollar is common.

Taxes & Refunds

In July 2000, the Australian government introduced a 10% goods and services tax (GST). We have included the GST in prices quoted in this book, unless otherwise noted.

If you purchase new or second-hand goods with a total minimum value of $300 from any one supplier within 28 days of departure from Australia, you are entitled to a refund of any GST paid. Contact the Australian Taxation Office (ATO; ☎ 13 63 20) for details.

POST & COMMUNICATIONS
Post

Australia Post (☎ 13 13 18) runs the country's mail system. Most post offices are open weekdays from 9am to 5pm, but you can often get stamps from newsagencies, or from some Australia Post retail outlets from 9am to noon Saturday.

Sydney's original general post office (GPO; ☎ 9244 3713) is at Mezzanine Level, 159–71 Pitt St and has been impressively refurbished. It's open from 8.15am to 5.30pm weekdays and 10am to 2pm Saturday.

There's another GPO at 130 Pitt St. Poste Restante and PO boxes are located at 310 George St, in the Hunter Connection Building near the Wynyard station entrance; it's open from 9am to 5pm weekdays.

Sending Mail It costs 45c to send a postcard or standard letter within Australia, while aerograms cost 78c.

Airmail postcards and letters (up to 50g) cost $1 to the Asia/Pacific region, and $1.50 to the rest of the world. There's a handy price guide at Australia Post's Web site (W www.auspost.com.au).

Receiving Mail The Poste Restante at 310 George St is open from 9am to 5pm weekdays and has computer terminals that enable you to check if mail is waiting for you. Remember to bring some identification. You can also have mail redirected to any suburban post office for a small fee.

AmEx and Thomas Cook (see Money, earlier) provide mail services for their clients. Alternatively, there's Travellers Contact Point (Map 5; ☎ 9221 8744), 7th floor, 428 George St, which is open 9am to 6pm weekdays and 10am to 4pm Saturday.

Telephone

Lonely Planet's eKno global communication service provides low-cost international calls – for local calls you're usually better off with a local phonecard. eKno also offers free messaging services, email, travel information, and an online travel vault where you can securely store all your important documents. You can join online at W www.ekno.lonelyplanet.com, where you will find the local-access numbers for the 24-hour customer-service centre. Once you have joined, always check the eKno Web site for the latest access numbers for each country and updates on new features.

Telstra Phone Centre, at 231 Elizabeth St, has booths of coin, phonecard and credit-card telephones. It's open from 7am to 11pm weekdays and from 7am to 7pm weekends and public holidays. The 24-hour Translating & Interpreting Service (☎ 13 14 50) at Level 25, 477 Pitt St, can help with language difficulties. For help in finding a number within Australia, call directory assistance (☎ 1223) or Yellow Pages Direct (☎ 13 13 19, business numbers only).

Local Calls Local calls from public phones cost 40c for unlimited time; most phones take coins and/or phonecards and credit cards. You can also make local calls from gold or blue phones (often found in hotels, shops, bars etc) and from payphone booths.

STD Calls The 02 code covers NSW and the ACT, 03 is for Victoria and Tasmania, 07 covers Queensland and 08 is for South Australia, Western Australia and the Northern Territory. There is no need to dial the area code when making local calls.

You can make long-distance (STD – Subscriber Trunk Dialling) calls from virtually any public phone. Many public phones accept Telstra phonecards, which come in denominations of $5, $10, $20 and $50, and are available from retail outlets that display the phonecard logo. Otherwise, use coins. STD calls are cheaper in off-peak hours – see the front of a local telephone book for the different rates.

Some public phones take only bank cashcards or credit cards.

International Calls You can make ISD (International Subscriber Dialling) calls from most STD phones.

To call Australia from abroad dial ☎ 61 and drop the zero from the area code.

Dial ☎ 0011 for overseas, the country code (44 for Britain, 1 for North America, 64 for New Zealand etc), the city code (020 for London, 212 for New York etc) then the telephone number. (For free international directory assistance, call ☎ 1225.) Off-peak

rates apply on weekends – between midnight Friday and midnight Sunday is the cheapest time to ring.

It's possible to make ISD calls through either of Australia's two main telecommunications companies, Optus or Telstra, from private phones in most areas. Phone Optus (☎ 1800 500 002, 9439 5602) for details on how to access its services.

Telstra rates for calls from public phones are higher than for calls from private phones. Call ☎ 12552 for international rates.

Country Direct gives travellers in Australia direct access to operators in nearly 50 countries, to make reverse-charge (collect) or credit-card calls. For a full list of countries hooked into this system, check the local *White Pages* telephone book.

There are several companies offering discounted international calls, especially around Kings Cross. A travellers' communications specialist with telephones and Internet access, the Global Gossip chain has numerous outlets in suburbs popular with travellers: Kings Cross (Map 7; ☎ 9326 9777) at 111 Darlinghurst Rd; Central (Map 8; ☎ 9212 1466) at 770 George St; Darlinghurst (Map 5; ☎ 9380 4588) at 108 Oxford St; Bondi (Map 11; ☎ 9365 4811) at 37 Hall St; and Glebe (Map 9; ☎ 9552 6966) at 317 Glebe Point Rd. Branches are generally open from around 9am to midnight.

Other Calls Many businesses and some government departments operate a free-call service from around the country with the prefix 1800. Other companies have six-digit numbers beginning with 13. Calls to these numbers are charged at the rate of a local call.

Phone numbers with the prefixes 014, 015, 017, 018, 041 or 040 are mobile or car phones, and cost more than calls to local numbers.

Numbers starting with 1900 are usually recorded information services provided by private companies. You'll pay by the minute and costs can mount quickly. Numbers starting with 1300 are also information lines, but dialling them costs the same as a local call.

Fax

You can send a fax from post offices and some agencies. To send one to another fax machine or postal address within Australia, post offices charge $4/1 per first page/subsequent page. If the fax is sent to a postal address, it goes first to the local post office and is either delivered by normal mail, or is collected by the recipient. International faxes, either to a private fax machine or the local mail service, cost $10/2.

If you're sending a fax to a fax machine, it's worth finding a business that offers a fax service because it's usually a lot cheaper than the post office. Kinko's (☎ 9267 4255) at 175 Liverpool St, opposite Hyde Park, charges $1.10 per page to send/receive local faxes, and is open 24 hours. You can receive faxes for 25c per page at Backpackers World (Map 7; ☎ 9380 2700, fax 9380 2900), 212 Victoria St, Kings Cross. The international dialling code for sending faxes is 0015.

Email & Internet Access

Internet 'cafes' have been popping up all over Sydney and the resulting price war is good news for travellers. Kings Cross has the highest concentration of Internet cafes, several of which are open 24 hours. Besides allowing you to access email and the Web, many offer word-processing, fax, scanning, and printing services too.

Global Gossip has numerous locations – see the entry under International Calls for details, earlier.

Most libraries offer free Internet access, but you need to book ahead. Many hostels are also getting wired up.

INTERNET RESOURCES

The World Wide Web is a rich resource for travellers. You can research your trip, hunt down bargain air fares, book hotels, check on weather conditions or chat with locals and other travellers about the best places to visit (or avoid!).

There's no better place to start your Web explorations than the Lonely Planet Web site (W www.lonelyplanet.com). Here you'll find succinct summaries on travelling to most places on earth, postcards from other travellers and the Thorn Tree bulletin board, where you can ask questions before you go or dispense advice when you get back. You can also find travel news and updates to many of our most popular guidebooks, and the subWWWay section links you to the most useful travel resources elsewhere on the Web.

Other useful Web sites are:

Active Sydney News, views and links for activist events around Sydney
W www.active.org.au
Australian Tourist Commission (ATC) Huge official site: maps, information etc
W www.australia.com
Izon's Backpacker Journal Full of backpacker-friendly information and useful links
W www.izon.com
State Transit Authority (STA) Information on bus, train, and ferry services
W www.sydneytransport.net.au
CitySearch The *Sydney Morning Herald*'s Internet entertainment, dining, accommodation and shopping service
W www.citysearch.com.au
YHA Australia Heaps of info on hostelling around Australia
W www.yha.org.au

BOOKS

Most books are published in different editions by different publishers in different countries. As a result, a book might be a hardcover rarity in one country and readily available in paperback in another. Fortunately, bookshops and libraries search by title or author, so your local bookshop or library is best placed to advise you on availability.

For information on Sydney's bookshops see the Shopping chapter.

Lonely Planet

Lonely Planet's *New South Wales* guide includes extensive coverage of the whole state, so if you plan to visit more of the state, check it out. Lonely Planet's *Bushwalking in Australia* details the walk in the Blue Gum Forest in the Blue Mountains. For extensive information on Sydney's eateries, get a copy of Lonely Planet's *Out to Eat – Sydney*.

If you are travelling elsewhere in Australia, Lonely Planet publishes *Australia,* individual state and city guides *(Melbourne, Islands of Australia's Great Barrier Reef, Victoria, Queensland, Tasmania, Northern Territory, Western Australia, Outback Australia),* the *Australian phrasebook* and the *Australia Road Atlas.*

Guidebooks

There's a good range of guidebooks concentrating on particular aspects of Sydney, including a number on exploring the city on foot. Joan Lawrence has written several books describing short walks in many Sydney suburbs, including *Balmain, Glebe and Annandale Walks, Eastern Suburbs Walks* and *North Shore Walks. Sydney by Ferry & Foot,* by John Gunter, describes walks mainly near the harbour.

If having a luxurious time full of heady delights is your aim, then *Sensual Sydney* by Kristen Sproule offers some good tips.

See the Cycling section of the Things to See & Do chapter for books on cycling and the boxed text 'For the Serious Foodie...' in the Places to Eat chapter.

Travel

A great book is *Sydney,* by Jan Morris, one of the best travel writers around. In Lonely Planet's *Sean & David's Long Drive,* an offbeat road book by Sean Condon, the protagonists visit Sydney.

History & Politics

A good introduction to Australian history is Manning Clark's *A Short History of Australia.*

Robert Hughes's best-selling account of the convict era, *The Fatal Shore,* is a very good read and a popular introduction for many Australians to their own history.

The Birth of Sydney, edited by Tim Flannery, is a fascinating anthology about Sydney's unruly early days as a convict settlement and its development as a thriving city about 100 years later, told through a variety of sources.

If you want to get a handle on Sydney's not-too-buried seamy side, grab a copy of John Birmingham's *Leviathan – The Unauthorised Biography of Sydney.*

Aboriginal History & Culture

Invasion to Embassy: Land in Aboriginal Politics in NSW 1770–1972 by Heather Goodall is an essential read for travellers through NSW who wish to understand the government policies that affected the Aboriginal peoples and their struggle for land.

The Man Who Sold His Dreamings by Roland Robinson provides the reader with Dreaming stories from the Aboriginal peoples of NSW. These intriguing stories explain the creation of the land and peoples of NSW.

Healing the Land by Judith Monticone raises some serious issues about the Reconciliation movement. While the horror of atrocities committed in the battle for settlement of Australia makes for unpleasant reading, it's nonetheless a very informative book.

Lonely Planet's *Aboriginal Australia & the Torres Strait Islands* is also a handy guide to the culture and history of Australia's Indigenous peoples.

Children's Books

Norman Lindsay's *The Magic Pudding* and May Gibbs' *Snugglepot & Cuddlepie* are classics for younger children. Lindsay's home near Springwood in the Blue Mountains (see the Blue Mountains section in the Excursions chapter) is now a museum, as is Nutcote, May Gibbs' house in Neutral Bay. For details on Nutcote see the Mosman & Around section in the Things to See & Do chapter.

General

There are some good coffee-table books about Sydney that make excellent souvenirs, such as *Above Sydney* by George Hall, which shows the city from an aerial perspective, with some great harbour shots.

NEWSPAPERS & MAGAZINES

The *Sydney Morning Herald* is one of the best newspapers in the country. It's a serious broadsheet, but also captures some of Sydney's larrikinism. The other big Sydney paper is the Murdoch tabloid, the *Daily Telegraph*.

Two national newspapers are available in Sydney: the *Australian*, a conservative daily that has an interesting weekend edition; and the business-oriented *Australian Financial Review*. There are also a healthy number of weekly newspapers for Australia's ethnic communities – some are published in English.

The *Bulletin* is a venerable, conservative weekly news magazine, which carries a condensed version of *Newsweek*. It was first published in 1880.

Widely available international papers include the *International Herald Tribune,* the *European* and the *Guardian Weekly*. *Time* produces an Australian edition, as does *Rolling Stone*.

RADIO & TV

Sydney's radio dial is crowded with stations. The Australian Broadcasting Commission (ABC) has Radio National (576 AM), 2BL (702 AM) and ABC Classic FM (92.9 FM). Triple J FM (105.7) is the ABC's excellent 'youth' station. There are also the SBS multilingual stations (1107 AM and 97.7 FM), the multicultural 2000 FM (98.5 FM) and the excellent subscriber-based 2MBS (102.5 FM). Koori Radio broadcasts on 88.9 FM.

Sydney has five free-to-air TV channels: channel two – the government-funded ABC station; seven, nine and 10 – standard commercial fare; and SBS – a UHF channel devoted to multicultural programs. SBS invariably has the best news, movies and arts programs.

PHOTOGRAPHY & VIDEO

Australian film prices are similar to those in the rest of the Western world, but if you arrive via Hong Kong or Singapore, it's probably worth buying film there.

Developing standards are high, with many places offering one-hour service for colour print film. Film is susceptible to heat, so protect your film by keeping it cool and having it processed as soon as possible. Dust and humidity also affect film.

The best photographs are taken early in the morning or late in the afternoon, especially in summer when the sun's glare tends to wash out colours.

Many camera shops also do repairs. One is Paxton's (Map 5; ☎ 9299 2999), 285 George St, which is a large camera and video store specialising in duty-free gear.

At airports, X-ray machines don't jeopardise lower-speed film, but it's best to carry your film and camera with you and ask the X-ray inspector to check them visually.

Overseas visitors thinking of purchasing videos should remember that Australia uses the Phase Alternative Line (PAL) system, which isn't compatible with other standards unless converted.

TIME

NSW uses Eastern Standard Time (as do Queensland, Victoria, the ACT and Tasmania), which is 10 hours ahead of GMT/UTC (Greenwich Mean Time).

Other time zones in Australia are Central Time (half an hour behind Eastern Standard, used in South Australia and the Northern Territory) and Western Time (two hours behind Eastern Standard, used in Western Australia). Broken Hill, in western NSW, uses Central Time.

At noon in Sydney it's 2am in London, 3am in Rome, 9am in Bangkok, 2pm in Auckland, 6pm the previous day in Los Angeles and 9pm the previous day in New York.

From the last Sunday in October to the last Sunday in March, NSW is on Eastern Summer Time, which is one hour ahead of standard time.

ELECTRICITY

Voltage is 220–240V and plugs are flat three-pin, but not like British three-pin plugs. Except in fancy hotels, it's difficult to find converters to take either US flat two-pin plugs or European round two-pin plugs used for electric shavers or hair driers. Adapters for British plugs are found in good hardware shops, chemists and travel agencies.

Sydney Harbour ferry

GILLIANNE TEDDER

Surf lifesaver, Bondi Beach

PAUL BIENSSEN

PAUL BIENSSEN

MICHAEL LAAMELA

Aboriginal art in the making

Young local lad

PAUL BIENSSEN

spot of pigeon feeding, Hyde Park

Cricket at the SCG – India vs Australia

Volleyball action, Bondi Beach

St John's ambo's, City to Surf fun run

Boats jostle for position at the beginning of the traditional Boxing Day Sydney to Hobart Yacht Race.

WEIGHTS & MEASURES
Australia uses the metric system. See the table at the back of this book if you need to convert measurements.

LAUNDRY
Most hostels and cheaper hotels have self-service laundry facilities, while the more expensive hotels will return your clothes washed, dried and neatly folded. Otherwise there are self-service laundrettes, and dry-cleaning places, many of which open daily. Washing costs around $2 per load, and drying another $2 for 30 minutes. Some laundrettes have attendants who wash, dry and fold your clothes for an additional fee. To find a laundrette, look in the *Yellow Pages* under 'Laundries – Self-Service'.

LEFT LUGGAGE
Luggage lockers are available at Central station. Small/medium/large lockers are available for $4/6/8 per 24 hours: If you lose your ticket, a replacement will cost you $5. The locker room is open from 6.30am to 9.45pm Monday to Saturday, and to 9.30pm Sunday. Unclaimed luggage is cleared out every fortnight, so if you want to store your gear for longer than two weeks you'll need to make other arrangements.

There are luggage lockers ($6/9 medium/large per 24 hours) at the Sydney Coach Terminal at Central station on Eddy Ave (Bay 14). You can access the lockers between 6am and 9.30pm. You may also be able to store luggage with some of the backpacker service specialists in Kings Cross.

HEALTH
There are no vaccination requirements for travel to Australia. If you are coming to Australia from a yellow-fever-infected country you will need proof of vaccination. It's always a good idea to keep childhood vaccinations, such as polio, tetanus and diphtheria, up to date.

Medical care in Australia is first class and only moderately expensive. A typical visit to the doctor costs around $35 to $50. Health insurance is strongly encouraged by the federal government for Australian residents, but there's usually a waiting period after you sign up before you can make a claim.

There's universal health care in Australia (for Australians and citizens of nations with reciprocal rights) and you can choose your own General Practitioner. Visitors from Finland, Italy, Malta, the Netherlands, New Zealand, Sweden, Ireland and the UK have reciprocal health rights and can register at any Medicare office. Seeing a doctor is simply a matter of finding one nearby – check the *Yellow Pages* under 'Medical Practitioners'.

If you have an immediate health problem, attend the casualty section at the nearest public hospital; in an emergency, call an ambulance (☎ 000).

It's a good idea to travel with a basic medical kit (including aspirin or paracetamol, antiseptic, elastic plasters etc), even when your destination is a country like Australia where first-aid supplies are readily available. Don't forget any medication you're already taking.

Health Precautions
The sun can be very intense in Australia and ultraviolet rays can burn you badly even on an overcast day. Australia has the world's highest incidence of skin cancer, so cover up and slather on the sunscreen. The sun is at its fiercest between 11am and 3pm, so be especially careful during this period.

Too much sunlight, direct or reflected (glare), can damage your eyes. Good-quality sunglasses that filter out UV radiation are important.

Dehydration or salt deficiency can cause heat exhaustion. Take time to acclimatise to high temperatures and make sure you drink sufficient liquids. Wear loose clothing and a broad-brimmed hat. Heatstroke occurs when the body's heat-regulating mechanism breaks down and body temperature rises to dangerous levels. If you arrive during a hot period avoid excessive alcohol and strenuous activity.

For advice on HIV/AIDS call People Living With HIV/AIDS (PLWH/A; ☎ 9361 6011, 1800 245 677), Level 1, Suite 5, 94 Oxford St, Darlinghurst; or contact the

AIDS Council of NSW (ACON; ☎ 9206 2000, 1800 063 060), 9 Commonwealth St, Surry Hills.

The contraceptive pill is available by prescription only, so a visit to a doctor is necessary first.

Salbutamol inhalers (Ventolin) are available without prescription, but you must give your name and address to the chemist (pharmacist).

Condoms are available from supermarkets, chemists, convenience stores, and vending machines in many toilets.

Vaccinations

Several places give vaccinations and advice, but you need to book an appointment.

The Travellers Medical & Vaccination Centre (Map 5; ☎ 9221 7133), 7th floor, 428 George St, above Dymocks bookshop, opens weekdays from 9am to 5pm and until noon Saturday.

Kings Cross Travellers' Clinic (Map 7; ☎ 9358 3066), Suite 1, 13 Springfield Ave, is open from 10am to 1pm and 2pm to 6pm weekdays and until noon Saturday.

Hospitals & Pharmacies

The city's public hospitals, many of which have casualty and out-patient departments, include:

Children's Hospital at Westmead (☎ 9845 0000) Hawkesbury Rd, Westmead
Prince Henry Hospital (☎ 9382 5555) Anzac Pde, Little Bay
Royal North Shore Hospital (☎ 9926 7111) Pacific Hwy, St Leonards
Royal Prince Alfred Hospital (☎ 9515 6111) Missenden Rd, Camperdown
St Vincent's Public Hospital (Map 6; ☎ 9339 1111) Victoria St, Darlinghurst
Sydney Children's Hospital (☎ 9382 1111) High St, Randwick
Sydney Hospital & Sydney Eye Hospital (Map 5; ☎ 9382 7111) Macquarie St

For pharmacies, check the *Yellow Pages* under 'Chemists – Pharmaceutical'. Some chemists with longer opening hours are:

Blake's Pharmacy (Map 7; ☎ 9358 6712) 28 Darlinghurst Rd, Kings Cross. Open from 8am to midnight daily.

Darlinghurst Prescription Pharmacy (Map 8; ☎ 9361 5882) 261 Oxford St, Darlinghurst. Open from 8am to 10pm daily & 11am to 6pm on public holidays.
Park Pharmacy (Map 9; ☎ 9552 3372) 321 Glebe Point Rd, Glebe. Open from 8am to 8pm daily.
Wu's Pharmacy (Map 5; ☎ 9211 1805) 629 George St. Open from 9am to 9pm Monday to Saturday, & 9am to 7pm Sunday & public holidays.

WOMEN TRAVELLERS

Sydney is generally safe for women travellers, although you should avoid walking alone late at night. Sexual harassment and discrimination, while uncommon, can occur and shouldn't be tolerated. If you do encounter infantile sexism from drunken louts in pubs or bars, the best option is to leave and choose a better place – there are plenty.

Some of the major women's organisations (which can direct you to local services) are:

Royal Hospital for Women (☎ 9382 6111) Barker St, Randwick
Women's & Girls Emergency Centre (Map 8; ☎ 9360 5388) 177 Albion St, Surry Hills
Women's Legal Resources Centre (☎ 9749 5533, 1800 801 501, indigenous clients ☎ 1800 639 784)
Women's Liberation House (☎ 9569 3819) 63 Palace St, Petersham

GAY & LESBIAN TRAVELLERS

Gay and lesbian culture is so strong in Sydney that it's almost mainstream. Oxford St, especially around Taylor Square, is the centre of what's probably the second-largest gay community in the world, and the suburbs of Newtown and Leichhardt are popular with Sydney's lesbians. Sydney is one of the top three holiday destinations for North American gays and lesbians. The Gay & Lesbian Mardi Gras in February/March is the biggest annual tourist event in Australia. It culminates in a spectacular parade along Oxford St, watched by over half a million people.

Despite this, there's still a strong anti-homosexual streak among 'dinkum' Aussies, even in Sydney, and violence against homosexuals isn't unknown, especially during school holidays.

For the record, it's legal in NSW for a man to have sex with a man over the age of 18, and for a woman to have sex with a woman over the age of 16. Gay activists are currently protesting the male age-of-consent laws. Laws in other states differ.

Free gay papers, *Sydney Xpress* and *Sydney Star Observer* and publications such as *Lesbians on the Loose (LOTL)* and *Homo* have extensive listings.

For information on tickets to the Gay & Lesbian Mardi Gras, contact the Mardi Gras office (☎ 9557 4332), 21-3 Erskineville Rd, Erskineville. There is a Web site at 🅦 www .mardigras.com.au. See Special Events later in this chapter for more information about the Mardi Gras.

Sydney is also to host the Gay Games in 2002. For further information, see the boxed text 'Gay Games 2002' in the Things to See & Do chapter.

For counselling and referral call the Gay & Lesbian Line (☎ 9207 2800, 1800 805 379), which operates from 4pm to midnight daily.

DISABLED TRAVELLERS
Useful Organisations
A good Web site to check out is 🅦 www .accessibility.com.au. The following organisations offer useful information and services for people with disabilities:

Australian Council for the Rehabilitation of the Disabled (Acrod; ☎ 9743 2699) 24 Cabarita Rd, Cabarita (industry association for disability service providers)
Deaf Society of NSW (☎ 9893 8555, 1800 893 855, TTY 9893 8858, TTY 1800 893 885) Level 4, 169 Macquarie St, Parramatta
Independent Living Centre (☎ 9808 2233, TTY 9808 2477, fax 9809 7132) 600 Victoria Rd, Ryde (equipment and information service for disabled and older people)
National Information & Communication Awareness Network (Nican; ☎ 02-6285 3713, 1800 806 769, fax 6285 3714, 🅦 www.nican .com.au) Suite 4, 2 Phipps Cl, Deakin, ACT, 2600 (information on recreation, tourism, sport and the arts for disabled people)
Paraplegic & Quadriplegic Association of NSW (Paraquad; ☎ 9764 4166) 33–5 Burlington Rd, Homebush

Royal Blind Society of NSW (☎ 9334 3333, 1800 424 359, TTY 9334 3260, Braille TTY 9334 3466) 4 Mitchell St, Enfield

Useful Publications
The following publications contain useful information on access for travellers:

Access for All A handy brochure published by the NPWS with information on wheelchair-friendly national parks in the Sydney area and its surrounds.
Accessing Sydney Available from Acrod NSW
Blue Mountains Access Guide Available from PO Box 189, Katoomba 2780
Easy Access Australia – A Travel Guide to Australia Available from PO Box 218, Kew VIC 3101

SENIOR TRAVELLERS
Travellers with an Australian Seniors Card are entitled to many discounts including public transport and admission fees. Few discounts apply to senior citizens from abroad, though some places may agree to give you a discount if you show your seniors card from home.

In your home country you may be entitled to interesting travel packages and discounts (on car hire, for instance) through organisations and travel agencies that cater to senior travellers. Start hunting at your local senior citizens' advice bureau.

For information on recreational and other activities contact the Seniors Information Service (☎ 13 12 44), 6th floor, 93 York St, Sydney. Each March there's a Seniors Week with exhibitions, concerts, seminars etc.

SYDNEY FOR CHILDREN
Try not to overdo things with your kids and consider using some sort of self-catering accommodation as a base. Include children in the planning process; if they've helped to work out where you're going, they'll be more interested when they get there. Include a range of activities. During school holidays many places put on extra activities for children; the Opera House has an interesting range of entertainment tailored to juniors.

Look for copies of *Sydney's Child,* a free monthly magazine listing activities and businesses catering for ankle-biters. The Sydney Visitors Centre at The Rocks and the Powerhouse Museum (see the Things to See & Do chapter) are among the many places that stock it.

For more general information see Lonely Planet's *Travel with Children*.

CULTURAL CENTRES

Among the many foreign cultural centres in Sydney are:

Alliance Française (☎ 9267 1755) 257 Clarence St
British Council (☎ 9326 2022) 203 New South Head Rd, Edgecliff
Goethe Institut (☎ 8356 8333) 90 Ocean St, Woollahra
Italian Institute of Culture (☎ 9392 7939) 1 Macquarie Place
Japan Cultural Centre (☎ 9954 0111) Level 12, 201 Miller St, North Sydney

DANGERS & ANNOYANCES

Sydney isn't a dangerous city but the usual big-city rules apply: Never leave cars or rooms unlocked, never leave luggage unattended, never show big wads of money, never get drunk in the company of strangers and never walk through parks alone late at night. Use extra caution in Kings Cross, which attracts drifters from all over Australia and gutter-crawlers from all over Sydney.

If you're unlucky enough to have something stolen, immediately report it to the nearest police station. If your credit cards, cash card or travellers cheques have been taken, notify your bank or the relevant company immediately (most have 24-hour 'lost or stolen' numbers listed under 'Banks' or 'Credit Card Organisations' in the *Yellow Pages*).

Swimming

It seems superfluous to mention it, but don't go swimming if you've been drinking alcohol. Wait 30 minutes after eating before you swim.

The surf lifesaving clubs aren't there for show – many people are rescued from the surf each year. Shark attacks are extremely rare. Some major beaches, especially around Sydney, have shark-netting to deter sharks from cruising along the beaches and checking out the menu. The more popular beaches have shark-spotting planes at peak times. If a siren sounds while you're swimming leave the water quickly but calmly.

There are a few poisonous marine animals (such as the blue-ringed octopus, which can be fatal) – basically, if you don't know what it is, don't touch it.

Some beaches are unsuitable for swimming because of pollution caused by stormwater runoff; some local radio stations give updates on the latest conditions. See the boxed text 'A Ripping Time' for details on what to do if you're stuck in a rip.

Snakes & Spiders

Snakes are protected. Although there are many venomous snakes in Australia, few are aggressive, and unless you have the bad fortune to tread on one you're unlikely to be bitten. Taipans and tiger snakes, however, will attack if alarmed.

To minimise your chances of being bitten, always wear boots, socks and long trousers

---

A Ripping Time

Sydney's harbour beaches offer sheltered water for swimming. Nothing beats being knocked around in the waves that pound the ocean beaches, where you're safe if you follow instructions and swim within the flags. There are some notorious but clearly signposted rips – even at Sydney's most popular beaches – so don't underestimate the surf just because it doesn't look threatening.

If you *do* get stuck in a rip:

• Don't panic.
• Don't shout yourself hoarse, as you'll swallow water. Wave your arm to attract the lifeguard's attention.
• Don't try to swim against it. This is how you get tired and cramped. It's best to let the rip take you along, as it's highly unlikely that you'll get swept far out to sea.

KN

The feared Sydney funnel-web spider spins a tube-like web around its burrow.

when walking through undergrowth where snakes may lurk. Don't poke your fingers into holes and crevices, and be careful when collecting firewood.

Snake bites don't cause instantaneous death and antivenenes are usually available. Keep the victim calm and still, wrap the bitten limb tightly, as you would for a sprained ankle, then attach a splint to immobilise it. Then seek medical help, if possible with the dead snake for identification. Don't attempt to catch the snake if there's even a remote possibility of being bitten again.

There are a few nasty spiders in Sydney, too, including the funnel-web, the redback and the white-tail. The funnel-web bite can be fatal and is treated in the same way as a snake bite. For redback bites, apply ice and seek medical attention. It's good to check your boots and shoes before putting your feet in them, and you may want to look under the toilet seat if you're using an outdoor toilet.

Ticks & Leeches
The common bush tick can be dangerous if left lodged in the skin because the toxin it excretes can cause paralysis and sometimes death. Check your body for lumps every night if you've been bushwalking. Remove a tick by dousing it with methylated spirits or kerosene and levering it out intact.

If you're out walking in muddy fields north of Sydney, periodically check yourself for leeches.

Bushfires
In dry, hot weather, bushfires can raze thousands of hectares of eucalypt forest. Be *extremely* careful of fire when camping in summer. Many catastrophic bushfires are started by people either accidentally or deliberately.

Apart from the real risk of dying in the fire, you can be hit with huge fines, and even jail sentences if you light a fire during a total fire ban. This includes stoves fuelled by gas or liquid. *Never* throw a cigarette butt out of a car.

Bushwalkers should take local advice before setting out. If there's a total fire ban in operation, delay your trip until the weather changes.

EMERGENCY
In a life-threatening emergency, dial ☎ 000. This call is free from any phone and the operator will connect you with the police, ambulance or fire brigade.

There are several police stations in the city, including one at 192 Day St (☎ 9265 6499), near Darling Harbour, another in The Rocks on the corner of George and Argyle Sts (☎ 9265 6318), and one in Kings Cross behind the El Alamein fountain at 1–15A Elizabeth Bay Rd (☎ 8356 0099).

Sydney Hospital (Map 5; ☎ 9382 7111) on Macquarie St, and St Vincent's (Map 6; ☎ 9339 1111) on the corner of Victoria and Burton Sts, Darlinghurst, are two of the many public hospitals with emergency departments (see the Health section earlier).

Foreigners (except those from countries that have reciprocal health agreements with Australia – see the Health section earlier) are charged at least $85 for a visit to casualty. They bill your home address, so you'll be treated before they see your money.

The Wayside Chapel (Map 7; ☎ 9358 6577, 24 hours), 29 Hughes St, Kings Cross, is a crisis centre that provides useful local information and can help solve problems. At the time of writing it had just opened a controversial injecting room, to allow addicts to shoot up in safety.

Some other useful emergency numbers include:

Pharmacy	☎ 9235 0333
Dentist	☎ 9369 7050
Interpreter Service	☎ 1300 651 500
Lifeline	☎ 13 11 14
Poisons Information	☎ 13 11 26
Rape Crisis Centre	☎ 9819 6565, 1800 424 017
Salvo Care Line	☎ 9331 6000
Youthline	☎ 9951 5522

LEGAL MATTERS

The legal drinking age is 18 and you may need photo ID to prove your age. Stiff fines, jail sentences and other penalties could be incurred if you're caught driving under the influence of alcohol. The legal blood-alcohol limit is 0.05%.

Traffic offences (illegal parking, speeding etc) usually incur a fine payable within 30 days.

The importation and use of illegal drugs (and that includes marijuana) is prohibited and punishable by imprisonment.

If you need legal assistance contact the Legal Aid Commission of NSW (☎ 9219 5000, 1800 806 913), 323 Castlereagh St, Haymarket; it has several suburban branches.

BUSINESS HOURS

Most offices and businesses are open weekdays from 9am to 5pm, some until 5.30pm. Banking hours are from 9.30am to 4pm Monday to Thursday and until 5pm Friday.

Most shops are open from 8.30am or 9am to 5pm or 5.30pm weekdays, with hours extended to 9pm or 9.30pm Thursday. Many shops open all day Saturday, but some close at noon. On Sunday, many shops close, but there are exceptions, especially in Kings Cross and Oxford St where delicatessens, milk bars and bookshops stay open late every day.

PUBLIC HOLIDAYS

On public holidays, government departments, banks, offices, large stores and post offices are closed. On Good Friday and Christmas Day, there is limited newspaper circulation and about the only stores you'll find open are convenience stores. Note that some consulates close for 10 days over the Christmas to New Year period.

Public holidays include:

New Year's Day 1 January
Australia Day 26 January
Easter (Good Friday/Easter Monday) March/April
Anzac Day 25 April
Queen's Birthday 2nd Monday in June
Bank Holiday 1st Monday in August
Labour Day 1st Monday in October
Christmas Day 25 December
Boxing Day 26 December

Most public holidays become long weekends (three days), and if a fixed-date holiday such as New Year's Day falls on a weekend, the following Monday is usually a holiday.

SPECIAL EVENTS

Major celebrations on the Sydney calendar are:

Spring
September
Royal Botanic Gardens Spring Festival Early or mid-September; includes concerts, brass bands and a plant market; display of spring flowers in David Jones' city store.
Festival of the Winds Second Sunday; kite-flying festival with a multicultural theme at Bondi Beach; includes competitions for the best home-made kites and music and dance performances.
Taylor Square Arts Festival Mid-September; wide range of events week-long, many involving local Oxford St businesses.
Rugby League Grand Final Held at Sydney Football Stadium.

October
Manly International Jazz Festival Labour Day long weekend; styles range from traditional and big band to fusion, bop and contemporary. Call ☎ 9977 1088 for details.

November
Kings Cross Carnival First weekend; includes busking competition, and glorious food and wine tastings.

Summer

December

Christmas Party 25 December; party on Bondi Beach, a favourite with travellers, improved by being made alcohol-free.

Sydney to Hobart Yacht Race 26 December; Sydney Harbour is crowded with boats farewelling yachts competing in the race.

New Years Eve 31 December; Circular Quay and Darling Harbour are popular spots to see this huge fireworks display.

January

Sydney Festival Most of January; wide range of events from inline skating and street theatre to huge, free concerts in The Domain. Call ☎ 8248 6500 or visit its Web site (W www.sydneyfestival .org.au).

Great Ferry Boat Race Australia Day (26 January); contested by the city's ferries, decorated with balloons and streamers for the race from the Harbour Bridge to Manly and back.

Survival Festival 26 January; an important celebration of Aboriginal and Torres Strait Islander survival, with music, art and performance. Alcohol-free and held at Waverley Oval in Bondi. Call ☎ 9241 3533 for details.

Flickerfest International short film festival, held at Bondi Pavilion. Call ☎ 9365 6877 for details.

January/February

Chinese New Year January or February; celebrated on the Lunar New Year (literally with a bang!) in Chinatown.

Hunter Vintage Festival January to March, Hunter Valley; attracts hordes of wine enthusiasts for tastings, and grape-picking and treading contests.

February

Tropfest The world's largest short-film festival, is held on one night in February each year in Sydney's Domain, Royal Botanic Gardens, and selected cafes on Victoria Street, Darlinghurst. For more information see The Domain section in Things to See & Do and the Free Entertainment section in the Entertainment chapter.

February/March

Gay & Lesbian Mardi Gras February and early March; attracts more visitors and generates more tourist dollars than any other event in Australia. The month-long festival includes a sports carnival, the Blessing of the Mardi Gras, theatre, an arts festival and *lots* of parties culminating in an amazing parade (first Saturday in March) and the Mardi Gras Party. Tickets normally sell out by mid-January, and are usually only available to Mardi Gras members, though interstate and overseas visitors can get temporary membership. See the Gay & Lesbian Travellers section earlier for details.

Autumn

March/April

Golden Slipper March; Sydney's major horse race, which is held at Rosehill.

Royal Easter Show Sydney Showground at Homebush Bay; 12-day event traditionally beginning with a massive parade of farm animals; has a distinctly agricultural flavour, but has plenty of events to entertain city slickers.

Sydney Cup April; the second-most major horse race (after Melbourne Cup), held at Randwick.

Winter

June

Sydney Film Festival At the magnificent State Theatre; subscribe to the whole season or buy tickets to special screenings. Call ☎ 9660 3844 for details.

Sydney Biennale In even-numbered years; international arts festival at the Art Gallery of NSW and other city venues.

July

Yulefest In the Blue Mountains; guesthouses and restaurants celebrate Christmas. If you're lucky there might be snow.

August

City to Surf Run Second Sunday; more than 40,000 runners pound the 14km from Park St in the city to Bondi Beach; some are deadly serious, some are in costume and in it for fun, and everyone gets their name and finishing position published in the paper; entry forms appear in the *Sun Herald* months before the race, but you can enter on the day (adult/under-16 $22/16.50).

DOING BUSINESS

Sydney is Australia's chief commercial, financial and industrial centre. Many major international companies have their Australian and Asia-Pacific headquarters here. With its harbour, road and rail network and Australia's busiest airport, Sydney is also an important transport centre. The Sydney Stock Exchange (☎ 9227 0000), 20 Bridge St, is the largest in the country. The State Chamber of Commerce (☎ 1300 137 153) is at Level 12, 83 Clarence St. A number of countries have set up trade promotion offices in Sydney; a list of these can be found in the *Yellow Pages* under 'Trade Centres' and 'Trade Commissioners'.

The *Australian Financial Review* and the *Business Review Weekly* are Australia's foremost publications on business and finance.

Many top-end and higher mid-range hotels provide business facilities (eg, conference rooms, private office space, secretarial services, fax/photocopying services, use of computers and Internet access). Some also provide specialist translation services.

A number of telecommunications services catering to travellers offer good business-oriented facilities – see Post & Communications earlier in this chapter.

WORK

Many backpacker hostels find work for guests, but much of it involves collecting for charities or door-to-door sales. A few hostels have telephones in the rooms, which makes job-hunting easier, and some backpacker specialists provide a voicemail service.

Alternatively, you could do as Sydney-siders do and get a mobile phone (prepaid services, rather than contracts, are the best option for travellers).

TNT Magazine lists private employment agencies that specialise in finding work for travellers, or look in the *Yellow Pages* under 'Employment Agencies'. There are also job noticeboards around Kings Cross.

The government-run Centrelink offices (☎ 13 28 50) have touch-screen computers listing jobs, but most of what's available for travellers is seasonal work like harvesting and fruit-picking. The main office is at 477 Pitt St. Overseas visitors must present their work permits.

The nationwide employment scheme, Job Network (☎ 13 62 68), is similarly geared towards Australian citizens, but it too may offer seasonal work. Employment National's Harvest hotline (☎ 1300 720 126) is another option. Be sure to re-confirm all the details with your prospective employer before you head off to the back of beyond for a picking spree.

There are strict regulations governing overseas visitors working in Australia. Call DIMA (☎ 9258 4599, 13 18 81; in Canberra ☎ 02-6264 1111) or visit its Web site (Ⓦ www.dima.gov.au) if you're in any doubt. (See the Documents section earlier.)

Getting There & Away

AIR
Departure Tax
There's a departure tax of $38 payable by everyone leaving Australia, which is incorporated into your air fare. Sydney has a 'noise' tax of $3.40 (see Ecology & Environment in the Facts about Sydney chapter); again, this is included in your air fare.

Other Parts of Australia
In 2000, two domestic carriers (Impulse and Virgin Blue) challenged the stranglehold of Qantas and Ansett, resulting in a domestic air fare price war. In May 2001, Qantas made Impulse an offer it couldn't refuse, and they joined forces, leaving Ansett and Virgin to try and continue the price war if they felt like it. The fares aren't as cheap as they were in late 2000, but they are cheaper than they were a few years ago. Airlines can be contacted at: Ansett (☎ 13 13 00, ⓦ www.ansett.com.au); Qantas (☎ 13 13 13, ⓦ www.qantas.com); Virgin Blue (☎ 13 67 89, ⓦ www.virginblue.com.au). There are also smaller airlines (Eastern Australia and Kendell etc) that are subsidiaries of Qantas and Ansett and cover regional areas.

Fares Few people pay full fare on domestic travel because the airlines offer a wide range of discounts. These come and go, and there are regular 'spot specials', so keep your eyes open. If you book and pay one, two or three weeks in advance, you'll get a corresponding discount off the standard return fare – the further ahead you book, the bigger the discount. There are also cheap Internet air fares, although these come with more conditions.

Ansett Airlines

As this book goes to press, Ansett Airlines has been placed into voluntary administration; its future is uncertain. So please check its status before making plans.

Interstate Distances

Travelling interstate from Sydney is a major journey unless you fly. The nearest capital is Canberra, 315km away, while Melbourne is 870km away by the shortest road route. To Brisbane it's almost 1000km; to Adelaide at least 1400km; Darwin is 4000km; and Perth is 4100km. Sydney to Darwin via Adelaide is 4450km, and it's nearly 5000km via Townsville.

International travellers (Australians and foreigners) can get a 25% to 40% discount on Qantas or Ansett domestic flights simply by presenting their passport and international ticket (any airline, one way or return) when booking the full economy fare. In many cases it'll be cheaper to take advantage of other discounts. Both Ansett and Qantas offer good discounts for YHA, VIP and ITC cardholders.

Air Passes If you book in advance you'll find that some discounted fares are cheaper than air passes and have fewer restrictions. However, air passes are worth checking out.

One good example is the Qantas M10 'Z' pass, which offers coupons for domestic one-way fares. A minimum of two coupons must be purchased overseas, and then up to eight coupons may be purchased in the first week in Australia. A sample fare under this system is Sydney-Uluru for $340 one way, as opposed to the full economy fare of $660. Check what's on offer before you travel, as many airlines insist on air passes being purchased overseas.

Other Countries
Most visitors to Australia arrive by air at Sydney's Kingsford Smith airport.

Air fares to Australia are expensive – it's a long way from anywhere and flights are often heavily booked. If you're flying to

Air Travel Glossary

Alliances Many of the world's leading airlines are now intimately involved with each other, sharing everything from reservations systems and check-in to aircraft and frequent-flyer schemes. Opponents say that alliances restrict competition. Whatever the arguments, there is no doubt that big alliances are the way of the future.

Courier Fares Businesses often need to send urgent documents or freight securely and quickly. Courier companies hire people to accompany the package through customs and, in return, offer a discount ticket, which is sometimes a bargain. However, you may have to surrender all your baggage allowance and take only carry-on luggage.

Fares Airlines traditionally offer 1st class (coded F), business class (coded J) and economy class (coded Y) tickets. These days there are so many promotional and discounted fares available that few passengers pay full fare.

Lost Tickets If you lose your airline ticket, an airline will usually treat it like a travellers cheque and, after inquiries, issue you with another one. Legally, however, an airline is entitled to treat it like cash and if you lose it then it's gone forever. Take very good care of your tickets.

Onward Tickets An entry requirement for many countries is that you have a ticket out of the country. If you're unsure of your next move, the easiest solution is to buy the cheapest onward ticket to a neighbouring country or a ticket from a reliable airline which can later be refunded if you do not use it.

Open-Jaw Tickets These are return tickets where you fly out to one place but return from another. If available, this can save you backtracking to your arrival point.

Overbooking Since every flight has some passengers who fail to show up, airlines often book more passengers than they have seats. Usually excess passengers make up for the no-shows, but occasionally somebody gets 'bumped' onto the next available flight. Guess who it is most likely to be? The passengers who check in late. If you do get 'bumped', you are normally offered some form of compensation.

Reconfirmation Some airlines require you to reconfirm your flight at least 72 hours prior to departure. Check your travel documents to see if this is the case.

Restrictions Discounted tickets often have various restrictions on them – such as needing to be paid for in advance and incurring a penalty to be altered or cancelled. Others are restrictions on the minimum and maximum period you must be away.

Round-the-World Tickets RTW tickets give you a limited period (usually a year) in which to circumnavigate the globe. You can go anywhere the carrying airlines go; with some tickets you can't backtrack. The number of stopovers or total number of separate flights is decided before you set off and they usually cost a bit more than a basic return flight.

Ticketless Travel Airlines are gradually waking up to the realisation that paper tickets are unnecessary encumbrances. On simple one-way or return trips, reservations details can be held on computer and the passenger merely shows ID to claim their seat.

Transferred Tickets Airline tickets cannot be transferred from one person to another. Travellers sometimes try to sell the return half of their ticket, but officials can ask you to prove that you are the person named on the ticket. On an international flight, tickets are compared with passports.

Australia at a busy time of year (Christmas time is notoriously difficult) or on a particularly popular route (eg, Hong Kong–Sydney or Singapore-Sydney), plan well ahead.

Advance-purchase fares and other special deals can reduce ticket prices considerably. When choosing a ticket consider its validity and the number of stopovers. As a rule, the cheaper the ticket, the fewer stopovers allowed. Sometimes paying more for a ticket is worth it to avoid having to change planes on the way to Australia or languishing in a foreign departure lounge for hours on end.

Qantas offers air passes that give reasonable discounts on flights within Australia, although they have complex rules and restrictions. See Air Passes under Other Parts of Australia earlier.

The approximate fares quoted in this chapter are for the high season.

Arriving & Departing Delays of arrival or departure are not uncommon at Kingsford Smith airport. Even when you're on the ground it can take ages to get through immigration and customs.

Travellers with Specific Needs If they're warned early enough, airlines can often make special arrangements for travellers, such as wheelchair assistance at airports or vegetarian meals on the flight. Children under two years can travel for 10% of the standard fare (or free on some airlines) as long as they don't occupy a seat. They don't get a baggage allowance. 'Skycots', baby food and nappies should be provided by the airline if requested in advance. Children aged between two and 12 can usually occupy a seat for half to two-thirds of the full fare, and do get a baggage allowance.

The disability-friendly Web site **W** www.everybody.co.uk has an airline directory that provides information on the facilities offered by various airlines.

Round-the-World Tickets If you're flying to Australia from the Northern hemisphere, round-the-world (RTW) tickets can be a real bargain, and often you won't pay

much more than a standard return fare. RTW tickets are put together by the airline alliances, Star Alliance & Oneworld, and are only valid for a limited period of time (usually one year). You can fly to any destination covered by the carrying airlines as long as you stay within the set mileage/number of stops; with some tickets you can't backtrack. The number of stopovers or total number of separate flights is determined before you travel.

An alternative type of RTW ticket is one put together by a travel agent using a combination of discounted tickets, which may allow for more flexibility. Another option is a multiple destination ticket which is generally cheaper than a RTW ticket and allows for a couple of stops en route to Australia.

Typical prices for RTW tickets are around £830 or US$1999.

Circle-Pacific Tickets Circle-Pacific fares are similar to RTW tickets, using a combination of airlines to circle the Pacific – combining Australia, New Zealand, North America and Asia. Some examples

---

Warning

The information in this chapter is particularly vulnerable to change: Prices for international travel are volatile, routes are introduced and cancelled, schedules change, special deals come and go, and rules and visa requirements are amended. Airlines and governments seem to take a perverse pleasure in making price structures and regulations as complicated as possible. You should check directly with the airline or a travel agent to make sure you understand how a fare (and ticket you may buy) works. In addition, the travel industry is highly competitive and there are many lurks and perks.

The upshot of this is that you should get opinions, quotes and advice from as many airlines and travel agents as possible before you part with your hard-earned cash. The details given in this chapter should be regarded as pointers and are not a substitute for your own careful, up-to-date research.

are Qantas–Northwest Orient, and Canadian Airlines International–Cathay Pacific.

As with RTW tickets, there are advance-purchase restrictions and limits on how many stopovers you can make. Typically, fares range between US$1499 and US$2199. A possible Circle-Pacific route is Los Angeles-Hawaii-Auckland-Sydney-Singapore - Bangkok-Hong Kong-Tokyo-Los Angeles.

The UK Discount air travel is big business in London. Advertisements for many travel agencies appear in the travel pages of the weekend broadsheet newspapers, in *Time Out*, the *Evening Standard* and in the free magazine *TNT*.

For students or travellers under 26 years, popular travel agencies in the UK include STA Travel (☎ 020-7361 6262, W www .statravel.co.uk), which has an office at 86 Old Brompton Rd, London SW7, and branches across the country; and Usit Campus (☎ 0870-240 1010, W www .usitcampus.co.uk), which has an office at 52 Grosvenor Gardens, London SW1, and branches throughout the UK. Both of these agencies sell tickets to all travellers but cater especially to young people and students.

The cheapest London to Sydney tickets are about £335/500 one way/return. They are usually available only if you leave London in the low season (March to June). In September and mid-December, fares go up about 30%; the rest of the year they're somewhere in between. It pays to shop around, as fares can vary a great deal.

From Australia, you'll pay from around $1000/1500 one way/return in the low season to London and other European capitals, with stops in Asia on the way.

North America There are a variety of connections across the Pacific from Los Angeles or San Francisco to Australia. Qantas, Air New Zealand and United Airlines all have direct 14½-hour flights to Australia. There are also numerous airlines offering flights via Asia, with stopover possibilities including Tokyo, Kuala Lumpur, Bangkok, Hong Kong and Singapore and via the Pacific, with stopover possibilities

including Nadi (Fiji), Rarotonga (Cook Islands), Papette (Tahiti), and Auckland (New Zealand).

Discount travel agents in the USA are known as consolidators (although you won't see a sign on the door saying Consolidator). San Francisco is the ticket consolidator capital of America, although some good deals can be found in Los Angeles, New York and other big cities.

You can typically get a return ticket from the west/east coast for around US$1000/ 1250. Council Travel and STA Travel are good sources of discount tickets in the USA and have lots of offices around the country; in Canada, Travel Cuts offers a similar service. Fares from Vancouver are similar to the US west-coast prices. Fares from Toronto are from around C$1770 to C$2000 return.

Council Travel (☎ 800-226 8624, W www .counciltravel.com), America's largest student travel organisation, has around 60 offices in the USA. STA Travel (☎ 800-777 0112, W www.statravel.com) has offices in Boston, Chicago, Miami, New York, Philadelphia, San Francisco and other major cities.

Travel CUTS (☎ 800-667 2887, W www .travelcuts.com) is Canada's national student travel agency and has offices in all major cities.

Typical one-way/return fares from Australia include: $1250/1650 to San Francisco, $1500/2100 to New York and $1130/ 1850 to Vancouver.

New Zealand Air New Zealand and Qantas operate a network of trans-Tasman flights linking Auckland, Wellington and Christchurch in New Zealand with most major Australian cities. You can also fly directly between many other places in New Zealand and Australia.

Another option for trans-Tasman travellers is the discount airline, Freedom Air (W www.freedomair.com), an Air New Zealand subsidiary. It operates direct flights between Sydney and Dunedin, Hamilton and Palmerston North and offer excellent rates all year round.

Flight Centre (☎ 09-309 6171) has a large central office in Auckland at National Bank Towers (corner Queen & Darby Sts) and many branches throughout the country. STA Travel (☎ 09-309 0458, W www.statravel .co.nz) has its main office at 10 High St, Auckland, and has other offices in Auckland as well as in Hamilton, Palmerston North, Wellington, Christchurch and Dunedin.

Asia Ticket discounting is widespread in Asia, particularly in Singapore, Hong Kong, Bangkok and Penang. There are numerous fly-by-nights in the Asian ticketing scene, so care is required. Asian routes have been caught up in the capacity shortages on flights to Australia. Hong Kong–Australia flights are notoriously heavily booked; those to/from Bangkok and Singapore are often part of the longer Europe-Australia route, so are also sometimes full. Plan ahead.

Typical one-way fares to Sydney include S$950 from Singapore, HK$7680 from Hong Kong. Typical one-way fares from Australia's east coast to Singapore, Kuala Lumpur or Bangkok start from $400 to $1290, and to Hong Kong from $600 to $1300.

You can pick up interesting tickets in Asia to include Australia on the way across the Pacific Ocean. Qantas and Air New Zealand offer discounted trans-Pacific tickets.

Africa Qantas & South African Airlines are the only airlines operating between Africa and Australia, although Air Mauritius flies once per week between Mauritius and Melbourne and once per week between Mauritius and Perth, with connections from other African cities. Other options from South Africa are via Asia but fares are about the same. Fares vary but from Perth to Johannesburg you can expect to pay A$1799/2299 return in the low/high season. A flight from Sydney to Harare or Johannesburg, via Perth, cost about $2460.

Other airlines that connect southern Africa and Australia include Malaysia Airlines (via Kuala Lumpur) and Singapore Airlines (via Singapore).

From East Africa the options are to fly via Mauritius or South Africa, or via the Indian subcontinent and on to South-East Asia, then connect from there to Australia.

South America Qantas is the only airline that flies into South America. It operates two services per week via Auckland. Both Aerolineas Argentinas and Lan Chile no longer operate flights to Australia.

For travel to Australia from other South American countries, Qantas combines with a plethora of South American carriers from most capital cities via Buenos Aires to Australia.

BUS

Sydney Coach Terminal (Map 8; ☎ 9281 9366) on the corner of Eddy Ave and Pitt St, near Central station, is open from 6am to 10.30pm daily. Greyhound Pioneer/ McCafferty's (☎ 13 20 30, 13 14 99) have offices on Eddy Ave, while Premier (☎ 13 34 10) and Firefly Express (☎ 9211 1644) have offices around the corner on Pitt St. Many bus lines stop in suburbs on the way in/out of the city, and some have feeder services from the suburbs. Greyhound Pioneer was recently bought out by Mc Cafferty's and the two companies will gradually be streamlined, although business names will remain separate.

Greyhound Pioneer/McCafferty's is the only national bus network. See its Web site at either W www.greyhound.com.au or W www.mccaffertys.com.au. For destinations along the Princes Hwy within NSW, Pioneer Motor Service (☎ 13 34 10, 24 hours) often has the best fares. There are a few other companies running less-extensive routes.

It pays to shop around for fares. Students, YHA members and, sometimes, backpackers, generally get discounts of at least 10% with many long-distance companies. On straight point-to-point tickets there are varying stopover deals. Some companies give one free stopover on express routes, while others charge a small fee. This fee might be waived if you book through certain agents, such as hostels.

GETTING THERE & AWAY

Major routes from Sydney are:

Canberra Murrays (☎ 13 22 51) has three daily express buses that take under four hours to reach Canberra and cost $35.20/24.20/18.70 adult/concession/child one way. Greyhound Pioneer and McCafferty's have frequent Canberra services, which cost $35/32/28.

Melbourne It's a 12- to 13-hour run to Melbourne via the Hume Hwy, the most direct route – longer still if you go via Canberra. McCafferty's adult one-way fare is $59 and Firefly Express charges $55; other companies charge around $60.

Brisbane It takes about 16 hours via the Pacific Hwy and the standard fare is around $80. You often need to book in advance. Some buses don't stop in all the main towns en route. Companies running the Pacific Hwy route to Brisbane include Greyhound Pioneer/McCafferty's and Premier. With Greyhound/McCafferty's the fare costs adult/YHA & VIP cardholder $85/77.

Northern NSW Fares between Sydney and destinations in northern NSW include: $62/56 to Port Macquarie (seven hours), $71/64 to Coffs Harbour (9½ hours) and $85/77 to Byron Bay (13 hours). Greyhound Pioneer and McCafferty's also have services to northern NSW via the inland New England Hwy, which take an hour or two longer but cost about the same. Book at their offices or at Sydney Coach Terminal.

Adelaide The trip from Sydney to Adelaide takes 20 to 25 hours and costs $115 (Greyhound/McCafferty's). Services run via Canberra or Broken Hill. Travelling Sydney-Melbourne-Adelaide with Firefly ($90) is cheaper than travelling Sydney-Adelaide with other companies.

Elsewhere in Australia The 52- to 56-hour trip to Perth (via Adelaide) costs $341/307 one way with Greyhound/McCafferty's. To Alice Springs it's about 42 hours (plus some waiting in Adelaide) and $275/248; all the way to Darwin (via Adelaide and Alice Springs) takes 67 hours and costs $455/400.

Bus Passes

If you're planning to travel extensively in Australia, check Greyhound Pioneer's excellent bus pass deals. If a bus pass is what you want, make sure you get enough time and stopovers.

Bus Tours

A good way of travelling between Sydney and Byron Bay is with Ando's Opal Outback Tours (☎ 1800 228 828), which takes five days and travels inland via Lightning Ridge. Tours depart Sydney every Sunday and include opal and gold mining; sheep shearing; optional horse riding; and accommodation in miners' cabins, outback pubs and cotton plantations. Now run by Ando's nephew, this tour has received good feedback. It costs $460/435 adult/YHA, ISIC, Nomads and VIP cardholders.

Pioneering Spirit (☎ 1800 672 422, W www.pioneeringspirit.com.au) runs a three-day bus trip from Sydney to Byron Bay via the coast for $235, including accommodation, breakfast and dinner, entry fees and wine-tastings. This tour departs Sydney every Friday; you need to book in advance.

Oz Experience (☎ 8356 1766, W www.ozexperience.com) is a party-loving backpackers' bus line offering frequent services along the east coast, with off-the-beaten-track detours to cattle stations and national parks. There are over 20 different tours, ranging in price from $65 to $1445 depending on distance, and tickets are valid for six to 12 months.

TRAIN

Interstate and principal regional services run to and from Central station (Map 8). Most people just call it Central, but it's also known as Sydney Terminal station.

Within New South Wales

Countrylink's rail network within NSW is the most comprehensive in Australia. Trains and connecting buses take you quickly (if not frequently) to most sizeable towns. Most Countrylink services have to be booked (☎ 13 22 32 from 7am to 9pm daily. W www.countrylink.nsw.gov.au).

Intrastate economy-class services from Sydney include: Albury ($85.80, seven hours); Armidale ($79.20, eight hours); Bathurst ($37.40, 3½ to four hours); Bourke ($97.90, 11 hours); Broken Hill ($116.60 15½ hours); Byron Bay ($97.90, 12¾ hours); Coffs Harbour ($79.20, 8½ hours); Cooma ($66, 5¾ hours); Dubbo ($66, 6½ hours); Orange ($45.10, 4¾ hours) and Tamworth ($71.50, 6¼ hours).

CityRail (Sydney metropolitan service) runs frequent trains south to Wollongong ($8.40 one way); west through the Blue Mountains to Katoomba ($11) and Lithgow ($16.60); north to Newcastle ($16.60); and southwest through the Southern Highlands to Goulburn ($24). Some duplicate Countrylink services, but are a little slower and much cheaper, especially if you buy a day-return ticket. You can't book seats on CityRail trains. Off-peak return fares are available after 9am weekdays and all day on weekends.

Other Parts of Australia

For interstate service information, bookings and recorded information on arrival/departure times call the Central Reservation Centre (☎ 13 22 32) or a Countrylink Travel Centre (same central number). There are Countrylink Travel Centres on the main concourse at Central station; at Circular Quay on Alfred St under the Cahill Expressway; at Shop W15, Station Concourse, Wynyard station (Map 5; ☎ 9224 4744); and in Town Hall station. These are fully fledged travel agencies and keep standard business hours, but you can buy a train ticket at the Central station office on the concourse from 6am to 9.35pm daily. You can also make phone bookings and then collect your tickets from a Countrylink Travel Centre or a train station.

Interstate trains can be faster than buses, and there are often special fares that make the prices competitive. On interstate journeys, you can arrange free stopovers if you finish the trip within two months (six months on a return ticket). Countrylink offers both XPT linking Sydney with Brisbane, Melbourne, Dubbo, Grafton and Murwillumbah) and Explorer (Sydney to Tamworth, Armidale, Moree and Canberra) services. There are discounts of up to 40% on all standard rail fares if you book two weeks in advance, but this time requirement is sometimes waived.

Train passes available through Countrylink are as follows: NSW Discovery Pass, which includes one month's economy train/bus travel with unlimited stops within NSW for $273.90; East Coast Discovery Pass, which includes six months' unlimited one-way economy-class travel on Countrylink and Queensland Rail (bus too) – Sydney to Cairns costs $247.50.

Interstate routes and standard fares from Sydney are:

Canberra $47.30/67.10 economy/1st class, three trains daily, four hours
Melbourne $110/154/231 economy/1st class/1st-class sleeper, twice daily, 10¼ hours
Brisbane $110/154/231 economy/1st class/1st-class sleeper, nightly, 14¼ hours. This train connects with a bus at Casino for passengers travelling to the far north coast of NSW, and Queensland's Gold Coast. You can also take the daily train between Sydney and Murwillumbah, just south of the Queensland border ($110/148.50 in economy/1st class). There's a bus from Murwillumbah to the Gold Coast.
Adelaide & Perth The twice-weekly *Indian Pacific* goes to Perth ($459/1199/1499 economy/holiday/1st-class sleeper, 65 hours) via Adelaide ($176/439/549, 25 hours). The 1st-class fares include meals.
Alice Springs The incredible *Ghan* travels weekly to Alice Springs ($390/785/1146 economy/holiday/1st-class sleeper, 45 hours).

CAR & MOTORCYCLE

There are four main road routes out of Sydney: the Sydney-Newcastle freeway/Pacific Hwy, which runs north to Newcastle and eventually to Brisbane (cross the Harbour Bridge and follow the Pacific Hwy to the start of the freeway in Hornsby); the Western Motorway, which runs west to Penrith and the Blue Mountains, and becomes the Great Western Hwy (follow Parramatta Rd west to Strathfield); the Hume Hwy, which runs south-west to Mittagong and Goulburn and on to Melbourne (follow Parramatta Rd west to Ashfield); and the Princes Hwy, running south to Wollongong and the south coast (follow South Dowling St south from Surry Hills).

See the Getting Around chapter for information on car rental.

Getting Around

The fairly short distances involved make walking a good way to explore the city and inner suburbs. There are several steep hills, but the climb is invariably short. See the Things to See & Do chapter for suggestions on walking routes.

The State Transit Authority (STA) of NSW controls most public transport in Sydney. Call ☎ 13 15 00 between 6am and 10pm daily for information about Sydney buses and ferries and CityRail, or visit its information booths at Circular Quay or Wynyard Park. Also check the front of the A–K *Yellow Pages* telephone directory. Children (under 16) pay half-price on STA services.

THE AIRPORT

Sydney's Kingsford Smith airport is about 9km south of the city centre. The international and domestic terminals are a 4km bus trip apart ($2.50 with STA). Ansett and Qantas have separate domestic terminals. In the arrivals hall at the international terminal there's an airport information desk and a branch of the NSW Travel Centre. All terminals have foreign-exchange facilities.

TO/FROM THE AIRPORT
Bus

Airport Express (☎ 13 15 00, W www .sydneybuses.nsw.gov.au) is a special STA service that travels to/from the airport via Central station, with bus No 300 continuing to Circular Quay and bus No 350 going to Kings Cross. The green-and-yellow Airport Express buses have their own stops. The one-way fare is $17.50/7/3.50 for a family/adult/child; a return ticket, valid for two months, is $30/12/6. The trip from the airport to Central station takes about 15 minutes, to Circular Quay or Kings Cross about 30 minutes.

These buses leave the airport for the city approximately every 10 minutes. Buses leave Circular Quay and Kings Cross for the airport every 20 minutes, but both stop on Eddy Ave at Central station along the way, so a bus leaves there every 10 minutes. The service runs from 5am to 9.30pm.

Some ordinary STA buses also service the airport, but don't run as frequently. These are bus No 100 to Dee Why, bus No 305 to Railway Square (via Redfern) and bus No 400 from Burwood to Bondi Junction.

Kingsford Smith Transport/Airporter (☎ 9667 0663) runs a door-to-door service between the airport and places to stay (including hostels) in the city and Kings Cross between 5am and 8pm. The fare is $7/11 one way/return. Heading out to the airport, you must book at least three hours before you want to be collected.

Train

There's a new train line that runs from city train stations to the airport terminals (domestic and international). Trains run from approximately 6am to 2am weekdays and 6.30am to 1.45am weekends. A one-way fare from Central station costs adult/child $10/7.

Taxi

Depending on traffic conditions, taking a taxi (via the traditional route) from the airport to Circular Quay costs $20 to $25, to Central station $15 to $20. The new Eastern Distributor road toll costs $3.20 for northbound traffic.

Car

Avis (☎ 9667 0667), Budget (☎ 9207 9160), Hertz (☎ 9669 2444), Delta Europcar (☎ 9207 9400) and Thrifty (☎ 9669 6677) have rental desks at the airport's international and domestic terminals.

DISCOUNT PASSES

The composite SydneyPass is great value if you intend to use different forms of transport. If you just want to get to places you're better off buying a TravelPass.

SydneyPass

The SydneyPass offers bus, rail and ferry transport, travel on the Sydney Explorer and Bondi & Bay Explorer buses, harbour ferry cruises and the Airport Express. Passes are valid for a week; a three-day SydneyPass costs $225/90/45 for family/adult/child travel, five days costs $300/120/60 and seven days costs $350/140/70. The trip back to the airport is valid for two months, but it must be your last trip because you then have to surrender the ticket.

TravelPass

The TravelPass offers cheap weekly, quarterly or yearly travel on buses, trains and ferries. It's designed for commuters, but is useful for visitors. There are various colour-coded tickets offering different combinations of distances and services. The Green TravelPass is valid for extensive bus and train travel, and all ferries except the River-Cat and the Manly JetCat (before 7pm). At $37 for a week, it's a bargain. If you buy a TravelPass after 3pm, your week begins the following day. TravelPasses are sold at newsagents, train stations and STA offices, but *not* on buses.

TravelTen & FerryTen

The colour-coded TravelTen ticket ($11) gives a sizeable discount on 10 bus trips. The blue ticket is valid for two zones. The FerryTen also allows 10 trips, starting at $26.30 for travel on the inner harbour.

Day Passes

The BusTripper pass ($8.30/4.25 adult/concession) allows unlimited travel on Sydney bus routes. The Bus/Ferry DayPass costs $13/6.50.

Combination Passes

Several transport-plus-entry tickets are available for STA services, and work out cheaper than paying separately. The ZooPass ($25/12.50 adult/child) pays for your ferry to/from Taronga Zoo, the short bus ride from the wharf to the zoo entrance, zoo entry and the Aerial Safari cable-car ride. The ZooLink ticket is similar to the ZooPass (see the Taronga Zoo section in the Things to See & Do chapter). There are similar passes for the National Aquarium in Darling Harbour and Oceanworld in Manly.

Darling Harbour has a composite ticket offering sightseeing, travel and admission to several attractions. See the Darling Harbour & Pyrmont section in the Things to See & Do chapter.

BUS

The bus information kiosk on the corner of Alfred and Pitt Sts (behind Circular Quay) is open daily. There are other offices on Carrington St (by Wynyard Park) and outside the Queen Victoria Building (QVB) on York St. For further information, call the bus, train and ferry Infoline (☎ 13 15 00).

Buses run almost everywhere, but they're slow compared to trains. However, some places – including Bondi Beach, Coogee, and the North Shore east of the Sydney Harbour Bridge – aren't serviced by trains. On the eastern suburbs line you can get a combination bus/rail ticket from some stations, which enables you to change from a train to a bus for a destination such as Bondi Beach. This works out cheaper than buying separate tickets.

Sydney is divided into seven zones, the city centre being zone 1. The main bus stops in the city centre are Circular Quay, Wynyard Park on York St and Railway Square.

Nightrider buses provide an hourly service after regular buses and trains stop running (generally, shortly after midnight). They operate from Town Hall station and service suburban train stations. Return and weekly train-tickets and some passes are accepted; otherwise most trips cost about $4, depending on distance.

Some useful bus routes from Circular Quay are:

destination	bus Nos
Balmain	441, 442, 445, 446
Bondi Beach	380, 382, 389
Coogee	314–16, 372–4, 377, X13, X74
Darling Harbour	443, 456, 500, 501, 506, 888

destination	bus Nos
Glebe	431–4
Kings Cross	200, 323, 324, 325–7, 333 (free bus)
La Perouse	393, 394, 398
Leichhardt	370, 413, 436–40, 445, 446, 468, 470
Newtown	355, 370, 422, 423, 426, 428
Paddington	378, 380, 382
Surry Hills	301–4, 375, 390, 391
Watsons Bay	325

For Manly, take bus No 151 or 169 from Wynyard Park.

Special Bus Services

Sydney Explorer The red Sydney Explorer is an STA bus that runs a two-hour circular route from Circular Quay to Kings Cross, Chinatown, Darling Harbour and The Rocks, linking many inner-city attractions. It runs approximately every 20 minutes, departing from Circular Quay from 8.40am to 5.22pm daily. There's an on-board commentary, you can get on and off as often as you like, and your ticket includes discounted entry to many attractions. This is a good way to orient yourself, as well as see a lot of sights.

The 22 Explorer stops are marked by green and red signs. It's cheaper to get to places on its route by ordinary bus (in fact, it's possible to walk around the circuit), but the Explorer is less hassle because you don't have to work out the routes for yourself. You can use the Explorer ticket on ordinary buses between Central station and Circular Quay or the Rocks until midnight, and the ticket entitles you to big discounts on some tours (conditions apply). You can buy a ticket ($75/30/15 family/adult/child) on the bus, from STA offices and elsewhere. A detailed map of the route comes with the ticket.

Bondi Explorer This operates along similar lines to the Sydney Explorer, but has a much larger route that includes Circular Quay, Kings Cross, Paddington, Double Bay, Vaucluse, Watsons Bay, the Gap, Bondi Beach and Oxford St. The circular route takes two hours, and if you want to get off at many of the 19 places of interest along the way you'll need to start early. The bus departs Circular Quay half-hourly from 9.15am to 4.15pm daily. The ticket ($75/30/15 family/adult/child) entitles you to use ordinary buses south of the harbour until midnight. A map comes with the ticket.

TRAIN

CityRail (☎ 13 15 00), Sydney's suburban rail network (Map 15), services a substantial portion of the city. It has frequent trains and is generally much quicker than the bus. Getting around the city centre by train is feasible (if disorienting). At Circular Quay, under the Cahill Expressway behind Wharf 5, is a CityRail booth, which is open from 9am to 5pm daily.

The rail system consists of a central City Circle and a number of lines radiating out to the suburbs. Stations on the City Circle (starting at the southern end) are, in a clockwise direction: Central, Town Hall (on George St between Bathurst and Druitt/Park Sts), Wynyard (York St at Wynyard Park), Circular Quay, St James (northern end of Hyde Park) and Museum (southern end of Hyde Park). A single trip anywhere on the City Circle or to a nearby suburb such as Kings Cross costs $2.20; an off-peak return trip costs $2.60. Most suburban trains stop at Central station and at least one of the other City Circle stations. A combined ticket for light rail and trains, called TramLink, is available at all stations.

Trains run from around 4am to about midnight, give or take an hour. After the trains stop, Nightrider buses (see Bus earlier) provide a skeleton service.

There are automated ticket machines at most train stations. The machines accept $5, $10 and $20 notes, and all coins except 5c coins. You can buy an off-peak return ticket for not much more than a standard one-way fare after 9am on weekdays and at any time on weekends.

MONORAIL

Sydney's Metro Monorail is the only above ground rail system in the world that operates through a major city. The Metro Monorail (☎ 8584 5288, W www.metromonorail.com.au) circles Darling Harbour and links it to the city centre. There's a monorail every three to five minutes, and the full loop takes about 14 minutes. A single trip costs $3.50/2.20 adult/ senior (free for children five and under), but with the day pass ($7) or family pass ($20) you can ride as often as you like between 7am (8am Sunday) and 10pm (until midnight Friday and Saturday).

METRO LIGHT RAIL
In the 1930s Sydney had more than 250km of tramway, but by the early 1960s the last tram (streetcar) had lowered its pantograph and that fine metaphor for a hasty departure, 'pulled out like a Bondi tram', became meaningless. However, in 1997 the tram made a return, albeit with its name changed to Metro Light Rail (MLR; ☎ 8584 5288, W www.metrolightrail.com.au). It's pretty much another monorail in terms of usefulness to most commuters, and it operates 24 hours between Central station and Pyrmont via Darling Harbour and Chinatown. The service runs to Lilyfield via the Fish Market, Wentworth Park, Glebe, Jubilee Park and Rozelle Bay from 6am to 11pm Sunday to Thursday (until midnight Friday and Saturday). Fares range from $2.20 to $4.50 for adults and $1.10 to $3.30 concessions.

CAR & MOTORCYCLE
Australians drive on the left-hand side of the road. The minimum driving age (for NSW) is 17 for 'P-plates', full licence at 18 years old. Overseas visitors can drive in Australia with their domestic driving licences, but must take a driving test to obtain a NSW driving licence if they take up temporary or permanent residency. Speed limits in Sydney are generally 60km/h, rising to 100 or 110km/h on freeways. Seat belts must be worn.

The blood-alcohol limit of 0.05% is enforced with random breath-checks and severe punishments. If you're in an accident (even if you didn't cause it) and you're over the alcohol limit, your insurance will be invalidated.

Parking
You'll need a street directory to drive around the city, but with such good public transport why bother? The city centre has an extensive and maddening one-way-street system; parking is hell in most of the inner city and tow-away zones lurk in wait. Carparks in the inner city area include: the Goulburn St Parking Station (Map 5; ☎ 9212 1522) on the corner of Goulburn and Elizabeth Sts; Royal Parking (Map 5; ☎ 9212 4332) at 81 Quay St, Haymarket; Grimes Parking (Map 5; ☎ 9247 3715) at 220 George St; The Rocks Space Station (Map 5; ☎ 9247 6222) at 121 Harrington St, The Rocks; and Kings Cross Car Park (Map 7; ☎ 9358 5000) on the corner of Ward Ave and Elizabeth Bay Rd. Many maps indicate with a 'P' where you can park your car. See also the *Yellow Pages* under 'Parking Stations'.

If you have a car, make sure that your hotel has parking (many cheaper places don't) or you'll have to pay for commercial parking, which is fairly expensive.

Rental
The larger companies' metropolitan rates are typically about $59/69/89 small-/ medium-/large-sized car a day. These rates sometimes also include insurance and unlimited kilometres.

There are usually discounts for rentals of three or four days or longer. Check the small print on your rental agreement to see exactly where you can take the car (some firms don't allow driving on dirt roads) and what your insurance covers.

The major companies – Avis (☎ 13 63 33), Budget (☎ 13 27 27), Hertz (☎ 13 30 39), Thrifty (☎ 1300 367 227) and Delta Europcar (☎ 1300 131 390) – have offices at the airport and around the city, generally on William St.

The *Yellow Pages* is crammed with other outfits. Many offer deals that seem like great value, but advertisements may be misleading, so read the small print *carefully* and ring around. We get scores of letters from frustrated car hirers.

There are plenty of places renting older cars, which range from reasonable transport

GETTING AROUND

to frustrating old bombs. Check the car thoroughly *before* you sign anything and check the fine print regarding insurance excess. One small company offering competitive rates is Bayswater Rental (☎ 9360 3622), 180 William St, Kings Cross, with small manual cars from $29 a day (for three to five days) including insurance and 100km free each day.

Motorcycle rentals are available from Bikescape Motorcycle Tours & Rentals (Map 8; ☎ 9699 4722, fax 9699 4733, e jimc@bikescape.com.au), on the corner of Abercrombie and Cleveland Sts, Chippendale, a five-minute walk from Central station. Rates start from $70 per day for a PGO 50 to $250 per day for a Honda ST1100 Pan Euro, with rates reduced for longer rental periods. There are interesting tours available, and equipment is supplied.

Automobile Associations
The National Roads & Motorists Association (NRMA), the NSW motoring association, provides 24-hour emergency roadside assistance, road maps, travel advice and insurance, and discounted accommodation. It has reciprocal arrangements with the other state associations and similar organisations overseas. If you belong to another motoring organisation, bring proof of membership with you. The NRMA's head office (Map 5; ☎ 13 21 32) is at 74–6 King St in the city.

TAXI
Taxis are easily flagged-down in the city centre and the inner suburbs. You'll find taxi ranks at Central, Wynyard and Circular Quay train stations; and just off George St, on Goulburn St. The four big taxi companies offer reliable telephone services: Taxis Combined (☎ 8332 8888, TTY 90203315), 9–13 O'Riordan St, Alexandria; RSL Cabs (☎ 13 22 11), 20 O'Riordan St, Alexandria; Legion (☎ 13 14 51), 77 Foveaux St, Surry Hills; and Premier Cabs (☎ 13 10 17) at Granville.

Taxi fares include a $1.10 telephone booking fee, $2.35 flagfall and $1.32 per kilometre. The waiting fee is $0.61 per minute, and there's a luggage charge of $0.10 per kilogram for luggage over 25kg (often waived) between 6am and 10pm. Between 10pm and 6am, a 20% surcharge is added to the bill. Tipping isn't mandatory but rounding-up the bill is common. If you take a taxi via the Harbour Bridge or tunnel (or any other toll road), expect to pay the driver's return toll.

Water Taxis
Water taxis are pricey, but a fun way of getting around the harbour. Companies include Water Taxis Combined (☎ 9955 3222, 9555 1155), which can transport up to 28 people from Circular Quay to Watsons Bay or Shark Island ($45 boat hire plus $7 per person) and to Clark Island ($35 plus $7 per person).

FERRY
Sydney's ferries (Map 16; ☎ 13 15 00) are one of the nicest ways of getting around. The picturesque, old, green-and-yellow boats are supplemented by speedy JetCats to Manly, and sleek RiverCats running up the Parramatta River.

All the harbour ferries (and the Cats) depart from Circular Quay (Map 5). The STA, which runs most ferries, has a ferry information office (which also sells tickets) on the concourse under the Cahill Expressway, opposite the entry to Wharf 4; it's open from 7am to 5.45pm Monday to Saturday, and 8am to 5.45pm Sunday. Many ferries have connecting bus services.

In getting to Manly you have the choice of a roomy ferry ($5.30/2.60 adult/child, about 30 minutes) or a JetCat ($6.60, no concessions, about 15 minutes). The ferry trip is more pleasant because you can walk around, and there's a basic snack bar on board. JetCats have only a small outdoor area, and if you're stuck inside the windows can be a long way away. The JetCat is the only craft running to Manly after 7pm, but you can take it for the normal ferry fare. If you're staying in Manly, consider buying a Manly FerryTen pass (10 trips for $38.80) or, better still, a Green TravelPass (see the Discount Passes section earlier).

Hegarty's Ferries (☎ 9206 1167) run from Wharf 6 at Circular Quay to wharves directly across the harbour: Lavender Bay, McMahons Point and two stops in Kirribilli. These services cater to peak-hour commuters and stop at 6.35pm weekdays and 6pm weekends. The one-way fare is adult/child $3/1.50. The Hunters Hill ferry stops at Balmain and Birchgrove.

You can catch a RiverCat upriver to Parramatta for $6.30/3.10.

See Map 16 for ferry routes.

BICYCLE

See the Cycling section in the Things to See & Do chapter for cycling tips, information on buying or hiring a bike, and recommended spots for a leisurely pedal.

Sydney is awash with bicycles on the last Friday of the month, when hundreds of cyclists (plus joggers and inline skaters) gather to travel through the city in peak-hour traffic. The event is called Critical Mass and the aim is to raise awareness of Sydney's traffic conditions. Cyclists meet from 5pm onwards at Hyde Park and everyone heads off together at 6pm. The route changes every month and the journey takes an hour or more. Call ☎ 9351 2627 or visit the Web site (W www .nccnsw.org.au/~cmass/index .shtml) for more information.

ORGANISED TOURS

There is a vast array of city and area coach tours. For details, check the free magazines at hotels, or ask at Australian Travel Specialists (Map 5; ☎ 9555 2700) at Circular Quay's Wharf 6; it's open from 7am to 9pm weekdays and 8am to 9pm weekends.

Australian Pacific Tours (☎ 9247 7222), AAT King's (☎ 1800 334 009), Newmans (☎ 1300 300 036), Murrays (☎ 13 22 51) and Great Sights Tours (☎ 1300 850 850) carry most tourists around town. You can join a half-day city or koala-cuddling tour (from around $50), or a full-day city tour

(from around $70). Many companies also offer tours outside Sydney to the Blue Mountains, Jenolan Caves, Hunter Valley, Canberra etc. See the Excursions chapter for some options.

Sydney Aboriginal Discoveries (☎ 9568 6880, W www.aboriginaldiscoveries.com .au) offers a variety of interesting tours focused on indigenous culture and history. Outings cost from $65.60, and the options include a harbour cruise, a camping trip, a walkabout tour, a feast of native Australian foods, and an Aboriginal philosophy meeting (adults only). We've had good feedback about these tours.

The National Parks & Wildlife Service (NPWS; ☎ 9247 5033) runs tours of Sydney's historic forts and islands. See Sydney Harbour National Park in the Things to See & Do chapter.

Blue Thunder Bike Tours (☎ 1800 800 184, 0416 117 239) and Eastcoast Motorcycle Tours (☎ 0408 618 982) show you Sydney from the back of a Harley-Davidson. Blue Thunder can take you up into the Blue Mountains, Kangaroo Valley or the Hunter Valley. With Eastcoast, a one-hour tour of the harbour costs $90; it also offers day trips out of the city. Both companies have set tours or you can plan your own itinerary.

Harbour Cruises

A wide range of cruises from Circular Quay offer relatively inexpensive excursions on the harbour. You can book most at Australian Travel Specialists (Map 5; ☎ 9247 7818), at Circular Quay's Wharf 6 (and at offices in Rozelle, Darling Harbour and AMP Tower). It's open from 7am to 9pm weekdays and 8am to 9pm weekends. Captain Cook Cruises (☎ 9206 1111) has its own booking office at Wharf 6.

STA ferries offer some good-value cruises, such as the 2½-hour trip that goes as far as Sydney Head and the Spit Bridge

GETTING AROUND

($55/22/11 family/adult/child, 1pm/1.30pm weekdays/weekends). For sparkling views of the city at night, there's a 1½-hour Harbour Lights cruise ($47.50/19/9.50, 8pm Monday to Saturday). There's also a one-hour morning cruise of the eastern bays ($37.50/15/7.50, 10am and 11.15am). These tours are included in the cost of a Sydney Pass. STA cruises depart from Wharf 5, and tickets can be bought from the ferry ticket offices at each wharf.

The Sydney Harbour Explorer ($55/25/12 family/adult/child), run by Captain Cook Cruises, is a service that stops at the Opera House, Watsons Bay, Taronga Zoo, The Rocks and Darling Harbour. Boats run every two hours from 9.30am to 3.30pm daily from Wharf 6.

Sail Venture Cruises/Matilda Cruises (☎ 9264 7377), Pier 26, Darling Harbour, has 2½-hour coffee cruises ($27/13.70 adult/child), buffet lunch cruises ($56.20/27.80) and dinner cruises ($94.50/49.50).

Sailing cruises are also offered on the *Bounty* (☎ 9247 1789), a replica of the ship lost by the infamous Captain Bligh in the famous mutiny – this one was made for the film starring Mel Gibson. It sails twice daily on weekdays and thrice daily on weekends. There is a choice of cruises available. Prices range from $53 for the 1½-hour Sunday brunch sail, to $99 for the 2½-hour daily evening dinner cruise. The boat leaves from Campbell's Cove at the Rocks. The *Svanen* (☎ 9698 4456) also sails from here.

Hitching

Hitching is never entirely safe in any country, and we don't recommend it. Travellers who decide to hitch should understand that they're taking a small but potentially serious risk. People who do choose to hitch will be safer if they travel in pairs and let someone know where they are planning to go.

The ideal combination for successful hitching is one female and one male. Any more makes things very difficult and two guys hitching together can expect long waits. It's not advisable for women to hitch alone, or even in pairs.

Look for a place where vehicles will be going slowly and where they can stop easily: the ideal location is on the outskirts of a town.

University and hostel notice boards are good places to look for hitching partners. Just as hitchers should be wary when accepting lifts, drivers who pick up travellers should also be aware of the risks.

Walking Tours
See Walking Tours in the Things to See & Do chapter for information on guided walking tours around Sydney.

Bicycle Tours
CTA Cycle Tours (☎ 1800 353 004) runs weekend day tours from about $50, including gear and ferry transport.

Things to See & Do

Highlights

- Boating on beautiful Sydney Harbour, whether by ferry, harbour cruise or pleasure craft
- Feasting your eyes on harbour and city views via a walk around Millers Point, Campbells Cove, Circular Quay and the Royal Botanic Gardens
- Bushwalking in Sydney Harbour National Park – spectacularly scenic and right in the city!
- Glamming up or grabbing a milk crate to experience the magic at Mardi Gras
- Seeing a show at the Sydney Opera House
- Interacting with the displays at the Powerhouse Museum or viewing the extensive Aboriginal and Torres Strait Island art collection at the Art Gallery of NSW
- Beach-bumming at one of the ocean or harbour beaches
- Taking time out to sit under a Moreton Bay fig in a waterside park
- Coming face-to-face with a shark at Sydney Aquarium
- Catching an outdoor film or music performance at one of the city's summer festivals
- Cruising through Chinatown and chowing down on a late-night supper or daytime yum cha

Most interesting things to see in Sydney are in the city centre or nearby inner suburbs. They're all easy to get to on foot or by public transport. (See also the Free Entertainment section in the Entertainment chapter.)

WALKING TOURS

Setting out on foot is a good way to explore Australia's largest city. See the boxed texts 'City Walkabouts' and 'Harbourside Walks' for walking suggestions.

Guided Walks

There are several guided walks in Sydney. **Maureen Fry** (☎ 9660 7157, 15 Arcadia Rd, Glebe) caters mainly for groups, but she can take individuals or fit you in with a group. A two-hour guided walk costs $16 per person, with a minimum of 10 people.

The Rocks Walking Tours (☎ 9247 6678, Shop K4, Kendall Lane, The Rocks; adult/child 10-16 years/family $16/10.70/41.25) offers guided 90-minute walks from the visitors centre at 10.30am, 12.30pm and 2.30pm weekdays, 11.30am and 2pm weekends. If you'd rather soak it up at your own pace, hire a Rocks Walking Adventure cassette (☎ 018 111 011).

Sydney Aboriginal Discoveries (☎ 9568 6880, 1/108 Norton St, Leichhardt) offers a variety of outings with an indigenous focus, including walkabout tours of city landmarks and sacred places.

Sydney Architecture Walk (☎ 0403 888 390, City Exhibition Space, Level 4, Customs House, Circular Quay; adult/student $20/12; 10am Wed & Sat) is a 2½-hour walking tour of Sydney's contemporary architecture.

SYDNEY HARBOUR (MAP 2)

The harbour has melded and shaped the Sydney psyche since the first days of settlement, and today it's both a major port and the city's playground. Its waters, beaches, islands and waterside parks offer all the swimming, sailing, picnicking and walking you could want.

Officially called Port Jackson, Sydney's extravagantly colourful harbour stretches some 20km inland to join the mouth of the **Parramatta River (Map 1)**. The headlands at the entrance are North Head and South Head. The city centre is about 8km inland and the most scenic area is on the ocean side. The harbour has multiple sandstone headlands, beautiful bays and beaches, numerous inlets

THINGS TO SEE & DO

City Walkabouts

One way to orient yourself is to start in **Hyde Park (Map 5)** at Museum station's Liverpool St exit. Walk north through the park past the **Anzac Memorial**. On the right, on College St, is the **Australian Museum**. From here William St (the eastward extension of Park St) heads east to **Kings Cross**. Across Park St, at the end of the avenue of trees, is the wonderful **Archibald Memorial Fountain (Map 5)**. To the north on College St is **St Mary's Cathedral**.

Keep heading north to reach **Macquarie St**, with its collection of early colonial buildings and, after a few blocks, **Circular Quay** and the **Sydney Opera House**. On the western side of Circular Quay, behind the **Museum of Contemporary Art**, George St meanders through **The Rocks**.

Walk north on George St, which curves around under the **Sydney Harbour Bridge** into Lower Fort St. Turn right (north) for the waterfront or left to climb **Observatory Hill**. From Fort St, Argyle St heads east, through the skinny **Argyle Cut** and back to The Rocks.

Nearby on Cumberland St you can climb stairs to the Harbour Bridge and walk across to **Milsons Point** on the North Shore, from where you can catch a train back to the city.

This walk covers about 7km and takes about 2½ to three hours.

It's also worth wandering along Oxford St from Hyde Park's southeastern corner to **Paddington (Map 8)**. You can catch a bus back to the city from Paddington, or, if you keep going to **Bondi Junction**, catch a train.

and several islands. **Middle Harbour** is a large inlet that heads northwest 2km inside the Heads.

At weekends the harbour is carpeted with the sails of hundreds of yachts, and following the 18-footer yacht races on Sunday is a favourite activity (from mid-September to late March). See the Spectator Sports section in the Entertainment chapter.

The best way to view the harbour is to persuade someone to take you sailing, take a harbour cruise or catch any one of the many ferries that ply its waters (see the Getting Around chapter). The Manly ferry offers vistas of the harbour east of the bridge, while the Parramatta RiverCats cover the west. You can also visit some of the small islands, which are part of Sydney Harbour National Park.

For details on some of Sydney's beaches see the boxed text 'Beaches' later in this chapter.

Sydney Harbour National Park

This national park (☎ 9337 5511, *Greycliffe House, Nielsen Park, Vaucluse*) protects the scattered pockets of bushland around the harbour and includes several small islands. It offers some great walking tracks, scenic lookouts, Aboriginal carvings, beaches and a handful of historic sites. On the south shore, the park incorporates South Head and Nielsen Park; on the North Shore it includes North Head, Dobroyd Head, Middle Head and Ashton Park. George's Head, Obelisk Bay and Middle Head, north-east of Taylors Bay, are also part of the park, as are the islands.

Islands Previously known as Pinchgut, **Fort Denison** is a small, fortified island off Mrs Macquaries Point. It was originally used as a punishment 'cell' to isolate troublesome convicts, until it was fortified in the mid-19th century during the Crimean War, amid fears of a Russian invasion. It now has a cafe, which may be one of the best places to have coffee in all of Sydney. (For places to enjoy great coffee see the boxed text 'Buzzing' in the Places to Eat chapter.)

The largest island in the bay, **Goat Island**, west of Sydney Harbour Bridge, has been a shipyard, quarantine station and gunpowder depot in its previous lives, and is now a filming location for the popular *Water Rats* TV show. Fort Denison and Goat Island are heritage sites, so you'll need to join a tour if you want to visit them – contact National Parks & Wildlife Service (NPWS; ☎ 9247 5033, Cadman's Cottage, 110 George St, The Rocks). Goat Island tours *(adult/concession $19.80/15.40; 12.30pm Mon, Fri, Sat & Sun)* depart from

Cadman's Cottage. There's also a *Water Rats* tour *(adult/concession $19.80/15.40; 11.45am Wed)*, and a Gruesome Tales tour *(admission $24.20; Sat night)* – this is not suitable for children under 12!

Clarke Island, off Darling Point, **Rodd Island**, at Iron Cove near Birkenhead Point, and **Shark Island**, off Rose Bay, make great picnic getaways, but you'll need to hire a water taxi or have access to a boat to reach them. To visit these islands you need a permit from Cadman's Cottage. Landing fees are $3 per person (GST not included, children under five free). These three islands are open from 9am to sunset daily.

THE ROCKS (MAP 5)

Sydney's first non-Aboriginal settlement was made on the rocky spur of land on the western side of Sydney Cove, from which the Sydney Harbour Bridge now crosses to the North Shore. It became known as The Rocks because of the prominent outcrops of sandstone on the hillside. Today the site is unrecognisable from the squalid and overcrowded place it was when the sewers were open and the residents were raucous.

Soon after settlement The Rocks became the centre of the colony's maritime and commercial enterprises. Warehouses and bond stores were built, and the area thronged with convicts, officers, ticket-of-leavers (convicts with permits to leave prison), whalers, sailors and street gangs; brothels and inns soon followed. (This is the spot to look for several of Australia's oldest pubs; for locations, see The Rocks section in the Places to Eat chapter.)

In the 1820s and 1830s the nouveaux riches built three-storey houses on what is now Lower Fort St (which overlooked the slums), but the area remained notorious right into the 20th century. In the 1870s and '80s the infamous Rocks 'pushes' used to haunt the area, snatching purses, holding up pedestrians, feuding and generally creating havoc. The area fell into decline when modern shipping and storage facilities moved away from Circular Quay, and slumped further following an outbreak of the bubonic plague in 1900 that led to whole streets being razed.

Harbourside Walks

At the entrance to the harbour, near Watsons Bay, there's a rather fine short walk around **South Head (Map 2)**. It begins at Camp Cove and passes by Lady Bay, Inner South Head and the **Gap** (a popular place for watching sunrises and sunsets), ending at Outer South Head. From Circular Quay, catch bus No 324 or 325 (or an infrequent ferry) to Watsons Bay.

There's a delightful 5km coastal walk running from Bondi Beach along the clifftops to Tamarama, Bronte, Clovelly and Coogee.

On the North Shore, the Sydney Harbour National Park includes the 4km **Ashton Park track**, which begins below Taronga Zoo and rounds Bradleys Head, skirting Taylors Bay to reach Clifton Gardens. Take the Taronga Zoo ferry from Circular Quay to get to Ashton Park. From Taronga, you can also wander west to **Cremorne Point** via a combination of parks, stairways, streets and pockets of bush.

One of the best walks in the park is the 8km **Manly Scenic Walkway**, which takes about four hours and follows the shore from Manly to Spit Bridge, from where there are buses back to the city centre. Points of interest, from the Manly end, include Fairlight, Forty Baskets and Reef Beaches (the latter, a nude beach, involves a swerve off the main track), and ancient Aboriginal rock carvings on a sandstone platform between the Cutler Rd Lookout and Grotto Point. The route can be tricky to discern at times, so grab a leaflet from the Manly Visitors Information Bureau (☎ 9977 1088). For more information call the National Parks & Wildlife Service (☎ 9977 6229) or Manly Municipal Council (☎ 9976 1500).

For a more urban waterside wander, head west of Hyde Park along Market St, which leads to Pyrmont Bridge (for pedestrians and the monorail only) and **Darling Harbour (Map 5)**. On the other side of Darling Harbour, Pyrmont Bridge Rd leads to the **Anzac Bridge** and **Sydney Fish Market (Map 9)**. If you continue along Pyrmont Bridge Rd you'll eventually end up in **Glebe (Map 9)**.

Sydney Harbour Ferries publishes a useful pamphlet detailing some picturesque harbourside strolls.

The construction of the Harbour Bridge two decades later resulted in further demolition.

The Rocks as we know it today was created by visionaries in the building industry and the union movement. Redevelopment began in the 1970s under the auspices of the Sydney Cove Redevelopment Authority and turned The Rocks into a sanitised, historical tourist precinct, full of narrow cobbled streets, fine colonial buildings, converted warehouses, tearooms and stuffed koalas. If you ignore the kitsch, it's a delightful place to stroll around, especially in the narrow backstreets and in the less-developed, tightly knit, contiguous community of Millers Point.

Orientation & Information

The main street leading into The Rocks is George St, which runs south through the city centre to Railway Square and was the colony's first 'street'. George St curves under the Harbour Bridge and meets Lower Fort St, which leads south to Observatory Park and north to the waterfront near Pier 1. Cumberland St is parallel to George St, and almost all of the area's attractions are jammed into the narrow paths and alleyways between the two streets. The Argyle Cut on Argyle St is the short cut between the eastern and western sides of the peninsula.

The **Sydney Visitors Centre** (☎ *9255 1788, 106 George St, The Rocks; open 9am-6pm daily*) has an exhibition on the colourful and shameful history of The Rocks and shows the video *Story of the Rocks* in its upstairs theatre.

The visitors centre has a good range of publications and souvenirs, and maps of self-guided walking tours for $2.20. The Rocks isn't large, but there are many small streets and hidden corners, so a map is handy. Make sure you see Millers Point on the western side of the Bradfield Hwy (the elevated Harbour Bridge approach road), where there are some charming old terrace houses and the Sydney Observatory.

Things to See & Do

The oldest house in Sydney is **Cadman's Cottage** *(1816; ☎ 9247 5033, 110 George St;*

open 9.30am-4.30pm Mon-Fri, 10am-4.30pm Sat & Sun), next door to the visitors centre. It was once the home of the last government coxswain, John Cadman. When the cottage was built, it was actually on the waterfront, and the arches to the south of it housed longboats. The cottage is now the home of the Sydney Harbour National Park Information Centre, which helps organise tours of the harbour islands.

Susannah Place *(☎ 9241 1893, 58-64 Gloucester St; open 10am-5pm Sat & Sun, daily in January; adult/child/family $7/3/17)* is a terrace of tiny houses dating from 1844. It's one of the few remaining examples of the modest housing that was once standard in the area, and there's a corner shop that sells wares from that period.

The Rocks has several interesting shopping centres. These include the **Argyle Stores** on Argyle St, which was originally built as a bond store between 1826 and 1881, but today houses shops, studios, and eateries; the **Rocks Centre,** also on Argyle St; and the **Metcalfe Arcade** on George St.

The work of Sydney artist Ken Done is displayed at the **Ken Done Gallery** *(☎ 9247 2740, 1 Hickson Rd, The Rocks; open 10am-5.30pm daily)* in a converted warehouse.

A short walk west along Argyle St through the **Argyle Cut** – a tunnel excavated by convicts through the hill – takes you to the other side of the peninsula and **Millers Point,** a delightful district of early colonial homes.

At the far end of the cut is **Garrison Church** (1848), the first church in Australia. Soldiers of the 50th Queen's Own Regiment once said their prayers in the church and the first prime minister of Australia, Edmund Barton, received his primary education in the parish hall that once stood here. Nearby is **Argyle Place** (an English-style village green), and the secular delights of the **Lord Nelson Brewery** and **Hero of Waterloo** hotels, which vie for the title of Sydney's oldest pub.

Further north is the **Colonial House Museum** *(☎ 9247 6008, 53 Lower Fort St; adult/child/family $1/0.50/2)*, a private house with colonial-era furniture and knick-knacks. It was closed for renovations at the time of writing, but should have reopened by the time you have this book in your hands.

Built in the 1850s, the historically and architecturally interesting **Sydney Observatory** (☎ 9217 0485, Watson Rd, Observatory Hill, The Rocks; admission free, day tours $3; night tours adult/child & concession/family $10/5/25; open 10am-5pm daily – booking essential) has a commanding position atop Observatory Hill overlooking Millers Point and the harbour. This was the second observatory to be built on the hill – the first was constructed in 1821. Before that, the hill's exposed position made it an ideal site for a windmill to grind wheat. The colony's first windmill was built here in 1796, but its canvas sails were stolen and the structure eventually collapsed.

The observatory has an interesting little exhibition about astronomy in Australia from the Aboriginal sky stories to the present day, with interactive displays and videos. Evening tours include the exhibition and a viewing through the telescopes, plus a talk.

Close by, the **National Trust Centre** (☎ 9258 0123, Watson Rd, Observatory Hill, The Rocks; adult/child $6/3; open 11am-5pm Tues-Fri, noon-5pm Sat & Sun) in the old military hospital houses the **SH Ervin Gallery**, which has changing exhibitions with an Australian theme.

The waterfront from Dawes Point to Darling Harbour was Sydney's busiest before container shipping and the construction of new port facilities at Botany Bay. Although Darling Harbour is redeveloped, many wharves and warehouses around Dawes Point are in a state of decay. **Pier 1** now houses a hotel and the Harbourside Brasserie (see the Entertainment chapter). **Pier 4** (also known as Wharf Theatre) is home to the renowned Sydney Theatre Company, the Bangarra Dance Theatre, The Australian Theatre for Young People (ATYP) and the Sydney Dance Company. Tours of the theatre company are held at 10am Thursday or by appointment and cost $5 – bookings are advisable (☎ 9250 1700 or inquire at the box office).

You can find the site of the **public gallows**, in use until 1804, and **Sydney's first jail** on Essex St. The Essex St gallows were given a second lease of life (so to speak) from 1820 to 1840 while the Darlinghurst Gaol was being built.

See the Walking Tours section in this chapter for guided walks around The Rocks.

SYDNEY HARBOUR BRIDGE (MAP 5)

From the northern end of The Rocks, the imposing 'coathanger' crosses the harbour at one of its narrowest points, linking the southern and northern shores and joining central Sydney with North Sydney. Although some people consider the bridge ugly, it's always been a popular icon, partly because of its sheer size, simplicity and symmetry, partly because of its function in uniting the city, and partly because it kept many people employed during the Depression.

The two halves of the mighty arch were built out from each shore, supported by cranes. After nine years of work, when the ends of the arches were only centimetres apart and ready to be bolted together, a gale blew up and winds of over 100km/h (62mph) set them swaying. But the bridge survived and the arch was soon completed.

The bridge cost $20 million, a bargain in modern terms, but took until 1988 to pay off! Normally, giving it a new coat of paint takes four years.

You can climb inside the southeastern stone pylon, which houses the **Pylon Lookout** (☎ 9247 3408; adult/concession/family $5/3/12; open 10am-5pm daily). The pylons may look as though they're shouldering the weight of the Harbour Bridge, but they're actually decorative. You can gain access to the lookout via the Argyle St stairs to Cumberland St, and then walk along the pedestrian footpath on the bridge to the pylon.

Cars, trains, cyclists, joggers and pedestrians use the bridge. At night there are also huge cockroaches and rats. The cycleway is on the western side, the pedestrian footpath on the eastern; stair access is from Cumberland St in The Rocks and near Milsons Point station on the North Shore.

The best way to experience the bridge is undoubtedly on foot; don't expect much of

Top of the Harbour

Sydney is a city of awe-inspiring views, but perhaps the most exciting one of all is that from the Harbour Bridge. It's nothing short of spectacular, and it's open to the public daily (previously, it was up to law-breaking dare-devils and maintenance workers to let us know what we were missing out on). From Bridgeclimb's office under the bridge, you'll receive instructions and guidance on how to climb 'the coathanger', plus your daggy grey jumpsuit and a hanky, hat and glasses holder (everything must be attached to your jumpsuit for reasons of safety).

You start the climb by walking along the approach span, which runs under the Bradfield Hwy. Then you ascend through the southeast pylon, emerging onto the southeastern arch. Slowly, slowly, you ascend, with commentary (via earphone) all the way. There's plenty of time to stop and admire the views of Circular Quay, the ferries, the harbour's islands and overhead helicopters. Your climb leader will take photos throughout the climb so that you have a souvenir of your adventure (prices are pretty high but it's the only way to get pictures of yourself on the bridge). Eventually, you reach the summit, which is breathtaking. You really do feel as though you're on top of Sydney. The descent via the southwestern arch is fun too, with good views of Balmain and the western side of the city.

All in all, the climb takes about three hours (go to the toilet before you start the climb – there are no comfort stops). Wear rubber-soled shoes and save the celebratory tipple for after the big event – you're breath-tested before beginning the climb. The relentless 'Disney-meets-corporate training exercise' enthusiasm of the staff will probably tax your strength more than the actual exertion of getting to the top, but it's truly worthwhile, even for jaded Sydneysiders.

Contact **Bridgeclimb** (☎ 8274 7777, W www.bridgeclimb.com.au, 5 Cumberland St, The Rocks; day climbs adult/concession $125/100 Mon-Fri, $150/125 Sat, Sun & public holidays, night climbs $150/125 Mon-Fri, $170/150 Sat, Sun & public holidays) for more details. Prices include a complimentary group photo on the bridge and all the equipment you'll need.

---

a view crossing by car or train. Driving south there's a $2.20 toll; there's no toll in the other direction.

If you don't suffer from vertigo (and you can afford the steep fee) you can climb to the peak of the bridge itself with a guided tour group – see the boxed text 'Top of the Harbour' in this chapter. If it's fabulous views you're after, see the boxed text 'City Views'.

The bridge shares Sydney's voluminous trans-harbour traffic with the **Harbour Tunnel**. The tunnel begins about half a kilometre south of the Opera House, crosses under the harbour to the east of the bridge and meets the Warringah Fwy (the road leading north from the bridge) on the northern side. There's a $2.20 southbound-only toll. If you're heading from the North Shore to the eastern suburbs, it's easier to use the tunnel; for Glebe, Pyrmont and Darling Harbour use the bridge.

SYDNEY OPERA HOUSE (MAP 5)

Australia's most recognisable icon sits dramatically on Bennelong Point on the eastern headland of Circular Quay. The Opera House's soaring shell-like roofs were actually inspired by palm fronds, but look a little like white turtles engaging in congress. Started in 1959, the Opera House was officially opened in 1973 after an operatic series of personality clashes, technical difficulties and delays. (See the boxed text 'Soap Opera House'.)

It's truly memorable to see a performance here, visit the Sunday market or sit at an outdoor cafe and watch harbour life go by. The Opera House itself looks fine from any angle, but the view from a ferry coming into Circular Quay is one of the best.

The Opera House (☎ 9250 7777, Bennelong Point) has four main auditoriums and stages dance, theatre, concerts and films, as well as opera. There's also a venue called

The Studio, which stages contemporary arts events. Over 2000 events are staged here every year.

There are tours (☎ 9250 7250) of the building, and although the inside isn't as spectacular as the outside, they're worth taking. The Front of House tour costs adult/senior/student $15.40/11.80/10.60. Tours are held approximately every half-hour from 8.30am to 5pm daily. Not all tours can visit all theatres at any given time because of the various activities taking place. You're more likely to see everything if you take a tour early in the day or go on a Sunday. There are also intermittent Backstage Pass tours ($25.20).

On Sunday there's a market near the front entrance selling Australian-made arts and crafts.

The bimonthly *Opera House Diary* details forthcoming performances and is available free at the Opera House.

Buying a Ticket

You can book tickets through the box office (☎ 9250 7777, fax 9251 3943, e bookings@ soh.nsw.gov.au; open 9am-8.30pm Mon-Sat & 2½ hours before Sun performance). You can also book by fax if you quote your credit card details (a service fee is charged) or by writing to the Box Office Manager, Sydney Opera House, PO Box R239, Royal Exchange, 1225. Children under five aren't admitted to most performances so check before you book.

Despite the price, popular operas sell out quickly, but there are often 'restricted view' tickets available for about $43. Some seats may have no view, which you might consider as an option for an opera performance. People under 27 qualify for Big Rush rates – otherwise – the price for standing room of restricted view tickets cost $33 on the day.

The Soap Opera House

The hullabaloo surrounding construction of the Sydney Opera House was an operatic blend of personal vision, long delays, bitter feuding, cost blowouts and narrow-minded politicking.

Sydney Opera House Design Competition

The NSW government held an international design competition in 1956, which was won by Danish designer Jørn Utzon, with plans for a $7 million building. Construction of Utzon's unique design began in 1959, but the project soon became a nightmare of cost overruns and construction difficulties. After political interference and disagreements with his consultants about construction methods, Utzon quit in disgust in 1966, leaving a consortium of three Australian architects to design a compromised interior. The parsimonious state government financed the eventual $102 million cost in true-blue Aussie fashion through a series of lotteries. The building was completed in 1973.

After all the brawling and political bickering, the first public performance staged was, appropriately, Prokofiev's *War & Peace*. The preparations were a debacle and a possum appeared on stage during one of the dress rehearsals.

In 1995, the resident Opera Australia staged *The Eighth Wonder*, dramatising the events surrounding the building of the Opera House.

CIRCULAR QUAY (MAP 5)

Circular Quay, built around Sydney Cove, is one of the city's focal points. Sydney Cove was the landing place of the First Fleet, and the first European settlement grew around the Tank Stream, which now runs underground into the harbour near Wharf 6.

The quay was created by a huge landfill built using convict labour between 1837 and 1844 and was originally called Semi Circular Quay. In the 1850s it was extended further, covering the Tank Stream, and was given its present name. Circular Quay was for many years the shipping centre of Sydney; early photographs and paintings show a forest of masts crowding the skyline. Today it's both a commuting hub and a recreational space.

There's no finer way of getting around Sydney than by ferry, and waiting for one on Circular Quay among the crowds and the buskers is an experience in itself.

Circular Quay is the departure point for all harbour ferries, the starting point of many city bus routes, and a train station on the City Circle. It has ferry and bus information booths, and a Countrylink Travel Centre (☎ 13 22 32). (See also the Getting There & Away chapter.) The elevated Cahill Expressway, running above Alfred St behind the ferry wharves, rather isolates the quay from the rest of the city and is one of the city's worst eyesores.

Circular Quay East runs out beside the Royal Botanic Gardens to Bennelong Point with the Opera House perched on the end. Along Circular Quay West is the small **First Fleet Park**, a good place to pause after pounding the pavements; the **Overseas Passenger Terminal**, where liners moor; and the little **Campbells Cove**, backed by the low-rise Park Hyatt Sydney.

The **Museum of Contemporary Art** (MCA; ☎ 9252 4033, 140 George St, The Rocks; admission free, exhibitions adult/child/family $9/6/18; open 10am-5pm daily), fronting Circular Quay West, is set in a stately Art Deco building. It has a fine collection of modern art (sculpture, painting, installations and the moving image) and temporary exhibitions on a variety of themes. The MCA store has good postcards and gifts, and the cafe serves classy food. There are free guided tours at 11am and 2pm weekdays and at noon and 1.30pm weekends.

For a more detailed listing of galleries around Sydney see the boxed text 'Galleries' in this chapter.

Customs House

Built in 1885, the grand old Customs House (☎ 9247 2285, 31 Alfred St; admission free; open 10am-5pm daily) has been totally revamped and offers a number of attractions for visitors, including: **Djamu Shop** (☎ 9320 6431, ground floor; open 9.30am-5pm daily), which showcases art, craft and books from Australian Aboriginal and Torres Strait Islander communities; **City Exhibition Space** (☎ 9242 8555, 4th floor), which has displays and exhibitions on Sydney's architecture; and **Object Galleries** (☎ 9247 9126, 3rd floor), which show international and Australian contemporary crafts and design. Cafe Sydney on the 5th floor has sweeping views of the quay.

MACQUARIE PLACE & AROUND (MAP 5)

Narrow lanes lead south from Circular Quay towards the city centre. At the corner of Loftus and Bridge Sts, under the shady Moreton Bay fig trees in Macquarie Place, are a cannon and anchor from the First Fleet flagship, HMS *Sirius*. Other pieces of **colonial memorabilia** in this interesting square include gas lamps, an ornate drinking fountain dating from 1857, a National Trust-classified gentlemen's convenience (not open) and an **obelisk**, erected in 1818, inscribed with the words 'to record that all the public roads leading to the interior of the colony are measured from it'.

The square has some pleasant outdoor cafes and is overlooked by the rear facade of the imposing 19th-century **Lands Department building**, on Bridge St, with its statues of surveyors, explorers and politicians.

Museum of Sydney

The excellent and dynamic Museum of Sydney (☎ 9251 5988, W www.hht.nsw.gov.au,

37 Phillip St; adult/child & concession/ family $7/3/17; open 9.30am-5pm daily), on the corner of Phillip and Bridge Sts, is built on the site of the colony's first and infamously fetid Government House (built in 1788). The museum uses installation and multiple-perspective art to explore Sydney's early history – including the early natural environment, the culture of the indigenous Eora people and convict life. It also has a good cafe and a gift shop.

Justice & Police Museum
Designed by colonial architect James Barnet, and completed in 1856, the museum *(☎ 9252 1144, 8 Phillip St; adult/child & concession/ family $7/3/17; open 10am-5pm Sat & Sun)* is in the old Water Police Station, on the corner of Albert and Phillip Sts. It was in use until 1979 and is now set up as a late-19th-century police station and court. It has various exhibits on criminal activity in New South Wales, including forensic evidence from famous crimes of the past, some nasty-looking weapons and lots of mug shots, so you can try and spot anyone you know.

CITY CENTRE (MAPS 5 & 8)
Central Sydney stretches from Circular Quay in the north to Central station in the south. The business hub is towards the northern end near Circular Quay, but most redevelopment is occurring at the southern end and this is gradually shifting the focus of the city.

Sydney lacks a true civic centre, but **Martin Place** lays claim to the honour, if only by default. This grand pedestrian mall extends from Macquarie St to George St and is lined by the monumental buildings of financial institutions and the colonnaded, Victorian, general post office (GPO). The Commonwealth Bank on the corner of Martin Place and Elizabeth St, and the Westpac Bank on George St opposite the western end of Martin Place, have impressive old banking chambers.

The street has a couple of fountains, plenty of public seating and an amphitheatre – a popular lunchtime entertainment spot, especially during January's Sydney Festival, when there's free entertainment daily.

Near the George St end of Martin Place is the **Cenotaph** commemorating Australia's war dead. This is where Sydney's Christmas tree is placed, in December's summer heat.

Barrack St, west of Martin Place, another pedestrian area, has fruit barrows and good views of Martin Place and the GPO. East of Martin Place are the delightful historic buildings of **Macquarie St** and the parks and gardens of the city centre's eastern edge (see the boxed text 'Green Gardens and Spaces' in this chapter).

The huge, sumptuous **Queen Victoria Building** *(QVB; ☎ 9265 6869, 455 George St; open 24 hours, shops open 9am-6pm Mon-Wed, Fri & Sat, 9am-9pm Thur, 11am-5pm Sun),* next to Town Hall, takes up the entire block bordered by George, Market, York and Druitt Sts. It houses about 200 shops, cafes and restaurants. It was built in 1898, in the style of a Byzantine palace, to house the city's fruit and vegetable market. They don't build markets like this any more! There are guided tours *(☎ 9265 6869)* at 11.30am and 2.30pm Monday to Saturday and at noon and 2.30pm Sunday. Outside the QVB is an imposing statue of Queen Victoria herself, and nearby is a wishing well featuring a small bronze statue of her beloved pooch, Islay (which, quite disconcertingly, speaks aloud in a deep baritone).

A few blocks south, the old civic locus used to be the plaza containing Town Hall and St Andrew's Cathedral, but traffic and insensitive development have diminished the area's authority. The sandstone wedding cake exterior of **Town Hall** *(1874; ☎ 9265 9189, 483 George St; open 8am-6pm Mon-Fri),* on the corner of George and Druitt Sts, is matched by the elaborate chamber room and concert hall inside. The **concert hall** *(☎ 9265 9007)* houses an impressive organ and is a venue for free, monthly lunchtime concerts. Across the open space to the south, **St Andrew's Cathedral** *(☎ 9265 1661),* dating from the same period, is the oldest cathedral in Australia. At the time of writing it was being restored, but the interior was almost finished and free concerts still take place.

Opposite the QVB, underneath the Sydney Hilton Hotel and the Royal Arcade, is the **Marble Bar** (☎ 9266 2000, Sydney Hilton Hotel, 259 Pitt St), an extravagant piece of Victoriana. The bar was built by George Adams, the founder of Tattersalls lotteries. When the old Adams Hotel was torn down to build the Hilton, the bar was carefully dismantled and reassembled. The city's other ostentatious building is the splendidly elaborate **State Theatre** (☎ 9373 6655, 49 Market St), to the north. It was originally built as a movie palace during Hollywood's heyday and is now a National Trust-classified building. Except for during the Sydney Film Festival in June, it stages only live shows. Tours of the opulent interior (☎ 9373 6660) run Tuesday to Sunday, and cost adult/concession $12/$8.

On Pitt St, a block south of Martin Place, is the busy **Pitt St Mall**, with shopping arcades and department stores nearby. The lovingly restored **Strand Arcade**, which houses speciality shops and designer clothing and wares, runs west off the mall to George St. On the eastern side of the mall is the modern **Skygarden** arcade. **Centrepoint**, at the bottom of the Sydney (AMP) Tower (see the 'City Views' boxed text in this chapter), is another large complex. Two large department stores, Grace Bros and the more upmarket David Jones, are nearby on Market St. Gowings, on the corner of Market and George Sts, is an old-fashioned-style department store catering mostly to men and boys.

To the southwest are the lively **Chinatown** and the much smaller **Spanish Quarter**. Chinatown, west of George St between Liverpool and Quay Sts, is a colourful and bustling area, encompassing Dixon St Mall and **Haymarket**, and the restored **Paddy's Markets** in Market City. The Spanish Quarter is along Liverpool St between George and Sussex Sts. A block east, **World Square**, a big hole in the ground for much of the late 1980s and 1990s, is slowly taking shape.

The dynamism of this part of the city is spreading south to breathe life back into the zone around **Central station** (1906) and **Railway Square** at the intersection of Broadway, George and Regent Sts on the city centre's southern periphery. At the turn of the 20th century, this was Sydney's business district. Running beneath Central from Railway Square is a long pedestrian subway, emerging at Devonshire St in Surry Hills. It's usually crowded with commuters (and buskers), but late at night it can be spooky.

DARLING HARBOUR & PYRMONT (MAP 5)

This huge, waterfront leisure park on the city centre's western edge was once a thriving dockland area with factories, warehouses and shipyards lining Cockle Bay. In a state of decline for many years, it was reinvented and opened in 1988. It had a shaky start and resembled a ghost town on many occasions, but further developments like Darling Walk and the snazzy wining-and-dining precincts of Cockle Bay wharf and King St wharf have attracted many more visitors. (See also the Darling Harbour & Pyrmont section in the Places to Eat chapter.)

The Harbourside shopping centre underwent a $50 million face-lift in the late 1990s, and although this is the supposed centrepiece, the real attractions are the aquarium, the state-of-the-art Powerhouse Museum, the IMAX Theatre and the lovely Chinese Garden.

Darling Harbour Visitors Centre (☎ 9281 0788, 33 Wheat Rd; open 10am-6pm daily) is under the elevated freeway near the IMAX Theatre.

Although the complex covers a large area it's possible to see it all on foot. If you're bent on seeing everything, consider the Darling Harbour Superticket (adult/child $29.95/19.50), which gives you a harbour cruise, entry to the aquarium and Chinese Garden, a cafe meal and a monorail ride. You can buy the Superticket at the aquarium, monorail stations, the Chinese Garden or through Matilda Cruises (☎ 9264 7377); it's valid for one month.

Harbourside

This large, graceful structure, Harbourside (☎ 9281 3999; open 10am-9pm daily), faintly reminiscent of public buildings from the reign of Queen Victoria, is basically a shopping centre. One of the main attractions

The Herb Garden, Royal Botanic Gardens

SIMON BRACKEN

Pausing for a moment atop the Harbour Bridge

MICHAEL LAANELA

Taxiing across the harbour

SIMON BRACKEN

sleepy kangaroo, Taronga Zoo

SIMON BRACKEN

Aboriginal dancer

MICHAEL LAANELA

GILLIANNE TEDDER

Sydney's monorail speeds by, Darling Harbour

SIMON BRACKEN

Star City Casino

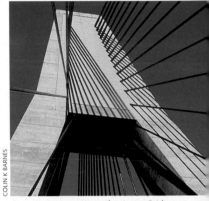

COLIN K BARNES

Stunning perspectives, the Anzac Bridge

NEIL SETCHFIELD

The 300m-high Sydney (AMP) Tower soars up and away from the Centrepoint shopping centre.

City Views

The most elevated view in Sydney is from **Sydney (AMP) Tower** (☎ 9231 1000; adult/child/family $19.80/13.20/55; open 9am-10.30pm Sun-Fri, 9am-11.30pm Sat), the 300m-high needle soaring from the Centrepoint shopping centre, on the corner of Market and Pitt Sts. The views extend west to the Blue Mountains and east to the ocean, as well as to the streets of inner Sydney below. To get to the tower enter Centrepoint from Market St and take the lift to the podium level where you buy your ticket.

The Harbour Bridge offers excellent views. You can get onto the bridge from a stone staircase off Cumberland St in The Rocks or from near Milsons Point train station on the North Shore. A footpath runs right across. If the view from the footpath isn't enough, you can climb the 200 stairs inside the south-east pylon for panoramic views of the harbour and city. For the intrepid view-seeker, Bridgeclimb (☎ 8274 7777, 5 Cumberland St, The Rocks) offers a breath-taking 1500m climb to the top of the bridge. (See the boxed text 'Top of the Harbour' for details.)

For a sea-level view of the Opera House, harbour and bridge, walk to **Mrs Macquaries Point**, at the headland east of the Opera House. The point has been a lookout since at least 1810, when Elizabeth Macquarie, wife of Governor Lachlan Macquarie, had a stone chair hewn from the rock so she could sit and watch ships entering the harbour and keep an eye on hubby's construction projects just across Farm Cove. The seat is still there today.

If you're in the vicinity of Kings Cross, the northern end of Victoria St in **Potts Point** is a good vantage point for views of the cityscape and its best-known icons, especially at night.

To get the best views of all, catch a **ferry** – the Manly ferries are especially good because they traverse the length of the harbour east of the Harbour Bridge. The ferries that travel west of the bridge (such as the Hunters Hill ferry – see the Ferry section in the Getting Around chapter for details) are also worth catching, both for the experience of cruising under the bridge and to see the narrow waterways humming with workday activity.

---

is **Gavala** (☎ 9212 7232), which has a gallery and retail shop of Aboriginal art and products. Performances (Aboriginal dance) can be arranged for groups, but bookings are essential.

Harbourside is close to Pyrmont Bridge (the old bridge that crosses Cockle Bay), a short walk west from the city centre via Market St, and it is also a stop on the monorail.

Sydney Aquarium

Near the eastern end of Pyrmont Bridge, this aquarium (☎ 9262 2300, W www.sydney aquarium.com.au, Aquarium Pier, Darling Harbour; adult/child/family $22/10/48; open 9am-10pm daily, last ticket sale at 9pm) displays the richness of Australian marine life and consists of three 'oceanariums' moored in the harbour: sharks, rays and big fish in one and Sydney Harbour marine life and seals in the others. There are also transparent underwater tunnels and informative, well-presented exhibits of freshwater fish and coral gardens.

Australian National Maritime Museum

It's not hard to spot the maritime museum (☎ 9298 3777, W www.anmm.gov.au, 2 Murray St, Darling Harbour; adult/child & concession/family $25/13/60 to see everything, $14/7/30 for limited access, $10/6/25 galleries admission; open 9.30am-5pm daily) at the western end of Pyrmont Bridge, with its billowing, sail-like roofs echoing the roof shapes of the Opera House. The museum tells the story of Australia's relationship with the sea, from Aboriginal canoes and the First Fleet to surf culture and the America's Cup.

The admission price varies depending on how much you want to see. Prices include guided tours, which take place on the hour 10am to 3pm daily.

Vessels moored at the wharves and awaiting exploration include a racing yacht, a Vietnamese refugee boat and the naval destroyer HMAS *Vampire*. There's an audiovisual display of sailing life, maritime craft demonstrations and entertainment.

Powerhouse Museum

Sydney's most spectacular museum (☎ *9217 0100*, W *www.phm.gov.au, 500 Harris St, Ultimo; adult/concession/child/family $9/3/ 2/20, admission free for children under 5, Australian Seniors Card holders & pensioners; open 10am-5pm daily),* is housed in a vast building that was once the power station for Sydney's now-defunct trams.

The museum covers the decorative arts, social history, science and technology with exhibits on anything from costume jewellery to space capsules to indigenous communication. The superbly displayed collections emphasise interaction and education through enjoyment, with video and computer activities, experiments, performances, demonstrations and films. It's no surprise that this museum is immensely popular with young and old. There are a variety of free tours, including a tour of the museum's highlights at 1.30pm weekdays. Guided tours in a community language can be booked (☎ 9217 0462). Special facilities are also available for disabled visitors, call ☎ 9217 0111 for details.

IMAX Theatre

The IMAX Theatre (☎ *9281 3300,* W *www .imax.com.au, Southern Promenade, Cockle Bay; adult/child $15/10; open 10am-10pm daily),* with its yellow-and-black chequered facade, rises up between two elevated freeways. It shows eye-popping, 45-minute feature films on its giant eight-storey screen every hour, on the hour. The films are so realistic that there's a sign warning patrons that they may experience physical discomfort during the screening.

Green Gardens and Spaces

Sydney has plenty of parks, many with harbour views, making it a wonderful city for a picnic or a stroll.

The **Royal Botanic Gardens**, The **Domain** and **Hyde Park** (see those sections in this chapter) border the eastern side of the city centre. There are also a few smaller parks in the city centre, which provide relief from the cement. **Wynyard Park** is a wedge of Victoriana on York St outside Wynyard station; the smaller **Lang Park** is a few blocks north; and **First Fleet Park** is north again, at Circular Quay. **Observatory Park**, on the western side of the Bradfield Hwy, is a pleasant place with old trees and good views.

There are two small parks at Elizabeth Bay, north-east of Kings Cross: the delightful **Arthur McElhone Reserve** opposite Elizabeth Bay House and **Beare Park**, down by the water. But the nearest swathe of green to the Cross is **Rushcutters Bay Park**, a pretty waterfront area to the east with workout facilities and good views of the yachts.

East of Surry Hills and south of Paddington are the adjacent **Moore Park** and **Centennial Park**, both large recreational areas (see under Paddington in this chapter).

Many headlands and bays on the North Shore have small parks, including **Blues Point**, Kirribilli's **Careening Cove**, Neutral Bay's **Anderson Park** and **Cremorne Point**, and Mosman's **Reid Park**. Finding them without a street directory can be difficult.

On the North Shore there's an 8km corridor of bushland called **Garigal National Park** stretching from Bantry Bay on Middle Harbour north to **Ku-ring-gai Chase National Park** at St Ives. **Lane Cove National Park**, between the suburbs of Ryde and Chatswood, is also on the North Shore. Both parks have extensive walking tracks and Lane Cove has lots of picnic areas. You may see lyrebirds in Garigal; the males make their spectacular mating displays from May to August.

See also Sydney Harbour National Park earlier in this chapter.

Chinese Garden

The exquisite 10-hectare Chinese Garden *(☎ 9281 0111; adult/child/family $4.50/2/10; open 9.30am-5.30pm daily),* the biggest outside China, is an oasis of tranquillity. It was designed by landscape architects from the Guangdong Landscape Bureau in Guangzhou (Sydney's sister city) to commemorate Australia's bicentenary in 1988.

After entering through the Courtyard of Welcoming Fragrance you'll see distinct geographical features: among them minimountains, wilderness, forest and a lake, interspersed with pavilions, waterfalls, lush plants and walls. Round off the experience with tea and Chinese cakes in the teahouse (open 10am-5pm daily) overlooking the lotus pond.

See also the boxed text 'Gardens and Green Spaces'.

Australia's Northern Territory & Outback Centre

This centre *(☎ 9283 7477, 28 Darling Walk, 1-25 Harbour St, Darling Harbour; open daily)* is both a tourist agency for the Northern Territory region, and a retail outlet for authentic Aboriginal and Australiana-type goods. Objects of interest include woomeras (spears), *kalis* (jumbo-sized boomerangs), musical clap sticks and bullroarers. There's also a free performance of Sounds of the Outback in its auditorium, featuring live didgeridoo and images of the Outback, although it's not an Aboriginal cultural performance. Times are 1pm, 3pm and 5pm Tuesday to Friday and hourly from 1pm to 5pm on weekends and public holidays.

Tumbalong Park & Around

The pleasant grassy area in the centre of the Darling Harbour complex is Tumbalong Park. The park has an amphitheatre that hosts free entertainment most lunchtimes and on weekends.

The **Sydney Convention & Exhibition Centre** *(☎ 9282 5000, Darling Dve),* on the western edge of the park, was designed by Australian architect Philip Cox, who also designed the aquarium, the maritime museum and the Sydney Football Stadium.

The centre's roofs are suspended from steel masts, continuing Darling Harbour's maritime theme.

South of the Chinese Garden, on the edge of Chinatown, is the **Sydney Entertainment Centre** *(☎ 9266 4800, 1900 957 333, Harbour St, Haymarket),* a venue for rock concerts and sporting events.

Motor World Sydney

Motor World Sydney *(☎ 9552 3375, Cnr Harris & Allen Sts, Darling Harbour; adult/child & concession/family $11/6/22; open 10am-5pm Wed-Sun & daily during school holidays),* is a short walk from the Powerhouse Museum. It has over 190 vehicles on display, from vintage beauties to Morris Minors.

Star City Casino

Built near the waterfront in Pyrmont on the north-eastern headland of Darling Harbour, the new casino complex *(☎ 9777 9000, 80 Pyrmont St, Pyrmont)* offers the usual gaudy assortment (check out the volcano!) of 24-hour gambling rooms, shops and theme bars, as well as two large theatres (the Lyric and the Showroom), a nightclub and a five-star hotel.

Sydney Fish Market (Map 9)

Fish auctions *(☎ 9660 1611 for tour information)* are held on weekdays at these markets west of Darling Harbour on the corner of Pyrmont Bridge Rd and Bank St, beside the approach roads to Glebe Island Bridge. It opens at 5.30am and lasts from three to six hours, depending on the size of the catch. The complex includes fabulous fish shops, fruit and vegetable stalls, delicatessens and several eateries.

Getting There & Around

The two main pedestrian approaches to Darling Harbour are footbridges from Market and Liverpool Sts. The one from Market St leads onto the lovely old Pyrmont Bridge, a pedestrian and monorail-only route that crosses Cockle Bay. It was famous in its day as the first electrically operated swing span bridge in the world.

Town Hall is the closest train station, from where it's a short walk down either Druitt or Market Sts.

Monorail The monorail (☎ 8584 5288) circles Darling Harbour and links it to the city centre. Some say its steel track, winding round the streets at 1st-floor level, ruins some of Sydney's best vistas. The initial uproar has died down, although you'll find its used more by tourists than locals. As a transport system, the monorail isn't great, but for sightseeing it's worth $3.50 ($7 for the whole day). Get off at Haymarket for the Powerhouse Museum or at Harbourside for Harbourside shopping centre, the National Maritime Museum and Pyrmont Bridge.

Bus & Train Bus Nos 433 and 888 connect Circular Quay with the Powerhouse Museum and the casino. The Sydney Explorer bus (see the Getting Around chapter) stops at five points around Darling Harbour every 20 minutes.

The Metro Light Rail transit (read tram) system runs from Central station to Darling Harbour and Pyrmont. A one-way fare is $2.20, return $3.50.

Ferry State Transit Authority (STA) ferries leave Circular Quay's Wharf 5 every 30 minutes from 7am to 8pm daily, and costs $4/2 adult/concession. They stop at Darling Harbour's Aquarium wharf, and the Pyrmont Bay wharf near the casino.

People Mover The People Mover (☎ 0408 290 515; adult/child $3.50/2.50; open 10am-5pm daily) is an incongruous, trackless, toy-town style minitrain that makes a 20-minute loop around Darling Harbour's sights.

MACQUARIE ST (MAP 5)

Sydney's greatest concentration of early public buildings graces Macquarie St, which runs along the eastern edge of the city from Hyde Park to the Opera House. The street is named after Governor Lachlan Macquarie, who was the first governor

to have a vision of the city extending beyond a convict colony. In the early 19th century he commissioned convicted forger Francis Greenway to design a series of public buildings. There are excellent views of Greenway's buildings from the 14th-floor cafeteria of the Law Courts building, on the corner of Macquarie St and Queens Square.

Hyde Park Barracks Museum & St James Church

These two Greenway gems, on Queens Square at the northern end of Hyde Park, face each other across Macquarie St. The barracks (1819) was built originally as convict quarters, then became an immigration depot and later an asylum for women. The barracks now house a museum (☎ 9223 8922, Queens Square, Macquarie St; adult/child/family $7/3/17; open 9.30am-5pm daily), with an exhibition that concentrates on the barracks' history and offers an interesting perspective on Sydney's social history.

St James (1819–24) was restored in the 1950s. It contains traditional stained glass, but also the more modern, striking 'creation window' in the Chapel of the Holy Spirit.

Sydney Mint Museum

This lovely building (1816) housing the Sydney Mint Museum (☎ 9217 0311, Macquarie St) was originally the southern wing of the infamous Rum Hospital. It was commissioned by Macquarie in 1814 and became a branch of the Royal Mint in 1854, the first to be established outside London. The museum has exhibits on the gold rush, coins, stamps, minting and a collection of decorative arts. At the time of writing, it was closed for renovations, but there are plans to reopen it.

Parliament House

Parliament House (1816; ☎ 9230 2047, Macquarie St; admission free; open 9am-5pm Mon-Fri), used by the Legislative Council of the colony from 1829, is still used by the NSW Parliament. This elegant two-storey, sandstone, verandaed building was originally the northern wing of the

Rum Hospital and is the world's oldest continually operating parliament building. There are free tours (☎ 9230 2111) at 10am, 11am and 2pm on non-sitting weekdays. The public gallery is open on sitting days; question time is at 2.15pm, Tuesday to Thursday.

Sydney Hospital & Sydney Eye Hospital

Just south of Parliament House is the country's oldest hospital (☎ 9382 7111, *Macquarie St*). Dating from the early 1880s, it was the site of the first Nightingale school, and the home of nursing in Australia. In front of the hospital is the bronze **Il Porcellino**, a copy of a statue of a boar in Florence, with water dripping from its mouth. Rubbing its polished snout – coupled with a donation that goes to the hospital – is said to grant you a wish.

State Library of NSW

The state library (☎ 9273 1414, *Macquarie St; galleries open 9am-5pm Mon-Fri, 11am-5pm Sat & Sun*) is more of a cultural centre than a traditional library. It has one of the best collections of early works on Australia, including Captain Cook's and Joseph Banks' journals, and Captain Bligh's log from the *Bounty*.

Conservatorium of Music

The conservatorium (☎ 9230 1222, *Conservatorium Rd*), at the northern end of Macquarie St, was built by Greenway as the stables and servants' quarters of Macquarie's planned new government house. However, Macquarie was replaced as governor before the rest of the new house was finished. Greenway's life ended in poverty because he couldn't recoup the money he had invested in the building.

The Writers' Walk

Every day at Circular Quay, thousands of feet pass over an odd but interesting collection of musings. Set into the promenade alongside the wharves is a series of round metal plaques – a selection of ruminations from a handful of Australian writers (and the odd literary visitor), reflecting on the place they call home.

Contributors include internationally acclaimed art critic and historian Robert Hughes; feminist, academic and author Germaine Greer; and writers Thea Astley, Peter Carey, Dorothy Hewitt and James A Michener.

Subjects range from indigenous rights and identity, to the paradoxical nature of glass; offerings range from eloquent poems addressing the human condition, to an irreverent ditty about a meat pie by Barry Humphries (associate of the famous Dame Edna Everage).

Several of the writers are Australians now living overseas. A wistful entry from the expatriate (and apparently homesick) author and entertainer Clive James reads:

In Sydney Harbour the yachts will be racing on the crushed diamond water under a sky the texture of powdered sapphires. It would be churlish not to concede that the same abundance of natural blessings which gave us the energy to leave has every right to call us back.

On one of James' visits to Sydney, he saw a group of Japanese tourists bowing over his plaque – believing it was the site of his grave!

SIMON BRACKEN

The conservatorium's students host concerts at venues around the city – including the popular, free Lunchbreak series (1.10pm Tuesday during term time) at St Andrew's Cathedral next to Town Hall.

Other Things to See

The Victorian townhouse, **History House** (☎ 9247 8001, 133 Macquarie St), built in 1853, now houses the Royal Australian Historical Society. The **Royal College of Physicians** (☎ 9256 5444, 145 Macquarie St) building, just up the street, is one of the last surviving verandaed Georgian townhouses in the city.

ROYAL BOTANIC GARDENS (MAP 5)

The Royal Botanic Gardens (☎ 9231 8111, Mrs Macquaries Rd; open 7am-sunset daily, visitors centre open 9.30am-5pm daily) encompass Farm Cove, the first bay east of Circular Quay. It has a magnificent collection of South Pacific plant life; an old-fashioned, formal rose garden; an arid garden featuring cacti and succulents; and a dark, dank bat colony complete with upside-down mammals.

The gardens were established in 1816, and include the site of the colony's first vegetable patch. There's a fabulous tropical display housed in the interconnecting **Arc** and **Pyramid glasshouses** (open 10am-4pm daily). It's a great place to visit on a cool, grey day. The multistorey Arc has a collection of rampant climbers and trailers from the world's rainforests, while the Pyramid houses the Australian collection, including monsoonal, woodland and tropical rainforest plants.

Free guided walks leave at 10.30am daily from the visitors centre and are extremely informative.

The **Trackless Train** (adult/child $10/5) is similar to Darling Harbour's People Mover and does a circuit of the gardens.

THE DOMAIN (MAP 5)

The Domain is a large, grassy area south of Macquarie St, which was set aside by Governor Phillip in 1788 for public recreation. It also contained Australia's first farm. It's separated from the Royal Botanic Gardens by the Cahill Expressway, but you can cross the expressway on the Art Gallery Rd bridge.

Today, it's used by workers for lunchtime sports and as a place to escape the bustle of the city. It's the Sunday afternoon gathering place for impassioned soapbox speakers who do their best to entertain or enrage their listeners. Free events are staged here during the Sydney Festival in January, as is the popular Carols by Candlelight at Christmas. The Domain is also the venue for the Tropfest film festival (see Free Entertainment in the Entertainment chapter).

ART GALLERY OF NSW (MAP 5)

The Art Gallery of NSW (☎ 9225 1744, Art Gallery Rd, The Domain; admission free; open 10am-5pm daily) is in the northeastern corner of the Domain, a short walk from the city centre. It has an excellent permanent display of Australian, European, Japanese and tribal art, and has some inspired temporary exhibits. It was built in 1880, but has modern extensions discreetly moulded into the hillside.

Free guided tours are held at 1pm and 2pm Monday, 11am, noon, 1pm and 2pm Tuesday to Friday and 11am, 1pm, 2pm and 3pm weekends. Tours of the Aboriginal and Torres Strait Island gallery run at 11am Tuesday to Friday and at 11am weekends, and there's a free Aboriginal dance performance at 12pm Tuesday to Saturday. There's a charge for some temporary exhibitions.

AUSTRALIAN MUSEUM (MAP 5)

Established only 40 years after the First Fleet dropped anchor, the Australian Museum (☎ 9320 6000, **W** www.austmus.gov.au, 6 College St; adult/concession/child/family $8/4/3/19; open 9.30am-5pm daily), across from Hyde Park, is a natural history museum with an excellent Australian wildlife collection and a fascinating insects and birds exhibition. One exhibition traces indigenous Australian history and the Dreamtime, in the words of Australia's first peoples.

Various tours are available (some free) and there are a range of events, from lectures, exhibitions and kids events.

Galleries

Don't miss seeing the Art Gallery of NSW and the Museum of Contemporary Art (MCA). Other galleries abound, especially in the inner eastern suburbs, where there is the highest concentration of art galleries in Australia.

The blue *Guide and Map to Art Galleries* is a free annual pamphlet with gallery listings, available from bookshops, cafes and galleries in the eastern suburbs. The *Sydney Morning Herald*'s Friday 'Metro' section lists galleries and art exhibitions, but for more detailed information look for the monthly *Art Almanac* ($2.20) at galleries and newsagents. Pick up a copy of *Paddington Galleries & Environs* from one of the many galleries in that suburb.

Galleries to look out for include the following:

Artspace (Map 6)
(☎ 9368 1899, *The Gunnery, 43-51 Cowper Wharf Rdwy, Woolloomooloo; open 11am-6pm Mon-Sat*) This gallery has changing contemporary avant garde exhibitions and is on a mission to liven things up in Sydney's art scene.

Australian Centre for Photography (Map 8)
(☎ 9332 1455, *257 Oxford St, Paddington; open 11am-6pm Tues-Sun*) This gallery has permanent and temporary exhibitions of photography in a very stylish, modern space.

Australian Galleries (Map 8)
(☎ 9360 5177, *15 Roylston St, Paddington; open 10am-6pm Mon-Sat*) With a good collection of Australian art, this place has some interesting paintings on display.

Boomalli Aboriginal Artists Co-operative
(☎ 9560 2541, *191 Parramatta Rd, Annandale; open 10am-5pm Tues-Fri*) Fans of Aboriginal art will enjoy visiting this space, although it's not on the traditional 'gallery rounds'.

Brett Whiteley Studio (Map 8)
(☎ 9225 1881, *2 Raper St, Surry Hills; adult/concession $7/5; open 10am-4pm Sat & Sun*) Brett Whiteley's former studio has been preserved with articles and paintings from his life.

The Cartoon Gallery (Map 5)
(☎ 9267 3022, *Shop 38, Level 2, QVB; open 10am-6pm Mon-Sat, until 9pm Thurs, until 5pm Sun*). This gallery features animation and comic-strip art, much of it for sale.

Coo-ee Aboriginal Art Gallery (Map 8)
(☎ 9332 1544, *98 Oxford St, Paddington; open 10am-6pm Mon-Sat, 11am-5pm Sun*) With a good range of Aboriginal art and objects, this friendly place will even arrange shipping if you decide to buy.

Ken Done Gallery (Map 5)
(☎ 9247 2740, *1 Hickson Rd, The Rocks; open 10am-5.30pm*) Colourful, naive art by a popular (especially overseas) designer.

Stills Gallery (Map 6)
(☎ 9331 7775, *36 Gosbell St, Paddington; open 11am-6pm Wed-Sat*) This gallery features current Australian photography.

Tin Sheds Gallery
(☎ 9351 3115, *154 City Rd, University of Sydney; open 11am-5pm Tues-Sat*) Contemporary works of art and architecture are shown here.

Wagner Art Gallery (Map 8)
(☎ 9360 6069, *39 Gurner St, Paddington; open 10.30am-6pm Mon-Sat*) Famous Australian art is featured in this corner terrace house.

HYDE PARK & AROUND (MAP 5)

The pleasant Hyde Park is large enough to offer a break from traffic and crowds, but retains a city feel.

At the northern end is the richly symbolic Art Deco **Archibald Memorial Fountain**. Sidney Archibald, founding editor of *Bulletin* magazine, bequeathed the fountain to the city. The statues are from Greek mythology. Near Liverpool St, at the southern end, is the dignified **Anzac Memorial** (1934), which has a small free exhibition of photographs and exhibits covering the wars Australians have fought in. There are tours at 11.30am and 1.30pm daily. Some pines near the memorial were grown from seeds gathered at Gallipoli.

St Mary's Cathedral (1882), across College St from the park's northeastern corner, took 14 years to build. Though you can hardly tell from the outside, it's one of the largest cathedrals in the world. A free tour of the cathedral and crypt is held at noon Sunday, departing from the College St entrance. Its spires are a recent addition and have added greatly to its architectural appeal.

The impressive 1873 **Great Synagogue** *(☎ 9267 2477, 166 Elizabeth St)* is diagonally opposite St Mary's, across the park on Elizabeth St north of Park St. A free 45-minute tour takes place at noon Tuesday and Thursday.

There's an entrance to **Museum station** in the southwestern corner of Hyde Park, near the park cafe. Many people dislike it, others find it a charming period piece. It depends on whether those dim tunnels of glazed tiles remind you of film noir or of a public toilet. Museum station and nearby renovated St James station date from the 1920s and were Sydney's first underground stations.

KINGS CROSS & AROUND (MAPS 6 & 7)

The Cross is a bizarre cocktail of strip joints, prostitution, crime and drugs, peppered with a handful of classy restaurants, designer cafes, upmarket hotels and backpacker hostels. It attracts an interesting mix of lowlife, sailors, travellers, inner-city trendies, tourists, and suburbanites looking for a big night out.

The Cross has always been a bit raffish, from its early days as a centre of bohemianism to the Vietnam War era, when it became the vice centre of Australia. Today, the Cross retains its risque aura, with a hint of menace and more than a touch of sleaze. Sometimes the razzle-dazzle has a sideshow appeal; sometimes walking up Darlinghurst Rd, the main drag, can be an unappetising experience. On a Friday or Saturday night in particular, it pays to watch where you're putting your feet, as pavement pizzas are often about.

However, there's much more to this insomniac region than sleaze. It's the travellers headquarters of Sydney, with many people beginning and ending their Australian travels here. It has Australia's greatest concentration of hostels and late-night Internet cafes; weary travellers can even pull up a milk crate along Darlinghurst Rd for a (therapeutic) Chinese massage. There are also many good places to eat, and entertainment that doesn't involve the sex industry. You don't have to walk far from the neon lights to find gracious old terraces in tree-lined streets.

Darlinghurst Rd is the trashy main drag. It dog-legs into Macleay St, which continues into the more salubrious suburb of Potts Point. Most hostels are on Victoria St, which diverges from Darlinghurst Rd north of William St, near the iconic Coca-Cola sign, which serves as a handy landmark.

The Cross is a good place to swap information and buy or sell things. Noticeboards can be found in hostels, shops and along Victoria St. At Kings Cross Car Market *(☎ 9358 5000, ⓦ www.carmarket.com.au; Cnr Ward Ave & Elizabeth Bay Rd)* travellers buy and sell vehicles.

The most notable landmark in Kings Cross is the thistle-like **El Alamein Fountain** in the brick-paved Fitzroy Gardens. The fountain is known locally as 'the elephant douche'. Bunkered down behind the fountain is a fortress-like police station *(☎ 8356 0099)*.

Nearby, to the north, in the suburb of Elizabeth Bay, is what was once known as 'the finest house in the colony'. **Elizabeth Bay House** *(1839; ☎ 9356 3022, 7 Onslow Ave; adult/child/family $7/3/17; open 10am-4.30pm Tues-Sun)*. It was meticulously restored by the Historic Houses Trust, and has fine views of the harbour. It was designed in English neoclassical revival style for the then colonial secretary of NSW, Alexander Macleay. It is refurbished with early 19th-century furniture, and the original colour scheme is reproduced.

The suburb of **Woolloomooloo**, wedged between the city and the Cross and affectionately known as 'the loo', is one of Sydney's older areas. It's crammed with narrow streets and was run-down in the early 70s, but was given a face-lift and is now a pleasant place to explore.

On Cowper Wharf Rdwy is **Harry's Cafe de Wheels**, the famous Woolloomooloo pie cart, which has been open since 1945. Nearby is the fingerpoint wharf, jutting into Woolloomooloo Bay, which has been redeveloped into a residential, hotel and restaurant complex. Opposite is the innovative **Artspace** gallery (see the boxed text 'Galleries' in this chapter for details).

If you're in for some tough-love style pampering, look no further than the popular **Ginseng Bathhouse** *(☎ 9368 1442, 111 Darlinghurst Rd, Kings Cross; adult/child aged 5-12 $22/11; open 10am-10pm Mon-Fri, 9am-10pm Sat & Sun)*, where men and women (in separate rooms) can enjoy the delights of hot and cold baths, a ginseng bath, wet and dry saunas, a tea room and a sleeping room. For extra money you can be scrubbed to within an inch of your circulation's life, and emerge on the mean streets of the Cross as smooth as a baby's bottom.

Getting There & Away
The simplest way to get to the Cross is on a CityRail eastern suburbs train from Martin Place, Town Hall or Central station. It's the first stop outside the city loop on the line to Bondi Junction.

The STA's Airport Express bus No 350 runs to Kings Cross, as does the private Kingsford Smith Transport (see the Getting Around chapter). From Circular Quay, bus Nos 200, 323–27 and 333 (a free service) run to Kings Cross; from Railway Square take bus No 311.

You can walk to the Cross from Hyde Park along William St in about 15 minutes. A longer, more interesting route involves crossing the Domain, crossing the pedestrian bridge behind the Art Gallery of NSW, walking past Woolloomooloo's wharf and climbing McElhone Stairs to the northern end of Victoria St.

INNER EAST (MAPS 6 & 8)
The lifeblood of Darlinghurst, Surry Hills and Paddington, **Oxford St** is a strip of shops, cafes, bars and nightclubs, and is one of the more happening places for late-night action. Its flamboyance and spirit are largely attributed to its vibrant and vocal gay community, and the route of the Sydney Gay & Lesbian Mardi Gras parade passes this way.

The main drag of Oxford St runs from the southeastern corner of Hyde Park to the northwestern corner of Centennial Park, though it continues in name into Bondi Junction. **Taylor Square**, at the junction of Oxford, Flinders and Bourke Sts, is the hub of social life in the area. (Be warned: tricky Oxford St street numbers restart west of the junction with South Dowling and Victoria Sts, on the Darlinghurst-Paddington border.) Southeast of Taylor Square, Darlinghurst Rd and Victoria St run north off Oxford St to Kings Cross, while Oxford St continues on through Paddington and Woollahra, eventually reaching Bondi Junction. Bus Nos 380 and 382 from Circular Quay, and No 378 from Railway Square, run the length of the street.

Darlinghurst
Darlinghurst is the inner-city mecca for groovy young things wanting to be close to the action and the good coffee. It's a vital area of trendy, self-conscious, urban cool, where every second person is an aspiring film-maker. There's no better way to soak up its studied ambience than to loiter in a few alfresco cafes and do as the others do. Darlinghurst encompasses the vibrant 'Little

Italy' of Stanley St in East Sydney, and is wedged between Oxford and William Sts.

Facing Taylor Square is **Darlinghurst Courthouse** (1842) and behind it is the **Old Darlinghurst Gaol**, where author Henry Lawson was incarcerated several times for debt (he called it 'Starvinghurst'). Today it houses East Sydney TAFE College.

The **Sydney Jewish Museum** (☎ 9360 7999, 148 Darlinghurst Rd; adult/student $7/5; open 10am-4pm Mon-Thur, until 2pm Fri, 11am-5pm Sun, closed Jewish holidays), on the corner of Burton St, has exhibits on the holocaust and Australian Jewish history. Give yourself about three hours to really soak up what you'll learn in this extraordinary place.

Surry Hills

South of Darlinghurst, Surry Hills, squeezed between the east side of Central station and South Dowling St, is a former working class neighbourhood that's undergoing gentrification. Originally the centre of Sydney's rag trade and print media, it's an interesting multicultural area with some good cafes and restaurants, and a handful of funky boutiques and record stores. The main attraction is the **Brett Whiteley Studio** (☎ 9225 1881, 2 Raper St; adult/concession $7/5; open 10am-4pm Sat & Sun), in a small lane in a quiet part of the suburb. The gallery, in the former studio of this renowned modern Australian painter, houses a selection of his paintings and drawings, and there are also poetry, music and tours at various times – call ☎ 9225 1740 for details and bookings of these events.

Surry Hills is a short walk south of Oxford St. Catch bus No 301–04, 390 or 391 from Circular Quay.

Paddington

Paddington, 4km east of the city centre, is an attractive inner-city residential area of leafy streets and tightly packed terrace houses. It was built for aspiring artisans in the later years of the Victorian era. During the lemming-like rush to the dreary outer suburbs after WWII, the area became a slum. A renewed interest in Victorian architecture, combined with a sudden recollection of the pleasures of inner-city life, led to the area's restoration during the 1960s. Today it's a fascinating jumble of beautifully restored terraces tumbling down steeply sloping streets. Paddington is a fine example of unplanned urban restoration, and it's full of trendy shops and restaurants, art galleries, bookshops and well-dressed people.

You can wander through Paddington's streets and winding laneways any time, although the busiest time is from around 10am Saturday, when the **Paddington Village Bazaar** (☎ 9331 2646), in the grounds of the Uniting Church on the corner of Newcombe and Oxford Sts, is in full swing. The crowds can be huge, although unfortunately, this market is not as creative and stimulating as it used to be.

The magnificent, restored **Juniper Hall** on Oxford St, diagonally opposite Paddington Town Hall, was built by Robert Cooper as a family home in 1824, with profits from his gin business. He named it after the juniper berries from which he distilled his gin. It's owned by the National Trust but isn't open to the public.

The **Australian Centre for Photography** (☎ 9332 1455, 257 Oxford St; open 11am-6pm Tues-Sun) has regular exhibitions, and is a good place to catch some art if you don't want to wander off Oxford St to the galleries scattered throughout Paddington.

There are free tours of the stately **Victoria Barracks** (☎ 9339 3000, Oxford St), between Oatley and Greens Rds; tours run at 10am Thursday, and include a performance by the military band (weather permitting).

The utilitarian **Moore Park** south of Paddington, bordering Surry Hills, has a playing field; a walking, cycling and skating track; a horse trail; a golf-driving range; and grass skiing. It's also home to the historic **Sydney Cricket Ground** (SCG; ☎ 9360 6601) and the **Sydney Football Stadium** (☎ 9360 6601). Sportspace Tours (☎ 9380 0383) offers behind-the-scenes guided tours of the facilities, which include historic displays featuring great players (and commentators) associated with sports played here. Tours are held at 10 am, 1pm and 3pm

Monday to Saturday (except on match days), and cost adult/child & concession/family $19.50/13/52 for 1½ hours.

Much of the former **Royal Agricultural Society's (RAS) Showgrounds** has been taken over by **Fox Studios** *(☎ 9383 4000, Lang Rd, Moore Park; admission free, backlot admission adult/concession/child over six years $24.95/19.95/14.95; open 10am-midnight daily, backlot 10am-5pm daily)*. As well as a professional film studio and backlot (with various tours), the complex has a big Hoyts cinema, plus shops, restaurants, live music venues, markets and sporting facilities.

Centennial Park, Sydney's biggest park, is further east again, south of Woollahra. It has running, cycling and horse tracks, barbecue sites, football pitches and more. You can hire bikes and inline skates from several places on Clovelly Rd, Randwick, near the southern edge of the park, or hire horses (about $35) from one of five stables situated around the park – contact the stable manager (☎ 9332 2809).

At the southern edge of the park is **Randwick Racecourse** *(☎ 9663 8400, Alison Rd, Randwick)*, and south of there is the **University of NSW**. The university is on Anzac Parade, which becomes Flinders St and runs into Taylor Square. Many buses run along Anzac Parade, including No 336 from Circular Quay.

EASTERN SUBURBS (MAPS 6 & 8)

The harbourside suburbs east of Kings Cross are some of Sydney's most expensive. The main road through this area is New South Head Rd, the continuation of William St.

Darling Point, east of Rushcutters Bay, was a popular place for the city's first merchants to build mansions. Inland is the suburb of **Edgecliff**, centred on New South Head Rd and boasting the highest per capita income in Australia. The wealthy harbourside suburb of **Double Bay** is further east. Double Bay's main shopping street is Bay St, which runs north off New South Head Rd and eventually leads to a quiet waterfront

park and the ferry wharf. Double Bay is worth a visit. There are plenty of cafes and patisseries that don't necessarily cost a fortune, and you can at least window-shop for some designer clothes.

There's a small beach near the ferry wharf and a saltwater pool to the east, near Seven Shillings Beach. The latter is actually part of **Point Piper**, the headland that separates Double Bay from **Rose Bay**. Rose Bay has a pair of longer beaches visible at low tide, though people rarely swim here. It's also serviced by ferries. Inland behind the wharf area is the posh Royal Sydney Golf Course.

Rose Bay curves north onto the peninsula that forms the southern side of the entrance to Sydney Harbour. On the harbour side of the peninsula is **Vaucluse**, probably the most exclusive suburb of all.

Vaucluse was a desirable address even in the colony's early days, so it's interesting to note that **Vaucluse House** *(1828; ☎ 9388 7922, Wentworth Rd, Vaucluse; adult/child/family $7/3/17; open 10am-4.30pm Tues-Sun)*, one of its finest mansions, was built by William Wentworth, a prominent explorer, patriot, barrister and vocal advocate of self-government. As a result of this free thinking, he suffered a sort of social ostracism.

Built in fine grounds in the Gothic Tudor style, it's an imposing, turreted example of 19th-century Australiana. Catch bus No 325 from Circular Quay and get off two stops after **Nielsen Park**, which is part of Sydney Harbour National Park.

Watsons Bay is nestled on the harbour side of the peninsula as it narrows towards South Head. On the ocean side is the **Gap**, a dramatic clifftop lookout. On the harbour north of Watsons Bay are the small fashionable beaches of **Camp Cove** and **Lady Bay** (nudist). At the tip of the peninsula is **South Head**, with great views across the harbour to North Head and Middle Head.

Getting There & Away

The closest suburb to a rail link is Double Bay, which is northeast of the Edgecliff train station on the eastern-suburbs line. Take the New South Head Rd exit from the station, turn right and follow New South Head Rd to the nearby corner of Ocean Ave. Head down to the corner of Cooper St, which leads to Bay St. Alternatively you could continue on New South Head Rd until you meet Bay St, but it's a less pleasant walk.

Ferries run from Circular Quay to Double Bay and Rose Bay and, on weekends, to Watsons Bay. See the Watson Bay section in the Places to Eat chapter for information on private boats to Watsons Bay. Bus Nos 324 and 325 run from Circular Quay to Watsons Bay.

INNER WEST (MAPS 4 & 9)
Balmain & Birchgrove

Once a tough, working-class neighbourhood, Balmain attracted artists in the 1960s and has been prime real estate for some time, rivalling Paddington in Victorian-era trendiness. There's nothing special to do or see, but there are some good places to eat, some great pubs and pleasant walks.

William Balmain was a high achiever who arrived on the First Fleet, and within a decade was principal surgeon, a magistrate and collector of customs. He was rewarded with several land grants, including the 220 hectares of headland which bear his name.

Most construction in Balmain occurred between 1855 and 1890, although there are colonial Georgian and early Victorian houses still standing. See the boxed text 'A Balmain & Birchgrove Stroll'.

Darling St, Balmain's spine, runs the length of the peninsula. It has bookshops, restaurants, antique shops, bakeries and boutiques. The Balmain markets are held from 8.30am to 4pm Saturday at St Andrew's Congregational Church at 223 Darling St.

The suburbs between Balmain and Glebe – **Annandale** and **Leichhardt** (its lesbian population dubs it 'dyke-heart') – also attract interesting people and have good eateries.

A major attraction when visiting Balmain is the journey on the Hunters Hill ferry from Circular Quay; it stops at Thames St, Darling St and Birchgrove wharves. Bus Nos 441, 442, 445 and 446 also come here.

Glebe

Glebe is southwest of the city centre, close to the University of Sydney. It has been going up the social scale in recent years, but still has a bohemian atmosphere. The main thoroughfare, Glebe Point Rd, runs the length of the suburb from Broadway to Glebe Point and offers affordable restaurants, interesting shops and Internet cafes. There are several good places to stay, and its proximity to the city makes it an interesting alternative to the Cross.

The area has been inhabited since the First Fleet's chaplain was granted the first church land (or glebe), covering an area of 160 hectares. Around 1826 the Church of England sold the land to wealthy settlers, who built mansions. After 1855 church land was leased for building downmarket housing, and it was subdivided. A century later the estate had deteriorated into slums. In the mid-1970s the federal government bought the estate and rejuvenated the area for low-income families, many of whom had lived here for generations.

Glebe's **Buddhist Temple**, on Edward St, was built by Chinese immigrants who arrived in Australia during the 1850s goldrush, and has been fully restored by Sydney's Chinese community. It welcomes visitors, but remember that it's a holy place. At the northern tip of Glebe Point Rd is **Jubilee Park** with views across the bay to Rozelle and back towards the city.

If all that walking, eating, drinking and frolicking is taking its toll on your body, you might like to visit the **Natural Health Care Centre** (☎ 9660 0677, 20 Glebe Point Rd; 1hr remedial massage $33, naturopathy, herbal medicine etc $20 without remedies; open 9am-5pm Mon, Fri & Sat, 9am-8pm Wed & Thur), where students of the Australian College of Natural Therapies fulfil practical components of their various courses, at a substantially reduced rate for you. You can get treatments such as osteopathy, naturopathy, reflexology, beauty therapy and even ear candling.

Getting There & Away From the airport you can take the Kingsford Smith Transport

A Balmain & Birchgrove Stroll

Balmain (Map 4) is full of pretty Victorian houses and offers some stunning views of Sydney Harbour. To get a feel for this attractive suburb with our walk, you can begin at either the Darling St wharf, the Yurulbin Point wharf, or if you want a shorter walk you can start from the corner of Darling and Rowntree Sts and walk towards either wharf.

From the Darling St wharf (which you can reach by ferry from Circular Quay or by bus from the city centre) walk up Darling St to No 10, which is the site of the **Shipwright's Arms Hotel** (also known as the Dolphin Hotel), a 19th-century meeting place and public house. At No 12 you'll find the **Waterman's Cottage** (c. 1841), where Henry McKenzie lived. He was kind enough to row Balmain dwellers over the harbour waters on request.

Turn left at Weston St and walk down to Peacock Point, a lovely park with great views of the city skyline and Darling Harbour. Around the point, go up Little Edward St, turn left at William St, then right into Johnston St. This part of Balmain has some interesting homes, both old and new. Continue up Darling St and turn left into Jubilee Place, where at No 1 you'll find the site where the famous winged keel of *Australia II* (which won the 1983 America's Cup) was made.

Walk through Ewenton Park and then along Grafton St to No 12b, **Hampton Villa**, where the former premier of NSW Sir Henry Parkes lived in the late 1880s. A right turn into Ewenton St, then a left turn into Wallace St will take you to **Clontarf** (1844) at No 4, an impressive restored house saved by local resident protests. Turn right at Adolphus St, which has **St Marys Hall** (c. 1851) at No 7, before reaching Darling St again.

At 179 Darling St stands the 1854 **Watch House**, which is the oldest surviving lock-up in Sydney. At No 181 is the 1854 **Presbyterian Church**. Further along the street you'll come to **The London Hotel** at No 234, which is a great old pub with an inviting veranda – perfect for quenching a walker's thirst with a beer (see the Entertainment chapter for details).

Across the road and up a bit is **St Andrew's Congregational Church**, the home of the delightful **Balmain markets** (see the Shopping chapter, later). There's a good stretch of shops and cafes all the way to Rowntree St. Near the corner of Darling and Rowntree Sts are some other Balmain buildings of note. The **Balmain Police Station** is next to the 1888 **Balmain Town Hall**, at No 370. In the library here, you can find historical information about the area and purchase walking maps. Across the road at No 391 is Balmain Fire Station (1891).

From Darling St turn north into Rowntree St. Follow Rowntree St to the junction with Ballast Point Rd. Turn right into Ballast Point Rd then left into Lemm St and follow it through to **Wharf Rd**, which has an attractive stretch of waterfront homes.

Follow Wharf Rd west and turn into The Terrace, which cuts through Birchgrove Park (a popular dog-walking haunt). Enter ritzy Louisa Rd from Rose St and start spending some Monopoly money on one of Sydney's most expensive streets. At Nos 12 and 14 you'll find **Keba** and **Vidette**, two impressive 1870s residences. Walking towards Yurulbin Point you'll pass **The Anchorage** at No 44, a large restored house with a 'widow's walk' on the roof. No 67 is **Birchgrove House** (c. 1810), which was the first residence built in the area. Louisa Rd winds down to the Birchgrove wharf at **Yurulbin Point** and an attractive reserve. There are good views up the harbour towards the Harbour Bridge from the point. From here you can take a ferry back to Circular Quay.

Yurulbin Point used to be called Long Nose Point but the name was changed to acknowledge the Aboriginal heritage of the area. Yurulbin means 'swift running water'. This area was occupied by the Wangal clan, of which Bennelong is thought to have been a member. (Bennelong was one of the many Aborigines captured by Arthur Phillip and taken to live in the Botany Bay settlement.)

Allow 1½ to two hours (dawdling and window-shopping taken into account) to walk from Darling St wharf to Yurulbin Point wharf.

bus (☎ 9667 6663); from the city and Railway Square bus Nos 431–34 run along Glebe Point Rd.

On foot, head south on George St and then Broadway, turning right into Glebe Point Rd about 1km southwest of Central station. A more interesting daytime walk begins at Darling Harbour's Pyrmont Bridge, which leads to Pyrmont Bridge Rd. After passing Sydney Fish Market (see under Darling Harbour & Pyrmont earlier) on Blackwattle Bay, follow the road past Wentworth Park. Turn right onto Burton St, and take the steps up to Ferry Rd, which leads into Glebe Point Rd. Turn left into Glebe Point Rd for shops and cafes, or turn right for Jubilee Park.

Newtown

Bordering the south of the University of Sydney, Newtown is a melting pot of social and sexual subcultures, students and home renovators. King St, the main drag, is packed with funky clothes shops, bookshops, cafes and an incredible amount of Thai restaurants. The backstreets are full of aerosol graffiti art, the cafes full of creative types. While it's definitely moving up the social scale, Newtown comes with a healthy dose of grunge and political activism, and harbours a few live-music venues. The best way to get there is by train, but bus Nos 355, 370, 422, 423, 426 and 428 from the city run along King St.

Leichhardt

Predominantly Italian, Leichhardt, southwest of Glebe, is increasingly popular with students, lesbians and young professionals. Its Italian eateries on Norton St have a citywide reputation (see the Places to Eat chapter for more details). Bus Nos 436–40 run here from the city.

INNER SOUTH (MAPS 8 & 9)

Southwest of Central station, the small suburb of **Chippendale** is a maze of Victorian terrace houses – an unscrubbed version of Paddington. South of Railway Square, near the corner of Lee (George) and Regent Sts, is the quaint neo-Gothic **Mortuary Station**,

where coffins and mourners once boarded funeral trains bound for Rookwood Cemetery, which is now in the city's western suburbs.

Chippendale borders the east of the **University of Sydney**, Australia's oldest tertiary institution. **Nicholson Museum** *(☎ 9351 2812, Building A14, Main Quadrangle, University of Sydney; admission free; open 10am-4.30pm Mon-Fri, closed public holidays & Jan)* displays Greek, Assyrian, Egyptian, Near Eastern and other antiquities.

Redfern, south of Central station, but on the eastern side of the tracks, remains predominantly working class, although more and more people are moving in and renovating. Redfern tends to buck the system, and relations between the police and the community (especially the large Koori community) are at times bad. The suburb (and nearby Waterloo) is also an area of Aboriginal self-reliance and defiance, with a strong sense of community; it has become something of a sanctuary from white authorities, but has suffered from problems associated with drug and alcohol use.

Some of the restored workshops at the site of the former Eveleigh Locomotive Workshops, corner of Garden and Boundary Sts, are home to the **National Technology Park and National Innovation Centre**. Some of the buildings contain Victorian steam-powered blacksmithing equipment, used by Wrought Artworks (☎ 9319 6190) to manufacture artefacts. The curious can wander in and watch them at work.

BONDI BEACH (MAP 11)

Although it's Australia's most famous beach, Bondi Beach isn't always as glamorous as tourist brochures might suggest. It still retains some working-class roots and successive waves of migrants have shaped aspects of the suburb. In recent years it has become much more fashionable and rents have skyrocketed. Today its unique flavour is a blend of old Jewish and Italian communities, dyed-in-the-wool Aussies, New Zealand expats, Irish and British working travellers and devoted surfers, all bonded by their love for the beach.

Orientation & Information

Campbell Pde is the main beachfront road where most shops, hotels and cafes are located. The corner of Campbell Pde and Hall St is the hub. The main road into Bondi Beach is Bondi Rd, which branches off from Oxford St east of the mall in Bondi Junction. This is the same Oxford St that begins at Hyde Park and runs through Darlinghurst and Paddington.

The post office is on the corner of Jacques Ave and Hall St. A little further up Hall St, you enter a small Jewish area, with kosher shops and the social Hakoah Club.

Although Bondi Beach is usually referred to simply as Bondi, the suburb of Bondi is actually inland, between Bondi Junction and Bondi Beach.

Things to See & Do

The main reason for coming is the beach, where you can swim, surf or just hang out. If the water's too rough there are sea-water swimming pools at either end, including a children's pool at the eastern end. **Bondi Pavilion** (☎ 9130 3325, Queen Elizabeth Dve, Bondi), on the esplanade, has change rooms and showers, as well as a theatre and gallery hosting cultural and community events.

Accessible **Aboriginal rock engravings** are a short walk north of Bondi Beach on the golf course in North Bondi. There's a beautiful coastal walking path, featuring teriffic views, leading south 5km along the cliff-tops to the beaches at Tamarama, Bronte and Coogee.

Getting There & Away

Bondi Junction is the terminus of the eastern suburbs CityRail line, and the nearest train station to Bondi Beach. From there, you can take bus No 380, 382 or 389 to Bondi and Bondi Beach. Alternatively, you can take these buses from Circular Quay or bus No 378 from Railway Square, which continues south to Bronte; bus Nos 378 and 380 run along Oxford St.

Buses stop along Campbell Pde terminating at Brighton Blvd in North Bondi.

TAMARAMA & BRONTE

South of Bondi, Tamarama (or 'Glamarama') is a lovely cove (with strong rips) popular with Sydney's 'beautiful people'. Get off the bus just before it reaches Bondi Beach; Tamarama is a five-minute walk down the hill.

At Bronte, south of Tamarama, there's a superb family-oriented beach hemmed in by a bowl-shaped park and sandstone headlands. A toy train chugs around during the warmer months, offering children's rides. Cafes with outdoor tables, picnic areas and barbecues make it the perfect place for a day of doing very little. Catch bus No 378 from Railway Square, or take a train to Bondi Junction and pick the bus up there. You can walk along the wonderful clifftop footpath from Bondi Beach or from Coogee via Gordon's Bay, Clovelly and the sun-bleached **Waverley Cemetery**.

COOGEE (MAP 10)

Coogee, about 4km south of Bondi Beach, is almost a miniature carbon copy, minus the crowds and glitzy development. While increasingly popular with visitors it still has a relaxed atmosphere, few airs and graces and a good sweep of sand.

The main beachfront street is Arden St, and the junction of Arden St and Coogee Bay Rd is the commercial hub of the suburb. Like Bondi, Coogee's main attraction is its beach and this is a great spot for snorkelling. From Coogee, the spectacular clifftop footpath runs north along the coast to Bondi Beach passing Gordon's Bay, Clovelly, Bronte and Tamarama. Coogee also boasts the delightful **Wylies Baths** and women-only **McIvers Baths**.

Getting There & Away

Bus Nos 373 and 374 run from Circular Quay; bus Nos 371 and 372 run from Railway Square; and bus Nos 314 and 315 run from Bondi Junction.

THE NORTH SHORE (MAP 3)

The North Shore is the unofficial but universally recognised name applied to the suburbs north of the harbour. The area's pretty bays and beaches, good shopping and eateries make it worthwhile leaving the cosmopolitan delights of the southern side to see how wealthier Sydneysiders live.

Kirribilli & Milsons Point

The Sydney residences of the governor general and the prime minister are on Kirribilli Point, east of the Harbour Bridge. The prime minister stays in **Kirribilli House** (1854) and the governor general in **Admiralty House** (1846). Admiralty House is the one nearer the bridge (and the one everyone dreams of living in if it came without the job).

To the north of Kirribilli Point is the **Royal Sydney Yacht Squadron** headquarters. Yachting has been popular on the harbour since the 1830s, and the Australian Yacht Club was formed in 1862.

Luna Park amusement park (*☎ 9922 6644, 1 Olympic Pl, Milsons Point)*, at Milsons Point on the edge of Lavender Bay immediately west of the Harbour Bridge, was at its peak in the 1930s, when thousands of people flocked across the harbour on the new bridge. The park closed in the 1970s after a fatal fire on the Ghost Train, and it has opened and closed a couple of times since. At the time of writing it was closed, but there are plans for it to reopen in 2003.

McMahons Point is a pleasant, sleepy suburb on the next headland west. It's tipped by **Blues Point Reserve**, named after the Jamaican-born Billy Blue, who ferried people across from Dawes Point in the 1830s and was famous for his cheeky sense of humour. Blues Point Tower was designed by the architect Harry Seidler. It was one of the first high-rise buildings on the harbour and is regarded by many as an eyesore. If you follow Blues Point Rd north from the ferry wharf it'll bring you to North Sydney. Clark Park is a pleasant spot for a picnic lunch in the sun, and is popular with nearby office workers. The views show why.

Kirribilli, Lavender Bay and Blues Point are serviced by ferries from Circular Quay. Other ways of getting here include walking across the bridge or taking a North Shore train to Milsons Point.

North Sydney & Crows Nest

North Sydney is northwest of the Harbour Bridge. The suburb's historical connections have become difficult to find since it became Sydney's second Central Business District (CBD).

The grand Victorian **North Sydney Post Office** (1889) is on the corner of Miller St and the Pacific Hwy, one of Sydney's busiest intersections (it seems to take an age for the lights to change...). To the left of the post office, along Mount St, is **Mary MacKillop Place** (*☎ 8912 4878, 7 Mount St, North Sydney; adult/concession/child/family $8.25/5.50/3.30/16.50; open 10am-4pm daily)*, with displays telling the life story of the girl from the bush who became a nun – and Australia's first saint. The building was blessed by Pope John Paul II, on the day (19 January 1995) of Mary MacKillop's beatification.

The 1880s **Sexton's Cottage Museum** (*Stanton Library; ☎ 9936 8400, 250 West St; admission free; open 1pm-4pm Thur)*, in St Thomas' Rest Park, next to the old St Thomas' Church, has displays relating to the early European settlement of the area.

Balls Head Reserve

Balls Head Reserve not only has great views of the harbour, but also ancient Aboriginal **rock paintings and carvings**, although they're not easily discernible. The park is two headlands west of the Harbour Bridge. Take a train to Waverton, turn left when you leave the station and follow Bay Rd, which becomes Balls Head Rd.

Hunters Hill & Woolwich

The elegant Victorian suburbs of Hunters Hill and Woolwich are on a spit at the junction of the Parramatta and Lane Cove rivers. In 1834, Mary Reiby built a riverside cottage here. She was followed in 1847 by the Joubert family, who operated a fleet of ferries for nearly 50 years. The Joubert brothers began to build houses, and it's said that 200 of them still stand.

The National Trust **Vienna Cottage** (*☎ 9817 2510, 38 Alexandra St, Hunters Hill; admission $4; open 10am-4pm 2nd &*

The illuminated dome of the Queen Victoria Building (QVB)

Sydney's Conservatorium of Music, Royal Botanic Gardens

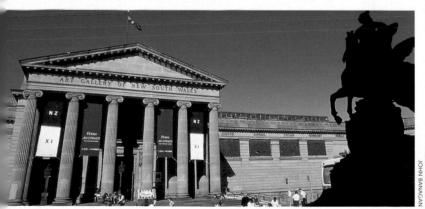

The Art Gallery of NSW exhibits Australian and international artworks.

Main Pond, Royal Botanic Gardens

An avenue of trees, Centennial Park

Walk, cycle or jog through one of Sydney's numerous parks and gardens.

4th Sun of the month) is a stone cottage built in 1871 by Jacob Hellman and is typical of the era.

Hunters Hill ferries from Circular Quay stop at Woolwich's Valencia St wharf.

Mosman & Around

East of the Harbour Bridge, Mosman, **Neutral Bay** and **Cremorne** have good shopping centres and some beautiful foreshore parks and walks. Mosman is on the large chunk of land separating Middle Harbour from the main harbour. Cremorne and Neutral Bay are further west. The beachside suburb of **Balmoral**, north of Mosman, faces Manly across Middle Harbour. It has three fine beaches (one with a shark net) and some famous restaurants.

You can walk north from Kirribilli, past Careening Cove, to Neutral Bay, where pleasant Anderson Park leads down to the waterfront. East of here is **Nutcote** *(☎ 9953 4453,* **W** *www.maygibbs.com.au, 5 Wallaringa Ave, Neutral Bay; adult/concession/child/family $7/5/3/17; open 11am-3pm Wed-Sun),* the former home of well-known and loved Australian children's author May Gibbs *(Snugglepot & Cuddlepie)*. It's now a museum, restored to its 1930s style, and has exhibits on her life and work. Volunteer guides can show you around and there are beautiful gardens. It's a short walk from the Neutral Bay (Hayes St) ferry wharf.

To the south is Kurraba Point. Off Bogota Ave you can pick up a footpath that runs through bushy gardens to the end of **Cremorne Point**. This is an excellent spot to picnic on the grass reserve or go for a swim, with great views of the harbour. The point is especially popular on Christmas Day and New Year's Eve as a vantage point for the annual fireworks. From here, you can continue up the other side to Mosman Bay and Taronga Zoo.

The main road through this area is Military Rd, which branches east off the Warringah Fwy (the northern side of the Harbour Bridge) near North Sydney. Military Rd crosses Middle Harbour at Spit Bridge then runs north, changing names several times. It bypasses Manly, eventually reaching **Palm Beach**, Sydney's northernmost beachside suburb.

Bus No 190 runs from Central station and the QVB to Palm Beach via Military Rd; bus No 175 from Wynyard runs to Brookvale via Cremorne and Mosman. Buses also run to Military Rd from the North Shore suburb of St Leonards.

Taronga Zoo

The 30-hectare Taronga Zoo *(☎ 9969 2777, Bradleys Head Rd, Mosman; adult/student/senior/child $16/11.50/10/8.50, child under 4 free; open 9am-5pm daily),* a short ferry ride from Circular Quay, has an attractive hillside setting overlooking the harbour. It houses over 2000 endangered and rare critters, including a substantial number of Australian ones.

Ferries to the zoo depart from Circular Quay's Wharf 2, half-hourly from 7.15am on weekdays, 8.45am Saturday and 9am Sunday. The zoo is on a steep hillside and it makes sense to work your way down if you plan to depart by ferry. If you can't be bothered to climb to the top entrance, take the bus or the Aerial Safari cable car. A ZooPass ticket, sold at Circular Quay and elsewhere, costs $25/12.50 adult/concession and includes return ferry rides, the bus to the entrance (and a bus to the top of the hill for those daunted by the climb) and zoo admission. A ZooLink ticket is similar to the ZooPass but includes train travel. (See also the Combination Passes section in the Getting Around chapter.)

MANLY (MAP 12)

The jewel of the North Shore, Manly, sits on a narrow peninsula that ends at the dramatic cliffs of North Head. It was one of the first places in Australia to be named by Europeans – Arthur Phillip named it after the 'manly' physique of the Aborigines he saw here in 1788. Sun-soaked Manly boasts all the trappings of a full-scale holiday resort and a sense of community identity, but isn't afraid to show a bit of tack and brashness to attract visitors. It makes a refreshing change from the prim upper-middle-class harbour enclaves nearby.

To get here from Circular Quay take a ferry ($5 one way, 30 minutes) or a JetCat ($6.30, 15 minutes). Both offer fantastic views of the city and harbour.

Orientation & Information

Manly straddles the narrow isthmus leading to North Head, and has both ocean and harbour beaches. The ferry wharf is on Manly Cove, on the harbour side, and The Corso (the main commercial strip) runs from here to the ocean, where Manly Beach is lined with Norfolk pines. Most of The Corso is a pedestrian mall.

Manly Visitors Information Bureau (☎ 9977 1088) is between the bus station and the wharf. It has useful, free pamphlets on the 8km Manly Scenic Walkway and transport information about the area.

Things to See

The long ocean beach north of the Corso is North Steyne Beach; the shorter stretch of beach running south is usually called Manly Beach, but it's technically South Steyne Beach. The beachfront road is called North Steyne and South Steyne. At the southern end of Manly Beach is the Manly Surf Life Saving Club, from which a path leads around the rocky headland to tiny Fairy Bower Beach, which has a small saltwater swimming pool. Further around is beautiful Shelly Beach. The large building on the hill southeast of the town centre is St Patrick's College (1889). Manly Hospital is nearby.

North Steyne Beach runs up to Queenscliff Beach, near the steep Queenscliff headland. There's a lifesaving club here as well. Around the headland (although not easy to get to on foot) is Freshwater Beach.

There's another stretch of sand on the harbour side at Manly Cove, backed by the East and West Esplanade. In the centre is Manly wharf, which was gearing up for a major redevelopment at the time of writing.

Oceanworld (☎ 9949 2644, West Esplanade; adult/concession/child/family $15.90/11/8/39.90; open 10am-5.30pm daily) is on the headland at the western end of Manly Cove. It's a good oceanarium and its program includes various tours –

including the Shark Tunnel Tour, Dangerous Australians and Venomous Marine Creatures. The glass tunnel lets you feel as though you really are walking underwater, without the bother of getting wet or eaten.

Manly Art Gallery & Museum (☎ 9949 1776, West Esplanade Reserve; adult/concession/under 18s $3.50/1.10/free; open 10am-5pm Tues-Sun), next to Oceanworld, has exhibitions on beach themes and local history (which are almost one and the same thing in Manly), with some fine Australian works and helpful staff.

See Harbourside Walks earlier in this chapter for details of the lovely Manly Scenic Walkway.

North Head

Spectacular North Head, at the Sydney Harbour entrance about 3km south of Manly, offers good views of the ocean, harbour and city skyline. The peninsula has dramatic cliffs, several coves and lookouts with views of the cliffs, the harbour and the city centre. Most of the headland is in the Sydney Harbour National Park; contact the NPWS office (☎ 9977 6522) near the Quarantine Station for information.

The Quarantine Station (☎ 9247 5033, North Head Scenic Dve, Manly) housed suspected and real disease carriers from 1832 to 1984 and many people died here. The station is run by the NPWS and you have to book a guided tour to visit. These 1½-hour tours are held on Monday, Wednesday, Friday, Saturday and Sunday; admission is adult/concession $11/7.70. The station is reputedly haunted and there are spooky three-hour ghost tours at night from Friday to Sunday that cost $27.50 weekdays and $22 weekends. Kids' ghost tours cost $13.20.

The centre of the headland is an off-limits military reserve, but you can visit the National Artillery Museum (☎ 9976 3855, North Fort Rd, North Head; adult/concession/child/family $6/4/3/12; open noon-4pm Wed, Sat & Sun) in North Fort.

Getting There & Away

See the Getting Around chapter for details on ferries to Manly. Alternatively, bus No

Gay Games VI – 25 October–9 November 2002

As Sydney shines in the afterglow of 'the best Olympic Games ever' it is with pride that it welcomes over 14,000 lesbian, gay, bisexual and transgender athletes from more than 60 countries – and thousands of their nearest and dearest – to gather and celebrate sport and culture. The Gay Games will make its first journey to the Southern Hemisphere in glorious and sunny Spring 2002, and will be staged in the very venues used for the Sydney 2000 Olympics. Team Sydney will have its biggest team ever at these games and is bursting with excitement!

Participation, Inclusion and Personal Best Gay Games VI is an international sports festival and a cultural festival of ideas, and is 'guaranteed to challenge, stimulate and extend boundaries'. These principles are not about winning but about welcoming all, participating and having fun doing it.

Spectators will have the opportunity to see 31 sports across 45 venues, including dancing, figure skating, ice hockey, martial arts, softball, soccer and tennis; and two weeks of cultural events. The Cultural Festival celebrates the international community's engagement with arts and ideas at every level of achievement. Together with the sports program it will demonstrate an energetic, intelligent, generous and well-rounded community with emphasis placed on tributes to the talent and creative energy of community groups. Special events will include the Quilt Memorial, a public display of quilt blocks from around the world. A Memorial Service and unfolding of the quilts will be held during the Games.

At the Zurich Eurogames in 2000, it was called the Rainbow Square; in Amsterdam, it was the Friendship Village; and in Sydney in 2002 it will be the City Hub, a city-based information centre and meeting place where participants, volunteers, visitors and locals can meet, get accreditation, socialise and buy tickets to the Cultural Festival and sporting events. Here you can enjoy works of comedy, cabaret and music.

For an overview of the Gay Games VI Sport and Cultural Festival schedule of events log on to W www.sydney2002.org.au.

Gina Tsarouhas

169 runs from Wynyard Park in the city. The No 135 bus from outside Manly wharf covers North Head; the one-way fare is $2.50.

SYDNEY OLYMPIC PARK

Sydney Olympic Park in the suburb of Homebush Bay, 14km west of the city centre, was the main venue for the 2000 Olympic Games. This is also the venue for the Gay Games VI, to be held from October to November 2002. See the boxed text 'Gay Games VI – 25 October–9 November 2002' in this chapter for more information.

Also here is the **Sydney Showground** (☎ 9704 1244, *1 Showground Rd, Sydney Olympic Park, Homebush Bay)*, the home of the Royal Easter Show.

The Sydney Olympic Explorer (adult/child $10/5) is a hop-on, hop-off service that makes pit-stops around the Olympic Park site, including the Sydney Superdome, Stadium Australia, the Tennis Centre, Sydney Aquatic Centre and Bicentennial Park. Buses leave from the Homebush Bay Information Centre every 10 to 15 minutes between 9.20am and 5pm daily.

The best way to get to Olympic Park is to catch a RiverCat (adult/child $19.20/9.60 return) from Circular Quay up the Parramatta River to the Olympic Park wharf. A return ticket includes the Olympic Explorer bus. You can also catch a train to Lidcombe or Strathfield stations, then board bus No 401 or 403.

ACTIVITIES

The *Sydney Morning Herald*'s Friday 'Metro' guide lists activities. Noticeboards at hostels are usually crammed with suggestions, and travel agencies often have good information on day trips.

Swimming

Given Sydneysiders' love of watersports, it should come as no surprise that there are more than 100 public swimming pools in Sydney, including the following.

Andrew 'Boy' Charlton Pool (Map 6) (☎ *9358 6686, Mrs Macquaries Rd; adult/ child & concession $2.75/1.30; open 6.30am-8pm daily, closed winter)* is a saltwater pool and is in the Domain on the edge of Woolloomooloo Bay, and is popular with the gay crowd. It was closed for redevelopment at the time of writing.

Bondi Icebergs (Map 11) (☎ *9130 3120, 1 Notts Ave, Bondi; club open 11am-9pm Mon-Wed, until 11pm Thur & Sun, until midnight Fri & Sat)* gets its name from the members' love of swimming in winter with blocks of ice in the pool. This place is an institution, but was closed for renovation at the time of writing, check with the management for pool opening hours.

North Sydney Olympic Pool (Map 3) (☎ *9955 2309, Alfred St South, Milsons Point; adult/child $3.50/$1.65; open 5.30am-9pm Mon-Fri, 7am-7pm Sat & Sun)* is an open-air, heated pool, which makes swimming in winter a lot more comfortable. It's popular with pre-work lap fanatics.

Sydney Aquatic Centre (☎ *9752 3666, Olympic Blvd, Homebush Bay; adult/child/ family $5.50/4.40/17.60; open 5am-9.45pm Mon-Fri, 6am-7.45pm Sat, Sun & public holidays, closes 1hr earlier May-Oct)* is the pool where so many world records were broken during the 2000 Olympics, and the facilities here are high-tech and world-class.

Victoria Park Pool (☎ *9660 4244, Cnr City & Parramatta Rds; adult/child/family $3/1.50/7; open 6am-7.15pm Mon-Fri, 7am-5.45pm Sat & Sun)* is an open-air, heated pool in a park next to Sydney University. It's handy to Glebe.

Leichhardt Park Aquatic Centre (☎ *9555 8344, Mary St, Leichhardt; adult/child/ concession $4.50/3.50/2.80; open 5.30am-8pm daily)* has multiple heated pools for a variety of speeds, including a diving tower.

Also check out the tiny **saltwater pool** at Fairy Bower Beach, Manly, and the two ocean-side pools at Coogee, one of which, **McIvers Baths**, is for women only, the other of which, **Wylies Baths**, is just ace.

Surfing

South of the Heads, the best spots are Bondi, Tamarama, Coogee and Maroubra. Cronulla, south of Botany Bay, is also a serious surfing spot. On the North Shore, there are a dozen surf beaches between Manly and Palm Beach; the best are Manly, Curl Curl, Dee Why, North Narrabeen, Mona Vale, Newport Reef, North Avalon and Palm Beach itself. Depending on your abilities, you should find a beach that suits you.

In Manly, surfboards and boogie-boards (wetsuits included) can be hired from the very friendly and knowledgable team at **Aloha Surf (Map 12)** (☎ *9977 3777, 44 Pittwater Rd, Manly; half/full day $20/40)*.

At Bondi Beach, you can hire surfboards and boogie-boards with wetsuit from **Bondi Surf Company (Map 11)** (☎ *9365 0870, Shop 2, 72 Campbell Pde; surfboards 2hrs/full day $30/60, boogie boards $20/ 50)*. Passport or credit card identification required.

Balmoral Windsurfing Sailing Kayaking & Kitesurfing School (☎ *9960 5344, 2 The Esplanade, Balmoral)* hires windsurfers for between $25 and $35 per hour.

Sailing & Boating

There are plenty of sailing schools in Sydney and even if you're not serious about learning the ropes, an introductory lesson is a fun way of getting onto the harbour.

The sociable **EastSail Sailing School** (☎ *9327 1166, d'Albora Marina, New Beach Rd, Rushcutters Bay)* runs a range of courses from introductory to racing level.

The friendly **Sunsail** (☎ *9955 6400, 23A King George St, McMahons Point)* has an introductory one-day course for $100 per person.

If you want to learn to sail a dinghy, contact **Northside Sailing School** (☎ *9969 3972, The Spit)*, which offers lessons and boat hire, plus a range of kids' activities.

Beaches

Sydney's two types of beach (harbour and ocean) are some of its greatest assets. They're hugely popular on warm weekends but Sydneysiders also swim before or after (or instead of) going to work. The beaches are easily accessible and usually good, although some post warnings that swimming is inadvisable after heavy rains because of stormwater run-off.

Swimming is generally safe, but at the ocean beaches you're only allowed to swim within the 'flagged' areas patrolled by the famed surf life-savers. Efforts are made to keep surfers separate from swimmers.

Shark patrols operate during the summer, and ocean beaches are generally netted. Try to keep the *Jaws* terrors in perspective – Sydney has only had one fatal shark attack since 1937. See also Dangers & Annoyances in the Facts for the Visitor chapter.

Many of Sydney's beaches are 'topless', but check to see what the locals are doing first. There are also a couple of nude beaches.

Harbour Beaches – South
Lady Bay Beach There are great views of the harbour for the nudists who frequent this little beach.
Camp Cove Near Lady Bay, this is a quiet family-friendly beach.
Shark Beach Despite the name, this beach is perfectly safe, as it's been netted. It's popular for picnics and family groups.

Harbour Beaches – North
Manly Cove A good suburban beach, with netting.
Reef Beach On the Scenic Walkway, this beach is *not* nudist, despite what you may have heard.
Clontarf Another popular and pretty beach for families.
Chinaman's Beach Gorgeous, peaceful and serene.
Balmoral Lovely, but the crowds can be a little too much.

Ocean Beaches – South
Bondi Beach Maybe not the biggest, nor the best, but there's something about Bondi that keeps thousands flocking here on a hot day.
Tamarama Also known as 'Glamarama'. Popular with models and the generically gorgeous. Watch out for the infamously strong rips here.
Bronte A fantastic beach, with lots of room for picnics and a good stretch of nearby cafes.
Clovelly Safe for swimming and a great spot for snorkelling.
Maroubra A large beach with good surf breaks, although the locals can be fierce about out-of-towners dropping in on their waves.

Ocean Beaches – North
Freshwater This is a nice beach, not too rough, and popular with local teenagers.
Curl Curl A well-balanced mix of family groups and surfers make this a quintessential Aussie beach.
Dee Why Big and popular with local families.
Collaroy The beach here is a good spot to unwind, with a relaxed atmosphere.
Narrabeen This is surfing turf, so if you want to learn, it might be best to wait before trying the breaks here.
Bilgola For some reason this beach seems like a bit of a secret for everyone except locals. Lovely.
Avalon Beach A big beach with good surf. Local residents told the producers of *Baywatch* (who wanted to film here) to shove it. Ten points.
Whale Beach Heavenly and remote, this gorgeous beach is smack bang in the middle of paradise.
Palm Beach The tip of Sydney and blissful. The fact that many scenes for *Home & Away* are filmed here doesn't detract from its astounding beauty.

THINGS TO SEE & DO

Diving

The best shore dives in Sydney are the Gordons Bay Underwater Nature Trail, north of Coogee; Shark Point, Clovelly; and Ship Rock, Cronulla. Popular boat dive sites are Wedding Cake Island, off Coogee; around the Sydney Heads; and off the Royal National Park. In Manly, you can make beach dives from Shelly Beach.

Plenty of outfits will take you diving and many run dive courses.

Pro Dive (☎ 9264 6177, 478 George St; ☎ 9665 6333, 27 Alfreda St, Coogee) has several outlets in and around Sydney, including in the city and in Coogee. Four-day diving courses cost from $395, boat dives cost $149 with gear ($99 without), and shore dives $105 with gear.

Dive courses are available at **Dive Centre Manly (Map 12)** (☎ 9977 4355, 10 Belgrave St, Manly; 'Learn to Dive' backpacker special $270). It also hires snorkelling gear and wetsuits. **Dive Centre Bondi** (☎ 9369 3855, 192 Bondi Rd, Bondi) is its branch in the eastern suburbs.

Scenic Flights

If you think Sydney looks beautiful from the ground or sea, a scenic flight will knock your socks off. Unfortunately, it'll cost ya. **Sydney by Seaplane** (☎ 1300 656 787, fax 9130 4896, e info@sydneybyseaplane .com, Barrenjoey Boathouse, Governor Phillip Park, Palm Beach; Imperial Peking Restaurant Jetty, Lyne Park, Rose Bay; adult/child from $85/45 to $585/220) has a variety of scenic flights (from 15 minutes to 90 minutes) and charter flights/packages that allow you to view areas such as Bondi Beach, Sydney Harbour, Palm Beach and the Hawkesbury River from on high.

Cycling

The steep hills, narrow streets and busy traffic don't make Sydney a particularly bicycle-friendly city. Some roads have designated cycle lanes but these often run between parked cars and moving traffic. Bicycle NSW (☎ 9283 5200, Level 2, 209 Castlereagh St) publishes a handy book called Cycling around Sydney ($11), detailing routes and cycle paths in and around the city. It also publishes booklets detailing cycle routes throughout NSW.

With less-hectic traffic and long cycle paths, both Manly and Centennial Park are popular pedalling spots. The Road Transport Authority (RTA) issues maps of metropolitan Sydney's cycle path network. You can pick them up at bicycle retailers or call ☎ 1800 060 607 or download them at the Web site (W www.rta.nsw.gov.au).

Bicycles can travel on suburban trains for concession rates during peak hours, and for free outside peak times. Cycling is prohibited in Darling Harbour and Martin Place. **Innes Bicycles (Map 5)** (☎ 9264 9597, 222 Clarence St) in the city, sells bicycles and does repairs.

You can rent hybrid bikes from the following places: **Woolys Wheels (Map 8)** (☎ 9331 2671, 82 Oxford St, Paddington; $33/day), across from the Victoria Barracks; **Manly Cycles (Map 12)** (☎ 9977 1189, 36 Pittwater Rd, Manly; $12/hour $25/day).

Most places require a hefty deposit, but accept credit cards. See the Getting Around chapter for cycle tours of Sydney.

Inline Skating

The beach promenades at Bondi and Manly are the favoured spots for skating, but Coogee and Bronte are becoming popular too. Centennial Park is a sensible choice for novice inline skaters, as the traffic is slow and one way.

Skates can be hired from **Manly Blades (Map 12)** (☎ 9976 3833, Manly Beach Plaza, 49 North Steyne; $12/hr, $18/2hrs, $25/day). It also offers lessons.

Jogging

The foreshore from Circular Quay around Farm Cove to Woolloomooloo Bay and through the Royal Botanic Gardens and the Domain is popular with joggers. Running across the Harbour Bridge is a popular way for North Shore residents to commute to work in the city.

Centennial Park and the promenades at Bondi Beach and Manly are the best jogging spots. The cliff trail between Bondi Beach and Bronte is also good.

Horse Riding

There are four outfits offering horse rides in Centennial Park – contact the stable manager (☎ 9332 2809) for details. They are based at the RAS Showgrounds (enter on the corner of Lang and Cook Rds). Prices start from around $35 per hour, and bookings are necessary.

Golf

The most central of Sydney's 40-odd public golf courses is **Moore Park (Map 8)** *(☎ 9663 3960, Centennial Ave; $27 Mon-Fri, $30 for 18 holes Sat & Sun)*.

Another public course is **Bondi** *(☎ 9130 3170, 5 Military Rd, North Bondi)*. **Hudson Park** *(☎ 9746 5702, Arthur St, Homebush)* is a golf-driving range at Homebush Bay.

Tennis

There are tennis courts for hire all over the city.

Jensen's Tennis Centre *(☎ 9698 9451, Prince Alfred Park)* is close to central station, and the courts have synthetic grass.

Miller's Point Tennis Court *(☎ 9256 2222, Kent St, The Rocks)* has hard courts.

Parklands Tennis Centre *(☎ 9662 7521, Cnr Anzac Pde & Lang Rd, Moore Park)* is close to Fox Studios and Paddington, and has synthetic grass and hard courts.

Places to Stay

Sydney offers a huge range of accommodation options – from budget to 'If you have to ask – you can't afford it'.

Hotel rates rise during the summer months (December to February), school holidays, long weekends and Mardi Gras (February/March). Cheaper rates are available in winter (June to September), so it's worth ringing around. Rates quoted here are generally for the high season, and all include GST unless otherwise indicated.

Many larger hotels include breakfast and parking and drop their rates on weekends. Mid-range and top-end hotels publish 'rack' (standard) rates, but there are often special deals and it's worth inquiring about these. Prices are usually quoted per room, depending on the facilities and/or the view.

For longer-term stays, there are places in the 'flats to let' and 'share accommodation' ads in the *Sydney Morning Herald* on Wednesday and Saturday. Hostel noticeboards are another good source. Serviced apartments often sleep several people; lower weekly rates can be inexpensive for a group.

Disabled travellers can get information on accommodation options in Sydney from Nican (☎ 02-6285 3713, 1800 806 769, fax 6285 3714, ⓦ www.nican.com.au) and *Accessing Sydney* (see Disabled Travellers in the Facts for the Visitor chapter for details).

PLACES TO STAY – BUDGET
Camping
Sydney's caravan parks, most of which also have sites for tents, are a fair way out of town. The following are 26km or less from the city centre.

Lane Cove River Caravan Park (☎ *9888 9133, fax 9888 9322, Plassey Rd, North Ryde*) Unpowered van sites $21/140 night/week, powered van sites $24/160, small double cabins $88, large cabins $98. Fourteen kilometres north of the city, this cheery place is happy to turn you into a happy camper.

Harts Caravan Park (☎ *9522 7143, 215 Port Hacking Rd, Miranda*) Unpowered sites $9 per person, double powered sites $24, vans $30-35 per night. This caravan park lies 24km south of central Sydney.

Lakeside Caravan Park (☎ *9913 7845, fax 9970 6385, Lake Park Rd, Narrabeen*) Unpowered van sites $22 per night for 2 people, powered van sites $28, cabins $100 per night a double, villas $170. This camping area is located 26km north of Sydney, in the prime real estate area of the northern beaches.

Sheralee Tourist Caravan Park (☎ *9567 7161, 88 Bryant St, Rockdale*) Unpowered/powered tent sites $20/25, powered van sites $25. This is the closest (albeit spartan) caravan park you'll find to Sydney, with only 13km separating you and the action.

The Grand Pines Caravan Park (☎ *9529 7329, fax 9583 1550, 289 The Grand Pde, Sans Souci*) Double powered sites $38.50, double vans from $55/250 night/week, cabins $66-88/385-600. Located on Botany Bay, this is a friendly, good-quality caravan park 17km south of Sydney.

Hostels
Sydney has a huge number of hostels. The largest concentration is in Kings Cross, but there are others in Bondi, Coogee, Glebe, Surry Hills and Manly. Facilities vary in the dorms, and many hostels also offer single, double and/or twin rooms. YHA hostels are sometimes better run and cleaner than many backpacker places. Some hostels have set hours for checking in and out, though all have 24-hour access once you've paid.

Many hostels offer reduced weekly rates, and most are acutely aware of the competition. The prices quoted here could easily fluctuate with demand. Hostelling International (HI) and YHA members usually receive discounts, as do members of VIP Backpackers International.

YHA hostels take members of any nationality, although Australians may find that other hostels won't take them unless they can prove that they're travelling.

The YHA's Membership & Travel Centre (☎ 9261 1111, ⓦ www.hostelbooking .com), 422 Kent St, can book you into any YHA hostel in Australia, and many others around the world. The centre is also a domestic and international travel agency. It's open from 9am to 5pm weekdays, 9am to 2pm Saturday.

As well as the backpacker-only hostels, many pubs and boarding houses fill spare rooms with bunks. Some are quite OK, but most lack the hostel atmosphere and the essential information grapevine. If you're staying in a pub and need a good night's sleep, check the location of the jukebox or band in the downstairs bar before choosing a room.

City Centre (Maps 5 & 8) Sydney's centre has a number of hostels, of varying standards. We've included the ones we think offer the best facilities for travellers and are safety conscious.

Sydney Central YHA (☎ 9281 9111, fax 9281 9199, ⓔ sydcentral@yhansw.org.au, 11 Rawson Place) Dorms \$24-29 per person, twins \$36 per person, doubles & twins with en suite \$40 per person. This massive hostel, on the corner of Pitt St and Rawson

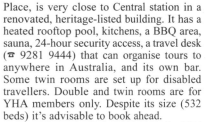

Place, is very close to Central station in a renovated, heritage-listed building. It has a heated rooftop pool, kitchens, a BBQ area, sauna, 24-hour security access, a travel desk (☎ 9281 9444) that can organise tours to anywhere in Australia, and its own bar. Some twin rooms are set up for disabled travellers. Double and twin rooms are for YHA members only. Despite its size (532 beds) it's advisable to book ahead.

Hotel Bakpak CB (☎ 9211 5115, fax 9281 9605, ⓔ infocb@bakpakgroup.com, 417 Pitt St) Beds in 4-8–bed dorm \$22/133 night/ week, singles \$45/300, twins \$54/350, doubles/triples/family rooms \$65/85/86. This rambling hotel first opened in 1908 and was once the largest residential hotel in the country. Now, it's a good budget hotel with plenty of dorms and knowledgable staff.

Hotel Bakpak Westend (☎ 9211 4822, fax 9211 5312, ⓔ reswestend@bakpakgroup .com, 412 Pitt St) Beds in 26-bed dorm \$19/133 night/week, 4-bed dorm with bathroom \$27/164.50, 6-bed dorm with bathroom \$24/164.50, doubles with bathroom \$76-82. This hostel includes breakfast in the price, is convenient to Central station, is big and is getting fixed up as the new owners take charge.

Crystal Palace Hotel (☎ 9211 1395, 789 George St) Beds in 4-bed dorm \$20/110 night/week, 13-bed dorm \$20/100. The dorm accommodation here was in the throes of renovation at the time of writing, and things were looking promising, with a brand-new kitchen and nice, high ceilings.

Y on the Park (☎ 9264 2451, fax 9285 6288, ⓔ yonthepark@ywca-sydney.com.au, 5-11 Wentworth Ave) Beds in 4-bed dorm \$29. Singles/doubles/triples with share bathroom \$68/93/105, with bathroom \$108/ 132/143. This YWCA takes young and not-so-young men, and has an enviable position, with Hyde Park across the road and both the city centre and Oxford St a short walk away. The standard is high, with simple but spotless well-furnished rooms and an adjoining cafe downstairs.

Wanderers on Kent (☎ 9267 7718, 1800 424 444, fax 9267 7719, ⓔ info@ wanderersonkent.com.au, 477 Kent St) Beds

Hotels vs Pubs

First-time visitors to Australia may be confused by the distinction between hotels and...well, hotels. There are three kinds. Until relatively recently, any establishment serving alcohol was called a hotel and was legally required to provide accommodation (usually pretty spartan and sometimes quite noisy). These hotels are also known as pubs (public houses). Private hotels are usually boarding-house-style places with similar facilities to pubs, but without a bar. These often have 'private' in their name to distinguish them from pubs. Hotels that provide accommodation with extra facilities, such as room service, are usually rated at three stars or higher. Sydney has a range of all three types of hotels.

in 10-bed/8-bed/4-6–bed dorm/doubles & twins $22/24/24.50/68. This new hostel has good rooms and great access to central Sydney. Security is very good, and there are electronic lockers, computer terminals, air-con, a cafe and bar, and even a solarium!

Kings Cross & Around (Maps 6 & 7)

Many of the fine old terrace houses along Victoria St have been converted into hostels. There are *heaps* of hostels in the Cross and there is little to distinguish many of them from each other – they seem to pop up overnight, and disappear just as quickly and in much the same way. Many hostels (and their staff) are extremely helpful in directing you to finding work or organising tours and social outings. Security, fire safety and comfort are only some of the good things to keep an eye out for, although the social life of a hostel can be of great importance to many travellers.

Highfield Private Hotel (☎ 9326 9539, fax 9358 1552, e highfieldhotel@bigpond.com, 166 Victoria St) Beds in 3-bed dorm $23/120 night/week, singles $45/270, doubles $60/360. A clean and welcoming hotel owned by a Swedish family, this place has good security and simple rooms (all share bathroom) with 24-hour access.

Original Backpackers (☎ 9356 3232, fax 9368 1435, e info@originalbackpackers .com.au, 160-2 Victoria St) Dorm beds $22/135 night/week, singles $30/210, doubles & twins with TV & fridge $55/330. Open 24 hours. A hostel for over 20 years, this really *is* the original backpackers in the area. A big 176-bed place in two historic houses, it has friendly staff, good security, safety and facilities (laundry, kitchen etc), plus Blinky the dog.

Travellers Rest Hostel (☎ 9358 4606, fax 9358 4606, 156 Victoria St) Dorm beds $20/124 night/week, twins $45/262, doubles with share bathroom $50/288, with bathroom $55/310. Travellers Rest is a comfortable hostel, with well-equipped rooms that have phone, fridge and TV, and all linen supplied. Some have balconies overlooking Victoria St.

Virgin Backpackers (☎ 9357 4733, 1800 667 255, fax 9357 4434, e stay@ vbackpackers.com, 144 Victoria St) Dorm beds $24/140 night/week, doubles $55/325. With modern fittings in the cafe and reception, this place is quite spiffy-looking for a hostel. The rooms have been fitted-out nicely and the communal areas are very good. Security and safety are good here too, and breakfast is included.

Eva's Backpackers (☎ 9358 2185, fax 9358 3259, 6-8 Orwell St) Dorm beds $20/120 night/week, doubles & twins $50/300. Eva's is a perennial favourite with many travellers, particularly Germans. It's family owned and operated, and is clean, considerate and well managed. There's a good rooftop barbecue area and a sociable kitchen/dining room. Often full, it's best to book ahead.

Sydney Central Backpackers (☎ 9358 6600, fax 9356 3799, 16 Orwell St) Dorm beds $22/132 night/week, doubles $57/342, twins $52/312. Cheery and reasonably tidy, this place has a great rooftop garden with nice views. The rooms aren't bad either, with fridge, fan, locker and sink. The doubles have TV.

Jolly Swagman Backpackers (☎ 9358 6400, 1800 805 870, fax 9331 0125, e stay@jollyswagman.com.au, 27 Orwell St) Dorm beds $22/126 night/week, doubles & twins $56/324, discounts for VIP members. This 134-bed hostel has 24-hour security and a social life that gets the thumbs-up from more than a few travellers. The rooms are modern and have lockers, fridges, reading lamps, fans and TV (no TV in dorms). Safety standards are high, and the staff is friendly and helpful with getting work and getting around. Recommended.

Nomad's The Palms Backpackers (☎ 9357 1199, fax 9331 3854, 23 Hughes St) Dorm beds/doubles $21/55. This is a small, low-key hostel with bathrooms attached to the dorms, and good facilities. The carpet is just like Grandma's.

The Blue Parrot Backpackers (☎/fax 9356 4888, 1800 252 299, 87 Macleay St, Potts Point) Dorm beds $24/140 night/ week. Brand spanking new at the time of writing, this place is neat as a new pin and admirably fire-safety conscious. The facilities are good, as are the prices.

***Rucksack Rest** (☎ 9358 2348, 9 McDonald St, Potts Point)* Dorm beds $20/120 night/week, doubles $45-50/270-300, twins $48/288. Long-established and tucked away down a relatively sedate cul-de-sac off Macleay St, the Rucksack Rest is quiet, clean, well run and a good place for longer stays. The rooms are fairly small but comfortable, and dorms sleep no more than three people.

***The Pink House** (☎/fax 9358 1689, ☎ 1800 806 384, ℮ info@pinkhouse.com .au, 6-8 Barncleuth Square)* Beds in 8-bed dorm $17.50/105 night/week, 6-bed dorm $21/126, 4-bed dorm $22/132, doubles $51/153. Close to the El Alamein fountain action, but far away enough to seem relaxed, this popular hostel has nice, light-filled rooms, 24-hour video surveillance and a leafy courtyard area. The building is a fine old mansion painted – you guessed it – pink.

***Backpackers Headquarters Hostel** (☎ 9331 6180, 79 Bayswater Rd)* Dorm beds $22/130 night/week. The pastel-hued 58-bed Backpackers Headquarters has very good security and good-quality rooms. Rooms on the side away from busy Kings Cross Rd are quieter. The communal rooms are tidy, and rates are lower for VIP members.

***Forbes Terrace** (☎ 9358 4327, fax 9357 3652, ℮ hotel@g-day.aust.com, 153 Forbes St, Woolloomooloo)* Dorm beds $19.80/107.80 night/week, singles $44/308, twins $66/462. Just west of the Cross, Forbes Terrace is clean and has a good courtyard area, although the bathrooms are showing their age. Rooms have TV, fridge and tea- and coffee-making facilities. Clean linen is supplied for free.

***Funk House** (☎ 9358 6455, fax 9358 3506, 23 Darlinghurst Rd)* Dorm beds $23/135 night/week, doubles $58/340, discounts for VIP members. This lively place is purple on the outside and every colour imaginable on the inside. It's also right in the thick of things, so the 24-hour security is a bonus. Rooms are good, if a little spartan, although most people seem to want to stay here for the atmosphere, which has been described as 'smoking'.

Surry Hills (Map 8) Surry Hills makes a good alternative to crowded Bondi and city-centre hostels. And it's close to both areas.

***Nomads Captain Cook Hotel** (☎ 9331 6487, fax 9331 7746, 162 Flinders St)* Beds in 10-12–bed/4-bed dorm/doubles & twins $19/24/60, weekly rates available. In a famous old pub on a *very* busy intersection, this place is handy and has good facilities if you want to catch a big game at the Sydney Football Stadium or Sydney Cricket Ground, but bear in mind that this is when things get crowded.

***Kangaroo Bakpak** (☎ 9319 5915, 665 South Dowling St)* Beds in 4-bed dorm $22/132 night/week, in 6-bed dorm $20/120, doubles $25/150 per person. Set in an old house, there's a relaxed and friendly vibe here, with pleasant communal areas and front rooms with balconies. It has another hostel at 461 Cleveland St, known as Gracelands. From Central station, take bus No 372, 393 or 395.

***Excelsior Hotel** (☎ 9211 4945, 64 Foveaux St)* Dorm beds $20/110 night/week, doubles $50/250, discounts for VIP members. Most rooms offer reasonable, simple pub accommodation (but the bands in the downstairs bar can be a bit raucous), and most dorms have between three and six beds. It's only a few blocks from Central station.

***Alfred Park Private Hotel** (☎ 9319 4031, fax 9318 1306, 207 Cleveland St)* Dorms with bathroom $18-25 night, $105-175 week (GST not included), singles with share/private bathroom $66/77-99, twins with bathroom $99. Close to Central station, this hotel occupies two adjacent houses. The rooms are plain but clean and vary in size and ambience. There's a nice courtyard and kitchen, and a balcony overlooking the park, and overall, it's a well-managed place.

Glebe (Map 9) The hostels, restaurants and entertainment options in Glebe make it a good area to stay in.

***Glebe Point YHA** (☎ 9692 8418, fax 9660 0431, ℮ glebe@yhansw.org.au, 262-64 Glebe Point Rd)* Beds in 5-bed dorm $22, 3-4–bed dorm $26, twins & doubles

$31 per person (nonmembers add $3.50 per person per night). This large, friendly hostel offers good facilities – kitchen, TV lounge, laundry and linen. The rooms are simple but clean, as are the bathrooms, and credit-card reservations are accepted.

Glebe Village Backpackers Hostel (☎ 9660 8133, e glebevillage@bakpak .com, 256-8 Glebe Point Rd) Beds in 4-bed dorm $24/144 night/week, 6-10–bed dorm $23/138, twins & doubles $60/360 per room, triples $27/162 per person. This bustling place is basic but popular, with a nice front courtyard, a social atmosphere and the usual hostel facilities.

Wattle House (☎ 9552 4997, fax 9660 2528, e stay@wattle-house.au.com, 44 Hereford St) Beds in 4-bed dorm/twins & doubles $25/70. A lovely Victorian house accommodating 26 people, this place is excellent – super-tidy, friendly and efficient. It's nonsmoking, alcohol-free and reservations are advised. It has a minimum stay of three nights, although this can be negotiated.

Alishan International Guest House (☎ 9566 4048, fax 9525 4686, e kevin@ alishan.com.au, 100 Glebe Point Rd) Dorm beds from $27. Spotless and surprisingly quiet, this is a good choice. See also Glebe under Places to Stay – Mid-Range.

Newtown See the entry for St Andrew's College under University of Sydney in the University Colleges entry, later in this chapter.

Billabong Gardens (☎ 9550 3236, fax 9550 4352, 5-11 Egan St) Dorm beds with share bathroom $20/125 night/week, with bathroom $23/135, doubles & twins with share bathroom $66/390, with bathroom $88/530. This lovely long-standing hostel is clean and quiet and has good word-of-mouth reviews from many travellers. There's a small solar-heated pool surrounded by thriving native plants, and a very good kitchen. Travellers can be picked up at the airport by arrangement. From Railway Square, catch bus No 422, 423, 426 or 428 up Newtown's King St, and get off at Missenden Rd. By train, go to Newtown station and turn right; Egan St is about four blocks along, on the left.

Bondi Beach (Map 11) There's a range of accommodation in Bondi, not all of it appealing, but with the beach on your doorstep you're unlikely to spend much time in your room. In summer, Bondi's already crowded streets fill to capacity with out-of-towners and long-term working-holiday makers.

Noah's Bondi Beach (☎ 9365 7100, 1800 226 662, fax 9365 7644, e noahs bondibeach@dragon.net.au, 2 Campbell Pde) Beds in 8-bed dorm $16/105 night/week, 6-bed dorm $18/115, 4-bed dorm $20/130, doubles $52/320, beach double $60/380. A well-run place in a great south Bondi location, the rooms are worn but clean. Most dorm rooms have TV and fridge, and there's a good lounge with pinball machines and a pool table. There's also a nightly $6.50 buffet if you're pinching pennies and hungry.

Lamrock Lodge (☎ 9130 5063, fax 9300 9582, 19 Lamrock Ave) Dorm beds $20/126 night/week, twins $55/330. This tidy, recently refurbished place offers good facilities like TV, microwave and fridge in each room and is open 24 hours.

Indy's (☎ 9365 4900, fax 9365 4994, 35a Hall St) Dorm beds $25/143.50 night/week for VIP members. With a relaxed, easy-going vibe, this hostel is probably the best backpacking option in Bondi. Facilities are good and it's security conscious.

Coogee (Map 10) It's further from the city than Bondi and other traveller centres, but Coogee's relaxed atmosphere and hostels make it a very popular spot. It's worth ringing hostels before arriving as they generally have limited office hours, eg, 8am to midday and then 4pm to 8pm. Security is also an issue at some of these places, so always place your valuables in a safe or a locker.

Wizard of Oz Backpackers (☎ 9315 7876, 172 Coogee Bay Rd) Dorm beds $23/135 night/week. Smack-bang on Coogee Bay Rd in a refurbished California bungalow, this place is laid-back and casual. Dorms sleep anything from four to fourteen people.

Coogee Beachside Accommodation (☎ 9315 8511, 178 Coogee Bay Rd) Doubles & twins $65. A good option for budget travellers looking for simple but clean accommodation in a converted house with kitchen facilities.

Surfside Backpackers Coogee (☎ *9315 7888, 186 Arden St)* Beds in 4-bed dorm $23/140 night/week, 16-bed dorm $20/110. Opposite the beach and main bus stop, the entrance is on Alfreda St. This is a big rabbit warren of a hostel with OK facilities and communal balconies with views of the beach. It's popular.

Coogee Beach Backpackers (☎ *9315 8000, 94-6 Beach St)* Dorm beds $22/132 night/week. A short, stiff walk up the hill at the northern end of the beach, this place occupies a Federation-era house and a modern block next door. There are common areas and a deck with great views of the ocean. At the time of writing, there was a big 'for sale' sign out front and the property may be redeveloped in the near future.

Indy's (☎ *9315 7644, 302 Arden St)* Beds in 4-bed dorm $25/133 night/week. This smaller hostel is on the hill at the southern end, in an old Victorian-era house. Ask to look at the rooms before you settle on a dorm, as the higher ones are better. It has a TV room and the usual cleaner-than-it-could-be shared kitchen. Breakfast and linen are included in the price.

Manly (Map 12) Manly has great ocean and harbour beaches and few city hassles, and is only 30 minutes by ferry (15 minutes by JetCat) from Circular Quay.

Manly Beach Hut (☎ *9977 8777, fax 9977 8766,* e *enquiry@manlybeachhut.com .au, 7 Pine St)* Dorm beds $28/170 night/ week. There are only a few dorm beds (with TV and video) available, but they are easily the best in the area. In fact, this charming house may well provide the best dorm accommodation in Sydney. The house is beautifully furnished and has a great garden area. Book ahead, as this place is *excellent*.

Manly Beach Resort Backpackers (☎ *9977 4188, fax 9977 0524,* e *manly bch@ozemail.com.au, 6 Carlton St)* Dorm beds $22/140 night/week, doubles $50/315. Although this is a motel, backpackers have their own section in a large house. Dorms

are spacious and clean, and the communal areas are in good shape.

Manly Astra Backpackers (☎*/fax 9977 2092, 68 Pittwater Rd)* Rooms $28/165 night/week per person. This quiet, well-managed place enjoys the benefit of long-term management and repeat stays from happy visitors. It's simple, scrupulously tidy accommodation geared to couples on longer stays.

Manly Backpackers Beachside (☎ *9977 3411, fax 9977 4379, 28 Raglan St)* Dorm beds $24/147 night/week, doubles & twins $70/448. About a block from the beach, this place has modern, reasonable dorm accommodation with lockers available, a good communal kitchen and well-tended bathrooms.

Steyne Hotel (☎ *9977 4977, fax 9977 5645,* e *stay@steynehotel.com.au, 75 The Corso)* Bunk in 4-bed dorm $38.50. Although relatively pricey, given the pretty ordinary quality of its rooms, it has a good, shared kitchen, and bistro-style meals available in the bar downstairs. Breakfast is included in the price. You're right in the heart of Manly here, so consider this if noise keeps you awake at night.

Northern Beaches It's not as handy for transport as many other areas of Sydney, so it's a good idea to call these places before you arrive, to check if a room is available. The location on Sydney's 'insular peninsula' is mighty picturesque though.

Avalon Beach Hostel (☎ *9918 9709, fax 9973 1322, 59 Avalon Pde)* Beds in 6-bed dorm $20/121 night/week, 4-bed dorm $22/ 138, doubles $50/300. The relaxed beachside suburb of Avalon is a nice area to stay in, although this hostel is simple in what it offers, with communal kitchen, laundry, TV room and ping-pong. It's good to book ahead before trekking all the way here.

To get here, catch bus No L90 from Town Hall or Wynyard Park in the city, or No L88 from Town Hall. Ask for Avalon Beach ($4.60, 1¼ hours).

Sydney Beachhouse YHA (☎ *9981 1177, fax 9981 1114, 4 Collaroy St, Collaroy)* Beds in 3-bed mixed dorm $20, 4-bed single-sex dorm $24, 6-bed dorm $23, doubles & twins $60, family room (sleeps 5) with bathroom $104. This friendly, clean place gets great reviews from travellers and is close to some of Sydney's best beaches.

Hotels & Guesthouses

A wide variety of accommodations fall into this category. There are some fine budget hotels and guesthouses, which work out only fractionally more expensive than hostels if you're travelling with friends. A refundable key deposit of about $20 to $30 is often required.

City Centre (Map 5) Sydney's centre doesn't offer a great depth of choice in this price range, and you might like to ask to see a room before you agree to spend the night.

The George Street Private Hotel (☎/fax 9211 1800, 700a George St) Singles/doubles/triples/quads with share bathroom $50/64/75/84, double with TV & bathroom $85. One of the better innercity budget hotels, it's sparsely furnished, clean and has cooking and laundry facilities.

Sydney Central Private Hotel (☎/fax 9212 1005, e scph@bigpond.com.au, 75 Wentworth Ave) Singles/doubles & twins with share bathroom $40/60, with bathroom $75/85, with bathroom & air-con $85/105. The rooms here vary in age, and the newer ones represent better value in terms of comfort and facilities (they have air-con). Still, the cheap rooms are mighty cheap. The traffic (road and train) can be noisy, but you're close to Central, should you need to catch an early train.

Criterion Hotel (☎ 9264 3093, fax 9283 2460, Cnr Pitt & Park Sts) Singles/doubles & twins with share bathroom $55/66, with bathroom $88/99. This large (definitely *not* boutique) pub offers simple accommodation at reasonable rates for its location.

The Rocks (Map 5) This is a lovely area to stay in Sydney, however, as much accommodation here is near pubs, you may wish to pack the earplugs.

Palisade Hotel (☎ 9247 2272, fax 9247 2040, 35 Bettington St) Doubles/twins

$98/108. Standing sentinel-like at Millers Point, the Palisade Hotel has nine solidly furnished rooms, some with breathtaking views of the harbour and its fine bridge. It's a lovely old heritage building (although the bathrooms reflect its age a tad), and it's in a part of The Rocks that has thankfully avoided (at the time of writing) that twee, 'ye olde worlde' tourist-trap feel.

Pyrmont (Map 9) This handy central suburb makes a good alternative to staying in the centre of Sydney.

The Woolbrokers Arms (☎ 9552 4773, fax 9552 4771, 22 Allen St) Singles/doubles & twins/triples $66/89/107. On the corner of Allen and Pyrmont Sts, this small and friendly 26-room hotel is close to Darling Harbour and offers reasonable motel-style B&B. Rooms vary in size, and all have TV and fridge. Bathrooms are separate, but they're numerous enough (14 in all) to ensure privacy.

Kings Cross (Map 7) There are some reasonable hotels in the heart of the Cross.

Cross Court Tourist Hotel (☎ 9368 1822, 203 Brougham St) Singles/doubles & twins $70/80. A friendly, well-run place with 20 rooms and some great views, this is one of the better small hotels in the area.

Bernly Private Hotel (☎ 9358 3122, fax 9356 4405, e bernly@bernlyprivatehotel .com.au, 15 Springfield Ave) Beds in 2-bed dorm $24.20/145.20 night/week, 4-bed dorm $22/132, singles/doubles & twins with share bathroom $49.50/55 night, $297/330 week, singles/doubles/triples with en suite $82.50/93.50/132 night, $495/561/792 week. This polite, larger-than-it-looks hotel has simple rooms with fairly old decor, 24-hour reception and a rooftop garden.

Springfield Lodge (☎ 9358 3222, fax 9357 4742, e springfield@wheretostay.com.au, 9 Springfield Ave) Singles/doubles with share bathroom $50/60 night, $250/300 week, en suite rooms $65/75 night, $325/375 week. In a nice-looking building with friendly reception, this hotel has simple, tidy rooms with polished floorboards, TV, fridge and clean bathrooms.

Potts Point (Map 6) Close to Kings Cross, but with just a bit less sleaze, Potts Point is a good central choice.

Challis Lodge (☎ 9358 5422, fax 8356 9047, e challislodge@wheretostay.com.au, 21-3 Challis Ave) Singles & doubles with share bathroom $45-55/225-275 night/week, with bathroom $70/325, with balcony $80/400. Challis Lodge is a pair of renovated cavernous terraces not far from the Cross. It's low-key and well maintained, and has simple, clean rooms with polished floorboards; those on the upper floors are quieter and get better light.

The Point Inn (☎ 9357 3878, fax 9357 1421, e pointinn@bigpond.com, 31 Challis Ave) Singles with share bathroom $40-50/240 night/week, with bathroom $70/420, doubles with share bathroom $60-70. This place is a quiet and friendly guesthouse in a great location. It's simple but spick and span.

Macleay Lodge (☎ 9368 0660, fax 9357 4742, 71 Macleay St) Singles with share bathroom $45/225 night/week, doubles $55/275. This place has good-value, tidy rooms with TV, fridge and tea- and coffee-making facilities, even though the heavy smoking at reception is a bit off-putting. Some en suite rooms are available.

Holiday Lodge (☎ 9356 3955, 55 Macleay St) Economy singles/doubles/triples $70/75/80, newer doubles/triples $86/98. Rooms are basic motel-style, with TV, fridge and bathroom, and some can accommodate five people ($12 extra per person per night).

Woolloomooloo (Map 6) There's really only one budget option in Woolloomooloo worth staying in.

Frisco Hotel (☎ 9357 1800, fax 9357 2020, e frisco@bigpond.com.au, 46 Dowling St) Singles & twins $55/335.50 night/week, doubles $66/412.50, family rooms $82.50/528. With prices like these, you could forgive the Frisco for being a bit shabby – but it's not. Rooms are clean and comfortable, and the location is enviable.

Newtown Newtown offers fewer choices than Glebe, but it definitely offers a more interesting atmosphere, and food options for budget-conscious travellers are superb.

Australian Sunrise Lodge (☎ 9557 4400, fax 9550 4457, 485 King St) Singles/doubles with TV & fridge $59/69, with bathroom $79/89. Although it looks ordinary from the outside, this is a clean, pleasant-enough place, with parquet floors and potted plants. It has simple motel-style rooms. Ask for a room away from King St, and preferably with a balcony. Turn left when you leave Newtown station.

Bondi Beach (Map 11) Hotels in Bondi are prone to summer price-hikes. Rates vary depending on demand; there are better deals when trade is slow.

Biltmore Private Hotel (☎ 9130 4660, 110 Campbell Pde) Dorm beds/singles/doubles $19/39/49. Nab a bed in the dorms (all prices are for share room) that face out over the beach and you'll happily forget that this place is a bit on the dark and dingy side. If you're in a single or double with no outlook – don't bother.

Hotel Bondi (☎ 9130 3271, fax 9130 7974, 178 Campbell Pde) Singles/doubles/triples $50/95/105, beach-view rooms $120-150. Hotel Bondi is the peach-coloured layer-cake on the beachfront. The rooms are small and tidy, but be warned – the Bondi Hotel below is a very popular nightspot (see Bondi Beach under Places to Stay – Mid-Range).

Bondi Lodge (☎ 9365 2088, 63 Fletcher St) Dorm beds $35/185 night/week, singles $70/340, twins $50/235 per person. Bondi Lodge is a short walk up the hill from the southern end of the beach, but close to neighbouring Tamarama Beach. It's clean and friendly, with spotless communal areas.

Coogee (Map 10) An increasingly popular alternative to Bondi, Coogee's hotels are of varied standards, so check the room if you're not sure about the facilities.

Grand Pacific Private Hotel (☎ 9665 6301, 64 Carr St) Singles/doubles $35/45 for the first 2 nights, $25/35 from the 3rd night. It's not very grand any more, but cute and charming in a dilapidated, down-at-heel

way, and the location is great. There are tea-
and coffee-making facilities, a kitchen for
guests' use and a laundry.

Coogee Beachside Hotel (☎ 9665 1162,
fax 9665 0365, 171 Arden St) Dorm beds
$25/150 night/week, doubles $70/420. The
rooms in this hotel are showing their age,
but it's clean and friendly and well located
at the northern end of the beach. Prices
include breakfast.

North Sydney & Kirribilli (Map 3)
Places to stay on the 'other side' don't offer
much in the way of bargains, but these are
the better options.

North Shore Hotel (☎ 9955 1012, fax
9955 4212, 310 Miller St) Rooms $95-120.
Opposite St Leonards Park, this pleasant old
house has good quality accommodation,
and each room has a bathroom and is well
maintained.

The quiet, leafy suburb of Kirribilli, north-
east of the bridge, has several guesthouses.

Tremayne Private Hotel (☎ 9955 4155,
89 Carabella St) Singles/doubles with bathroom $220/300 per week. This is a large
guesthouse originally built as accommodation for country girls attending school in
Sydney. Some rooms have harbour views,
which make up for the rather shabby state
of the rooms. Share accommodation is also
available, and there are nightly rates for a
minimum two-night stay.

Kirribilli Court Private Hotel (☎ 9955
4344, fax 9929 4774, 45 Carabella St)
Dorm beds $15/90 night/week, singles
$40/180, doubles & twins $50/250. With its
mock-Tudor frontage, leafy surrounds and
collection of travellers enjoying the front
garden, this place has a relaxed atmosphere,
although the rooms are fairly ordinary and
the bathrooms are shared.

Glenferrie Lodge (☎ 9955 1685, 12a
Carabella St) Beds in a 3-bed dorm $27/
145 night/week, singles $35-50 night, $175-
250 week, doubles & twins $65-75 night,
$330-380 week. In a large, old house, this
hotel has clean rooms with a fridge and
helpful, friendly management.

Neutral Bay Motor Lodge (☎/fax 9953
4199, 45 Kurraba Rd, Neutral Bay) Singles/

doubles/permanent rooms $77/88/160 per
week. On the corner of Kurraba Rd and
Hayes St, near the Hayes St ferry wharf, this
is a quiet, friendly guesthouse with a communal kitchen and clean, simple rooms with
older-style furniture. All rooms are with
share bathroom. Parking is available.

University Colleges
Many residential colleges accept casual
guests. Those listed accept nonstudents and
both men and women. Unless otherwise
stated, rooms are available during holidays
only, mainly the long mid-December to
late-January break, and you'll need to book
in advance.

Although most places quote meal-
inclusive rates, it's often possible to negoti-
ate a lower bed-only rate. Ask about rates
for longer stays, which might be cheaper.

University of Sydney (Map 9) This uni
is southwest of Chippendale, close to Glebe
and Newtown.

International House (☎ 9950 9800, fax
9950 9804, 96 City Rd) Singles $53/68
student/nonstudent (all meals included),
singles/doubles with bathroom $83/95
student, $104/125 nonstudent. This is a
big modern university college with standard university rooms and all meals are
included.

Sancta Sophia College (☎ 9577 2100,
fax 9577 2388, 8 Missenden Rd) Singles/
twins with shared bathroom $55/85, rooms
with bathroom $66. Pretty Sancta Sophia
has rooms available (mostly during the
summer holidays) for nonstudents, and all
with breakfast.

St Andrew's College (☎ 9557 1133, fax
9261 1969, Carillion Ave) Adults/under 18s
$23/11, doubles & twins $28/13.50. This
college is known as Sydney Summer YHA
between early December and early February. You can contact YHA's Membership &
Travel Centre (☎ 9261 1111); see under
Hostels, earlier, for details.

St John's College (☎ 9394 5200, fax 9550
6303, 8a Missenden Rd) B&B singles
$79/330 night/week. Rooms are available
year-round. St John's is one of the older

colleges on campus and things will be much quieter if you stay during the holiday season.

Wesley College (☎ 9565 3333, fax 9516 3829, Western Ave) Singles $50.60/63.80 B&B/full board, doubles $38.50/52 per person. Right in the middle of the university, Wesley College has about 14 double rooms and a number of single rooms.

Women's College (☎ 9517 5000, fax 9517 5006, 15 Carillon Ave) B&B singles/doubles $55/80, with dinner $62/94, full board $70/110, less for students and YHA members. Women's College offers accommodation during the three university holidays. Call or fax for reservations.

University of NSW This university is only a short bus-ride from the southern ocean beaches and Oxford St.

International House (☎ 9663 0418, fax 9313 6346, Gate 2, High St) $50 per person per day with share bathroom and all meals.

New College (☎ 9662 6066, fax 9381 1909, Cnr Barker St & Anzac Pde) Accommodation only $49.50 per person, B&B $55, full board $66.

Kensington Colleges (☎ 9315 0000, fax 9315 0011, Gate 6, High St) Twins $25/27.50 YHA members/nonmembers (summer only). The three Kensington Colleges, Basser, Baxter and Goldstein offer YHA accommodation in the summer holidays.

Shalom College (☎ 9663 1366, fax 9313 7145, Gate 14, Barker St) B&B singles with share bathroom $44/55 students/nonstudents.

PLACES TO STAY – MID-RANGE

This section covers places charging from about $80 to $180 for a double. It's a wide price span, and standards vary accordingly. At the higher end of the price scale, you'll have a good bathroom and all sorts of facilities at your disposal.

Hotels & Motels

This is a category that offers wildly diverse standards of accommodation. You may find some real bargains, other rooms may be quite spartan.

City Centre (Maps 5 & 8) The following places offer good value in this price range.

Grand Hotel (☎ 9232 3755, fax 9232 1073, 30 Hunter St) Singles/doubles & twins/triples/family rooms $80/100/110/120. A pretty good innercity pub is the heritage-listed Grand Hotel, where prices are more than reasonable for the location. Rooms are quite modest, sizes vary and all have TV, fridge, and tea- and coffee-making facilities.

Sydney Vista Hotel (☎ 9274 1222, 1800 652 090, fax 9274 1274, e Sales@ vistahotels.com.au, 7-9 York St) Rooms from $160, with breakfast & car parking from $175. This hotel has a good, central location, although the rooms are not exactly inspiring. It has apartments with kitchenettes and faxes for longer stays.

Aaron's Hotel (☎ 9281 5555, 1800 101 100, fax 9281 2666, e aarons@acay.com .au, 37 Ultimo Rd) Standard doubles $115 Sun-Thur, $125 Fri & Sat, deluxe doubles $125 or $135. Right in the heart of Chinatown and very close to Darling Harbour, this hotel has plain, clean, light-filled rooms (all with bathroom) that you open with a spiffy card instead of a key.

Southern Cross Hotel (☎ 9282 0987, 1800 221 141, fax 9211 1806, 111 Goulburn St) Rooms $145. This hotel has a rooftop pool and garden and the rooms are good. It's on the corner of Goulburn and Elizabeth Sts, within walking distance of Hyde Park, Oxford St and Darling Harbour.

Country Comfort Sydney Central (☎ 9212 2544, fax 9281 3794, Cnr George & Quay Sts) Doubles $184. The location of this hotel couldn't be less 'country', but it is comfortable, despite the very low ceilings and the rather outdated pseudo-rural decor. Specials and packages are frequently available.

The Rocks (Map 5) If you don't mind a little pub noise, there are some good places to stay in this area.

Lord Nelson Brewery Hotel (☎ 9251 4044, fax 9251 1532, e hotel@lordnelson .com.au, 19 Kent St) Rooms with share bathroom/en suite $160/180. This is a swish boutique pub with its own brewery, in a historic sandstone building in the less-obviously touristy part of The Rocks. All rooms have fax machines and Dataport facilities.

Mercantile Hotel (☎ 9247 3570, fax 9247 7047, 25 George St) Singles/doubles & twins with share bathroom $80/110, doubles & twins with bathroom & spa $140. This green-tiled hotel is a restored pub with a strong Irish connection. It's right near the bridge and the rooms are good; all with breakfast.

Pyrmont (Map 5) *Glasgow Arms Hotel*
(☎ 9211 2354, fax 9281 9439, 527 Harris St) Singles/doubles $110/140. On the western side of Darling Harbour, across the road from the Powerhouse Museum, this hotel has nice rooms (with bathroom and breakfast) in a renovated old-style pub with a good atmosphere.

Hotel Ibis (☎ 9563 0888, fax 9563 0833, 70 Murray St) Rooms with Pyrmont view $130-140, with Darling Harbour view $155. Overlooking the harbour, the Hotel Ibis is between the Mercure and the Novotel, which bear a striking similarity in style (big, modern) and service (young, enthusiastic).

Kings Cross & Around (Maps 6 & 7)
The following options are good value for this area, and are safety conscious.

O'Malley's Hotel (☎ 9357 2211, fax 9357 2656, 228 William St) Singles/doubles & twins/triples $82.50/93.50/121. This is a friendly Irish pub with traditionally decorated, well-furnished rooms (with bathroom and breakfast). It's also surprisingly quiet, given its location, so book ahead.

Madison's Central City Hotel (☎ 9357 1155, 1800 060 118, fax 9357 1193, e reservations@centralcityhotel.com.au, 6 Ward Ave, Elizabeth Bay) Doubles & twins/suites $104.50/126.50. The friendly 40-room Madison's Hotel is in a refurbished 1930s building with good, straightforward rooms with en suite.

Hotel 59 (☎ 9360 5900, fax 9360 1828, e hotel59@enternet.com.au, 59 Bayswater Rd) Singles/doubles $105/115. This small friendly hotel in the quiet stretch of Bayswater Rd has charming rooms and

friendly staff. There's also a small cafe. Reservations are a good idea, as nice places like this fill up quickly.

Royal Sovereign Hotel (☎ 9331 3672, fax 9360 6196, e royalsov@solotel.com.au, Cnr Liverpool St & Darlinghurst Rd) Doubles $77. This 19-room hotel above the popular Darlo Bar has natty rooms with TV and share bathroom at a very reasonable price.

Manhattan Park Inn (☎ 9358 1288, fax 9357 3696, e manhattan@khll.com, 8 Greenknowe Ave) Standard/view double rooms $88/110 (maximum 2 people). This 1927 Art Deco-era building has 140 rooms and good service, although a view makes all the difference between ordinary and better-than-ordinary accommodation.

Victoria Court Hotel (☎ 9357 3200, fax 9357 7606, 122 Victoria St) Rooms $85-180. This is a quiet hotel with old-fashioned service and comfortable rooms in a lovely pair of renovated Victorian houses. There's security parking, and a pleasant courtyard.

Edgecliff, Darling Point & Rushcutters Bay (Map 6)
Up a notch on the social scale from Potts Point and Kings Cross, this is a lovely part of Sydney for visitors and residents alike.

Bayside (☎ 9327 8511, fax 9327 7808, 85 New South Head Rd, Rushcutters Bay) Rooms $155. A Flag franchise, this hotel has standard, comfortable rooms, and it's worth checking for specials, particularly if you're a member of the travel or hospitality industry.

Lodge Motel (☎ 9328 0666, fax 9328 0555, 38-44 New South Head Rd, Rushcutters Bay) Singles/doubles $65/75, twins/triples/quads/family $79/89/99/115. Rooms at this four-storey motel each have TV, kitchenette and bathroom, plus there's parking. The building's layout means it can get pretty noisy though, thanks to New South Head Rd.

Darling Point Boutique Hotel (☎ 9327 3207, fax 9327 3688, 2b Mona Rd, Darling Point) Rooms $132/385 night/week. Situated near New South Head Rd and close to Edgecliff station, the renovated rooms here have minikitchens with fridge and microwave, and some have good views. There's also a pleasant roof garden with spa, sauna and harbour views.

Metro Motor Inn (☎ *9238 7977, 1800 004 321, fax 9360 1216, 230 New South Head Rd, Edgecliff)* Roadside rooms $108/630 night/week, harbourside rooms $118/665. Although rooms are ordinary on the decor front, some have great harbour views. Packages are available.

Double Bay This swanky area is a good place to stay.

Savoy Double Bay Hotel (☎ *9326 1411, fax 9327 8486, 41-5 Knox St)* Rooms $119-149, suites $189. This pleasant, friendly hotel is small but in a good location.

Darlinghurst (Map 5) Close to nightlife and the city, Darlinghurst gets very busy during the Mardi Gras.

Oxford Koala Hotel (☎ *9269 0645, 1800 222 144, fax 9283 2741, Cnr Oxford & Pelican Sts)* Standard/superior rooms $135/155, apartments $185. This 1970s-era large hotel is gradually getting dragged into the modern day design-wise, and still offers pretty good value for its location and nice staff.

Paddington (Map 8) Paddington is a sensible option for those who wish to stay in the eastern suburbs.

Sullivans Hotel (☎ *9361 0211, fax 9360 3735,* e *sydney@sullivans.com.au, 21 Oxford St)* Standard/garden rooms $125/140. This handy, friendly and tidy hotel is a good choice, although the bustle of Oxford St may be a bit much for some light sleepers.

Surry Hills (Map 8) The hotels here are handy to the city and also to the eating areas of Surry Hills.

City Crown Lodge International (☎ *9331 2433, fax 9360 7760,* e *citycrow@bigpond.com, 289 Crown St)* Rooms $85-100. A little south of Oxford St, this place offers the usual standard motel accommodation.

Cambridge Park Inn (☎ *9212 1111, fax 9281 1981,* e *reservations@cambridge parkinn.com.au, 212 Riley St)* Standard

rooms/suites with breakfast $132/154. Prices seem to have gone down here over the years, which must qualify as some sort of miracle, especially given that standards have been maintained. It's not an attractive building – but the rooms are well appointed and there's a heated pool, spa, sauna and gym.

Balmain (Map 4) Balmain is not brimming with accommodation options.

Balmain Lodge (☎ *9810 3700, fax 9810 1500, 415 Darling St)* Rooms $79/350 night/week. In a handy Balmain location and with good security and rooms, this place is worth considering if you want to stay in the area.

Glebe (Map 9) Close to transport and 'Eat Street', Glebe has long been a popular choice for travellers.

Alishan International Guest House (☎ *9566 4048, fax 9525 4686,* e *kevin@alishan.com.au, 100 Glebe Point Rd)* Singles/doubles from $90. In a big old house in the centre of Glebe, this place is clean, quiet and well run, with good communal areas and a room that can accommodate disabled travellers.

Haven Inn (☎ *9660 6655, fax 9660 6279, 196 Glebe Point Rd)* Rooms $140-170. On the corner of Wigram Rd, Haven Inn has decent rooms in pastel shades with fridge and good bathrooms. There's a heated swimming pool, secure parking and a restaurant/bar.

A-Line Hotel (☎ *9566 2111, fax 9566 4493, 247-53 Broadway)* Twins & doubles/triples/family rooms $99/132/165. On busy Broadway, this hotel has clean, nice rooms with bathroom, TV and fridge. Some off-street parking is available.

Hotel Unilodge (☎ *9338 5000, 1800 500 658, fax 9338 5111,* e *reservations@unilodge.com.au, Cnr Broadway & Bay St)* Singles/doubles/triples/family rooms $150/170/195/220. This swanky-looking joint offers good value for its larger rooms, and has impressive facilities and amenities, such as a business centre and an indoor lap pool.

Bondi Beach (Map 11) This vibrant beachside suburb offers several accommodation options to suit this price range.

Hotel Bondi (☎ 9130 3271, fax 9130 7974, 178 Campbell Pde) Beach-view doubles $120, beach-view suites $125-150, family suites $170-190. The rooms and their bathrooms are clean and the views are great, but take note that the Bondi Hotel below can be a noisy nightspot.

Bondi Beachside Inn (☎ 9130 5311, fax 9365 2646, 152 Campbell Pde) Standard/ocean-view rooms $100/120. This place has clean, plain apartment-style rooms, with good kitchenettes and views. It's open 24 hours, and cheaper rates can be negotiated for stays of seven or more nights.

Beach Road Hotel (☎ 9130 7247, 71 Beach Rd) Singles/doubles/family rooms $70/85/120. This refurbished hotel is a large pub two blocks back from the beach. Heavy on the beach-themed decor, it has several bars, a couple of eateries and a nightclub. Rooms are clean and bright with clean bathrooms, and air-con and TV.

City Beach Motor Inn (☎ 9365 3100, 1800 358 884, fax 9365 0231, 99 Curlewis St) Singles/doubles/family rooms $140-185/195/1955. This Best Western hotel offers US-style motor inn accommodation and good facilities close to the beach and has parking.

Ravesi's (☎ 9365 4422, fax 9365 1481, Cnr Campbell Pde & Hall St) Rooms $116-325, depending on view and room features. With only 16 rooms, Ravesi's is popular and it's easy to see why. Rooms are in great condition, the place is right on the beach and the views are straight from heaven. There may be specials in the off-season, so ask.

Coogee (Map 10) Coogee's a perfect place to walk along the beach, stop for coffee and meander back to a comfortable hotel.

Coogee Bay Boutique Hotel (☎ 9665 0000, fax 9664 2103, 9 Vicar St) Heritage hotel singles/doubles $89/99, heritage suites/boutique rooms $105-169/180. Singles and doubles here have air-con, fridge, TV, telephone and en suite. Right in the centre of Coogee, there are rooms available in the original Coogee Bay Hotel and the newer, fancier wing. Enter from Vicar St, parallel to Arden St. If noise bothers you, you'd be better off staying away from the older hotel area.

Dive Hotel (☎ 9665 5538, fax 9665 4347, 234 Arden St) Standard/balcony/ocean-view rooms $150/160/190. Rooms include bathroom and kitchenette. This delightful, small boutique hotel is beautifully decorated in a modern style that retains interesting original tilework and a sense of beach-house space.

Manly (Map 12) Because Manly's a beach resort, many places have seasonal and weekend deals; ring around to find out what's on offer.

Manly Beach Hut (☎ 9977 8777, fax 9977 8766, e enquiry@manlybeachhut.com.au, 7 Pine St) Twins $70/395 night/week, doubles with share bathroom $110/590, with bathroom $120/690, with bathroom & kitchen $130/790. This place has excellent doubles and twins available, and there are plans to turn the neighbouring building into an annexe that has mostly double and twin rooms. The standards are high, and the quality, cleanliness and atmosphere are all first-rate. There are wheelchair-accessible bathrooms too.

Steyne Hotel (☎ 9977 4977, fax 9977 5645, e stay@steynehotel.com.au, 75 The Corso) Singles $88-121, doubles $110-176. Rooms here are OK and mostly come with older-style share bathroom, although there are some fancy suites with views and bathrooms (and higher rates). Be aware that noise levels can be high here.

Manly Lodge (☎ 9977 8655, fax 9976 2090, 22 Victoria Pde) Doubles/twins/suites from $144/159/195. This is a quaint, nice guesthouse with a holiday atmosphere and a vaguely Spanish appearance. Rooms have TV, video, fridge, air-con and bathroom; some have spas. There's also a communal sauna, spa and gym, and a pleasant outdoor area.

Manly Beach Resort (☎ 9977 4188, fax 9977 0524, e manlybch@ozemail.com.au, 6 Carlton St) Singles/doubles & twins/triples from $115/140/150. All rooms include continental breakfast. This is a reasonable

1970s-era motel with good security and car parking. There are also family rooms available and one studio.

Periwinkle Guest House (☎ *9977 4668, fax 9977 6308, 18-19 East Esplanade)* Singles/doubles/triples with share bathroom $99/126.50/148.50 night, $517/682/847 week (based on 2-week stay outside of public holidays and peak season), with bathroom $132/165/187 night, $715/880/1039.50 week. This is a beautifully restored Victorian house facing the harbour beach at Manly Cove. Rooms are elegant and well appointed, and there's a stylish but cosy kitchen. Laundry facilities are available.

Manly Paradise Motel (☎ *9977 5799, 1800 815 789, fax 9977 6848,* e *enquiries@ manlyparadise.com.au, 54 North Steyne)* Rooms $140-170. This friendly motel is on the beachfront, has a rooftop pool and undercover parking. Rooms have air-con, TV, bathroom, and tea- and coffee-making facilities – although ocean views are of the side-on variety. There's a lot of repeat business from guests, which is always a good sign.

Serviced Apartments

Serviced apartments – which can be anything from a hotel room with a fridge and a microwave, to a full-size apartment – can be good value, especially for families.

City Centre (Map 5) The city centre is a popular place to stay.

Hyde Park Inn & Serviced Apartments (☎ *9264 6001, 1800 221 030, fax 9261 8691, 271 Elizabeth St)* Standard singles/doubles/triples/quads/quins $143/159.50/176/192.50/209, deluxe rooms $159.50/176/192.50/209/225.50. This friendly complex of air-con serviced apartments offers rooms that can sleep between one and five, and has some nice views of Hyde Park.

Sydney Park Inn (☎ *9360 5988, fax 9360 1085, 2-6 Francis St, East Sydney)* Singles/doubles/triples $99/115/125. Near Hyde Park and Oxford St, these fully equipped studios (with breakfast) are complete with air-con, kitchenette, TV and video. Some rooms have better light than others.

Darling Harbour (Map 5) Popular with package tourist and casino fans, this is close to all of Sydney maritime attractions.

Savoy Apartments (☎ *9267 9211, fax 9262 2023,* e *accom@savoy.com.au, 37-43 King St)* Apartments for stays of less than 3 nights $165 per night, for more than 3 nights $150, for more than 28 days $130. Good-sized apartments are available here. Each apartment includes kitchen bathroom, balcony and laundry facilities. There is parking, but it costs $16.50 per day.

Pacific International (☎ *9284 2300, fax 9264 8698,* e *packent@pacificint.com.au, 433 Kent St)* Doubles $275, $25 per extra person. This is a handily located serviced apartment complex with good rooms (which sleep up to four) and facilities. Specials are also available.

The Waldorf (☎ *9261 5355, 1800 023 361, fax 9261 3753, 57 Liverpool St)* 1-bedroom/2-bedroom apartments from $170/220 per night. Weekly rates from $900. These fully equipped apartments come with internal laundry, kitchen, bathroom and living areas. There's also a rooftop pool, spa, sauna and free car parking.

Potts Point & Elizabeth Bay (Map 6) These areas are good places to stay if you want to be close to the action.

Oakford Potts Point (☎ *9358 4544, fax 9357 1162, 10 Wylde St)* Studio/1-bedroom apartments with pool views $166/187, with harbour views $199.50/209. Situated on the steep northern continuation of Macleay St, the apartments here are very well appointed and the views can be grand.

Seventeen Elizabeth Bay Rd (☎ *9358 8999, fax 9356 2491, 17 Elizabeth Bay Rd)* 1-bedroom apartments $160/980 night/week, 2-bedroom apartments $205/1225. This small 35-room place is nicely decorated and is within easy walking distance of the sights of Kings Cross and the eastern suburbs.

PLACES TO STAY – TOP END

This section covers accommodation costing from around $170 a night. There are lots of five-star and four-star establishments to choose from. Travel agencies in other states or countries can book many of these, and will have access to special deals and packages.

Hotels

City Centre (Map 5) Top-end hotels in Sydney are luxurious and generally offer water views.

Sydney Hilton (☎ 9266 2000, fax 9265 6065, 259 Pitt St) Rooms $275-1200. In the heart of the city, rooms here are good, although the hotel is not as flash looking as it was in the 1970s. Specials are often available. The historic Marble Bar is downstairs (see Things to See & Do chapter).

Menzies Hotel (☎ 9299 1000, 1300 363 600, fax 9290 3819, 14 Carrington St) Weekend packages from $180. This hotel is popular with business executives who want to stay right in the CBD and take advantage of in-house babysitter and interpreter services.

Wentworth Hotel (☎ 9230 0700, fax 9228 9133, 61-101 Phillip St) Rack/package rates from $300/195. Within walking distance of Circular Quay and the Macquarie St museums, this is a good option for those who want to be right in the city. Service is smooth as silk, although some rooms feel a little cramped.

Sheraton on the Park (☎ 9286 6000, fax 9286 6686, 161 Elizabeth St) Rooms $446-5500. Overlooking Hyde Park, this friendly hotel has a big, brash and flash lobby with enormous marble columns. Its good rooms have views of the city and park, and packages are available. Big-name stars such as Michael Jackson and the Spice Girls have stayed here. Say no more.

Sydney Marriott (☎ 9361 8400, 1800 025 419, fax 9361 8599, e ressmh@smh .mirvac.com.au, 36 College St) Standard deluxe rooms from $400, executive & junior/king suites $650/810. This smart, professional hotel, across the road from Hyde Park, offers luxury rooms and some lovely views. Packages are available, making a stay here significantly cheaper than the rack rates would suggest.

Hyde Park Plaza Hotel (☎ 9331 6933, 1800 222 442, fax 9331 6022, e reservationhydeparkplaza@mirvachotels .com.au, 38 College St) Studio/1-bedroom/

2-bedroom/3-bedroom suites $169/247/ 316/388. This place is close to Hyde Park, the city and Oxford St, and the staff are helpful and friendly. Rooms are good, and impressive reductions in tariff are available for stays of 21 days or more.

The Rocks & Circular Quay (Map 5)

This is an excellent area to stay in, particularly at the top end, where standards are high and the noise-proofing is excellent.

The Russell (☎ 9241 3543, fax 9252 1652, 143a George St) Singles with share bathroom $115-165, doubles with share bathroom $130-180, singles with bathroom $200-245, doubles with bathroom $215-260. In a superb location, this is a small, friendly hotel with rooms straight out of a Laura Ashley catalogue, pleasant lounge areas and a sunny rooftop garden.

The Stafford (☎ 9251 6711, fax 9251 3458, 75 Harrington St) Double & twin studios $235/1470 night/week, executive studios $275/1715, terraces $295/1855. The studios here are quite comfortable, and there are also nicer terrace houses available (for a minimum stay of three nights).

Harbour Rocks Hotel (☎ 9251 8944, 1800 251 210, fax 9251 8900, e harbo@ ozemail.com.au, 34-52 Harrington St) Standard rooms $198-220, with views $242-264. The Harbour Rocks occupies restored 19th-century buildings and is a charming boutique hotel. Rooms with a view take in the Opera House and Sydney Harbour.

Regent (☎ 9238 0000, 1800 022 800, fax 9251 2851, 199 George St) Doubles $408-528, double suites $572-4356. Easily one of the main contenders for the title of Best Hotel in Sydney, with luxurious rooms, Four Seasons beds, extraordinarily professional staff and knock-out views (city, Opera House, or harbour – take your pick). Packages are available, with different offers and extras.

Observatory Hotel (☎ 9256 2222, fax 9256 2233, e email@observatoryhotel.com .au, 89-113 Kent St) Packages $365-8550. The lovely Observatory Hotel is on the Millers Point side of the Bradfield Hwy.

It has plush rooms and is large for a boutique hotel, but small for a five-star.

ANA Hotel Sydney (☎ *9250 6000, fax 9250 6250, 176 Cumberland St)* Rooms $430-675, suites $705-4800. The ANA has 563 stylish and spacious rooms, all with a view of some sort. This place is so plush that it can trumpet that the bathroom mirrors are the 'mist-free' sort, on top of all the other luxuries. Packages and specials are available too.

Sydney Park Hyatt (☎ *9241 1234, 13 12 34, fax 9256 1555,* e *sydney@hyatt.com .au, 7 Hickson Rd)* Rooms $667-777, suites $886-5474. The super-luxurious Park Hyatt has one of the best locations in Sydney – snaking along the waterfront at the edge of Campbells Cove, almost under the Harbour Bridge and facing the Opera House. Watch out for discounted weekend packages that can offer substantial discounts. If you need a 24-hour butler service, then this is the hotel for you.

Sir Stamford at Circular Quay (☎ *9252 4600, 1300 301 391, fax 9252 4286,* e *reservations@sscq.stamford.com.au, 93 Macquarie St)* Rooms $539-605, suites $703-3270. On the site of one of the city's old venereal disease clinics, Sir Stamford does everything possible to rid itself of such sordid connotations. This nice brick building is tastefully furnished, and there's even a red carpet from the kerb to the hotel door. The staff are courteous and helpful.

Hotel Inter-Continental (☎ *9253 9000, 1800 221 828, fax 9240 1240,* e *sydney@ interconti.com, 117 Macquarie St)* Rooms $385-505 depending on the view, suites from $775. There are weekly rates and package deals in this hotel in a beautiful sandstone building that once housed the treasury. Service is five-star fantastic and you may not want to leave.

Darling Harbour (Map 5) Close to
excellent shopping and right on the water, Darling Harbour is a very popular place to stay.

Four Points Hotel Sheraton (☎ *9299 1231, 1800 074 545, fax 9299 3340, 161 Sussex St)* City-view/harbour-view rooms from $319/340. You know the drill as soon as you walk into a place with a lobby as big as this – it's luxury all the way. With over 600 deluxe rooms and bilingual staff, you could probably organise a coup here (and all from the comfort of your bed). Packages and specials are available.

Novotel Sydney on Darling Harbour (☎ *9934 0000, fax 9934 0099, 100 Murray St)* Rooms $280-345, suites $406-544. A hotel with good views of Darling Harbour and the city, this 530-room hotel is behind Harbourside (although somewhat cut off from it all – you need to walk across covered footbridges to get there) and has a swimming pool, spa, gym and tennis court. Packages and specials are available.

Furama (☎ *9281 0400, 1800 800 555, fax 9281 1212,* e *rsvn.fhdh@furama-hotels .com, 68 Harbour St)* Standard twins & doubles with breakfast $175, corporate rooms/executive suites/corporate suites $205/ 235/265. In a renovated 19th-century woolstore (and a modern extension), the Furama Hotel is directly opposite Sydney Entertainment Centre and has your standard 'big hotel' amenities.

Darlinghurst (Maps 6 & 7) These very
groovy hotels are setting new standards for luxury seekers in this area.

The Kirketon (☎ *9332 2011, fax 9332 2499,* e *info@kirketon.com.au, 229 Darlinghurst Rd)* Junior/premium/executive rooms $220/275/365. Supremely modern and swanky, but retaining a friendly atmosphere, this hotel is part of a new breed of luxury accommodation in the area.

L'Otel (☎ *9360 6868, fax 9331 4536,* e *hotel@lotel.com.au, 114 Darlinghurst Rd)* Rooms $150-210, with balcony from $250. This hip, stylish 16-room place is friendly and very well appointed. Rooms have IDD telephone, fax and data-port connections for modems, and a general air of subdued smartness. Weekly and monthly rates are available.

Medusa (☎ *9331 1000, fax 9380 6901,* e *info@medusa.com.au, 267 Darlinghurst Rd)* Deluxe/premium deluxe/grand rooms $270/320/385. This 18-room hotel is pure

Sydney. Glamorous, well-situated, a little bit flashy, a lot sexy, professional and decadent. You could lose yourself (or any number of people) in the beds here.

Potts Point (Maps 6 & 7) There are some excellent places to stay in this area.

Simpsons of Potts Point (☎ 9356 2199, fax 9356 4476, 8 Challis Ave) Standard singles/doubles $175/195, large rooms $195/215. Definitely worth a look if you're after a bit of luxury. This hotel is in a superb old house (1892) a short walk from Kings Cross. Rooms here are large, quiet and well furnished and the management is charming.

Regents Court (☎ 9358 1533, fax 9358 1833, e regcourt@iname.com, 18 Springfield Ave) Side rooms/front rooms $187/203. This is a stylish boutique hotel in a converted Art Deco apartment block close to the Cross. The good-sized rooms each have a small kitchenette, natty black-and-white bathrooms, TV and video. The Italian-style rooftop garden is a great place to relax.

Landmark Parkroyal (☎ 9368 3000, fax 9357 7600, 81 Macleay St) Rooms from $174, with view $201. Intermittent specials can really reduce the rates at this big 470-room hotel, which is popular with package tourists and flight crews.

Kings Cross (Map 7) The following hotel is in a good location and close to transport:

The Crescent on Bayswater (☎ 9357 7266, 1800 257 327, fax 9357 7418, e crescent@kepland.com.au, 33 Bayswater Rd) Room/suite $220/242. This hotel, in a huge brick building, is close to everything and includes breakfast and parking. For light-sleepers, you'll be pleased to know it has double-glazing on the windows. Specials and packages are available.

Woolloomooloo (Map 6) This suburb is a perfect choice for water-lovers.

W Sydney (☎ 9331 9000, fax 9331 9031, e wsydney.sales@whotels.com, 6 Cowper Wharf Rdwy) Rooms $390-550, lofts $550-1500. Packages and specials available. Taking pride of place in the

redevelopment of fingerpoint wharf, this modern luxury hotel is more hip than stuffy, and targets a young, affluent clientele. Rooms have all the high-tech gadgetry you could hope for, and the service is friendly.

Double Bay There are some lovely places to stay in Double Bay.

Sir Stamford (☎ 9363 0100, fax 9363 0100, 22 Knox St) Rooms $325-350, suites $460-540. With its navy blue decor and Biedermeier furniture, this luxury hotel perches above the Cosmopolitan shopping centre. Reception is on the 3rd floor and rooms are very comfortable. Various packages are offered, so check availability if you want top-end savings.

Stamford Plaza Double Bay (☎ 9362 4455, fax 9362 4744, 33 Cross St) Rooms $249-314, suites from $400. The plush Stamford Plaza used to be the Ritz Carlton, and still maintains a pretty ritzy vibe. Its packages are worth looking into.

Coogee & Bondi Beach (Maps 10 & 11) Top-end options in Sydney's most popular beach areas include:

Coogee Sands Apartments (☎ 9665 8588, fax 9664 1460, e info@coogeesands.com.au, 165 Dolphin St, Coogee) Studios and apartments $225-295. This renovated four-star hotel in a prime location offers pleasant accommodation with 10 days' complimentary parking.

Swiss Grand (☎ 9365 5666, 1800 655 252 fax 9365 5330, Cnr Campbell Pde & Beach Rd, Bondi) Suites $297-1650. Deals and packages available. One of the main advantages of staying here is that when you're on the balcony feasting your eyes on the view you can't see what an architectural monstrosity this place is. The inside is faux lavish and grand, but the friendly service is genuine.

Manly (Map 12) Manly's top-end hotels reward guests with good views.

Manly Pacific Parkroyal (☎ 9977 7666, fax 9977 7822, 55 North Steyne) Package rooms $229-377. This big hotel has full-frontal views of the beach and is Manly's fanciest place to stay. There's a gym, heated rooftop pool, spa, sauna and undercover parking.

Radisson Kestrel *(☎ 9977 8866, fax 9977 8209, 8-13 South Steyne)* Rooms $239-279, suites $249-439. This luxury hotel offers guests a choice of views (ocean or Manly) and room styles (standard, and suites of varying sizes) in two separate buildings, in a good location in Manly's south.

Milsons Point (Map 3) For comfort across the bridge, try:

Duxton Hotel *(☎ 9955 1111, 1800 807 356, fax 9955 3522, 88 Alfred St, Milsons Point)* Deluxe/superior/suites $240/266/305. Across from Milsons Point station, Duxton is a modern, stylish, four-star hotel with lovely views of Lavender Bay or Kirribilli. It's oriented to business travellers, with easy access to North Sydney and the city. Packages are available.

Serviced Apartments

The Rocks & City Centre (Map 5) Serviced apartment can be sensible choices for longer stays, and there are several excellent options in these central areas.

Quay West Sydney *(☎ 9240 6000, fax 9240 6060, 98 Gloucester St)* 1-bedroom standard/deluxe/harbour view apartments $260/275/360, 2-bedroom $420, suites $575-715. Situated in The Rocks, these fine-looking apartments have views of Sydney Harbour or the city, as well as a kitchen and laundry, and 24-hour room service. There's even a Roman-style swimming pool.

The Carrington Apartments *(☎ 9299 6556, fax 9299 2727, 57-9 York St)* 1-bedroom/2-bedroom apartments $220/275, for 7-20–day stays $132/176, more than 21 days $121/154. Reception is on the 10th floor of this 11-storey building. The rooms here feature furniture from more decorating phases than you can possibly imagine. NRMA, RACV, RACT and RACQ members and corporate guests get good discounts.

The York *(☎ 9210 5000, fax 0290 1487, e york@acay.com.au, 5 York St)* Studio apartments $214.50-242, 1-bedroom apartments $264-280.50, 2-bedroom apartments $313.50-440. The serviced apartments (which include free car parking) here are spacious and some have good views of the city. The outdoor heated pool on the 6th floor has views of the Harbour Bridge.

Darling Harbour (Map 5) Convenient transport and proximity to services make Darling Harbour a good place to base yourself in Sydney.

Southern Cross Executive Suites *(☎ 9268 5888, fax 9268 5666, 38 Harbour St)* 1-bedroom/2-bedroom/3-bedroom apartments $175/230/295. With a monorail station right underneath, this hotel offers easy access to Darling Harbour and the CBD, plus it has nice rooms with good kitchens.

Darlinghurst (Map 4) Serviced apartments in Darlinghurst are packed to capacity during Mardi Gras. Get in early.

Parkridge Corporate Apartments *(☎ 9361 8600, fax 9361 8666, e Parkridge@ hotel-apartments.com.au, 6-14 Oxford St)* 1-bedroom apartments $175/155/120 night/ week/month, 2-bedroom apartments $210/ 185/140, 2-bedroom executive apartments $240/190/160. Close to Hyde Park and offering great Mardi Gras views (at much higher prices), the suites at this well-managed complex are good. Rates can be negotiated during quiet periods.

Manly (Map 12) Fancy catching the ferry to work?

Grande Esplanade *(☎ 9976 4600, fax 9976 4699, e Grandeesplanade@bigpond .com, 54a West Esplanade)*. Studio/2-bedroom apartments $199/259 night. This hotel is directly opposite the ferry terminal and offers good accommodation for the business traveller, with prices decreasing the longer the stay.

Places to Eat

With great local produce, innovative chefs, reasonable prices and BYO licensing laws, eating out is one of the great delights of Sydney. The city has a huge variety of eateries; this chapter is just an introduction to the vast number on offer.

Many restaurants serve 'modern Australian' (or Mod Oz) food – an amalgamation of Mediterranean, Asian and Californian cooking practices that emphasises lightness, freshness and healthy eating. It's a hybrid style, shaped by migrant influences, climatic conditions and local produce. In Sydney this style has filtered down from sophisticated restaurants to modest corner bistros, so you can savour it whatever your budget.

There are thousands of fast-food options in Sydney. You'll find them on main streets and near train stations in most suburbs. In popular tourist areas such as Bondi, Manly and Kings Cross, you can't avoid them. Some offer reasonable food at good prices, but you should always avoid food that looks as though it's spent quite some time waiting for a customer.

Cafes tend to serve a near ubiquitous diet of focaccia, pide bread, filled croissants and sandwiches, and vegetarian options can be lacking in imagination, although portions are generous and full of flavour.

Sydney also has many food courts, which are handy places to sample a range of cuisines at very good prices. They're popular places, so you can generally rely on the food being fresh. Crowds are also a good indication of a shop's quality.

Even if you can't afford to dine at the top end, there are scores of restaurants and bistros serving decent food at good mid-range prices. Eating at modest Chinese, Indian and Vietnamese restaurants can be almost as cheap as eating at home. Pub counter-meals are also worth considering for solid, inexpensive fare, and the many brasserie-style eateries are cheaper than formal restaurants. See also the boxed text 'GST' in this chapter.

We've included some of Sydney's better restaurants in this chapter, as many travellers want to sample at least one 'good' restaurant during their time in Sydney. We've also included a boxed text 'Meals with A View' for those who want to eat well *and* drink in the sights. Of course, there's nothing stopping you from taking a sandwich to one of Sydney's vantage points if you want to save some money.

CITY CENTRE (MAPS 5 & 8)

There's no shortage of places for a snack or a meal in the city centre, but many, especially those north of Liverpool St, close in the evenings. They're clustered around train stations, in shopping arcades and tucked away in the food courts at the base of office buildings.

Restaurants

VII (☎ 9252 7777, 7 Bridge St) Lunch (fixed price menus) $65/85/110, dinner $110/140. Open noon-1.30pm Tues-Fri, 7pm-9pm Tues-Sat. If you're hankering for truly fine cuisine, then the labour-intensive delights at VII will have your mouth watering. The food is modern Australian, but influences from as far as Japan and France are detectable, and the service is impeccable. Make reservations for the weekend well in advance.

Sushi e (☎ 9240 3041, Level 4, Establishment, 252 George St) Entrees $7.50-15.50, mains $23.50-33.50. Open 6pm-11pm Tues-Thur, noon-2.30pm Thur & Fri, 7-midnight Fri & Sat. It may be expensive, but the sushi here is incredibly fresh, hand-picked and beautifully prepared. Be seduced by the salmon belly ($9.50), which is seared with a blow torch to draw out the natural flavours.

Est (☎ 9240 3010, Level 1, Establishment, 252 George St) Entrees $22-29, mains $33-77. The buzz is big about this place and the decor and menu show why. Light, smooth and swanky, this is Sydney at the new millennium's 'power lunch'.

Sosumi *(☎ 9229 7788, GPO, 1 Martin Pl)* Plates $4.50-8. With a little trolley that whizzes past you, laden with tasty Japanese goodies, this place is handy for a quick lunch – although the plate prices can be racked up pretty quickly! Unlimited green tea costs $3.50.

The Summit *(☎ 9247 9777, Level 47, 264 George St)* Entrees $17-34, mains $30-51. Open 6pm-late. Straddling the lurex border between a 1970s space-age dining room and everyone's fond memories of kitsch food with a marvellous view, the Summit has kept the prawn cocktail on the menu, but made sure it's a good dish. Everything else is stylish and tasteful. At last, a revolving restaurant that's not revolting.

Tetsuya's *(☎ 9267 2900, 529 Kent St)* Set menu (14 courses): dinner and Sat lunch $155 per person; Fri lunch $100. Open noon-1.30pm Fri & Sat, 7pm-8.30pm Tues-Sat. With its lounge bar, Japanese-style garden, and large rooms dotted with artwork, Tetsuya's new home is welcoming. Each course of this Japanese/French degustation is exhilarating: venison parcels rolled around foie gras, tuna cocktail with wasabi, confit of ocean trout with roe. Book well in advance.

International Revolving Restaurant *(☎ 8223 3800, Level 1, Centrepoint Tower)* 3-course menu $72.50. Open 5pm-11.45pm Tues-Sat. If high-altitude rotation doesn't make you queasy, you'll enjoy the magnificent view, although the food is not renowned for its magnificence.

Level 2 Revolving Restaurant *(☎ 8223 3800, Level 2, Centrepoint Tower)* Buffet dinner adult/child $47.50/19.50. Open 11.30am-3.30pm Mon-Sun, 5pm-11.45pm Mon-Sat, until 10.30pm Sun. With an all-you-can-eat buffet, offering a selection of meats, seafood and Asian dishes (with little for vegetarians), this place is a cheapish alternative to the usual 'dining with a great view' price question. Diners aren't charged for the ride to the top of the tower, so you're ahead in the money already. Bookings are recommended.

Slip-Inn *(☎ 9299 4777, 111 Sussex St)* Pizza $12-18. Open lunch & dinner Tues-Fri for restaurant & pizza bar, open lunch Mon-Fri for noodle bar. This place is worth visiting even if you don't eat, but it's worth bearing in mind that you can satisfy both your beer gut and your pizza gut at the same time.

Forty One *(☎ 9221 2500, Level 41, Chifley Tower, 2 Chifley Sq)* Set menus $98-125. Open noon-2pm Mon-Fri, 7pm-10pm Mon-Sat. In the 'treat yourself' league, Forty One offers welcoming service and some extraordinarily fine dining. The salad of quail, smoked duck and foie gras is delectable, although the desserts are a little too cloying for our tastes.

Banc *(☎ 9233 5300, 53 Martin Pl)* Entrees $26-48, mains $38-45. This refined restaurant is famous for its wine list, which resembles a telephone book in size. The food is just as wonderful, with a quail salad ($28) that'll leave you breathless. It's worth saving room for the desserts. This place is splendid and one of the best places to eat in Sydney, hands down .

Bodhi *(☎ 9360 2523, Lower level, Cook & Phillip Park, 2-4 College St)* Yum cha $3-5.50, entrees $6.50-14.50, mains $9.90-17.20. You'd never guess that this was a vegan temple, given the slick and minimal surroundings, but the wholesome (and to be honest, sometimes a tad bland) yum cha gets Sydney's health-conscious hungry. Simple, almost ascetic eating was never this stylish. You'll find another branch of Bodhi *(☎ 9212 2828, 181 Hay St)* near the Capitol Theatre.

Sydney's Spanish Quarter consists of a small group of restaurants and bars along Liverpool St, between George and Sussex Sts.

Capitan Torres *(☎ 9264 5574, 73 Liverpool St)* Tapas $3.50-11. Open noon-3pm & 5.30pm-11pm Mon-Sat, noon-3pm & 5.30pm-11pm Sun. This is a great, convivial bar, serving tapas and seafood (since 1973).

Casa Asturiana *(☎ 9264 1010, 77 Liverpool St)* Tapas $3.50-8.20. Open noon-3pm & 5.30pm-11pm Mon-Sat, noon-3pm & 5.30pm-11pm Sun. This place specialises in northern Spanish cooking, and reputedly has the best tapas in Sydney.

Don Quixote *(☎ 9264 5903, 545 Kent St)* Entrees $7.50-19, mains $18-27.50. Open

Meals with a View

If you want to combine two of Sydney's great passions (food and views), then look no further than this Top 10. It's in alphabetical order, and detailed reviews are provided in individual entries in this chapter.

Aria (☎ 9252 2555, 19/2 Circular Quay East) **Map 5** Top-end prices, but what a position! Still, it's cheaper than living here.

Aqua Dining (☎ 9964 9998, Cnr Paul & Northcliff Sts, Milsons Point) **Map 3** Try seeing the city from this swanky place on the North Shore. After all, you get the bridge and the city lights in one hit, and you can have a swim afterwards.

Bather's Pavilion Cafe (☎ 9969 5050, 4 The Esplanade, Balmoral) Basically, it's heaven: views of Balmoral and many romance-minded dining companions.

The Boathouse on Blackwattle Bay (☎ 9518 9011, End of Ferry Rd, Glebe) **Map 9** With a delightful position in Glebe, diners have blissful views of the Anzac Bridge.

Bennelong (☎ 9250 7548, Sydney Opera House) **Map 5** Turn that old cliche of dinner and a show into something meaningful. Do it at the Sydney Opera House.

Forty One (☎ 9221 2500, Level 41, Chifley Tower, 2 Chifley Sq) **Map 5** Luxury dining on all levels. Even the toilets here are renowned, due to the superlative view.

Otto (☎ 9368 7488, 6 Cowper Wharf Rdwy, Woolloomooloo) **Map 6** Woolloomooloo offers some great water views and Otto takes advantage of its position on the finger wharf. The ritzy boats at the marina make it all feel very 'Monte Carlo'.

The Summit (☎ 9247 9777, Level 47, 264 George St, City Centre) **Map 5** Dining here will make you feel as though the world is revolving around you – and that's because it is. This is one revolving restaurant that breaks the rules (by serving good food).

Yulla (☎ 9365 1788, Level 1, 38 Campbell Pde, Bondi) **Map 11** Last but not least, there's Yulla, with heavenly views of Bondi and – believe it or not – affordable prices.

noon-3pm & 6pm-11pm. With entertainment on Friday and Saturday night, and a reputation for providing filling Spanish meals to happy diners, Don Quixote has been a Spanish staple for years. For $250 and 24 hours' notice, you and 10 of your nearest and dearest can partake of the *Toston Sancho Panza* (whole suckling pig).

Ru-Yuan Vegetarian Restaurant (☎ 9211 2189, 768 George St) Lunch $5.50-7. This is a clean and simple place serving tasty vegan Chinese food at bargain prices for the health-conscious and the hungry.

Malaya on George (☎ 9211 0946, 761 George St) Laksa $15.50, curry $16.50-22. Open noon-3pm Mon-Fri, 5.30pm-10pm Mon-Sat. On the corner of Valentine and George Sts, this is a modern, spacious Malay/Chinese eatery. It's licensed and has an eye-watering beef rendang ($16.50).

Pho Pasteur (☎ 9212 5622, 709 George St, Haymarket) Dishes $6-8.80. Open 10am-9pm. Pho Pasteur will serve you the best *pho* (noodle soup) in the city centre,

and this is why it's almost always packed. You won't have to wait long for a table, or for a steaming, delicious bowl.

Mother Chu's Vegetarian Kitchen (☎ 9283 2828, 367 Pitt St) Dishes $7-$14. Open noon-3pm Mon-Sat, 5pm-10pm daily. This good, cheap Asian restaurant serves vegan food, so if you need a tofu hit, this is the place.

Cafes

Obelisk Cafe (Macquarie Pl) Baguettes $7.50, Turkish sandwiches $9.50. Situated – surprise, surprise – near an obelisk, this place has outdoor tables and good sandwiches and coffee.

MoS Cafe (☎ 9241 3636, 37 Phillip St) Entrees $3-18, mains $7-26. Open 7am-9pm Mon-Fri, 8.30am-5pm Sat & Sun. This is not your standard museum cafeteria; it has a smart menu and smart service to match.

Bambini Trust Cafe (☎ 9283 7098, St James Trust Bldg, 185 Elizabeth St) Entrees $16-23, mains $28-29. Open 7am-10pm

Mon-Fri. Far-removed from your average cafe, the Bambini Trust, with its walnut panelling, upholstered benches and art is like an old-fashioned European experience, with good food and nice staff.

Bar Cupola *(☎ 9283 3878, Shop G29, Queen Victoria Bldg)* Lunch $3.85-8.25. This bar serves some of the best coffee in Sydney and Italian-style sandwiches and sweets.

Zenergy *(☎ 9261 5679, 68 Druitt St)* Entrees $2-3.50, mains $3-7. Near Clarence St, this cafe is part of a small chain serving wholesome vegetarian fare – cheap and tasty sandwiches, salads and vegie burgers.

Pubs

Brooklyn Hotel *(☎ 9247 6744, Cnr Grosvenor & George Sts)* Entrees $6-29, mains $28.50-30. Open noon-3pm Mon-Fri. The Brooklyn is a popular pub for business lunches, where a good steak is always appreciated. You can smoke at the bar, but there's a nonsmoking area for dining as well. Bar food is available and the chef, Ian Fortini creates some exciting dishes.

Supermarkets & Shopping Centres

On Pitt St Mall there's reasonably priced food in **Mid City Centre** food court, and in the **Centrepoint** food court. They serve Mexican, Italian, Thai etc for less than $10. There is a range of eateries below street level of the **Queen Victoria Building (QVB)**, which forms an arcade through to Town Hall station. Many of these eateries remain open after the shops have closed.

Woolworths *(☎ 9264 1927, Cnr Park & George Sts)* This supermarket is close to Town Hall station and sells fresh and prepared food at cheap prices.

Coles Express *(☎ 9221 3119, 388 George St)* With long opening hours, this supermarket is handy for picking up provisions when in town and there is a selection of prepared food.

CHINATOWN (MAPS 5 & 8)

Chinatown is a dense cluster of mostly Chinese restaurants, cafes, fast-food outlets and shops catering to the Chinese community. There are also Thai, Vietnamese, Japanese and Korean eateries. Officially, Chinatown is confined to the pedestrian mall on Dixon St, but its culinary delights have spilled over into the surrounding streets, especially around Haymarket.

You can break the bank at some outstanding Chinese restaurants, or eat well for next to nothing in a food court. Weekend yum cha makes such a popular brunch that you may have to queue for it.

Restaurants

BBQ King *(☎ 9267 2586, 18-20 Goulburn St)* Entrees $4.40-8.80, mains $8.80-26. Open 11.30am-2am. As the name suggests, you come here for barbecue, and a lot of people would agree that this place is king. It's old-school, with laminex tables and folding chairs. There may be a queue, but it won't last long, and the great duck is worth the wait. Try the spinach with garlic, too.

Lam's Seafood Restaurant *(☎ 9281 2881/2, 35-7 Goulburn St, Haymarket)* Entrees $4-23.80, mains $15-market price seafood. Open noon-4am. Quick lunch? Luxurious banquet? You can do both here. Popular with locals, visitors and anyone in-between, Lam's has an extensive menu and staff who know a thing or two about getting the most out of the kitchen.

Marigold Citymark *(☎ 9281 3388, Levels 4 & 5, 683-9 George St, Haymarket)* Dim sum $2.40-4.60, yum cha specials $5.70. This 800-seat yum cha palace serves lunchtime yum cha daily and has an extensive menu of other dishes. Join the hordes.

Golden Century Seafood Restaurant *(☎ 9212 3901, 393-99 Sussex St, Haymarket)* Open noon-4am. With lots of fish tanks displaying your nervous-looking dinner, this place is a favourite late-night eating spot for many of Sydney's chefs and hotel workers. The flavours are exotic and engaging, the service fast and slick.

Silver Spring *(☎ 9211 2232, Level 1, 477 Pitt St, Haymarket)* Entrees $5-15.80, mains $13.80-market price seafood. Open 10am-3pm (yum cha), 5.30pm-11pm (a la carte). Something of a yum cha mothership on weekends, this place offers a mind-boggling array of dishes from the a la carte menu too. Get a group together and have a feast.

Kam Fook Shark Fin Restaurant *(☎ 9211 8388, Level 3, Market City, 9 Hay St)* Dishes $11-market price seafood. Open 10am-5pm (yum cha) daily, 5.30pm-11pm Sun-Thur, until midnight Fri & Sat. This enormous place can seat about 800 people, and regularly gets filled to capacity for its yum cha sessions. Ask the waiter to recommend dishes and you'll be duly rewarded with succulent offerings. As you'd expect, shark fin is the speciality.

Cafes

Chinese Noodle Restaurant *(☎ 9281 9051, Shop 7, Prince Centre, 8 Quay St)* Dishes $6-8.80. At this intimate, busy eatery decorated with grapes and Persian rugs, the noodles are handmade in traditional northern Chinese style – and the crowds are glad of it.

Emperor's Garden BBQ & Noodles *(☎ 9281 9899, 213-5 Thomas St)* Dishes $3.50-9. This is a popular Chinese eatery specialising in meat and poultry dishes (marinated duck tongue $6) and has a great little window area where you can choose your takeaway goodies.

Food Courts

Harbour Plaza Food Court *(Cnr Dixon & Goulburn Sts, Haymarket)* Dishes $5-8. Open 10am-10pm. The pagoda-style Harbour Plaza has a wide range of cheap Asian meals available.

Market City Shopping Centre *(☎ 9212 1388, Level 3, 2-13 Quay St, Sydney)* Dishes $3.50-10. This mammoth place has a fresh produce market on the first level, a factory outlet on the second level and more food from more places than you can imagine on the third level. You'll find Paddy's Markets and Kam Fook here too (see the Shopping chapter, and Restaurants entry earlier in the Chinatown section).

Sussex Centre *(401 Sussex St, Sydney)* Dishes $5-7. Open 9am-10pm. The food court here has a range of cheap, tasty dishes, making it a sensible choice for those who want to eat and run.

Dixon House Food Court *(Cnr Little Hay & Dixon Sts, Haymarket)* Dishes $5-8. This food court offers a selection of about 20 vendors, with low, low prices.

DARLING HARBOUR & PYRMONT (MAPS 4, 5, 8 & 9)

The biggest concentration of eateries is at ***Cockle Bay wharf*** **(Map 5)**, officially heralded as one of Sydney's newest dining precinct. Most are fairly slick: the view from the promenade is all white tablecloths, potted palms, polished glasses, and lots of chrome.

Across the water at ***Harbourside*** **(Map 5)**, are a handful of expensive restaurants and a swag of fast-food outlets, and not a great deal in-between. Many of the eateries around Darling Harbour are aimed at the tourist trade, but with an outdoor table on a sunny day, who cares? Wander around and take your pick.

Further up towards Millers Point, near Cockle Bay wharf, is the ***King St wharf*** **(Map 5)**, with more swanky-looking eateries than you can poke a stick at. They all have menus outside, so you can wander along the water's edge and take your pick.

Restaurants

Zaaffran *(☎ 9211 8900, Level 2, 345 Harbourside, Darling Harbour)* **Map 5** Entrees $11.50-13.50, mains $15-29. Open noon-2.30pm Tues-Sun, 6pm-9.30pm Sun-Thur, until 10pm Fri & Sat. In a city with a million cheap Indian joints, this place stands out. The food is expertly cooked and it makes good use of its location in Darling Harbour (generally populated by substandard, tacky restaurants). The chicken korma ($23.50) and beef vindaloo (23.50) remind you that these well-known dishes need not be ordinary or bland.

Chinta Ria...The Temple of Love *(☎ 9265 3211, Roof terrace, Cockle Bay wharf, 201 Sussex St)* **Map 5** Dishes $11-18 Perched on a leafy rooftop at the northern end of Cockle Bay wharf, this Malaysian place serves tasty, reasonably priced meals with great style. Its laksa is definitely worth sampling if you want to assuage a craving

Blackbird (☎ 9283 7385, Balcony level, Cockle Bay wharf) **Map 5** Entrees $4.50-9.90, mains $7.90-16.90. Open 8am-late. With 11 varieties of pizza, budget-minded prices and spunky staff, dining here is a pleasant experience, especially when you can go play around the bay before or after.

Doyle's at the Markets (☎ 9552 4339, Sydney Fish Market) **Map 9** Dishes from around $11. This is a bistro, serving meals like fish of the day with chips, and seafood baskets, but it also does takeaway. There's seating outside and it's a seafood lover's haven on a sunny day.

Fast Food, Cafes & Pubs

Most of the *fast-food outlets* at Harbourside are in the food court on the ground floor.

Hennessy's (☎ 9660 0332, 16 Harris St, Pyrmont) **Map 4** Breakfast $3.50-13, dishes $10.50-12.50. Open 8am-4pm. Tucked away down the end of Harris St, the charming Hennessy's has good, light meals (salads $6.50-13) and hearty breakfasts.

Masuya (☎ 9566 2866, Cnr Allen & Harris Sts, Pyrmont) **Map 9** Entrees $5.80-8.80, mains $9.80-15.80. Open noon-2pm

Tues-Fri, 5.30pm-10pm Tues-Sun. This place offers good-value no-frills Japanese food that's handy for take-aways as well as sit-down lunches and dinners. The *bento* (lunch) boxes are great value.

Glasgow Arms Hotel (☎ 9211 2354, 527 Harris St, Ultimo) **Map 5** Burgers $12. Away from Darling Harbour proper, near the Powerhouse Museum, you can eat with the locals here. It has a good bistro and the burgers will easily fuel a trip around the Powerhouse.

Kopitian Cafe (☎ 9282 9883, 592 Harris St, Ultimo) **Map 8** Lunch specials $6.50. Open 11am-3.30pm & 5.30pm-midnight Mon-Sat, 5.30pm-midnight Sun. This place gets Malay hawker-style cuisine right, and it's cheap to boot. Fill up on good curry, korma and rice for lunch, or sample the other dishes that your neighbours are devouring.

CIRCULAR QUAY (MAP 5)

Many cafes and restaurants that line the quay, especially on the western side, have good views of the harbour.

Restaurants

Doyle's at the Quay (☎ 9252 3400, Overseas Passenger Terminal, Circular Quay West) Mains $26-34.20. Doyles at the Quay is definitely not a local fish-and-chipper, but a place to enjoy good-quality seafood and a harbour view.

Aria (☎ 9252 2555, 19/2 Circular Quay East) Entrees $28-32, mains $38-44. Open noon-3pm Mon-Fri, 5.30pm-11.30pm Mon-Sat, 6pm-10pm Sun. With some of the best views in Sydney, it's fitting that this place also has some of the best food. Chef Matthew Moran deserves the accolades he receives, with a veal rack that takes us straight to heaven.

Sydney Cove Oyster Bar (☎ 9247 2937, Circular Quay East) Oysters $13-25. Open noon-midnight. In a sunny spot close to the Opera House, this place offers Australian produce and wine, with oysters served in a variety of ways for a quintessential Sydney experience.

There are three restaurants in the Opera House complex. *Concourse* (☎ 9250 7300)

and *Harbour* (☎ 9250 7191) are good but the best of the bunch is the Bennelong.

Bennelong (☎ 9250 7548, Sydney Opera House) 2/3 courses $55/66. Open 5.30pm-late Mon-Sat. Upstairs at the Opera House complex, maximising the building's stunning architecture, this restaurant is chic but accessible. There's often live jazz, and the cocktail lounge is open till around midnight.

Cafes

Rossini (☎ 9247 8026, Wharf 5, Alfred St, Circular Quay) Dishes $4-18. Clive James is a fan of this Italian cafeteria-style eatery, with a range of easy dishes and decent prices.

MCA Cafe (☎ 9241 4253, 140 George St, The Rocks) Entrees $12.50-16.50, mains $18-25. At the slick Museum of Contemporary Art's MCA Cafe, the outside tables have eye-catching views of the quay and Opera House. The prawn, pea and chilli risotto ($21.50) is creamy and full of juicy, plump prawns. Whoever dressed to mixed-leaf salad could give a masterclass. The service is also praiseworthy.

Portobello Caffe (☎ 9247 8548, Circular Quay East) Dishes $8.50-14.50. On the eastern side of Circular Quay next to Sydney Cove Oyster Bar, this cafe serves pastries and pasta, and expensive coffee; it has some outdoor tables with wonderful views.

Fast Food

For fuel rather than views, there are lots of cheap stalls on the wharves as you head towards the ferries, although most of what's on offer has a high grease count.

THE ROCKS (MAP 5)

Here, too, the cafes and restaurants are aimed mainly at tourists, but there are some good deals available, especially in the numerous pubs where most bar meals are around $12 or less.

Restaurants

Sailors Thai (☎ 9251 2466, 106 George St) Entrees $16-22, mains $20-33. Open noon-2pm Mon-Fri, 6pm-10pm Mon-Sat. Lurking in the former Sailors' Home (and current Sydney Visitor Information Centre) is one of the best kitchens to produce Thai food in all of Sydney. It's a stylish, beautifully run place and is definitely worth a visit.

Rockpool (☎ 9252 1888, 107 George St, The Rocks) Entrees $31-35, mains $42-45. This place is always featured in the 'best of' lists, and with good reason. It's one of the most famous and most highly regarded restaurants in Sydney, and its influence is considerable. Many would say Mod Oz cuisine took off from here. Neil Perry is the 'super chef' and no-one at Rockpool is going to let their reputations be tarnished. The seafood dishes are always great, so treat yourself and someone close to you.

Antibar (☎ 9241 3700, Level 3, Argyle Stores, 18-24 Argyle St, The Rocks) Antipasto $5.50-48, mains $16.50-24.50. Enter this renovated warehouse haven of fine Italian food and fresh produce via the Argyle Stairs and Gloucester Walk. Stefano Manfredi's cooking for bel mondo (the more upmarket restaurant in the building) can be inspired, and the antipasto can make for a great snack, especially with a coffee or beer at the Antibar.

Volnay (☎ 9696 2656, Level 1, Le Meridien, 11 Jamison St) Entrees $15-24, mains $19-48. Open noon-2pm & 6.30pm-10pm Mon-Fri, 6.30pm-10pm Sat. When it seems that all of Sydney's eateries are doing the 'fusion' thing, with competing exotic influences, Volnay serves good French food in understated, elegant surrounds. Try the ravioli of snails (drunk on Moet & Chandon! – $15).

Fast Food, Cafes & Pubs

There's a small food hall in the modern *Clocktower Square Shopping Centre*, on the corner of Harrington and Argyle Sts.

The Hero of Waterloo (☎ 9252 4553, 81 Lower Fort St) Dishes $6.60-16.50. In this historic pub in The Rocks, you can get old-fashioned pub grub, such as steak and bangers and mash.

Lord Nelson Brewery Hotel (☎ 9251 4044, 19 Kent St, Millers Point) Dishes $10-25. On the corner of Kent and Argyle Sts, this place does decent pub grub of the upmarket sausage, pie and pasta variety.

HOMEMade CHICKEN & ASPARAGUS Pie

HOMEMade CHICKEN & MUSHROOM Pie

HOMEMade PEPPER Steak Pie

HOMEMade SPINACH & RICOTTA CHEESE Pie

HOMEMade BLUEBERRY MUFFIN

Delicious pies for sale in a bakery shop window, The Rocks

greengrocer's wares

A vogue display of fruit and veg, Woollahra

Serving up seafood at the Sydney Fish Market

SIMON BRACKEN

Outdoor cafe, Museum of Contemporary Art

SIMON BRACKEN

Chill out with a cone, Bondi Beach

MICHAEL LAANELA

Enjoying a liquid lunch at an outdoor cafe

SIMON BRACKEN

Something for everyone, Newtown

SIMON BRACKEN

Priceless city views in plush surrounds

KINGS CROSS & AROUND (MAPS 6 & 7)

The Cross has a multitude of fast-food joints serving quick fare (good for soaking up beer) and easily found on the main drags. There are tiny cafes servicing locals and travellers, and some swanky top-notch eateries.

Restaurants

New York Restaurant (☎ 9357 2772, 18 Kellett St) Joints $5.50, grills $5-8. Open 11.30am-2.30pm & 4pm-8pm. No, marijuana joints aren't $5.50, but a joint of meat is. This place, with hilariously old-school decor and prices, is one of the cheapest and simplest places to nosh on down.

Bourbon & Beefsteak (☎ 9358 1144, 24 Darlinghurst Rd) Steaks $21.50-27.25. Open 24 hours. With its splendidly tacky and jumbled Las Vegas decor, this place is a touristy but surreal spot to quell the late-night munchies. It serves breakfast (and alcohol) 24 hours a day, and does a decent steak.

Lime & Lemongrass (☎ 9358 5577, 42 Kellett St) Entrees $6.60, mains $10.90-14.25. This place has good Thai food at decent prices, and is close to the cute little bars and cafes in Kellet St.

Bayswater Brasserie (☎ 9357 2177, 32 Bayswater Rd) Entrees $8.50 22.50, mains $16.50-29. This is a classy but casual restaurant with excellent service where if you choose carefully you needn't spend a fortune. Try the bar at the back if you want to relax before dining.

Salt (☎ 9332 2566, e info@saltrestaurant .com.au, Kirketon Hotel, 229 Darlinghurst Rd) Open noon-3pm Mon-Fri, 6pm-11pm daily. Gourmet pleasure seekers can be found inside Salt's mauve and chrome walls where greedily they pour over the menu and haggle for space with those usually found on the celebrity A-list. For those after an orgasmic mouth experience, the supple braised suckling pig with star anise, pickled cucumber and green papaya ($25.50) should be tried. The masterful combinations get better in the baked breast of guinea fowl with parmesan and sage, fragrant pumpkin and pine nuts, celery and currants ($38.50). Licensed, no BYO.

Fast Food, Cafes & Pubs

Cafe Hernandez (☎ 9331 2343, 60 Kings Cross Rd) Sandwiches $4.90, focaccia $7. Open 24 hours. With a delightful old-world atmosphere and some of the best coffee in Sydney, Hernandez has been attracting everyone from taxi drivers coming off the night shift to arty students for years. Be warned though, there's no bathroom.

Mum's Thai (☎ 9331 1577, 57 Bayswater Rd) Dishes $4.90-14.50. Mum's Thai has a good menu with a range of Thai seafood and vegetarian dishes, with many options for around $7.

Piccolo Bar (☎ 9368 1356, 6 Roslyn St) Snacks from about $4. Open since 1950, this is a late-night haven in a shoebox for those who keep their own hours and don't mind a bit of smoke.

Lamour Café (8 Roslyn St) Snacks $4-13.50. Open till about 3am. They didn't mind if anyone smoked, and some colourful language was used to describe both NSW's smoking laws and the council's attempts to pretty up Roslyn St with more concrete. The decor can only be described as 'shoebox kitsch', but this place gets pretty groovy late at night. A breath of fresh air, despite the smoke. (See the boxed text 'No Smoke Without Fire' in this chapter.)

Dean's Cafe (☎ 9368 0953, 5 Kellett St) Dishes $6.70-14.50. Open late. The cosily bohemian Dean's Cafe serves irresistible nachos and a good selection of drinks. It's a great place to satisfy the munchies or unwind after a big night out.

Vinyl Lounge (☎ 9326 9224, 17 Elizabeth Bay Rd, Elizabeth Bay) Baguettes $7.20-8.50. This gay-friendly, French-owned cafe has quite a following, and a sip of the coffee shows why. It's relaxing and friendly and close to Kings Cross's sights.

Ash's Cafe (☎ 9361 5543, 86 Bayswater Rd, Rushcutters Bay) Entrees $8-15.50, mains $15.95-21.70. Open 7am-10.30pm Tues-Fri, 9am-10.30pm Sat, 9am-6pm Sun. This relaxed, chic little place is a great spot to enjoy good breakfasts and friendly service. It's nice to follow up a satisfying meal here with a walk around the nearby park at the water's edge. Recommended.

For the Serious Foodie...

Looking for the best bite for your buck? Lonely Planet's *Out to Eat – Sydney* is the best guide to Sydney's value eateries for any budget; if you're staying a while it will quickly repay your investment. The book takes its food seriously, but offers a fresh approach, with independent, wickedly unstuffy opinions on heaps of hand-picked restaurants, bars and cafes in Sydney.

POTTS POINT & WOOLLOOMOOLOO (MAPS 6 & 7)

Victoria St, which leads north from the Kings Cross junction into Potts Point, has some good fashionable cafes and restaurants. There's also a cluster of more upmarket cafes and restaurants on Macleay St, which is the northern extension of Darlinghurst Rd.

Restaurants

Otto *(☎ 9368 7488, 8 Cowper Wharf Rdwy, Woolloomooloo)* Pasta $18-32, primi piatti $19-26, piatti principali $28-36. Situated with lovely marina views from the old finger wharf development, this is fine Italian dining in smart surrounds.

Macleay St Bistro *(☎ 9358 4891, 73a Macleay St)* Mains $21.50-28. Open 6pm-11pm. This long-established restaurant has a modern Australian menu with excellent mains such as char-grilled eye fillet with beetroot crisps and horseradish cream ($27.50).

The Pig & The Olive *(☎ 9357 3745, 71a Macleay St)* Pizza $13.50-19. Open 6pm-11pm Mon-Sat, until 10pm Sun. With its terracotta walls and pig-themed decorations, this place serves out-of-the-ordinary pizzas with scrumptious and inventive toppings, such as roasted walnut with peppers, mushroom and leek.

Fast Food, Cafes & Pubs

Harry's Cafe de Wheels *(☎ 9347 3074, Cowper Wharf Rdwy, Woolloomooloo)* Pies $2.10-3.80. Open till 1am Mon-Wed, 3am Thur, 4am Fri & Sat, midnight Sun. This must be one of the few pie carts in the world to be a tourist attraction. Open late since 1945, with pies and mash galore. Photos here prove that anyone and everyone comes to Harry's – even Pamela Anderson. As with many tourist attractions, the food's not that brilliant – many regard the hotdogs to be better than the pies.

Frisco Hotel *(☎ 9357 1800, 46 Dowling St, Woolloomooloo)* Mains $12-19. Popular with sailors from the nearby naval base, this pub also serves meals. There's a bistro downstairs, and an upstairs restaurant with a balcony. Monday and Tuesday are 'spag nights'.

Delectica *(☎ 9380 1390, 130 Victoria St, Potts Point)* Breakfast $3.50-9.50, lunch $8-13. This lovely place is modern and airy and has truly charming service. You might be amid backpacker chaos, but you won't feel like it. And the food is lovely too.

Spring Espresso Bar *(☎ 9331 0190, 65 Macleay St, Potts Point, Enter via Challis Ave)* Breakfast $3.50-8.50, snacks $7.50-12.50. For life-changingly great coffee and good snacks, try the diminutive and bustling Spring.

La Buvette *(☎ 9358 5113, 2 Challis Ave, Potts Point)* Breakfast $3.30-10.10, sandwiches $6.60-7.70. This charming place serves very good coffee and delicious goodies, especially at breakfast time.

No Smoke Without Fire

If Melbourne is Paris, then Sydney is Los Angeles (or so many Melburnians would have you believe). And Sydney *does* share some similarities with LA. There's the growing smog problem, the body-consciousness, the huge waiter-cum-actor population, and now, the smoke-free restaurant. As of July 2000 and the advent of the NSW Smoke Free Environment Act you can smoke at pubs, bars and outdoor tables (and why not? – the smog's already there). But you cannot smoke in any Sydney restaurant or cafe, and there are some hefty fines to discourage you.

DARLINGHURST & EAST SYDNEY (MAPS 5, 6 & 7)

Ranging from the budget to the pricey, this area has the greatest concentration of cafes and restaurants in Sydney. In Darlinghurst, most are either on Oxford St or on Victoria St. In East Sydney, they're mainly on Stanley St between Riley and Crown Sts and are mostly Italian style.

Restaurants

Govinda's (☎ 9380 5155, 112 Darlinghurst Rd, Darlinghurst) **Map 6** Dinner & movie $15.90. Open 6pm-10.30pm. The smart Hare Krishna Govinda's serves healthy vegetarian food. It offers an all-you-can-gobble smorgasbord, which also gives you admission to its cinema upstairs (see under Eastern Suburbs in the Entertainment chapter).

Sel et Poivre (☎ 9361 6530, 263 Victoria St, Darlinghurst) **Map 6** Entrees $7.50-14.90, mains $15.90-24.50. Open 7am-11pm. For reasonably priced, good quality French cooking, Sel et Poivre is a handy spot to locate in Darlinghurst. The always reliable paté ($9.50) with Melba toast and *cornichons* is a good start.

bonne femme (☎ 9331 4455, 191-3 Palmer St, East Sydney) **Map 5** Entrees $15, mains $25. Open 6pm-11pm Tues-Sat, noon-3pm Fri, 6pm-10pm Sun. It might not be owned by a femme anymore, but the homme in charge has made sure that the quality has not suffered. It's all rich, delicious French-inspired comfort food. And for the price, it's more than comfortable.

Beppi's (☎ 9360 4558, Cnr Stanley & Yurong Sts, East Sydney) **Map 5** Pasta $16-26, seasonal specials $18-32. In East Sydney the charming and long-standing Beppi's has been supported for many years by those seeking top-notch Italian food. The food is always worth savouring (even a simple dish such as filled mushrooms marinated and baked with mixed herbs is memorable – $16) and the service is polished.

Two Chefs (☎ 9331 1559, 115 Riley St, East Sydney) **Map 5** Lunch special $28.50 for 2 courses, mains $25.50-27.50. This is a small, stylish restaurant that's popular for lunch. The fixed-price menu is good value.

The Edge (☎ 9360 1372, 60 Riley St) **Map 5** Mains $22-25. The Edge serves modern Australian food in a light, pleasant space with a bar, and an outside seating area.

Fast Food & Cafes

The northern end of Victoria St, near Kings Cross, has plenty of eateries.

Bar Coluzzi (☎ 9380 5420, 322 Victoria St) **Map 6** Coffee $2.50-3. You come here for coffee, not food, and it's almost a meal in itself, so robust is the flavour. Coluzzi has achieved legendary status, and if you have to have coffee in Darlinghurst, this is the place.

Una's Coffee Lounge (☎ 9360 6885, 340 Victoria St) **Map 6** Mains $10.90-15.90. Open until 11pm. A true stayer, Una's has almost 30 years of experience in serving European comfort food and heavenly all-day fry-ups for brekkie.

Bills (☎ 9360 9631, 433 Liverpool St) **Map 6** Breakfast $5-13.50, lunch $16.50-18. Open 7am-3pm Mon-Sat. This place has a large communal table and a great selection of glossy magazines for its glossy clientele. You've *got* to try the famous ricotta pancakes.

Burgerman (☎ 9361 0268, 116 Surrey St) **Map 6** Burgers $5.95-9.15. For an excellent meal-in-a-bun (in stylish surrounds), try the licensed Burgerman, where delicious, healthy burgers are served.

Fez (☎ 9360 9581, 247 Victoria St) **Map 6** Entrees $7.50-10, mains $10-24. The food at this busy cafe has a Middle-Eastern flavour, with tasty dips and soups. Also good is the fried haloumi cheese with smoked tomato, white beans and mint-and-lemon dressing ($16).

fu manchu (☎ 9360 9424, 249 Victoria St) **Map 6** Mains $11-18. This is the original fu (see the other under Bondi Beach & Around later), and some of the best eating in Darlinghurst. The steamed BBQ pork or vegetarian buns ($5 for two) are plump little parcels from paradise.

Bandstand Cafe (☎ 9360 9266, 301 Victoria St) **Map 6** Sandwiches $7.50, lunch mains $7-11.50. On Green Park, this cafe has a tranquil setting, despite being squeezed

Buzzing

A fast-paced city like Sydney needs its coffee, in some form or other. And while it seems like everyone is doing cocaine at night, in the day they're drinking coffee. Here are our five favourite places (in alphabetical order) to get it:

Cafe Niki (☎ 9319 7517, 544 Bourke St, Surry Hills) **Map 8** Perhaps we're piss-weak, but the coffees we had here had us foaming at the mouth. Strong.

Bar Coluzzi (☎ 9380 5420, 322 Victoria St, Darlinghurst) **Map 6** To many Sydney-siders, coffee didn't exist until the Coluzzi came along. Pull up a seat and get a superb macchiato.

The Health Emporium (☎ 9365 6008, 263-5 Bondi Rd, Bondi) **Map 11** It may not sit on any recognisable coffee beat, but what David does with all the crazy health-conscious requests (weak soy flat white anyone?) is truly admirable. He can do proper coffee too.

Love in a Cup (106 Glenayr Ave, Bondi) **Map 11** Maybe not the greatest coffee you'll ever have, but when a smiling face presents it to you with a love-heart traced in the crema, you understand why it's called Love in a Cup. Heartwarming stuff.

Spring Espresso Bar (☎ 9331 0190, 65 Macleay St, Potts Point, Enter via Challis Ave) **Map 6** In the line of duty (honest!), we came here at least half a dozen times. Never a dud. Always perfect.

into a renovated bandstand. It serves coffee, cakes and basic light meals, and you can sit outside.

Le Petit Creme (☎ 9361 4738, 116 Darlinghurst Rd) **Map 6** Breakfast from $5. This is a popular French-style cafe, with some alfresco tables. It can get full quickly, so arrive early or be prepared for a bit of a wait.

Fishface (☎ 9332 4803, 132 Darlinghurst Rd) **Map 6** Mains $17.50-24.50. This small and appealing place serves delicious sea-food, like classy beer-battered fish and chips, and fills quickly in the evening. It's so good you can forgive it for the bum-numbing chairs.

Tum Tum Thai (☎ 9331 5390, 199 Darlinghurst Rd) **Map 7** Lunch specials $6.50-9, stir fries $8.80-11. Seating is limited at this long-time popular Thai joint, but the food's good and the casual atmosphere is nice.

DOV Cafe (☎ 9360 9594, 252 Forbes St) **Map 6** Entrees $8.50-14.50, mains $12.50-23. A popular BYO place in a sparse-yet-inviting sandstone building, DOV serves delicious Mediterranean and Israeli-inspired food (chopped liver anyone?). It has a long list of tasty cold dishes, and good cakes. It's also open for breakfast, and you can sit outside.

No Names (☎ 9360 4711, 2 Chapel St, Enter via Stanley St) **Map 5** Dishes from $5. The ultra-cheap No Names is above the Arch Coffee Lounge, near Riley St; there's no sign outside indicating it's here. Walk past the pool table and pinball machines right to the back, then climb the stairs. It serves filling spaghetti meals and large salads.

Bill & Toni's (☎ 9360 4702, 74 Stanley St) **Map 5** Entrees $7.50, mains $11. No one comes here for fine dining, OK? You come here because it's a tradition, it's cheap as chips, it's no-frills and it's good fun. You get your orange cordial for free and service that's lightning-fast and everyone leaves with a smile.

Divino (☎ 9360 9911, 70 Stanley St) **Map 5** Mains $18-22. For something more stylish than the cheaper Stanley St options, try this licensed, mid-range cafe, with its white table-cloths, blackboard menu and nice-looking waiters (if you happen to notice this sort of thing...).

Palati Fini (☎ 9360 9121, 80 Stanley St) **Map 5** Primi piatti $9-12, secondi piatti $17-21. The BYO Palati Fini is popular for a number of reasons: the food's good; it's unpretentious; a lovable old guy sings (well) at your table if the mood takes him. The risotto with seafood is worth trying, as is any pasta dish.

OXFORD ST & AROUND (MAP 8)
Restaurants

Sol (☎ 9380 4400, Level 1, Cnr Flinders & Oxford Sts, Darlinghurst) Entrees $12.50-16, mains $23-26. Situated smack-bang in the midst of bustling Taylor Square, this Mod Oz restaurant serves very good corn-fed chicken and barramundi dishes, often flavoured with Asian spices. The Thai-baked barramundi in banana leaf with lemon ginger rice and laksa sauce ($26) is a high point.

Balkan (☎ *9360 4970, 209 Oxford St, Darlinghurst)* Dishes $17.90-19.90, grills $18.90-25.90. The long-established Balkan is a continental restaurant specialising in meat, meat and more meat. The traditional *raznjici* (assortment of spicy meats) and *cevapcici* (spicy minced meat rolled into skinless sausages) are worth getting your tongue around.

Grand Pacific Blue Room (☎ *9331 7108, Cnr South Dowling & Oxford Sts, Padding-ton)* Entrees $13-17. Mains $14-23. In the mood for northwestern Chinese cuisine but in no mood to traipse down to Chinatown? Then try this place. It used to serve your standard 'cool spot' Mod Oz dishes, but the times have changed, and while it's still a cool spot for cocktails and socialising, the menu reflects a more laid-back, late-night-snack ethos. Skip the desserts, but dive into the hung shaw lamb ($17).

Fast Food, Cafes & Pubs

Oxford St is teeming with cafes, bars and takeaway joints. If you're after really cheap food, it's hard to beat the Indian diners that give you a choice of two or three dishes and rice, usually for less than $7. There are also lots of Thai places and kebab stops that are easy to find between College St and Taylor Square. We've selected the places that stand out from the crowd and offer something different.

Cafe Belgenny (☎ *9360 0043, 197b Campbell St, Surry Hills)* Lunch $5.30-9.50. Open 7.30am-5pm Mon-Fri, 8am-5pm Sat. This is a stylish little urban cafe behind Taylor Square, with a relaxed air, good coffee and cakes, groovy magazines, and tasty toasted pide.

Maltese Cafe (☎ *9361 6942, 310 Crown St, Surry Hills)* Pastizzi $0.50, pasta $5-6. For pasta on the cheap, visit this low-key cafe where you can fill up very cheaply.

The pastizzi are delicious and make handy, cheap snacks.

SURRY HILLS (MAP 8)

Surry Hills is an interesting multicultural dining area. Crown St is its main food thor-oughfare, but it's a long street with cafes and restaurants in clusters. The biggest bunch is between Cleveland and Devonshire Sts, both of which also have a number of eater-ies. It's a great area for innovative, inspired cooking and also for the new 'staples' that keep residents and travellers alike happy: good Thai takeaway, great Turkish pizza and tasty Lebanese dips.

Restaurants

Billy Kwong (☎ *9332 3300, 3/355 Crown St)* Mains $14-23. Superlatives don't cut it for this wonderful Chinese restaurant. Chef Kylie Kwong prepares delicious and imagi-native fare in a tiny, teahouse-style setting that's worth the splurge and the wait (no reservations, so get in early). Mum's Lemon Chicken is so good you'll want to be adopted by the Kwong family.

Prasit's Northside on Crown (☎ *9319 0748, 413 Crown St)* Mains $16.90-27.90. Larger and pricier than its other incarnation, Prasit's Northside Thai Takeaway (☎ *9332 1792, 395 Crown St)*, this place has a gor-geous gold-and-purple colour scheme, some great dishes and helpful service. The con-dom salad ($27.50) gets its name from the appearance of the transparent rice noodles it features – not from any strange ingredients.

MG Garage (☎ *9383 9383, 490 Crown St)* Entrees $9-29, mains $28-52. Open for lunch from noon Mon-Fri, 6.30pm-late Mon-Sat. Would you like a sports car with your entree? At MG Garage this is possible, although we're not sure how many people have actually succumbed to the combina-tion restaurant/showroom temptation. If you've come for wonderful food, intelligent service and smart surroundings you've made the right choice. This place is brilliant.

Thai Tha Poh (☎ *9699 2829, 666 Crown St)* Dishes $8.50-15.40. A good local Thai eatery with heavy pine furniture, the food here is fresh, colourful and flavoursome.

Tandoori Rasoi (☎ *9310 2470, Cnr Bourke & Cleveland Sts)* Mains $5.90-13.90. With good tandoori on offer, this nice place has good food, served in a former halal butcher shop.

Alio (☎ *8394 9368, 5 Baptist St, Redfern)* Entrees $15, mains $20-28. Open noon-3pm Tues-Fri, 6pm-10pm Mon-Sat. The homemade pasta here is worth travelling for, even though this part of Redfern is generally regarded as Surry Hills The linguini with garlic and chilli ($15) is bursting with salty flavour, so hurry over here.

Cafes

Bills 2 (☎ *9360 4762, 359 Crown St)* Lunch mains $13.50-18, dinner mains $18.50-22.50. This is an airy, stylish modern cafe open for breakfast, lunch and dinner, and it isn't as expensive as it looks. There are great breakfasts, and yummy, cheap snacks like toasted coconut bread.

Lemon (☎/*fax 9380 5242, 393 Crown St)* Breakfast $2.80-10.50, dishes $6-13. This quirky cafe does great things with haloumi cheese (in salad or for breakfast). It's a nice place, with friendly staff and a relaxed vibe.

Rustic Cafe (☎ *9318 1034, 560 Crown St)* Pasta $8.80-14.20. This vibrant place, on the corner of Crown and Devonshire Sts, is a great pit-stop. The menu is varied and prices are reasonable: dishes include yam chips, pastas and rump steak. There's a bar upstairs with sunny window seats.

Melograno Cafe (☎ *9698 9131, 572 Crown St)* Breakfast $3.50-7, meals $7-10.50. Melograno is a good little place that serves a wicked steak sandwich (with relish, tomato, spinach and mustard) with uncomplicated friendliness.

Mohr Fish (☎ *9218 1326, 202 Devonshire St)* Fish & chips $7.50, mains $16-20. At this likeable, small and ever-popular designer fish-cafe, you can get fantastic seafood mains and excellent fish and chips. Oh my goodness the chips!

il baretto (☎ *9361 6163, 496 Bourke St)* Entrees $4.50-12, mains $8-18. Open 8am-4pm & 6pm-10pm Tues-Sat, 8am-4pm Sun. This smart-looking BYO local has mastered the art of making great homemade gnocchi,

and it keeps the customers coming back for more. In fact, all the pasta dishes are worthy.

Cafe Niki (☎ *9319 7517, 544 Bourke St)* Mains $8.90-12.90. This great little cafe has all sorts of tempting goodies to eat and some seriously powerful coffee.

The Prophet (☎ *9698 7025, 274 Cleveland St)* Entrees $4-16.50, mains $9.50-16.50. Open noon-3pm daily, 5pm-10pm Sun-Thur, 5pm-11pm Fri & Sat. In business for 22 years, The Prophet is the pick of the Lebanese bunch on this strip. The mixed plates ($16.50) are tasty and filling, with veg and meat options.

Erciyes (☎ *9319 1309, 409 Cleveland St)* Pizza $9-10. Open 10am-midnight. Turkish pide is popular along Cleveland St, especially at Erciyes, diagonally opposite the junction with Crown St. The food is good value and very tasty. Its vine leaves are out of this world.

Maya Masala (☎ *9699 8663, 470 Cleveland St)* Meals $5.50-8.90, thali $10. Open 10am-10.30pm. For a fancy sugar-fix there's Maya, an Indian sweet shop that also sells a fantastic thali. Try the delicious *gulab jamun* (a rose-water syrup-soaked dumpling), which is a sugar hit that won't hurt your hip pocket (less than $2).

Maya Da Dhaba (☎ *8399 3785, 431 Cleveland St)* Entrees $3.50-14, mains $5.90-13. Serving better than average Indian fare, the popular Maya eateries also provide good value. The andrakhi lamb chops ($9.90) arrive sizzling and juicy, so tuck in. Homestyle Indian never tasted so good.

BYO What?

You'll find many restaurants advertising that they're BYO. The initials stand for 'Bring Your Own', which means that the restaurant isn't licensed to serve alcohol, but you are permitted to bring some with you. This is a real bonus for wine-lovers on a budget, as you can bring your own bottle of wine and not pay any mark-up. Many restaurants charge a small fee for corkage, which can be from as little as $1. Some licensed restaurants are also BYO, but they tend to charge a higher corkage fee.

PADDINGTON (MAP 8)

Oxford St continues east from Darlinghurst through Paddington, but be aware that locating restaurants can be tricky, as the street numbers begin again at the junction with South Dowling St.

Restaurants

Bistro Lulu (☎ 9380 6888, 257 Oxford St) Entrees $12.50, mains $15-22.50. Open noon-3pm Thur-Sat, 6pm-11pm Mon-Sat. This handy bistro keeps relaxed hours and offers great food in a warm, inviting atmosphere. Mains are hearty (grilled sirloin $22.50), but there's also delicate and imaginative starters and desserts.

Darcy's (☎ 9363 3706, 92 Hargrave St) Primi piatti $14.50-25, secondi piatti $30-38. Well-cooked Italian food and attentive service keep locals flocking here. If you want to try an old favourite, the steak Dianne ($31) is bovine heaven (for you, not the beef).

Bistro Moncur (☎ 9363 2519, Woollahra Hotel, Cnr Moncur & Queen Sts, Woollahra) Entrees $15.50-18.90, mains $24.70-33. Open noon-3pm Tues-Sun, 6pm-10.30pm Tues-Sat, 6pm-9pm Sun. With a stark black-and-white mural running the length of one wall and a menu that never fails to impress, Bistro Moncur has been an old favourite with those who appreciate smart food in smart surroundings. Try the quail stuffed with green Sicilian olives, roasted with belly bacon and served with polenta ($29).

Buon Ricordo Ristorante (☎ 9360 6729, 108 Boundary St) **Map 6** Primi piatti $20-25, secondi piatti $33-44. The authentic Italian food, excellent wine list and considerate service has made this place popular for years. Reservations are advised.

Cafes & Pubs

Arthur's Pizza (☎ 9331 1779, 260 Oxford St) Entrees $5.50-7.50, mains $11.90-21.80. With friendly, snappy service and a long list of pizzas both simple and sophisticated, Arthur's has a loyal clientele.

Sloanes Cafe (☎ 9331 6717, 312 Oxford St) Dishes $5-16.50. This is a modern little cafe with a large vegetarian selection and a gorgeous courtyard. The breakfasts are good and so are the homemade muffins ($2.75).

Hot Gossip (☎ 9332 4358, 436 Oxford St) Dishes $3-14. The rejection of minimalist decor is quite a relief in trendy Paddo, and this is a lovely place to refuel and relax. It has three rooms with cosy seats and its menu is filled with simple goodies.

Grand National Hotel (☎ 9363 4557, 161 Underwood St) Entrees $13.90-18.50, mains $22.50-28. Open noon-3pm & 6pm-10.30pm Tues-Sat. The 'Nash' has pub grub with a difference – it's inventive and consistently stylish for one. With well-chosen wine recommendations adding even more punch to the experience, this place is easily first past the post in the Paddo pub stakes.

And the Dish Ran Away with the Spoon (☎ 9361 6131, 226 Glenmore Rd) Burgers $5-8. Open 8am-10pm. It's hard to believe that the 'skinny burger' ($6.60) is low-fat, as it tastes too good to be true. In this charming little place, locals pack in to eat lunch and graze on great pasta and growth-hormone-free organic chooks.

Royal Hotel (☎ 9331 2604, 237 Glenmore Rd) Dishes $12.90-30. At Five Ways (the junction of Glenmore Rd and Goodhope, Heeley and Broughton Sts), there are great views from the iron laced balcony at this hotel. Follow the chain of painted elephants upstairs and enjoy the food, which is top-end pub nosh.

Bellevue Hotel (☎ 9363 2293, 159 Hargrave St) Dishes $10.50-31. This place has a loyal local following and does a hearty spin on pub grub – in comfy surroundings.

Jones The Grocer (☎ 9362 1222, 68 Moncur St, Woollahra) Baguettes $6.60, salads $4.90-7.90. This joint is always jumping and with the lovely food on display it's easy to see why. This is one of Sydney's favourite places to stock up on fancy deli goods. There's also a Bondi branch at 36 Campbell Pde (☎ 9130 1100).

Sea Cow (☎ 9332 2458, 110 Boundary St) **Map 6** Mains $11.50-16. Open 5pm-9.30pm Mon-Thur, noon-9.30pm Fri & Sat, noon-9pm Sun. A fancy, modern version of a fish-and-chippery with big French windows and tables inside and out. This is in a

PLACES TO EAT

nice, quiet part of Paddington, if the frenzy of Oxford St is wearing you out.

GLEBE (MAP 9)

Glebe Point Rd was once *the* place to grab a bite to eat, but in recent years it's become a little less adventurous and is better known for budget eating. There are lots of Thai and Indian places to choose from, mostly at very reasonable prices, and the cafe scene here is still vibrant, thanks to its proximity to Sydney University.

Restaurants

The Boathouse on Blackwattle Bay (☎ 9518 9011, End of Ferry Rd) Entrees $21-23, mains $35-38. Easily the best restaurant in Glebe, and one of the best restaurants in Sydney, the Boathouse has stunning views of Blackwattle Bay and Anzac Bridge, and seafood so fresh it may as well have jumped onto your plate from the water. Try the signature dish, snapper pie. There's also a great wine list, to help you drink in the view. Reservations are definitely recommended.

Spanish Tapas (☎ 9571 9005, 28 Glebe Point Rd) Entrees $6.50-17, mains $19-20. Open 6pm-11pm. There's quite a party vibe here, with average to great tapas dishes, low lights, music and a convivial bunch of diners.

Tanjore (☎ 9660 6332, 34 Glebe Point Rd) Entrees $5.50-14.90, mains $10.90-16.50. Open noon-2.30pm Tues-Fri, noon-3pm Sun, 5pm-11pm daily. A pioneer of South Indian food in Australia, Tanjore attracts a range of locals, Indian food lovers and celebrities. Everything is cooked to order and the *masala dosai* (Sunday lunch special – $12.90) is fantastic.

Different Drummer (☎ 9552 3406, 185 Glebe Point Rd) Tapas $8-14. Open for dinner nightly except Mon. This is a fun place to try good tapas (like king prawns in chilli and ginger) and have a few drinks in relaxed surrounds. We once saw a bride, complete with her overnight bag, propping up the bar after her nuptials.

Perry's Gourmet Pizzas (☎ 9660 8440, 381 Glebe Point Rd) Super Supreme Pizza $9.50-20.90. Very handy to the nearby hostels and well priced, Perry's offers free delivery and is BYO.

Cafes

Badde Manors (☎ 9660 3797, 37 Francis St) Mains $11.50. Badde Manors is a long-established and well-known local haunt. It can be pretty hectic here, so don't take offence if the staff are a tad brusque – it's called Badde Manors for a reason. The cakes and tarts look sexy.

Brunch (☎ 9566 1625, 144a Glebe Point Rd) Breakfast $10-15. Open 8am-5pm. Need a heart-starting cup of good coffee and a really good breakfast? Look no further.

Iku Wholefoods (☎ 9692 8720, 25a Glebe Point Rd) Entrees $2.50-3.80, mains $4-8.60. Open 11.30am-9pm Mon-Fri, 11.30am-8.30pm Sat, 12.30pm-7.30pm Sun. This stalwart of healthy eating offers wonderful vegan and vegetarian food in a relaxed, small setting (takeaway is a good idea) and bargain prices. There are other branches at 62 Oxford St, Darlinghurst (☎ 9380 9780), at the rear of 168 Military Rd, Neutral Bay (☎ 9953 1964), at 612a Darling St, Rozelle (☎ 9810 5155) and 279 Bronte Rd, Waverley (☎ 9369 5022).

Wood Glen Cafe (☎ 9518 6002, 92 Glebe Point Rd) Entrees $6.50-8.70, mains $12-14. The food here is vegan/vegetarian, and it's not short on flavour. The mushroom pie ($14), filled with shitake, Swiss and oyster mushrooms and wrapped in a polenta crust with kumera mash is substantial and hearty.

BALMAIN (MAP 4)

Balmain's Darling St has many restaurants dotted along it – from cheap noodle spots to fine French-style bistros – and it manages to achieve the rare feat of being a busy 'foodie' destination *and* a laid-back, local hang-out.

Canteen (☎ 9818 1521, 332 Darling St) Baguettes $7.20-10.50. Open 7am-5pm Mon-Sat, 8am-5pm Sun. This airy, popular place serves simple fare and is good for breakfast and snacks.

Tuk Tuk Real Thai (☎ 9555 5899, 350 Darling St) Entrees $2.25-10.50, mains $12.50-20. Open 5.30pm-10pm Tues-Sun.

With its own genuine Tuk Tuk parked outside, this Thai restaurant hums with activity and has a legendary banana-flower salad ($17.50). It can get busy, so book ahead or plan to take away.

mofo (☎ 9555 5811, 354 Darling St) Mains $4-11. Open 8am-7.30pm Mon-Fri, 8am-4.30pm Sat. With a slightly chaotic, but friendly and easy-going atmosphere, there are good dishes at this vegetarian restaurant. Menus are presented on old 45s.

LEICHHARDT
Leichhardt is Sydney's 'Little Italy', with a good reputation for Italian food and great coffee. The street bustles on weekend nights; it's a short ride from George St on bus No 438 or 440.

Grind (☎ 9568 5535, 151 Norton St) Entrees $6-7.50, mains $9.50-18.50. Open 7am-10.30pm Tues-Thur, 7am-11pm Fri, 8am-11pm Sat, 8am-10.30pm Sun. This place occupies a prime position on Norton St, and there's a balcony too, so enjoy the good pasta dishes and big breakfasts while you watch 'il mondo' go by.

Elio (☎ 9560 9129, 159 Norton St) Entrees $12.50-14.50, mains $16.50-29. Open 6pm-midnight daily, noon-3pm Sun. With personal, attentive and informed service, Elio offers high-quality pasta dishes, although the mains were a little overcooked for our taste.

Bar Italia (☎ 9560 9981, 169-71 Norton St) Entrees $3-4.50, mains $8-14.50. This enormously popular restaurant, cafe and gelateria offers pasta mains and bar snacks, but one of its biggest drawcards is its famous gelato. The outdoor courtyard, good honest food and a little red wine makes for a very enjoyable meal.

Grappa (☎ 9560 6090, Shop 1, 267-77 Norton St) Entrees $13.50-23.50, mains $13-55. Open noon-3pm Tues-Fri & Sun, 6pm-10pm Mon-Thur, 6pm-11pm Fri & Sat, 6pm-9.30pm Sun. This nice-looking eatery, with a large open kitchen, snazzy bar and elegant decor is perfect for a more swanky dining experience. There's a good range of dishes, and seventeen varieties of grappa, hence the name.

NEWTOWN
Newtown's King St is regarded by many as 'Eat Street' and it's easy to see why. There seem to be dozens of Thai restaurants alone! You can sample a range of different cuisines here, from African to Italian, and Indian to Vietnamese, and many places are suited to tight budgets.

Restaurants
Rosalina's (☎ 9516 1429, 30 King St) Pasta $8.50-13.50, mains $13.50-16. Cuter than cute, Rosalina's is like a cliched 'little Italian place' from central casting, complete with dodgy mural. Charming service, homemade vino and great pasta make it very popular on weekends, so book ahead.

Green Gourmet (☎ 9519 5330, 115-17 King St) Lunch buffet $8, tofu mains $13.80. Spotlessly clean and kind to animals, Green Gourmet offers great Chinese-Malaysian vegetarian fare at good prices.

Linda's Backstage Restaurant (☎ 9550 6015, Newtown Hotel, 174 King St) Entrees $9-12.50, mains $16-18.50. Open noon-3pm Sun, 6pm-late Tues-Sun. This place is a good gay pub with drag shows and the added bonus of a great little restaurant out the back. Chef Linda Robertson uses the freshest ingredients and Southeast Asian and European influences to make her diners happy.

Bacigalupo (☎ 9565 5238, 284 King St) Entrees $6.50-11, mains $9.50-14. If traipsing along King St has caused your tummy to rumble, Bacigalupo's mammoth blackboard full of good pasta dishes and hearty specials will ease the pain.

Rambutan Bush (☎ 9550 6025, 467 King St) Entrees $5-6.50, mains $11.90-16.50. Open 6pm-10pm Tues-Sun, noon-3pm Sat & Sun. A simply decorated place, this restaurant offers refuge to those wishing to escape from the profusion of Thai joints on King St. The straightforward menu offers regular favourites, but also some more interesting sambals; the peanut sauce is highly recommended.

Fast Food & Cafes
Efes Turkish Pizza (☎ 9516 4276, 124 King St) Entrees $4.50-8, mains $7.50-15. Open

11am-midnight. No flash-arse 'gourmet' or wood-fired pizzas here – its all straightforward, cheap-as-chips Turkish pizza delights. *Sucuklu* (spicy Turkish sausage, garlic and eggs in a golden pizza casing with a mix of fetta, mozzarella and haloumi cheeses – $8) is just one of the options.

Singapore Gourmet (☎ 9550 6453, 520 King St) Dishes $3-13. Open 5.30pm-10.30pm Thur-Sat, 5.30pm-10pm Sun-Wed. The decor and the prices here haven't changed in years, and that makes good eating for the budget conscious, with big servings of mee goreng ($6.50) and seafood laksa ($8.50) raising smiles all round.

DOUBLE BAY

This exclusive neighbourhood has some excellent places to eat, and is a favourite with those who like to dress up for lunch.

Arte e Cucina (☎ 9328 0880, 2 Short St) Entrees $2.60-19, mains $16-28. Fancy combining a bit of Australian art with some good Italian cooking? This place has John Olsen on the walls and a range of good dishes on the plates. Try the crostini ($2.80), spread with delicious chicken-liver paste and then move onto the great antipasto selection.

Botticelli (☎ 9363 3266, 21 Bay St) Primi piatti $14.50-16.50, secondi piatti $19.50-27. This popular restaurant has great Italian food. It's a good place for a romantic dinner – former Australian prime minister Bob Hawke and his biographer Blanche d'Alpuget celebrated their nuptuals here, but don't let that put you off.

Roberto's at The Oak (☎ 9327 1470, 28 Bay St) Entrees $6.50-19.50, mains $13.50-26. Open noon-3pm & 5pm-10.30pm Mon-Sat, noon-3pm & 5pm-10pm Sun. Blonde-on-blonde sums this place up. Incongruous decor in a nice old pub doesn't promise much, but the food and service are both very good here. The tuna carpaccio is delightful.

Spice market (☎ 9328 7499, 340 New South Head Rd) Entrees $1.50-9, mains $10-15. Squeeze behind one of the communal tables and revel in the slick surroundings and the smells of fresh, modern Thai cooking. A

great range of vegetarian dishes makes this a good option for animal lovers.

BONDI BEACH & AROUND (MAP 11)

Unless you're flat broke, starving in Bondi is hard to do. There are numerous cafes and restaurants on busy Campbell Pde and nearby streets near the beach and in North Bondi. We've selected what we think are the best ones, but if you're really pinching the pennies, there are lots of less-than-salubrious takeaways and (very) greasy spoons in the neighbourhood.

If you're serious about great food with great value, see also the boxed text 'For the Serious Foodie...', earlier.

Restaurants

Ploy Thai (☎ 9300 6604, 8 Campbell Pde) Entrees $2-5.50, mains $9.50-13.90. Open 11am-10.30pm. A cut above the other Thai restaurants in the area, this quirky place offers great standard curries, but also enough tempting choices to persuade you to sample other Thai flavours. Try the duck larb ($13.90).

Point of View (☎ 9365 5166, 1/34 Campbell Pde) Tapas $9.50-14.50, mains $14-25. Open 6pm-midnight Tues-Fri, 9am-midnight Sat & Sun. With a downstairs bar with old-school hip-hop DJs and a restaurant upstairs offering interesting meals, Point of View is a popular Bondi hang. The tapas is good stuff, and goes well with a jug of sangria.

Yulla (☎ 9365 1788, Level 1, 28 Campbell Pde) Breakfast $5.50-9.50, lunch & dinner $7.50-18.50. This is Israeli/Middle-Eastern food done right (the hummus must be the best we've ever had). When you combine the food, the beach views and the more-than-reasonable prices, those kibbutz nightmares fade into oblivion.

Hugo's (☎ 9300 0900, 70 Campbell Pde) Mains $30-34. Hugo's is well-known among Bondi dwellers as a good place to have a better-than-average-meal in swish 'look at me' surrounds. It's not cheap, and can seem a bit 'sceney', but once you've tried some of the food and had one of the daiquiris, you won't care.

Gelbison (☎ 9130 4042, 10 Lamrock Ave) Entrees $3-14.90, mains $9.50-18.90. Open 5pm-11pm. An old favourite with many beach-bums looking for great pasta and pizza, Gelbison never seems to change, and in Bondi, that's a rare thing. Enjoy.

fu manchu (☎ 9300 0416, Level 1, 80 Campbell Pde) Noodles & noodle soups $11-14.50. Craving really good Chinese-Malaysian food? fu manchu will set you right with its heavenly sang *chio bao* ($10 for two) and Nonya chicken and potato curry with roti bread ($15).

Sean's Panaroma (☎ 9365 4924, 270 Campbell Pde) Entrees $14-19, mains $32-39. This excellent small restaurant serves wonderful, seasonal meals within carshot of the pounding waves. The wild barramundi, braised with basil and spinach ($33) is worth writing home about.

Cafes

Love in a Cup (106 Glenayr Ave) Breakfast from $5. This place is as cute as a bug's ear and the staff may well be the sweetest in Sydney. It's tiny and the menu is limited because of this, but once you're tried the fantastic 'Love eggs' or the heavenly 'Love waffles', you'll be too in love to notice.

Brown Sugar (☎ 9365 6262, 100 Brighton Blvd) Breakfast $4.40-11.50, lunch $5.50-15.50. Open 7.30am-4pm Mon-Sat, 9am-4pm Sun. This cramped space really churns out brekkie to the smooth set on weekends – and one bite of the eggs will tell you why. It's much less frantic on weekdays, and the lunch dishes are truly tasty.

The Health Emporium (☎ 9365 6008, 263-5 Bondi Rd) Snacks $3-7. This friendly cafe has good, healthy munchies, such as pies and nori rolls, and fresh juices, and it also stocks a tantalising array of organic fruit and vegies. Thankfully, it's not totally health-conscious – the life-changing qualities of a really good coffee are understood here.

COOGEE (MAP 10)
Restaurants

Erciyes 2 (☎ 9664 1913, 240 Coogee Bay Rd) Pizza $8.50-9.50. Open 10am-11pm. This spic and span offshoot of Erciyes in Surry Hills offers great Turkish pizza and a range of dips and kebabs. It's BYO, does fast food and also offers belly dancing on Friday and Saturday.

A Fish Called Coogee (☎ 9664 7700, 229 Coogee Bay Rd) Fish & chips from $6, BBQ baby lobster $18.90. Open 11.30am-9.30pm. This great little fishmongers sells fresh fish cooked 'so many different ways'. Grab some takeaway fish and chips and sit on the beach, because the tables here are often full.

Rice (☎ 9664 6655, 100 Beach St) Noodles $9-13.50. Open noon-late. Perhaps the flashest looking noodle joint in Sydney, this stunning place serves noodles to your specifications and also curries, salads, stir fries and meat dishes.

Jack & Jill's Fish Cafe (☎ 9665 8429, 98 Beach St) Fish & chips $12. Open 5pm-9pm Tues-Sat, noon-8pm Sun. This homey, simple place serves good seafood dishes at reasonable prices. Next door to Rice, it's away from the madding crowd, but close to the northern end of Coogee Beach.

Fast Food & Cafes

There are numerous fast-food outlets on Coogee Bay Rd offering cheap eats, but you're better off hitting the cafes for healthier food, sunnier demeanours and outdoor tables.

Cafe Congo (☎ 9665 3101, 208 Arden St) Mains $10-17. Open 8am-9.30pm Wed-Sat, 8am-6pm Sun & Mon. This tropical-looking cafe doesn't specialise in African food, but you'll feel like you're in the jungle. There's aerosol art on the walls and the staff will put simple Italian and Mexican-style dishes in your belly.

Coogee Cafe (☎ 9665 5779, 221 Coogee Bay Rd) All-day eggs breakfast $6.60-11.60. Open 8am-5pm Mon, 8am-10.30pm Tues-Sun. This busy, beach-themed cafe has harried service but remains popular.

Cozzi Espresso Cafe (☎ 9665 6111, 233 Coogee Bay Rd) Pasta $10-14. Open 7am-10pm. This is a nice-looking little cafe that offers good light snacks, pasta and dinner.

WATSONS BAY

The Doyles have been a presence in Watsons Bay since 1885, and they're still going strong. It's a touristy experience though, and the prices are quite ludicrous. If you *must* have fish and chips here, go to the pub, not the overpriced restaurants.

Doyle's Watsons Bay Hotel (☎ 9337 4299, 2 Military Rd, Watsons Bay) Fish & chips about $20-25. You can enjoy great views from this pub, with its fun beer garden. Those with a fish aversion can also chow down on a steak sandwich ($10.80). Grab a beer and enjoy this very Sydney experience.

Getting There & Away
On weekdays at lunchtime, you can catch Doyle's own water taxi from the Harbour Master's Steps on the western side of Circular Quay. The taxi costs $6/10 one way/return, and services run between 11.15am and 3.45pm. An ordinary water taxi would cost about $60 between four people. Ferries run from Circular Quay to Watsons Bay every two hours on weekends, from 9.15am to 5.15pm. For the non-nautical, bus Nos 324 and 325 run from Circular Quay.

NORTH SHORE
North Sydney (Map 3)
North Sydney Noodle Market (☎ 9440 2242, 0412 335 660, Civic Centre Park, Cnr Miller & McLaren Sts) Prices $5-13. Open Oct-Apr. This market is a praiseworthy attempt to capture the atmosphere of Asian street-food markets. Numerous stalls serve a variety of Southeast Asian and North Asian food.

Isshin Japanese Restaurant (☎ 9922 4370, 121 Walker St) Entrees $4-12, mains $10-17. Open noon-2.30pm Mon-Fri, 6.30pm-10pm Tues-Sat. Solid, simple and unpretentious, Isshin serves good Japanese food with plenty of good-value specials to assuage your appetite.

To's Malaysian Gourmet (☎ 9955 2088, Shop 3, lower ground floor, Oracle Plaza, 181 Miller St) Entrees $1.20-7.40, mains $6-8.70. Open 11am-6pm Mon-Wed, 11am-7pm Thur & Fri, 11.30am-3pm Sat. If it's laksa you're after, come here. Over 100 bowls of it are served a day, and many people say it's the best in Sydney.

Prasit's Northside Thai (☎ 9957 2271, 77 Mount St) Entrees $10.50-22.50, mains $19-25. Open noon-3pm Mon-Fri, from 6pm Tues-Sat. On the corner of Elizabeth Plaza, this is a licensed Thai restaurant with good, spiced fish cakes and famous jungle curry.

Milsons Point (Map 3)
The Old Fish Shop (☎ 9460 2698, 96 Alfred St) Breakfast $3.50-5.80, focaccia $5-7, pizza $11. Decorated with chillies and garlic, like its sister restaurant in Newtown, this place proudly proclaims 'The coffee is good – we drink it ourselves'. The custard tarts are sublime.

Aqua Dining (☎ 9964 9998, Cnr Paul & Northcliff Sts) Entrees $17-25, mains $25-70. Open noon-2.30pm & 6.30pm-9.40pm Mon-Fri, 6.30pm-10.30pm Sat, noon-2.30pm Sun. See things differently and go to the North Shore, where the lights of the city skyline (and the bridge) captivate diners at this first-rate restaurant above an Olympic-sized pool.

Balmoral
In the quiet suburb of Balmoral, you'll find a number of good restaurants and cafes, most with good views across the harbour.

Bather's Cafe (☎ 9969 5050, 4 The Esplanade) Mains $18.50-27. Open 7am-11pm. With an eclectic decor (get a load of the beach cabin-style children's toilet!) and flavoursome Mediterranean food, this cafe is a more budget-conscious treat than the Pavilion for those who want fine food in a lovely suburb. For the full upmarket experience make a booking at the adjoining Bather's Pavilion. (See the boxed text 'Meals with a View' in this chapter.)

Watermark (☎ 9968 3433, 2a The Esplanade) Entrees $19-27, mains $28-42.50. Open 8am-10.30am, noon-3pm & 6.30pm-10.30pm Mon-Fri, 8am-10.30am, 12.30am-3.30pm & 6.30pm-10.30pm Sat & Sun. With some wonderful views Watermark, at the junction with Botanic Rd, has well-heeled patrons who don't mind forking out good money to eat in a converted changing room. The service is efficient, the food is Asian-inspired and Platinum American

Express cardholders are given first preference for window seating. Says it all really.

Awaba Cafe (☎ 9969 2104, 67 The Esplanade) Mains $8.50-22. Open 8am-5pm Mon-Wed, 8am-10pm Thur-Sat, 8am-5pm Sun. Awaba is a good choice if you want the Balmoral experience without the frightening prices. It's big, white and airy, and the food is delicious. Try the chilli salted squid ($16.50), which is lightly battered and delicious.

MANLY (MAP 12)
Restaurants

Alhambra Cafe & Tapas Bar (☎ 9976 2975, Shop 1, 54 West Esplanade) Mains $15-21.50. Open noon-3pm & 6pm-10pm Mon-Fri, noon-5pm & 6pm-10.30pm Sat & Sun. Vibrantly decorated in the Moorish style, this place offers excellent tapas (if not exactly cheap) and there's classical Flamenco dancing Thursday, Friday and Saturday nights.

Wi Marn Thai (☎ 9976 2995, 47 North Steyne) Lunch $9.90, mains $14.40-24. Wi Marn offers reasonably priced, Thai meals that are full of flavour. The seafood dishes are good, and with a great beach location, it all adds up to a pleasantly fishy encounter.

The Bower Restaurant (☎ 9977 5451, 7 Marine Pde) Mains from $25. Open 8am-10.30am & noon-3pm. Follow the foreshore path east from the main ocean beach to reach this small restaurant, within spray's-breath of tiny Fairy Bower beach. It has wonderful breakfasts, and main courses of modern (and delicious) Australian food. And yay! – it's BYO too.

Le Kiosk (☎ 9977 4122, 1 Marine Pde, Shelly Beach) Entrees $17-19, mains $28-35. Open noon-2.30pm & 6.30pm-9pm Mon-Thur, noon-2.30pm & 6.30pm-9.30pm Fri, noon-3pm & 6.30pm-10pm Sat, noon-3pm & 6.30pm-9pm Sun. At Shelly Beach, this upmarket restaurant specialises in heavenly, masterful cooking, with romance

everywhere you look. Bookings are advised, especially on weekends.

Malacca Straits (☎ 9977 6627, 49 Sydney Rd) Entrees $3.30-6, mains $10.90-18.90. The decor might not be very lively, but the flavours of the Thai and Malay food compensate. The sesame prawns on toast ($5.90) are a yummy snack.

Armstrong's Bar & Restaurant (☎ 9976 3835, Shop 213, Manly wharf) Entrees $10.50-14.50, mains $18.50-26. Open 10am-10pm. On Manly wharf, at the western end, Armstrong's has a good reputation for Mod Oz seafood. Carnivores will find something to eat too, but with great calamari and well-done fish and chips, why not get fishy for the day? If you feel the earth move, it's probably the ferry docking.

Fast Food & Cafes

In Manly, you don't have to go any further than the wharf to eat for $5 to $10; The Corso is jammed with places, and there are others along North and South Steyne.

Blue Water Cafe (☎ 9976 2051, 28 South Steyne) Entrees $5-12, mains $10-22. Open 7.30am-10pm Mon-Fri, 7.30am-10.30pm Sat & Sun. With huge portions, an entree should be enough for most at this bustling, popular cafe in a prime position.

BarKing Frog (☎ 9977 6307, 48 North Steyne) Snacks $5-14, lunch mains $11-19, dinner mains $19-25. Open 8am-10pm Mon-Thur & Sun, 8am-11pm Fri & Sat. This is a fashionable bar and cafe with good coffee, serving good, basic snacks and well-cooked mains. The eggs BarKing Frog ($13.50) is a tasty way to start the day.

Fresh (☎ 9977 7705, Shop 1, 49 North Steyne) Dishes $6-7. For quick, healthy and tasty budget fare, try Fresh. It gets packed and there's indoor and outdoor seating, so hurry up and chow down. Even the normally dubious vegie burger is great in the hands of these guys.

Entertainment

With a thriving arts and cultural scene and plenty of nightlife, Sydney has something for everyone. Attractions range from gay dance clubs, comedy, live bands in crowded pubs and films at one of the many cinemas, to opera and ballet at the Opera House and shows at the city's many theatres. Call the City of Sydney infoline (☎ 9265 9007) for information on current events.

One of the best sources of 'what's on' information is the *Sydney Morning Herald*'s 'Metro' section. It's published on Friday and lists happenings for the week ahead. The free weekly *Sydney City Hub* is a street-smart rag bursting with news on music and arty events. For more-specialised music listings pick up one of the free and widely available weekly papers, such as *Drum Media*, *Revolver* or *3D World*.

Ticketek (Map 5; ☎ 9266 4800), 195 Elizabeth St, is the city's main booking agency for theatre, concerts, sports and other events. Phone bookings can be made 7.30am to 10pm weekdays, 9am to 4pm Saturday, and 9am to 8pm Sunday. It also has agencies around town and publishes a bimonthly *Entertainment Guide*.

Halftix (Map 5; ☎ 9286 3310), 201 Sussex St, sells discounts seats to shows. Halftix is open daily except Sunday. You can also book through its Web site at Ⓦ www.halftix.com.au.

Try to catch something at the Sydney Opera House (SOH, see Performing Arts later) – in addition to opera and ballet, it hosts a wide range of musical events, live theatre, films, children's entertainment and even rock concerts.

FREE ENTERTAINMENT

On summer weekends there's free music performances in many parks, especially in *The Domain* during the Sydney Festival (January). There's often free lunchtime music in the *amphitheatre* at Martin Place (12.15pm to 1.15pm); at Darling Harbour's *Tumbalong Park amphitheatre*; and at

St Andrew's Cathedral next to the Town Hall (Tuesday at 1.10pm during the school term), courtesy of students from the Conservatorium of Music. Over the Labour Day long weekend (early October), there are free outdoor jazz concerts at the Manly International Jazz Festival. You can be entertained by buskers around the Opera House and Circular Quay, in The Rocks and Kings Cross, and along The Corso in Manly. Alternatively, you can listen to the mad and the erudite venting their obsessions at Speakers' Corner in The Domain on Sunday afternoon.

There's a free *Aboriginal dance performance* at the Art Gallery of NSW, at noon Tuesday to Saturday. See also the boxed text 'Aboriginal Performance' in this chapter.

Tropfest (☎ *9368 0434*, Ⓦ www.tropfest .com.au) is the biggest short-film festival in the world and draws huge crowds to The Domain in the Botanic Gardens and various locations on Victoria St, Darlinghurst, on one evening in February. There is always a compulsory prop in each entry (which encourages creativity and discourages cheating) and some pretty famous people from the film world are involved in the judging.

PUBS WITH MUSIC

Sydney doesn't have an especially dynamic pub music scene, but there are enough pubs offering live music for you to be able to find something most nights of the week. Five-star hotels often have famous cabaret artists, and sometimes more adventurous acts, at prices that aren't outrageous as long as you watch your alcohol intake. A few of the many venues are listed here; for other places with music on the menu, see Pubs & Bars in this chapter.

The Annandale (☎ *9550 1078, Cnr Parramatta Rd & Nelson St, Annandale)* Thankfully, the Annandale was rescued from the live music graveyard and once again features bands in this great venue.

The Basement (☎ 9251 2797, 29 Reiby Pl, Circular Quay) **Map 5** This place has good food, good music (plus the odd spoken-word gig) and sometimes big international names.

Bridge Hotel (☎ 9810 1260, 135 Victoria Rd, Rozelle) One of the last bastions of pub entertainment, and also one of the best, with comedy (stand-up and theatre) and good live music (including some big names in blues).

The Cat & Fiddle Hotel (☎ 9810 7931, 456 Darling St, Balmain) Open nightly. It has bands: jazz, blues, pop, rock, metal etc and has been recently refurbished.

Golden Sheaf Hotel (☎ 9327 5877, 429 New South Head Rd, Double Bay) This hotel offers groovy live music and the odd DJ. There's also good food available and the beer garden is a popular spot to hang out.

Harbourside Brasserie (☎ 9252 3000, Pier 1, Hickson Rd, Dawes Point) **Map 5** Open nightly. This great venue has live music every night (from funk to jazz to pop and salsa) and is almost under the Harbour Bridge.

Hopetoun Hotel (☎ 9361 5257, 416 Bourke St, Surry Hills) **Map 8** This great little venue offers flexibility for artists and patrons alike and it features an array of modern musical styles.

Lansdowne Hotel (☎ 9211 2325, 2 City Rd, Chippendale) **Map 9** The Lansdowne ain't what it used to be, having succumbed to the urge to renovate and whack in some pokies instead of bands. There's still some live music however, and a cocktail lounge.

Marlborough Hotel (☎ 9519 1222, 145 King St) **Map 9** 'The Marli' is a big Art Deco Newtown pub with bands and trivia nights.

Metro Theatre (☎ 9287 2000, 624 George St) **Map 5** Not really a pub at all (although you can drink here), but it's easily the nicest place to see local and international acts in comfort. Raves are sometimes held here too.

Sandringham Hotel (☎ 9557 1254, 387 King St, Newtown) At the time of research the Sando was being renovated. However, once the renovations are complete, there'll be live music again.

Selina's (☎ 9665 0000, Coogee Bay Hotel, Cnr Coogee Bay Rd & Arden St, Coogee) **Map 10** Selina's has rock (often top Australian and international bands), which you can pay a fair bit for; the main nights are Friday and Saturday, but there are cheaper bands on other nights.

Strawberry Hills Hotel (☎ 9698 2997, 453 Elizabeth St, Surry Hills) **Map 8** This place (once the home of regular jazz gigs) features the Eclipse Alley Five from 3pm to 7pm on Saturday afternoon.

NIGHTCLUBS

Dance music is huge in Sydney, and you'll find beats of almost every description if you're prepared to seek them out. Sydney has some truly great, local DJs, as well as touring internationals from overseas. However, nightclubs can be fickle things and exclusive clubs or specific nights can pop up and then vanish in the blink of an eye. Check the street press mentioned at the start of this chapter, and fliers in record stores, for up-to-the-minute information.

The Cauldron (☎ 9331 1523, 207 Darlinghurst Rd, Darlinghurst) **Map 7** On the corner of Farrel Ave, this is a long-running, slick club with a (sometimes) strict door policy. The music can be good, with some DJs who know how to please.

Cave (☎ 9566 4755, Star City Casino, Pirrama Rd, Pyrmont) **Map 5** This is a flashy, fleshy joint for those who like their R&B. The dress code is geared more towards labels and sex appeal, rather than comfort.

Bristol Arms Retro Hotel (☎ 9262 2391, 81 Sussex St) **Map 5** Having trouble with all this new-fangled music? Relax – you're back in disco heaven, with this popular place providing the soundtrack to much young love.

China White (☎ 9358 4676, 22 Bayswater Rd, Kings Cross) **Map 7** The music here tends towards trance and hard house, but there's a chill-out room if you need to take the edge off. Friday hosts Plastic and Saturday hosts Vinyl.

Club 77 (☎ 9361 4981, 77 William St, Kings Cross) **Map 5** On the strip better known for hire-car offices and hookers, Club 77 offers dance music nights that cater to almost every taste. It's a straightforward, unfussy and fun experience, refreshingly free of attitude.

EP1 (☎ *9358 3990, 1 Earl Pl, Kings Cross*) **Map 7** Tucked-away and easy on door policy, this place has popular nights for partying backpackers and disco fans, with Carwash Disco on Wednesday and Saturday nights.

Home (☎ *9266 0600, Cockle Bay wharf, 101 Wheat Rd, Darling Harbour*) **Map 5** A monster-sized pleasuredome over three levels, with a sound system that makes other clubs sound like they're plugged in to transistor radios. The cover charge is $25 and even with a capacity of 2000 people, this place gets packed. Some gay nights happen here too. (For Gay & Lesbian venues, see also the boxed text 'Gay Daze & Nights' in this chapter.)

Hugo's Lounge (☎ *9357 4411, Level 1, 33 Bayswater Rd, Kings Cross*) **Map 7** Kings Cross is home of the seedy nightspot, but Hugo's Lounge brings the area a much-needed bit of class. There's good food on offer here and the eye-candy is pretty sweet.

Mint (☎ *9233 5388, 53 Martin Pl*) **Map 5** In the oh-so-stylish Banc/Wine Banc emporium, this place is smooth and space age but without the 'stick up its bum' atmosphere that often mars beautiful-looking establishments. The music covers rare groove, electronica and foreign rhythms – and everyone's having a good time.

Mr GoodBar (☎ *9360 6759, 11a Oxford St, Paddington*) **Map 7** This hanky-sized club is still attracting gorgeous young things after many years of sizing up the punters at the door. Its Thursday night groove-fest, Step Forward, has a relaxed vibe and is easily its best night.

Q Bar (☎ *9360 1375, Level 2, 44 Oxford St*) **Map 5** This place had its heyday in the mid-1990s, but it's still going strong and the door policy can be ferocious at times. Get past the bouncers, hop into the lift and decide whether you want to play pool or dance. The music screeches at you and you'll need to screech to be heard.

Slip-Inn (☎ *9299 1700, 111 Sussex St*) **Map 5** Warren-like and full of different rooms for different drinking moods, this place also houses the Chinese Laundry (entry at 3 Slip St), which has great DJs.

You can eat, drink and be merry here with disconcerting ease, especially if you like a good-looking crowd.

Soho Bar & Lounge (☎ *9358 6511, 171 Victoria St, Kings Cross*) **Map 7** In an old Art Deco pub, this place has played host to numerous Sydneysiders' social lives. There are pool tables, relaxed drinking lounges and DJs playing everything from funk to breakbeat, house to nu (!) energy.

PUBS & BARS

Pubs and bars are an important part of Sydney's social scene. Try going to a few during the week because they often have a totally different atmosphere on the weekends, when the roving hordes are out on the town. Pubs vary from the traditional (with tiled walls), to the modern and minimalist. See the boxed text 'Blow up the Pokies Indeed' for an idea of how Sydney pubs are changing.

The Rocks & Circular Quay (Map 5)

There are some nice, old pubs in The Rocks, but determining just *how* old they are seems to be a less-than-exact science. The Hero of Waterloo and Lord Nelson Brewery Hotel are probably Sydney's best-known pubs, and two of its busiest. Both vie for the title of 'Sydney's oldest pub' – while other equally ambitious establishments lay claim to the title of 'oldest continually operating pub'.

Fortune of War (☎ *9247 2714, 137 George St, The Rocks*) Opposite the back of the MCA, this pub claims to hold Sydney's oldest hotel licence. It's a nice pub with a historical feel, but keeps the corny 'olde world' touches to a minimum.

Hero of Waterloo (☎ *9252 4553, 81 Lower Fort St, Millers Point*) On the corner of Windmill St, the Hero of Waterloo has music on weekends, including traditional Irish music. It also has its original dungeon, where drinks would sleep off a heavy night before a stint on the high seas.

Lord Nelson Brewery Hotel (☎ *9251 4044, 19 Kent St, The Rocks*) The Lord Nelson is an atmospheric pub that brews its own beers (Quayle Ale, Trafalgar Pale Ale, Victory Bitter, Three Sheets, Old Admiral,

MICHAEL LAANELA

MICHAEL LAANELA

GREG ELMS

GREG ELMS

GREG ELMS

eld along Oxford Street, Sydney's colourful Gay & Lesbian Mardi Gras attracts hundreds of thousands f participants and spectators every year.

A busker 'performs'

Graffiti with a message

Bringing music to the street

One of Pitt Street's eclectic performing artists

Striking contemporary art with attitude on a Sydney wall

Waiting for customers at a late-night bottleshop, Oxford Street

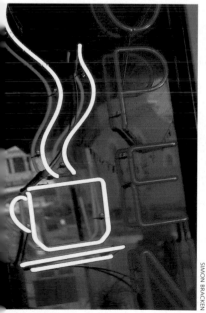

Open for coffee, Newtown

One of many 'colourful' clubs, Kings Cross

Woolloomooloo's famous pie cart, Harry's Cafe de Wheels – established 1945

Late night off the main drag of Kings Cross

Nelsons Blood and The Lord's Water). It might be wise not to sample them all in one sitting.

Mercantile Hotel (☎ 9247 3570, 25 George St, The Rocks) One of Sydney's best places for Guinness and regular, live Irish music is the beautifully green-hued Mercantile Hotel, near the bridge. It gets frantic here on St Patrick's Day.

Palisade Hotel (☎ 9247 2272, 35 Bettington St) Standing sentinel-like at Millers Point, the Palisade Hotel has breathtaking views of the harbour and its fine bridge. It's a lovely old heritage building in a part of The Rocks that has avoided becoming a tourist trap. See also Places to Stay.

Bennelong (☎ 9250 7548, Bennelong Point) If you're dressed up and keen for a cocktail, some jazz and a swanky setting, the bar at the smart Bennelong restaurant in the SOH is a great choice.

City Centre (Map 5)

Marble Bar (☎ 9266 2000, Hilton Hotel, 259 Pitt St) All walnut and marble, this place is the antidote to Sydney's blonde wood, white paint and stainless steel fixation – and there's music too! The music covers a range of styles, from jazzy to rock to whatever, almost every night of the week.

Establishment (☎ 9251 9933, 252 George St) This cavernous establishment, with an impressive marble bar, proves that the art of drinking a smart cocktail after a hard day in the city is not dead. The noise can only be described as a dull roar, so try and escape to Hemmesphere upstairs.

Forbes Hotel (☎ 9299 3703, 30 York St) At the intersection of York and King Sts, the charming, multistorey Forbes Hotel, with leadlighting, wood-panelled walls and a tiny wrought-iron balcony, is traditional and cosy, and popular with city workers.

Hotel CBD (☎ 9299 1700, 75 York St) A five-level alcoholiday for those who've had a tough day making money in the – where else? – CBD. The ground-floor bar gets crowded after work, but there are quieter options upstairs, and a good restaurant.

Scruffy Murphy's (☎ 9211 2002, 43-9 Goulburn St) There are *a lot* of Irish and

English backpackers in Sydney, and this place seems to be a home away from home for many of them. It's all faux-Irish fittings, real Irish patrons and rivers of English and Irish beer. If rowdy and raucous is your thing, then this is your pub.

Century Tavern (☎ 9264 3157, 640 George St) Hooray for the Century Tavern! Old-fashioned (right down to the original standard-issue carpet and curved glass windows looking down onto the street) and resolutely uncool, this place hangs onto its roots with pride.

Civic Hotel (☎ 8267 3181, Cnr Pitt & Goulburn Sts) It's nice to see a renovated pub not be turned into a sad excuse for a bad Irish theme park/pub or meat market catering to suits with architectural pretensions. This place looks spiffy – but it could also pass for extraordinarily well preserved.

Darling Harbour & Pyrmont (Maps 5 & 9)

Pyrmont Bridge Hotel (☎ 9660 6996, 96 Union St, Pyrmont) Pleasantly unpretentious beside the Darling Harbour and casino glitz, this 24-hour pub has good, cheap nosh and is popular with hospitality workers.

Quarrymans Hotel (☎ 9660 1448, 216 Harris St, Pyrmont) On the corner of Harris St and Pyrmont Bridge Rd, this pub has been spruced up in recent years and has some good beers on tap.

Dundee Arms Tavern (☎ 9299 1231, 161 Sussex St) In an old sandstone building that's part of the Four Points Sheraton, this upmarket pub is in a heritage-listed sandstone building from the 1850s, with great food and boutique beer.

Kings Cross & Around (Maps 5, 6 & 7

Kings Cross and the surrounding areas have plenty of watering holes.

Kings Cross Hotel (☎ 9358 3377, 248 William St, Kings Cross) **Map 7** This huge, rowdy pub, at the junction of Victoria St, Darlinghurst Rd and William St, is a boozy hang-out for backpackers and predominantly young out-of-towners, with 24-hour drinking on Friday and Saturday.

Mansions Hotel (☎ 9358 6677, 18 Bayswater Rd, Kings Cross) **Map 7** On the corner of Kellett St, this is a cavernous, modern place with pool and jukeboxes, although not much in the way of atmosphere.

Old Fitzroy Hotel (☎ 9356 3848, 129 Dowling St, Woolloomooloo) **Map 6** With a little theatre that showcases mostly local works, this is a friendly, sociable pub that's popular with backpackers.

Woolloomooloo Bay Hotel (☎ 9357 1177, 2 Bourke St, Woolloomooloo) **Map 6** This big pub has eating options and a choice of bars. The Sunday fixture Milk 'n' 2 Sugars is popular with DJ enthusiasts.

Water Bar (☎ 9331 9000, 6 Cowper Wharf Rdwy, Woolloomooloo) **Map 6** This luxurious bar straddles the gap between stylish and spacious. The cocktail list is long, the ceilings are high and the chairs are comfy.

Darlo Bar (☎ 9331 3672, Cnr Liverpool St & Darlinghurst Rd) **Map 6** Occupying its own tiny block, this is surely the narrowest pub in Sydney. It's pretty much a neighbourhood pub, but it's a very interesting neighbourhood. The service is friendly and the furniture is retro mix 'n' match.

Green Park Hotel (☎ 9380 5311, 360 Victoria St, Darlinghurst) **Map 6** South of the Cross, this hotel, with its tiled walls and bar, is a popular local watering hole and a cool hang-out for pool-shooters. The last dose of renovations provided much-needed drinking space and better toilets.

East Village (☎ 9331 5457, 234 Palmer St, East Sydney) **Map 5** As tarted-up, groovy inner-city pubs go, this is a very good one. The display of booze is impressive and the decor is modern without being chilly. It's close to the Italian restaurants of Palmer St too.

Oxford St & Around (Maps 5 & 8)

Burdekin Hotel (☎ 9331 2066, 2 Oxford St) This is one of a number of busy pubs along Oxford St. It has a stylish, small cocktail bar called the **Dug Out**, which you'll find at the back entrance, down a short flight of stairs.

Kinselas (☎ 9331 3299, 383 Bourke St, Darlinghurst) In what used to be a funeral parlour, this place has come back from the dead more times than we can recall. The downstairs part is poker machines and bad carpet, but the bar upstairs is stylish, modern and incredibly popular with the bright young things. The cocktails are good too.

Rose Shamrock & Thistle (☎ 9360 4662, 27-33 Oxford St, Paddington) **Map 8** This charming little pub keeps its easy-going charm and is popular with nearby art students and young locals.

Fringe Bar (☎ 9360 3554, 106 Oxford St) Housed in the Unicorn Hotel and popular with 20-somethings looking for weekend fun, you may have to queue here when it's busy.

Palace Hotel (☎ 9361 5170, 122 Flinders St) On the junction with South Dowling St, this is a great pub for socialising, with pool tables, an Art Deco ambience, good beer, a Thai restaurant (Mai Thai) and, best of all, no pokies!

Glebe (Map 9)

Friend in Hand Hotel (☎ 9660 2326, 58 Cowper St) At this unique, bric-a-brac filled pub you can enjoy poetry slams (Bardfly – Tuesday) or crab racing (Wednesday). Or just beer.

Gay Daze & Nights

Sydney has one of the biggest gay and lesbian populations in the world, so it's definitely Australia's playground when it comes to being out and getting about. For gay men, nightlife options tend to be 'take your pick', but for lesbians, partying options are lamentably slim. Places seem to open and close fast for the Sapphic crowd – you might want to check that girl-friendly places and nights are still operating before you venture out.

The scene can change quickly, but here's a starter list:

ARQ (☎ 9380 8700, 16 Flinders St, Darlinghurst) This big, flash club has a 24-hour licence and good lighting, which should be compulsory in more places.

Annie's Bar (☎ 9360 4714, Carrington Hotel, 563 Bourke St, Surry Hills) **Map 8** Enter this relaxed watering hole via the side of the Carrington Hotel. It's a chilled place, and very much a low-key 'local' for recoveries.

Bank Hotel (☎ 9557 1692, 324 King St, Newtown) This trendy hotel has a beer garden, pool tables, a Thai restaurant and a cocktail bar. It's also a popular lesbian hang-out.

Barracks Bar (☎ 9360 6773, 1 Flinders St, Darlinghurst) We couldn't sample this one, as it's a men-only joint, but sources tell us it's chock-a-block with leather and handle-bar moustaches, and if that's your cue to shout 'Who's your daddy?', then join the queue.

The Beresford Hotel (☎ 9331 1045, 354 Bourke St, Darlinghurst) **Map 8** Tired and emotional? Need a hand? There's an enormous one on the awning at the Beresford. One could curl up and sleep in it if one wasn't so intent on partying hard in that vague period known as 'recovery'. A rite of passage.

The Exchange Hotel (☎ 9331 1936, 34 Oxford St, Darlinghurst) **Map 5** This long-running temple of drinking and dancing has quite a few gay entertainment options, from the Lizard Lounge (popular with lesbians and friends) and Phoenix ('predom' men).

Flinders Hotel (☎ 9360 4929, 63 Flinders St, Darlinghurst) **Map 8** If this place was empty for most of the year it would still be profitable, thanks to the passing trade (no pun intended) that swamps this place on the holidays (Mardi Gras, Inquisition, Sleaze). Get down and get back up again.

Icebox (☎ 9331 0058, 2 Kellett St, Kings Cross) **Map 7** There's a popular queer night here called Milkbar, which has a good reputation and may prove to be a stayer.

Imperial Hotel (☎ 9519 9899, 35 Erskineville Rd, Erskineville) You might think Priscilla – Queen of the Desert was inspired by the drag on Oxford St, but think again. This is where it came from, and it's world-class. Surprisingly late hours too. There's The Hole on Wednesday for lesbians.

Lansdowne Hotel (☎ 9211 2325, 2 City Rd, Chippendale) **Map 9** How many lesbians does it take to change a light bulb? Find out here on Friday nights at the 40 Watt Club.

Midnight Shift (☎ 9360 4463, 85 Oxford St, Darlinghurst) **Map 8** It's hard to believe that a gay scene existed before this place (also nicknamed the Midnight Shirtlift). The ground floor is quite pubby, but upstairs it's a licence to booze, cruise and boogie.

Newtown Hotel (☎ 9557 1329, 174 King St, Newtown) In Sydney's other gay enclave, the Newtown does a roaring trade with gay folk who just want to go to the local and have a good time. The drag acts are good, too.

Oxford Hotel (☎ 9331 3467, 134 Oxford St, Darlinghurst) **Map 8** With an industrial hardcore theme going on at ground level and the luxe ambience of Gilligan's cocktail bar upstairs, this place covers the bases on Taylor Square. Occasionally the bouncers have been known to use ridiculous lines, such as 'We've had a broken glass tonight, so no-one with open-toed shoes is allowed in for safety reasons', to exclude women from entering.

Gay Daze & Nights

Stonewall (☎ 9360 1963, 175 Oxford St, Darlinghurst) **Map 8** Nicknamed 'Stonehenge' by those who find it a little too ancient for their liking, this place is usually pumping and pumped-up. Wednesday nights are Malebox nights, which should be self-explanatory. Get a number, look at everyone else's number, write a note and wait for someone to write you a note. Bet No 69 is fought-over. For women there's Girl's Night Out on Thursday.

The Taxi Club (☎ 9331 4256, 40-2 Flinders St, Darlinghurst) **Map 8** Chances are, if you can't remember the end of last night you finished it off at the Taxi Club. Refreshingly seedy after all these years, this place is a national treasure that no tourist brochure's going to tout. Mind the stairs.

Balmain (Map 4)
London Hotel (☎ 9555 1377, 234 Darling St) Open 11am-midnight Mon-Sat, noon-10pm Sun. A good place for a cleansing ale, especially after a trawl through the nearby Saturday market at St Andrew's.

Monkey Bar (☎ 9810 1749, 255 Darling St) Open noon-midnight Mon-Sat, noon-10pm Sun. On the corner of Darling and Ford Sts, this busy bar attracts a young crowd and offers bar snacks if you get peckish. There's also a restaurant on the premises.

Riverview Hotel (☎ 9555 8337, 29 Birchgrove Rd) This Balmain local was once owned by Australian swimming legend Dawn Fraser (a Balmain icon if ever there

Dawn Fraser is an Aussie icon: the first woman swimmer to win gold medals in three consecutive Olympic games.

was one). It's quiet and low-key and a bit of a treasure.

Surry Hills (Map 8)
Cricketers Arms Hotel (☎ 9331 3301, 106 Fitzroy St) A cruisy, cosy vibe fills this place with locals and those appreciative of good DJ skills. There are open fireplaces too.

Dolphin on Crown Hotel (☎ 9331 4800, 412 Crown St) The ground level bar of this pub is a good place for a drink, but there's also a nice little cocktail bar upstairs and two eating areas serving tasty food and snacks.

The Clock (☎ 9331 5333, 470 Crown St) Once a seedy dive, this now-airy pub symbolises the steady gentrification of Surry Hills. There's also a good restaurant upstairs.

Woollahra (Map 8)
Lord Dudley Hotel (☎ 9327 5399, 236 Jersey Rd) The Lord Dudley is as close as Sydney *really* gets to an English pub atmosphere, with dark walls and wood and good beer in pint glasses.

Newtown
Bank Hotel (☎ 9557 1692, 324 King St) This trendy hotel has a beer garden, pool tables, a Thai restaurant and a cocktail bar. It's also a popular lesbian hang-out.

Botany View Hotel (☎ 9519 4501, 597 King St) At the St Peter's end of King St, this good Art Deco pub has Guinness on tap.

GAMBLING
Australians love to gamble, and Sydney provides plenty of opportunities for punters to be separated from their cash.

Star City Casino *(☎ 9777 9000, 80 Pyrmont Rd, Pyrmont)* **Map 5** Open 24 hours. This huge casino, theatre, retail, restaurant and hotel complex is on the waterfront in Pyrmont, on the north-eastern headland of Darling Harbour. A free shuttle bus connects The Rocks and city centre with the casino, or you can catch the ferry to the Pyrmont Bay wharf, just across the road from the casino. There's a hundred and one ways to gamble here, and it can get packed on weekends.

Horse & Greyhound Racing

Sydney has four horse-racing venues.

Canterbury Park *(☎ 9930 4000, King St, Canterbury)* Canterbury Park is south-west of the city centre.

Rosehill Gardens *(☎ 9930 4070, Grand Ave, Rosehill)* Rosehill Gardens is near Parramatta and is one of Sydney's most famous racecourses.

Royal Randwick Racecourse *(☎ 9663 8400, Alison Rd, Randwick)* The closest horse-racing venue to the city, Royal Randwick is near Centennial Park and attracts some glamourous types, plus the usual array of 'colourful' racing identities.

Warwick Farm *(☎ 9602 6199, Hume Hwy, Warwick Farm)* Warwick Farm is near Liverpool.

Horse racing alternates between these tracks throughout the year. However, it's more colourful and exciting during the spring and autumn carnivals, when major events like the Golden Slipper at Rosehill or the Sydney Cup at Randwick take place.

A little down the social scale, but with a die-hard following is trotting/pacing (harness racing) meetings and greyhound racing.

Harold Park Paceway *(☎ 9660 3688, Ross St, Glebe)* **Map 9** Close to the city, the Harold Park trots are easy to get to.

Wentworth Park *(☎ 9552 1799, Wentworth Park Rd, Glebe)* **Map 9** This is Australia's premier greyhound-racing complex, with skinny, fast dogs chasing tin hares.

Pokies

Coin-fed gambling machines known as 'pokies' (short for poker machines) is a very common form of gambling. They're *everywhere*. You'll find them in many pubs and in leagues, RSL (Returned Servicemen's League) and other clubs, which they help to keep profitable.

COMEDY

The comedy scene isn't too healthy in Sydney at the moment, although some pubs have stand-up nights. Check entertainment listings in newspapers and the street press.

Sydney Comedy Store *(☎ 9357 1419, Fox Studios, Moore Park)* **Map 8** In its

Blow up the Pokies Indeed

To many, Sydney's once-thriving rock music scene has lost its mojo, due to the resistable rise of pokies As the state government realised that gambling revenue was quite an income-earner, more and more pokies began to appear in Sydney's pubs and clubs. And if you've got a stage filled with performers who aren't making the punters spend enough on beer, It seems obvious to remove the stage, whack in some pokies and watch the coins disappear into the slots. So instead of the raucous sound of live music, publicans can now enjoy the sound of increasingly whizz-bang pokies. Sydney band The Whitlams summed up the situation beautifully with their song *Blow up the Pokies*, which you might hear live if music-friendly pubs survive the pokie takeover.

MW

newish home in Fox Studios, this specially built comedy venue has improv, stand-up and open-mike nights.

CINEMAS

Cinema tickets generally cost between $10 and $15, with discounts for Seniors Card holders and students (proof required). Mainstream cinemas usually have cheaper tickets on Tuesday, while independent cinemas generally have cheaper tickets on Monday.

City Centre (Map 5)

City Greater Union Hoyts Village Complex (☎ 9273 7431, 505-25 George St) **Map 5** This behemoth is what happens when you join three already-large cinema complexes. Still amalgamating at the time of research, it should offer every mainstream movie on current release.

State Theatre (☎ 9373 6655, 49 Market St) **Map 5** Tucked between Pitt and George Sts, the glorious State Theatre is the main venue for the Sydney Film Festival, held annually in June.

Dendy (☎ 9233 8166, 19 Martin Pl) **Map 5** With a good bar and well-chosen movies, this branch of the Dendy chain was the first one the Dendy people opened, and it got the ball rolling.

Dendy (☎ 9252 8879, Shop 9, 2 Circular Quay) Right near the Opera House, this is a lavish new cinema with a great bar.

North Shore

Cremorne Hayden Orpheum Picture Palace (☎ 9908 4344, 308 Miliary Rd, Cremorne) At the junction of Military and Cremorne Rds, this is a fabulous Art Deco gem with an original organ and a bar.

Greater Union (☎ 9969 1988, 9 Spit Rd, Mosman) On Mosman's busy main drag, this cinema plays popular current releases.

Manly Twin Cinemas (☎ 9977 0644, 43 East Esplanade, Manly) **Map 12** This is your standard local cinema – it does the job without all the fancy trappings of some new cinemas, and ticket prices can be surprisingly low.

Inner West

Dendy (☎ 9550 5699, 261 King St, Newtown) This cinema is handy for those wishing to see films close by, saving a trip into town.

Valhalla (☎ 9660 8050, fax 9660 7220, 166 Glebe Point Rd, Glebe) **Map 9** The Valhalla has been an on-again, off-again cinema in the last few years, but it's still going, although it now gears itself to live performance, too.

Eastern Suburbs

Ritz Theatre (☎ 9611 4811, 43 St Paul's St, Randwick) This restored Art Deco cinema shows mainstream films at good prices. It's close to Coogee on bus Nos 373 and 314.

Fox Studios (☎ 9383 4000, Moore Park, Paddington) **Map 8** This new film and entertainment complex has a whopping 16 Hoyts cinemas. There are 12 for mainstream films and four for specialist and art-house screenings.

Academy Twin Cinema (☎ 9361 4453, 3a Oxford St, Paddington) **Map 8** This is a small cinema with art-house and independent offerings.

Verona Cinema (☎ 9360 6099, Upstairs, 17 Oxford St, Paddington) **Map 8** This cinema also has an excellent cafe and bar, with views over Oxford St.

Govinda's Movie Room (☎ 9380 5155, 112 Darlinghurst Rd, Darlinghurst) **Map 6** Open from 6pm, movies 7.30pm & 9.30pm. Ticket $15.90. South of Kings Cross, the cushioned Movie Room above Govinda's restaurant shows mainstream blockbusters, art-house fare and old favourites. The price includes an all-you-can-eat smorgasbord at Govinda's. See also Govinda's entry in the Darlinghurst & East Sydney Restaurants section in the Places to Eat chapter.

Chauvel Cinema (☎ 9361 5398, Cnr Oxford St & Oatley Rd, Paddington) **Map 8** This cinema, associated with the Australian Film Institute (AFI), plays quality releases, new and old, and also has themed festivals (Jewish, Queer etc).

Moonlight Cinema (☎ 1900 933 899, 13 61 00 for bookings, Centennial Park) **Map 8** Centennial Park is the outdoor venue for this excellent twilight cinema, which has screenings of popular films and classics during summer (around November to early March), after sundown.

Flickerfest (☎ 9365 6877, Bondi Pavilion, Bondi Beach) **Map 11** This is a well-regarded touring international short-film festival and competition held at the Bondi Pavilion in early January. See also Free Entertainment earlier in this chapter for information on Tropfest.

PERFORMING ARTS

Sydney Opera House (SOH; ☎ 9250 7777, Bennelong Point) **Map 5** The SOH is the performing arts centre of Sydney. Opera Australia, the Australian Ballet, Sydney Symphony Orchestra, Sydney Philharmonia Choirs, Musica Viva Australia and the Sydney Theatre Company (STC) stage regular performances here. See also Arts in the Facts about Sydney chapter.

For more information on companies' programs contact:

Australian Ballet (☎ 9252 5500,
  W www.australianballet.com.au) 18 Hickson Rd, The Rocks
Opera Australia (☎ 9699 1099,
  W www.opera-australia.org.au) 480 Elizabeth St, Surry Hills
Musica Viva Australia (☎ 8394 6666,
  W www.mva.org.au) 120 Chalmers St, Surry Hills
Sydney Dance Company (☎ 9221 4811,
  W www.sydneydance.com.au) Pier 4, Hickson Rd, Walsh Bay
Sydney Philharmonia Choirs (☎ 9251 2024,
  W www.sydneyphilharmonia.com.au) Pier 4, Hickson Rd, Walsh Bay
Sydney Symphony Orchestra (☎ 9334 4644,
  W www.sso.com.au) Level 5, 52 William St, East Sydney

A recent addition to the performance spaces in Sydney has been the *City Recital Hall (box office, ☎ 8256 2222, W www.cityrecitalhall .com, Angel Pl)* **Map 5** This is a purpose-built 1200-seat venue that hosts live music performances.

THEATRE

Sydney may not have a distinct theatre district, but it has numerous theatres and a vigorous calendar of productions. These range from Broadway and West End shows at mainstream theatres to experimental theatre at smaller inner-suburban venues. Most tickets cost from $25 to $60.

Sydney Opera House (box office ☎ 9250 7777, Bennelong Point) **Map 5** The SOH has three main theatres: the *Drama Theatre* regularly puts on plays by the STC; the *Playhouse* offers a range from Aboriginal performances to Shakespeare; the *Studio* venue hosts interesting contemporary arts and musical events.

Wharf Theatre (☎ 9250 1700, Pier 4, Hickson Rd, Walsh Bay) **Map 5** The STC, the city's top theatre company, has its own venue here, as does the Australian Theatre for Young People (ATYP) and the Bangarra Dance Theatre.

Capitol Theatre (☎ 9320 5000, 17 Campbell St, Haymarket) **Map 5** Lavishly restored after being saved from demolition, this theatre is home to big-name concerts and musicals.

Her Majesty's Theatre (☎ 9212 3411, 107 Quay St) **Map 8** This 1970s concrete blob houses mainstream theatrical fare, although at the time of research it appeared to be closed for renovations.

Theatre Royal (☎ 9224 8444, MLC Centre, King St) **Map 5** This theatre generally hosts big musicals and big names, with over 1100 seats. Recent refurbishments should take it out of the 1970s.

State Theatre (☎ 9373 6655, 49 Market St) **Map 5** A sight in itself is the lush and opulent State Theatre between Pitt and George Sts – they don't make them like this any more!

Ensemble Theatre (box office ☎ 9929 0644, W www.ensemble.com.au, 78 Mc Dougall St, Kirribilli) **Map 3** On the North Shore, the small Ensemble Theatre presents mainstream theatre, generally with well-known Australian actors, in a great setting on the waterfront at Careening Cove, a few blocks from Milsons Point station.

National Institute of Dramatic Art (NIDA; ☎ 9697 7600, 215 Anzac Pde, Kensington) NIDA, near the University of NSW, regularly stages excellent productions by its

ENTERTAINMENT

students. Previous graduates include Geoffrey Rush, Mel Gibson, Judy Davis and Cate Blanchett.

Footbridge Theatre *(☎ 9692 9955, University of Sydney, Parramatta Rd, Glebe)* **Map 9** This 700-seat venue often has drama, dance and musical performances and some truly woeful university revues.

Seymour Theatre Centre *(☎ 9351 7940, Cnr Cleveland St & City Rd, Chippendale)* **Map 9** This centre houses three theatres offering a variety of performances (drama, music etc) year-round.

Belvoir St Theatre *(☎ 9699 3444, 25 Belvoir St, Surry Hills)* **Map 8** This theatre is something of a home for original and often experimental Australian theatre. The excellent resident production company is known as Company B.

Stables Theatre *(☎ 9361 3817, 10 Nimrod St, Kings Cross)* **Map 7** Home of the Griffin Theatre company, this place often stages Australian works and hosts the occasional Sunday night cabaret.

New Theatre *(☎ 9519 3403, 542 King St, Newtown)* Although it has been around since the 1930s, the nonprofessional New Theatre produces some cutting-edge drama in addition to more-traditional pieces.

SPECTATOR SPORTS
You'll find vocal crowds and world-class athletes in action on just about every weekend of the year.

Football
The football season runs through autumn and winter (March to September).

Sydney is one of the world capitals of rugby league. The main competition, run by the National Rugby League, is the Telstra Premiership, which includes interstate sides.

The other big rugby league series (all three games of it annually) is the State of Origin, played in Sydney and Brisbane. The NSW versus Queensland game generates a lot of passion.

Rugby union is known as 'the running game' and has a reputation for attracting a more upper-crust following than rugby league. The Wallabies (the Australian rugby

Aboriginal Performance

Dance and song have always played an important part in the culture of Australia's indigenous peoples (both Torres Strait Islanders and Aborigines) and the stories expressed through these activities draw upon ancient myths and spiritual links with the land.

Aboriginal traditional dance is sometimes performed by the community-oriented **Aboriginal Dance Theatre Redfern** *(☎ 9699 2171, 88 Renwick St, Redfern)* **Map 8**, which has been operating for over 20 years, and also runs courses and workshops. Call to see if any performances or tours are planned.

The acclaimed **Bangarra Dance Theatre** *(☎ 9251 5333, Pier 4, Hickson Rd, Walsh Bay)* **Map 5** regularly performs indigenous song and dance, fusing ancient and modern styles. It's one of Australia's premier dance companies, and performances are definitely worth catching.

The **National Aboriginal and Islander Skills Development Association** *(Naisda; ☎ 9252 0199, ⓦ www.naisda.com.au, 3 Cumberland St, The Rocks)* **Map 5** is an indigenous performing arts college that presents regular performances at the Sydney Opera House and its college centre in The Rocks, including dance, song and spoken word.

At Harbourside in Darling Harbour, **Gavala** *(☎ 9212 7232)* **Map 5** presents Aboriginal dancers who perform traditional dances, play didgeridoos and recount stories, although you need to call and book for a group to see this. There's also a free Aboriginal dance performance at the Art Gallery of NSW, at noon Tuesday to Saturday.

union team) are world-beaters. You can occasionally see them in action against international teams.

Australian Rules football is a unique, exciting sport run by the Australian Football League (AFL). The Sydney Swans are Sydney's team, although North Melbourne's Kangaroos also play 'home' games at the Sydney Cricket Ground (SCG).

AFL is generally played at the SCG, and rugby league and union are played at various suburban venues as well as the following:

Sydney Football Stadium (SFS; Map 8; ☎ 9360 6601, for match information ☎ 1900 963 133) Driver Ave, Moore Park
Sydney Cricket Ground (Map 8; ☎ 9360 6601, for match information ☎ 1900 963 133) Driver Ave, Moore Park
Stadium Australia (☎ 8765 2000) Olympic Blvd, Homebush Bay

Tickets to most games start at about $23.

Soccer is gaining in popularity, thanks in part to the success of the national team and to the high profile of some Aussies playing overseas. The national league is only semiprofessional and games attract a relatively small following. In the past, most clubs were ethnically based, but they now appeal to the broader community. As well as at Stadium Australia, games are played at various grounds. For information, contact Soccer Australia (☎ 9267 0799, W www.socceraustralia.com.au), at 3/447 Kent St, Sydney.

Cricket
The SCG (☎ 9360 6601, for match information ☎ 1900 963 133, Driver Ave, Moore Park) **Map 8** This is the venue for sparsely attended Pura Cup (interstate) matches, well-attended test (international) matches and sell-out World Series Cup (one-day, international) matches. Local district games are also played here. The cricket season in Australia is from October to March.

Tennis
White City (☎ 9360 4113, 30 Alma St, Paddington) **Map 8** The grass courts here are home to Tennis NSW and the NSW Open, a tournament that takes place in January and often sees big names preparing for the Australian Open, which is held in Melbourne.

Basketball
Australia's basketball league has all the razzamatazz of US pro basketball (and quite a few US players as well) and is very popular with children and teenagers. The basketball season runs from April to November and games are played on weekends at the Sydney Entertainment Centre. The teams in Sydney are the Kings (men) and the Flames (women). Call the NSW Basketball Association (☎ 9746 2969) for details.

Netball
Netball doesn't have as high a profile as basketball in Australia, but it's wildly popular and the Australian national team is often ranked as the best in the world. The Sydney Swifts and the Sydney University Sandpipers are the city's representatives in the Commonwealth Bank Trophy.

The netball season runs from April to August. You can get information about where to see matches from Netball Australia (☎ 9633 2533, W www.netball.asn.au), at 19–21 Wentworth St, Parramatta.

Surf Life Saving Carnivals
The volunteer surf life-saver is one of Australia's icons. Australia was one of the first places in the world to have surf life-saving clubs. Despite the macho image often associated with life saving, many surf life-savers are female. You can see life-savers in action each summer at surf carnivals held all along the coast. Check at a local surf life-saving club for dates or contact Surf Life Saving NSW (☎ 9984 7188, W www.surflifesaving.com.au), PO Box 430, Narrabeen NSW.

Yachting
On weekends, hundreds of yachts weave around ferries and ships on Sydney Harbour. Many are racing, and the most spectacular are the speedy 18-footers. The 18-footer races carry big prize money and the boats are covered in sponsors' logos, like racing cars. The 18-footer racing season runs from mid-September to late March.

Sydney Flying Squadron (☎ 9955 8350, 76 McDougall St, Milsons Point) **Map 3** The oldest and largest 18-footer club is the Sydney Flying Squadron. You can catch a ferry from there to watch skiff racing from

2pm to 4pm on Saturday between October and April, and costs $12/8 adult/child.

The greatest yachting event on Sydney Harbour is the Boxing Day (26 December) start of the Sydney to Hobart Yacht Race. The harbour is crammed with competitors, media boats and a huge spectator fleet. Special ferries are scheduled by Sydney Ferries to follow the boats; call the Infoline ☎ 13 15 00 in November to find out when tickets go on sale.

Shopping

While Australia excels at myriad kitsch souvenirs involving koalas, boomerangs and the Opera House, you *can* find mementoes of your time in Australia that won't cause embarrassment. Check that your souvenir was actually made in Australia, and make sure that you'll be allowed to leave the country with it, as customs regulations are strict. Check the Customs section in the Facts for the Visitor chapter for more details.

WHAT TO BUY
Aboriginal Art
It's only in the last few decades that Aboriginal artists have begun using Western materials like canvas and acrylic paints. These works have quickly gained wide appreciation. The paintings depict traditional stories and ceremonial designs, and some have particular spiritual significance.

Much of the Aboriginal art available in Sydney, especially traditional styles, comes from other areas of Australia, and because it captures the essence of the Australian outback, it makes a wonderful reminder of a trip to Australia.

The best works range in price from $500 to $1500, but among the cheaper artworks on sale are prints, baskets, small carvings and beautiful screen-printed T-shirts produced by Aboriginal craft cooperatives. Although there are numerous commercial rip-offs, Sydney has some reputable outlets selling Aboriginal art and crafts, which pay the artists properly. It's worth shopping around and paying a few dollars more for the real thing.

A large range of traditional and contemporary Aboriginal art is available from several outlets.

Aboriginal Art Shop (☎ 9247 4344, Upper Concourse, Sydney Opera House) **Map 5** There's a good selection of Aboriginal art here as well as pieces from Papua New Guinea and quality gift items.

Aboriginal & Tribal Art Centre (☎ 9247 9625, 117 George St, The Rocks) **Map 5** Opposite the MCA, this gallery has great Aboriginal art and can organise overseas packing and postage.

Australia's Northern Territory & Outback Centre (☎ 9283 7477, Shop 28, Darling Walk, 1/25 Harbour St, Darling Harbour) **Map 5** This tourist centre has a good range of authentic Aboriginal products, such as boomerangs and didgeridoos.

Boomalli Aboriginal Artists Co-operative (☎ 9698 2047, 191 Parramatta Rd, Annandale) With a range of artists working through this cooperative, there's an interesting range of style and techniques on show.

Coo-ee Aboriginal Art Gallery (☎ 9332 1544, 98 Oxford St, Paddington) **Map 8** This two-storey shop has handmade souvenirs (such as didgeridoos, boomerangs, clothing, fabric and jewellery) and artworks, and shipping can be arranged for overseas buyers.

Gavala Art Shop & Cultural Centre (☎ 9212 7232, Harbourside, Darling Harbour) **Map 5** With a nice gallery and retail store, Gavala is a popular attraction with many visitors to Darling Harbour.

Hogarth Galleries Aboriginal Art Centre (☎ 9360 6839, 7 Walker Lane, Paddington) **Map 8** Open 11am-5pm Tues-Sat. Established in 1973, this gallery has monthly exhibitions.

Balarinji, an Aboriginal clothing company that combines Aboriginal art with modern graphic design, has a store at the airport (☎ 9700 7322), and a design studio in Customs House (☎ 9252 0047). Aboriginal athlete (and gold medallist at the 2000 Olympics) Cathy Freeman promotes its clothing, and its distinctive, brightly coloured work has adorned the bodies of two Qantas 747s.

Australiana
The term 'Australiana' describes the things you buy as gifts for the folks back home or to remember your visit by, and which are supposedly representative of Australia. Arts, crafts, T-shirts, designer clothing and

bush gear are sold practically everywhere. Apart from the usual kitsch there's much that's of high quality, with prices to match, though you can pick up the odd bargain. Check out the huge range in The Rocks and Darling Harbour to see what's available, then compare prices in other areas.

For Australian-made, environmentally-friendly souvenirs we recommend the first two places. Both have T-shirts, posters and other good-quality souvenirs.

Wilderness Society Shop (☎ 9233 4674, *1st floor, Centrepoint*) **Map 5** In the shop-till-you-drop precinct, this store will remind you that there are more interesting things to own than a new pair of shoes.

Australian Conservation Foundation Shop (*ACF;* ☎ 9247 4754, *33 George St, The Rocks*) **Map 5** This friendly shop has heaps of environmentally-friendly gift ideas.

Australian Geographic (☎ 9212 6539, *Shop 428, Harbourside, Darling Harbour;* ☎ 9231 5055, *Shop 34, Centrepoint, Cnr Pitt & Market Sts;* ☎ 9221 8299, *Sydney Arcade, George St*) **Map 5** This company has three stores that are full of Australian memorabilia and more than a few wacky items.

Gardens Shop (☎ 9231 8125, *Royal Botanic Gardens Visitors Centre*) **Map 5** This shop has souvenirs, posters, and books on Australian flora.

The Ken Done Gallery (☎ 9247 2740, *1 Hickson Rd, The Rocks*) **Map 5** Poster prints and silkscreen prints by Sydney artist Ken Done are available from his gallery.

The Australian Wine Centre (☎ 9247 2755, *Goldfields House, 1 Alfred St*) **Map 5** Shop open 9.30am-6.30pm Mon-Sat, 11am-5pm Sun; wine bar open 9.30am-6.30pm Mon-Thur, 9.30am-7pm Fri. Downstairs in Goldfields House, behind Circular Quay, this centre has wines from every Australian wine-growing region. It will package and send wine overseas.

Aussie Clothing The must-buy Aussie item (for many tourists and Aussies alike) is an Akubra, a brand of the classic stockman's hat. These are sold everywhere tourists converge, but if you want good advice and the right size, try some of these shops.

Strand Hatters (☎ 9231 6884, *8 Strand Arcade, Pitt St Mall*) **Map 5** This excellent shop sells a variety of hats, none very cheap, but the staff are friendly and knowledgable.

RM Williams (☎ 9262 2228, *389 George St*) **Map 5** This is an established manufacturer and distributor of Aussie outdoor gear, such as Driza-bones (oilskin riding coats), elastic-sided boots and moleskin trousers.

Thomas Cook Boot & Clothing Company (☎ 9232 3334, *129 Pitt St*) **Map 5** This shop sells a range of Aussie outdoor clothing and accessories. There's also an outlet at 790 George St, near Central station.

Many companies that produce surfing equipment also make a range of beach clothing (see Outdoor Gear later).

Opals The opal is Australia's national gemstone, and opals and opal jewellery are popular souvenirs. Precious opal exhibits a play of colour. It comes in several varieties, including jelly (transparent opal with little colour), crystal (jelly with more colour), white, milky (somewhere between crystal and white) and black (transparent to opaque opal with a dark background colour). Potch is opal without a play of colour and hence has no value.

Prices can be astronomical; over $2000 a carat or $3000 for a black opal, but you can pay as little as $50 for a stone of lower quality. The price depends on the flaws and the brilliance of colour.

Much less expensive are nonsolid opals. Doublets are precious opals stuck (by a jeweller) to a potch of nonprecious opal. Domed doublets are worth more than flat doublets because the section of precious opal is thicker. Triplets are flat doublets with a dome of glass or quartz crystal stuck on top, protecting and magnifying the opal. Many Sydney jewellers and duty-free shops sell opals, especially in The Rocks or the Queen Victoria Building (QVB Map 5). Have a look in *Opal Fields* (☎ 9247 6800, *190 George St;* ☎ 9264 6660, *Shop 19, QVB*), *Opal Minded* (☎ 9247 9885, *36-64 George St*), or *Opal Beauty* (☎ 9241 4050, *22 Argyle St, Rocks Centre;* ☎ 9264 8772, *Shop 39, QVB*).

Fashion

Oxford St is the perfect place to rack up some serious credit-card bills: from the Centennial Park end to the city, there are a string of Australian designer stores, including the following:

Zimmermann (☎ 9360 5769, 24 Oxford St, Woollahra) **Map 8** This tiny shop is responsible for half the eye-catching swimsuits on Bondi Beach, and is deservedly popular.

Scanlan & Theodore (☎ 9361 6722, 443 Oxford St, Paddington) **Map 8** A smart-looking, airy shop with interesting, beautifully-made clothes from one of Australia's best fashion houses.

Saba for Men (☎ 9331 2685, 270 Oxford St) **Map 8** This is the place to go for smart, fashionable, yet affordable men's clothing.

Collette Dinnigan (☎ 9360 6691, 33 William St, Paddington) **Map 8** Stunningly beautiful clothing that will have you both drooling and sweating. Dinnigan is one of Australia's most successful designers internationally, and this lost-boudoir of a shop shows why.

The Corner Shop (☎ 9380 9828, 43 William St, Paddington) **Map 8** This treasure-trove of a boutique stocks a mix of excellent second-hand clothes for women and the sort of designer imports that send Australia's foreign debt soaring. The handbags look almost edible.

For funky streetwear and slightly less daunting price-tags, try the Oxford St end of Crown St.

Wheels & Doll Baby (☎ 9361 3286, 259 Crown St) **Map 8** If you're given 10 minutes to come up with an outfit that'll have others believing you're the lost member of Aerosmith/The Velvet Underground/Blondie, then look no further.

Drag Bag (☎ 9380 8222, upstairs, 185 Oxford St) **Map 8** If you want to get *really* dressed up, on the corner of Taylor Square, Drag Bag sells sparkly glamwear for the gay crowd, including wigs, shoes, jewellery and make-up. It also does full make-overs (guys and girls).

For quirky threads from Asian designers, there are scores of excellent little *boutiques* in the numerous shopping arcades in and around Chinatown.

Newtown's King St is full of second-hand clothing stores, including the following:

Chiconomy (☎ 9557 4072, 399 King St, Newtown) This place has great second-hand gear for everyday use and that special one-off party outfit.

Scraggs House of Fashion (☎ 9550 4654, 551e King St, Newtown) Scraggs has some excellent 1970s fashions on offer, and great frocks from the last 50 years or so.

Cheap *factory outlets* and *seconds stores* abound both in Redfern, on the corner of Regent and Redfern Sts, and in western Surry Hills (from Albion St, head south towards Redfern). Here you'll find everything from bikinis to ball gowns – although the emphasis is on utilitarian clothing, underwear and footwear, rather than on cutting-edge fashion.

Antiques

Look for early Australian colonial furniture made from cedar or Huon pine; Australian silver jewellery; ceramics, either early factory pieces or studio pieces (especially anything by the Boyd family); glassware, such as Carnival glass; and Australiana collectables and bric-a-brac, such as old signs, tins, bottles etc – anything featuring the Opera House, Harbour Bridge or kookaburras.

Updated annually, *Carter's Price Guide to Antiques in Australia* is an excellent price reference. Also available is the free, large-format quarterly magazine *Antiques in New South Wales*.

Queen St in Woollahra is the main centre for antiques in Sydney.

Woollahra Antiques Centre (☎ 9327 8840, 160 Oxford St) **Map 8** Opposite the eastern end of Centennial Park, this is an agglomeration of 50 shops.

Sydney Antique Centre (☎ 9361 3244, 531 South Dowling St, Surry Hills) **Map 8** Open 10am-6pm. This centre has dozens of shops and stalls stocking antique everything, including the kitchen sink.

Craft & Design

You'll find many shops and galleries displaying crafts by local artists. The local craft scene is especially strong in the fields of ceramics, silver jewellery and stained glass.

Society of Arts & Crafts of NSW (☎ 9241 1673, Metcalfe Arcade, 80-84 George St) **Map 5** To see some of the best arts and crafts, drop in here. It houses a gallery and a sales outlet.

Australian Craftworks (☎ 9247 7156, 127 George St) **Map 5** In the old police station, this craft centre is worth checking out.

Cohav (☎ 9557 1218, 371 King St, Newtown) This shop crafts and sells lovely handmade silver jewellery set with semi-precious stones.

Puppet Shop at The Rocks (☎ 9247 9137, 77 George St, The Rocks) From the ceiling of this wonderful shop dangles all manner of stringed things and bizarre, jointed toys. Kids love this shop, and grown-ups do, too.

Dinosaur Designs (☎ 9223 2953, Shop 77, Strand Arcade) **Map 5** Dinosaur Designs is noted for its excellent range of inexpensive jewellery and homewares made from jewel-coloured resins. It also sells good silver jewellery. Other outlets are at 339 Oxford St, Paddington (☎ 9361 3776) **Map 8** and at Argyle Stores, 18–24 Argyle St, The Rocks (☎ 9251 5500) **Map 5**.

Outdoor Gear

Australians are among the world's keenest travellers, so it's no surprise that Sydney's outdoor and adventure shops carry an excellent range of both Australian-made and imported gear. In many cases, local products are cheaper than imports, and of equal quality.

There's a good selection of shops on Kent St, near Bathurst St and the YHA Membership & Travel Centre. Among the Australian firms here are three shops worth visiting.

Kathmandu (☎ 9261 8901, Cnr Bathurst & Kent Sts) **Map 5** With backpacks and trekking gear for all levels, this is a decent place to stock up on equipment.

Paddy Pallin (☎ 9264 2685, 507 Kent St) **Map 5** With skiing and camping gear on offer and knowledgeable staff, this shop is a good choice for outdoor enthusiasts.

Mountain Designs (☎ 9267 3822, Ⓦ *www.mountaindesigns.com, 499 Kent St)* **Map 5** This busy shop has a good range of backpacks and sleeping bags and other mountaineering equipment.

It's also worth checking out 'disposal' stores (listed in the *Yellow Pages*) which handle ex-army gear.

Australia produces some of the world's best surfing equipment; there are shops selling it at major surf beaches. See Surfing under Activities in the Things to See & Do chapter.

Mambo Friendship Store (☎ 9331 8034, Verona Cinema complex, 17 Oxford St, Paddington) **Map 8** Mambo is noted for producing quirky, off-the-wall designs that also prove to be hard-wearing and good value. The casual shirts of the Australian Olympic team were designed by popular Mambo designer and artist Reg Mombasa. To see the complete range of goodies (which also includes watches and backpacks), visit Mambo in Paddington, or at 80 Campbell Pde, Bondi (☎ 9365 2255) **Map 11**.

Hot Tuna (☎ 9361 5049, 180 Oxford St, Paddington) **Map 8** Hot Tuna has its own emporium stacked with gear, which includes bikinis, boardshorts, rashies (rash vests) and bags.

Other manufacturers include Billabong, Piping Hot, Hot Buttered and Rip Curl (excellent for wetsuits), whose products are available from surf shops and department stores. See also 'Surfing Equipment & Supplies – Retail' in the *Yellow Pages*.

Duty-Free

Prices for duty-free shopping in Sydney compare favourably with the rest of the world. Remember that a duty-free item may not have had much duty on it originally and might be cheaper in an ordinary store. Look around before buying. Duty-free shops abound in the city, and include:

City International Duty Free (☎ 9232 1555, 88 Pitt St) **Map 5**
Downtown Duty Free (☎ 9241 5844, 22 Pitt St) **Map 5**

Harbourside Duty Free (☎ *9283 8900, 249 Pitt St)* **Map 5**
DFS Galleria (☎ *1800 789 780, 155 George St)* **Map 5**

Music
Big stores selling recorded music include *HMV* and *Sanity*, with branches in the city and throughout the suburbs. Specialist music stores include:
The ABC Shop (☎ *9333 1635, Shop 48, QVB)* **Map 5** This shop is the national broadcaster's retail outlet. It sells CDs and cassettes associated with its programming.

For dance and electronic music, Oxford St is the place to go.
Central Station (☎ *9361 5222, 46 Oxford St, Darlinghurst)* **Map 5** With an enormous range of dance music on offer, you can create any mood you'd care to orchestrate here.
Reachin' Records (☎ *9380 5378, 80 Oxford St, Darlinghurst)* **Map 8** This record store is on the corner of Crown and Oxford Sts and was started by one of Sydney's best DJs, the highly regarded Sugar Ray.
Good Groove (☎ *9331 2942, 350 Crown St, Surry Hills)* **Map 8** This is a very funky little record shop, with an eclectic offering and cool staff.
Red Eye Records (☎ *9299 4233, 66 King St)* **Map 5** This is a huge store stocking music of almost every genre, from blues and jazz to world music, funk, country and pop. The staff have good import connections, and are adept at hunting down hard-to-find releases.

For others see the *Yellow Pages* under 'Compact Discs, Records & Tapes'.

Books
Dymocks (☎ *9235 0155, 424-30 George St)* **Map 5** Open 9am-6.30pm Mon-Wed & Fri, 9am-9pm Thurs, 9am-6pm Sat, 10am-5pm Sun. Dymocks' main store is enormous, with a huge range of stock and a cafe. Dymocks has several other city stores and it's great for finding textbooks for courses.
Angus & Robertson (☎ *9235 1188, Imperial Arcade, 168 Pitt St)* **Map 5** Under

renovation at the time of research, this monster chain makes a point of stocking all of the titles chosen for Oprah's book club (and lots of Lonely Planet titles), if that's what turns you on.

There are plenty of bookshops catering to more specialised tastes.
The Travel Bookshop (☎ *9261 8200, Shop 3, 175 Liverpool St)* **Map 5** Open 9am-5pm Mon-Fri, 10am-5pm Sat. This is a good shop specialising in travel books and maps.
Abbey's Bookshop (☎ *9264 3111, 131 York St)* **Map 5** Open 8.30am-7pm Mon-Wed & Fri, 8.30am-9pm Thurs, 9am-5pm Sat, 10am-5pm Sun. The friendly Abbey's Bookshop, opposite the QVB, has a wide range of literature, including many foreign-language titles.

Oxford St (Maps 5 & 8) has a handful of excellent bookshops.
The Bookshop Darlinghurst (☎ *9331 1103, 207 Oxford St)* **Map 8** Open 9.30am-11pm Mon-Wed, 9.30am-midnight Thur-Sat & 11am-midnight Sun. This small bookshop specialises in gay and lesbian literature.
Ariel (☎ *9332 4581, 42-4 Oxford St, Paddington)* **Map 8** Open 9am-midnight. Ariel focuses on art and design, and provides seating for comfortable browsing.
Berkelouw's Books (☎ *9360 3200, 19 Oxford St, Paddington)* **Map 8** Open 10am-midnight. Berkelouw's specialises in second-hand and antique books, has a good travel section and the added attraction of a small cafe.

Other good bookshops include:
Gleebooks (☎ *9660 2333, 49 Glebe Point Rd, Glebe; ☎ 9552 2526, 189 Glebe Point Rd, Glebe)* **Map 9** Open 8am-9pm. Gleebooks at the 49 Glebe Point Rd outlet is worth checking out for new books, as is its other outlet, at No 189, for second-hand and children's books (open 10am-9pm).
Pentimento (☎ *9810 0707, fax 9810 3094, e pentimento@bigpond.com.au, 275 Darling St, Balmain)* Open 10am-10pm Mon-Sat, 11am-10pm Sun. Pentimento is a lovely Balmain bookshop with a great range of art/design books and well-picked fiction.

Gould's Book Arcade (☎ 9519 8947, 32 King St, Newtown) This is easily the largest bookshop in Newtown; it's jam-packed, from wall to wall and floor to ceiling, and Bob is quite a character.

Lesley McKay's Bookshop (☎ 9327 1354, fax 9327 7347, 346 New South Head Rd, Double Bay) Open 9am-10pm Mon-Sat, 10am-10pm Sun. This is one of Sydney's best bookshops, with an excellent range of fiction, nonfiction and hardcover titles. The great reputation of the staff here is well deserved. There's also a children's bookshop next door at No 344, and a smaller branch on the corner of Queen and Moncur Sts, Woollahra.

Nicholas Pounder (☎ 9328 7410, 1st floor, 346 New South Head Rd, Double Bay) Nicholas is one of Sydney's best-known second-hand booksellers, and has tomes on more strange topics than you knew existed, as well as first editions and rarities.

WHERE TO SHOP

The most fashionable shops tend to be around Oxford St, which, in Paddington east of the Royal Women's Hospital, is packed with boutique clothing stores. There are several groovy clothes shops wedged between the cafes and restaurants at the Oxford St end of Crown St.

Newtown's King St is popular for grunge shopping, alternative-lifestyle fashions, creative furnishings and second-hand books and clothes. Bondi is a good place to look for a swimsuit or beach fashions.

If you're looking for bargains, there are several factory clothing outlets and seconds shops in Redfern and in Surry Hill's southwest.

Military Rd, between Neutral Bay and Mosman, is one long stretch of shops, catering to the surrounding affluent suburbs.

Shopping Centres

Queen Victoria Building (QVB; ☎ *9264 1955, 455 George St)* **Map 5** The magnificent QVB, with dozens of shops on four levels, is the city's most beautiful shopping centre. You'll find *Jag*, *Guess*, *Osh Kosh*, *Jigsaw*, *Crabtree & Evelyn*, *Portmans*, *Country*

Road, *Esprit* and *Oroton* here, among others. The lower level, which connects to Town Hall station, also has food bars, shoe repair shops, drycleaners and newsagents to service the rushing commuters.

Strand Arcade (☎ 9232 4199, Pitt St Mall) **Map 5** Several leading Australian fashion designers and craftspeople have shops in the impressive, carefully restored Strand Arcade. Built in 1892, it's between Pitt St Mall and George St. Designer boutiques include *Dinosaur Designs*, *Third Millennium*, *Wayne Cooper*, *Lili*, *Von Troska*, *Black Vanity*, *Rox* and *Love & Hatred*. Other city arcades include the *Royal*, beneath the Hilton Hotel, the *Imperial*, connecting Pitt St Mall and Castlereagh St.

The Galeries Victoria (☎ 9286 3742, 500 George St) **Map 5** Across the road from the QVB, this place has lots of boutiques, including a great *Mooks* store. You can also cut through George St to Pitt St through here.

Centrepoint Shopping Centre (☎ 9231 1000, Cnr Pitt & Market Sts) **Map 5** Centrepoint, beside the Imperial Arcade and beneath AMP Tower, has four storeys of fashion and jewellery shops. You can cut through Pitt St to Castlereagh St through here, and there are also connecting above-ground walkways with David Jones and Grace Bros.

Nearby is the seven-storey *Skygarden* **Map 5**, which has a number of art galleries and shops. At the renovated *MLC Centre*, on the corner of King and Castlereagh Sts, you'll find some of the world's top names in fashion and accessories.

The Argyle Stores (☎ 9251 4800, 18-24 Argyle St, The Rocks) **Map 5** is a huge shopping area, as is *The Rocks Centre*, on the corner of Playfair and Argyle Sts. *Harbourside* at Darling Harbour has many stores on its two floors.

Broadway Shopping Centre (☎ 9213 3333, Cnr Broadway & Bay St, Glebe) **Map 9** This centre is in the old Grace Bros buildings and has dozens of shops, a food court, a Hoyts cinema complex and two 24-hour supermarkets.

The biggest shopping centre in North Sydney is *Greenwood Plaza* **Map 2**, above North Sydney station.

Department Stores

Gowings (☎ 9287 6394, 45 Market St)
Map 5 Gowings is Sydney's oldest (1868)
department store. Although it's a men's
outfitters, a lot of women shop here for
well-priced basics like Bonds T-shirts,
Blundstone boots and flannelette pyjamas.
It's on the corner of Market and George Sts.

*Grace Bros (☎ 9238 9111, 1800 626 611,
436 George St)* **Map 5** This seven-level
Grace Bros is one of Sydney's largest stores
and sells just about everything. Grace Bros
also has suburban stores around Sydney.

*David Jones (☎ 9266 5544, Cnr Elizabeth
& Market Sts)* **Map 5** Considered the city's
premier department store, with two locations
on Market St, it's a good place to look for top-
quality goods. The one on the corner of
Castlereagh and Market Sts has menswear,
electrical goods and a food hall with luxury
food items. The Elizabeth St store sells
women's and children's goods. David Jones
also has suburban stores around Sydney.

Markets

Sydney's markets offer a range of goods, to
suit a variety of tastes. While some are quite
touristy, there are also a few where you'll
feel as though you're in a groovy, open-air
boutique at sale time.

*Paddington Village Bazaar (☎ 9331
2646, St John's Church, 395 Oxford St)*
Map 8 Open 10am-4.30pm Sat. One of

Paddington Village Bazaar, held every Saturday
morning

Sydney's most popular markets, it offers
everything from vintage clothing and funky
designer fashions, to jewellery, massage,
food and holistic treatments. More unusual
wares include temporary henna-tattoos, but-
terflies under glass, and hammocks. Don't
even think about finding a place to park –
this is one for public transport.

*Paddy's Markets (☎ 1300 361 589, Cnr
Hay & Thomas Sts)* **Map 8** Open 9am-
4.30pm Sat & Sun. There are two Paddy's
Markets. The one on the corner of Hay and
Thomas Sts in Haymarket, in the heart of
Chinatown, is a Sydney institution where
you'll find the usual market fare at rock-
bottom prices, alongside less predictable
wares such as wigs, board games, cheap
cosmetics, mobile phones and live budgies.
There's also a good selection of fresh fruit,
vegetables and seafood. Paddy's Market in
Flemington, on Parramatta Rd near Sydney
Olympic Park, operates (along with the
huge Sydney fruit and vegetable market) on
Friday and Sunday.

*Craft market (☎ 9255 1717, George St,
The Rocks)* **Map 5** Open 10am-5pm Sat &
Sun. At the top end of George St, under the
bridge, this market is closed to traffic. A
little on the touristy 'Australiana' side, it's
still good for a browse – wares include jewellery, antiques, souvenirs, fossils, gems,
crystals, retro postcards, musical instru-
ments and a good selection of juggling
paraphernalia.

*Balmain Markets (☎ 0418 765 736, St
Andrew's Church, 223 Darling St)* **Map 4**
Open 8.30am-4pm Sat. This is a really good
local market, offering stuff like handmade
candles, kids' clothing and essential oils,
and it's a great spot to hunt out fashion
accessories.

*Glebe's weekend market (☎ 4237 7499,
Glebe Public School, Cnr Glebe Point Rd &
Derby Pl)* **Map 9** Open 10am-4pm Sat. This
market has an assortment of books, clothing, ceramics, glassware, leather goods,
herbal teas, oddities and curios. The crowds
can be heavy.

*Bondi Beach Market (☎ 9315 8988,
Bondi Beach Public School, Cnr Campbell
Pde & Warners Ave)* **Map 11** Open 9am-

4pm Sun. At the northern end of Campbell Pde, this market is good for hip clothing, swimwear, jewellery, furniture, knick-knacks, bric-a-brac and beautiful-people watching.

Kirribilli Markets (☎ *9922 4428, Bradfield Park North, Milsons Point)* **Map 3** Open 7am-3pm 4th Sat every month. This popular monthly market has new and old bits and pieces for sale and a nice atmosphere.

Excursions

Sydney sprawls over a coastal plain, hemmed in by rugged country on three sides and by the Tasman Sea on the fourth.

The city is at the centre of the largest concentration of people in Australia, with more than 100 people per sq km from Wollongong to Newcastle. More than two-thirds of New South Wales' (NSW) population is crammed into this area; and about a quarter of all Australians live within 150km of Sydney.

This might sound like a recipe for overcrowding, but the region has historic small towns, stunning waterways, uncrowded beaches, superb national parks and vast tracts of forest. The proximity of Sydney also means that public transport is pretty good, so day trips are feasible even without a car.

You will find the following places on Map 1.

WILDLIFE PARKS
In addition to the large national parks on Sydney's fringes, there are several outer suburban places where you can see native animals. The larger parks are listed here, but you can also meet indigenous critters at the Australian Reptile Park near Gosford (see Central Coast later in this chapter).

Waratah Park
Popular Waratah Park (☎ 9450 2377, Namba Rd, Duffys Forest; adult/child $14.80/7.80; open 10am-5pm) on the edge of Ku-ring-gai Chase National Park, is a good place to see native fauna. The TV series Skippy was filmed here in the 1960s. Petting times are hourly from 11am to 4pm. You can get here on Forest Coach Lines' (☎ 9450 1236) bus No 284, which meets trains at Chatswood station, but there are only three buses on weekdays, fewer on weekends.

Koala Park Sanctuary
If a tactile koala encounter is all you're after, head for Koala Park Sanctuary (☎ 9484 3141, Castle Hill Rd, West Pennant Hills; adult/child $14/7; open 9am-5pm) in north-

western Sydney. The koalas are fed at 10.20am and 11.45am, and at 2pm and 3pm. Take a train to Pennant Hills station, and from there catch any bus No 661 to 665.

Featherdale Wildlife Park
Featherdale Wildlife Park (☎ 9622 1644, 217-29 Kildare Rd, Doonside; adult/child aged 4-14 $15/7.50; open 9am-5pm) has a wide variety of native fauna, including koalas. It's between Parramatta and Penrith. From the city, take a train to Blacktown, then catch bus No 725 from the station.

Wonderland Sydney
This amusement park (☎ 9830 9100, Wallgrove Rd, Eastern Creek; adult/child aged 4-13 $44/29.70 for both amusement parks, adult/child $16.5/9.90 for wildlife park; Wonderland open 10am-5pm, wildlife park open 9am-5pm) off the Western Motorway (M4) west of the city, includes the large Australian Wildlife Park, which houses all sorts of native Australian animals.

There are also pools and water slides at the amusement park next door, so bring your cossie (swimsuit) in summer.

BOTANY BAY NATIONAL PARK

Many first-time visitors to Sydney mistakenly believe that the city is built on the shores of Botany Bay. Sydney is actually built around the harbour of Port Jackson, some 10km to 15km north of Botany Bay, although the city's sprawling southern suburbs now encompass the bay too. Botany Bay National Park is in two locations (Kurnell and La Perouse), on either side of the entrance to Botany Bay.

Botany Bay is the place where Captain Cook first stepped ashore in Australia. The bay was named by Joseph Banks, the expedition's naturalist, in honour of the many botanical specimens he found here. Cook's landing place is marked by monuments on The Monument Track, a 2km-long walk at Kurnell.

Bushwalks are possible on both sides of the park and offer visitors the chance to feel as though they are a million miles from busy Sydney.

The **Discovery Centre** (☎ 9668 9111; admission $6 per car; open 10am-3pm) in the park has material relating to Cook's life and expeditions, an exhibition about the first contact between Cook's *Endeavour* crew and the Aboriginal people of the area, and information on the surrounding wetlands. The park is open from 7am to 7.30pm. From Cronulla station (10km away), take bus No 987.

La Perouse (Laperouse in French) is on the northern side of the bay entrance, at the spot where the French explorer of that name arrived in 1788, just six days after the arrival of the First Fleet. He gave the Poms a good scare – they weren't expecting the French to materialise in this part of the world quite so soon! Laperouse and his men camped at Botany Bay for a few weeks, then sailed off into the Pacific and vanished. Many years later the wrecks of their ships were discovered on a reef near Vanuatu.

The La Perouse area has strong links with the Aboriginal community. The **Laperouse**

Museum & Visitor Centre (☎ 9311 3379; adult/child $5.50/3.30; open 10am-4pm Wed-Sun) has an interesting Aboriginal gallery, as well as Laperouse expedition relics and antique maps. You can book guided tours by phoning ☎ 9247 5033.

There's a monument at La Perouse commemorating the explorer, built in 1828 by French sailors searching for him.

Bus Nos 394 and 398 run here from Circular Quay.

ROYAL NATIONAL PARK

The Royal National Park (Princes Hwy; $10/20 per car for 1/2 days, pedestrians & cyclists free; visitors centre ☎ 9542 0648, Farnell Rd; open 8.30am-4.30pm) features dramatic cliffs, secluded beaches, heathlands and lush rainforest and is the oldest gazetted national park in the world. It begins at Jibbon Point, 30km south of Sydney, and stretches 20km southward to Bulgo. A road runs through the park, with detours to the small township of Bundeena on Port Hacking, to the beautiful Wattamolla beach, and on to windswept Garie beach. There's a large network of walking tracks (some with disabled access), including a spectacular and highly recommended 26km coastal trail that runs the length of the park.

The sandstone plateau at the park's northern end is a sea of low scrub. Tall forest can only be found in the river valleys and on the park's southern boundary on the edge of the Illawarra escarpment. In late winter and early spring the park is carpeted with colourful wildflowers.

You can hire row boats, canoes, kayaks, aqua bikes and normal bikes at the **Audley Boat Shed** (☎ 9545 4967, Farnell Rd; row boats, canoes & kayaks $14/26 1 hr/day, aqua bikes $11 for 30 min, bikes $11/26 1 hr/day).

Garie, **Era**, **South Era** and **Burning Palms** are well-known surf beaches; swimming and surfing at Marley beach is dangerous (Little Marley is safe). Garie beach has a surf-lifesaving club and **Wattamolla Beach** has a calm lagoon for swimming.

A walking and cycling trail follows the Port Hacking River south from Audley, and other walking tracks pass tranquil, freshwater swimming holes. You can swim in **Kangaroo Creek** but not in the Port Hacking River.

The road through the park and the off-shoot to Bundeena are always open, but the gates to the beach roads close at sunset.

The park surrounds the sizeable town of **Bundeena**, on the southern shore of Port Hacking. Bundeena has its own beaches and you can walk for 30 minutes to **Jibbon Head**, which has a good beach and Aboriginal rock art. Bundeena is the starting point of the famous 26km-long coastal walk.

Places to Stay

The only *camping ground* accessible by car is at Bonnie Vale, near Bundeena, where sites start at $7.50/4 per adult/child. Free bush camping is allowed in several areas – one of the best places is Burning Palms beach – but you must obtain a permit (for a small fee) beforehand from the visitors centre.

Beachhaven Bed & Breakfast (☎/fax 9544 1333, 13 Bundeena Dve) 1-night stay $130-150 Mon-Thur, $175-200 Fri-Sun, 2-night stay $330-380 Sat, Sun & public holidays. Offering a choice of 'Tudor Suite' or 'Beachhouse', this quirky place gets good feedback and is right on Horderns Beach.

Garie Beach YHA Hostel (☎ 9261 1111 for bookings) Beds $8 for YHA members only. This small, basic (no electricity or phone) and secluded hostel is close to one of the best surf beaches in NSW. You need to book, collect a key and get detailed directions from the YHA Travel Centre (☎ 9261 1111) at 422 Kent St, Sydney. Don't forget to bring all your own supplies, as the nearest food store is 10km away.

Getting There & Away

Train The Sydney-Wollongong railway line forms the western boundary of the park. The closest station is Loftus, with a 2km walk to the visitors centre. There's a tram from Loftus to the park on Sunday and public holidays. Bringing a bike on the train is a good idea because there's a 10km ride along Lady Carrington Dve, a vehicle-free forest track about half an hour's ride from

Sutherland station. The stations of Enga-dine, Heathcote, Waterfall and Otford are on the park boundary and have walking trails leading into the park.

Car & Motorcycle From Sydney, take the Princes Hwy and turn off south of Loftus to reach the northern end of the park. From the south, enter via Otford on the coast road north of Wollongong. It's a beautiful drive through thick bush and there are great views from Lawrence Hargrave Lookout at Bald Hill, just north of Stanwell Park on the park's southern boundary. There's a third entrance at Waterfall, just off the Princes Hwy.

Ferry A scenic way to reach the park is to take a train from Sydney to the suburb of Cronulla (changing at Sutherland on the way; $4), then the Cronulla National Park Ferries (☎ 9523 2990) boat to Bundeena in the north-eastern corner of the park (adult/child $3.10/1.55). Ferries depart from the Cronulla wharf, just below the train station. Cronulla National Park Ferries also offers daily Hacking River cruises in summer and a reduced timetable in winter (adult/child $14/10).

KU-RING-GAI CHASE NATIONAL PARK

This 15,000 hectare national park *(general inquiries ☎ 9472 8949; $10 per car)*, 24km north of the city centre, borders the southern edge of Broken Bay and the western shore of Pittwater. It has that classic Sydney mixture of sandstone, bushland and water vistas, plus walking tracks, horse-riding trails, picnic areas, Aboriginal rock engravings and spectacular views of Broken Bay. The park has over 100km of shoreline. There are several through-roads and four entrances.

Kalkari Visitors Centre (☎ 9457 9853), on Ku-ring-gai Chase Rd about 2.5km into the park from the Mt Colah entrance, is open 9am to 5pm. The road descends from the Kalkari Visitors Centre to the picnic area and information centre at Bobbin Head on Cowan Creek, then heads south to the Turramurra entrance.

If you're lucky, you might get to see or hear a lyrebird in the Ku-ring-gai Chase National Park.

At Bobbin Head, **Halvorsen Boats** (☎ 9457 9011) rents row boats for $20/55 per hour/day. Eight-seater motorboats cost $55/125.

The best places to see **Aboriginal engravings** are on the Basin Track and Garigal Aboriginal Heritage Walk at West Head.

It's unwise to swim in Broken Bay because of sharks, but there are safe netted **swimming** areas at Illawong Bay and the Basin.

Elevated parts of the park offer superb views across inlets such as Cowan Creek and Pittwater. From **West Head** there's a fantastic view across Pittwater to Barrenjoey Head. You may also see lyrebirds at West Head during their May to July mating season.

Places to Stay

Camp Sites (☎ 9974 1011) Camp sites adult/child $9/4.50 per person (book in advance). Camping is permitted at the Basin on the western side of Pittwater. It's a walk of about 2.5km from West Head Rd, or a ferry (☎ 9974 5235) or water taxi (☎ 0428 238 190) ride from Palm Beach.

Pittwater YHA Hostel (☎ 9999 2196, Towlers Bay) Dorm beds adult/child under18 $19/13, doubles/twins $25 per person, Sat night about $5 extra. Nonmembers pay $3.50 more for temporary YHA membership. This idyllic, beautifully situated hostel, a couple of kilometres south of the Basin, is noted for its friendly wildlife. Book ahead and bring food.

Halvorsen Boats (☎ 9457 9011, fax 9457 8089, Bobbin Head) 8/11m houseboats 2-7 days $570-1215/$750-2100. These boats are a beautiful way to enjoy the area; you'll need to book. The 8m boats sleep five and the 11m boats sleep nine. A three-day booking is quite a bit cheaper than a two-day weekend booking, so ask for a full list of price options.

Getting There & Away

There are four road entrances to the park: Mt Colah, just off the Pacific Hwy; North Turramurra, in the park's south-west; and Terrey Hills and Church Point, in the south-east.

Bus From Wynyard station in the city, take bus No 190, L90 or L88 (which starts at Railway Square) to Mona Vale, then pick up bus No 155 or 156 to Church Point. Bus No 190 continues north to Palm Beach (the trip from Wynyard takes about an hour). Bus Nos 155 and 156 run from Manly.

Shorelink Buses (☎ 9457 8888) has a fairly frequent bus No 577 service from Turramurra train station to the nearby park entrance ($2.90).

STA buses service the Terrey Hills and Church Point entrances, but it's quite a walk to the Pittwater YHA Hostel or the camp sites from these entrances.

Ferry The Palm Beach Ferry Service (☎ 9974 5235) runs to the Basin hourly from 9am to 5pm Monday to Thursday, 9am to 8pm Friday and 9am to 6pm Saturday, Sunday and public holidays (adult/concession and child $8/4). Palm Beach & Hawkesbury River Cruises (☎ 9997 4815) depart from Palm Beach for Bobbin Head (via Patonga) at 11am daily, returning at 3.30pm (adult/concession/child $30/24/15 return).

To get to the Pittwater YHA Hostel get Church Point Ferries (☎ 9999 3492) to take you from Church Point to Halls wharf ($6.50 return); the hostel is a 10-minute uphill walk from here.

MACQUARIE TOWNS AREA

Windsor, Richmond, Wilberforce, Castlereagh and Pitt Town are the five 'Macquarie Towns' established by Governor Lachlan Macquarie in 1810 on fertile agricultural land on the upper Hawkesbury River.

The Hawkesbury Visitors Centre (☎ 4588 5895, Bicentennial Park, Ham Common, Windsor Rd, Clarendon), across from the Richmond Royal Australian Air Force (RAAF) base, is the main information centre for the upper Hawkesbury area; it's open 9am-1pm and 1.30pm-5pm Monday to Friday, 10am-3pm on Saturday, and 9am-1pm on Sunday. In Richmond the National Parks & Wildlife Service (NPWS; ☎ 4588 5247) is at 370 George St.

Windsor

Set on the banks of the Hawkesbury River, Windsor has many fine old colonial buildings. The **Hawkesbury Museum & Tourist Centre** (☎ 4577 2310, 7 Thompson Sq; adult/senior & student/child $2.50/1.50/0.50; open 10am-4pm) is in a building that dates from the 1820s, and was used as the Daniel O'Connell Inn during the 1840s. There are a variety of displays in the museum.

Windsor's other old buildings include the convict-built **St Matthew's Church** (1820), designed, like the old courthouse (1822), by convict architect Francis Greenway. George St has other historic buildings and the **Macquarie Arms Hotel**, built in 1815 under orders from the governor, claims to be the oldest pub in Australia (several other pubs in Sydney disagree).

On the edge of town is the tiny **Tebbutt's Observatory**, which used to feature on the $100 note.

Wilberforce & Around

Tiny Wilberforce, 6km north of Windsor, is on the edge of the riverflat farmland. **Hawkesbury Heritage Farm** (☎/fax 4575 1457, Rose St; adult/child/family $11/6.50/27.50; open 10am-5pm Thur-Sun) is a collection of old buildings gathered to form a small historical park. It includes **Rose Cottage** (1811), probably the oldest surviving timber building in the country. There are

also animals and various animal displays. Next door is **Butterfly Farm** (☎ 4575 1955, Wilberforce Rd; open 10am-5pm), an insect museum with swimming and go-karting. You can get here by public transport – take a CityRail train to Windsor and then a (very infrequent) Westbus No 668 or 669 – phone ☎ 9890 0000 or ☎ 13 15 00 to check times.

The originally Presbyterian (now Uniting) **Ebenezer Church** (☎ 4579 9350, Coromandel Rd; open 10am-3.30pm, service 8am Sun) 5km north of Wilberforce (turn right off Singleton Rd), is said to be the oldest church in Australia (1809) still used as a place of worship. There's a small museum and gift shop and Devonshire tea is available. The old **Tizzana Winery and Bed & Breakfast** (☎ 4579 1150, 518 Tizzana Rd; open noon-6pm weekends & public holidays, or by appointment) is near Ebenezer and has tastings and cellar sales.

Pitt Town & Around

Pitt Town, a few kilometres north-east of Windsor, is another Macquarie Town. Its old buildings include the restored **Bird in Hand Hotel** (☎ 4572 3372, Bathurst St), which was built in 1825. North of Pitt Town on the road to Wisemans Ferry is the small **Cattai National Park** (☎ 4572 3100, Wisemans Ferry Rd). It comprises two parts: Cattai Farm, containing First Fleet assistant surgeon Thomas Arndell's 1821 cottage; and Mitchell Park (2km east), with pristine forest and walking trails.

A truly interesting site in the area is **Rouse Hill Estate** (☎ 9627 6777, fax 9627 6776, Guntawong Rd, Rouse Hill; adult/child & concession/family $6/3/15; open 10am-3pm Thur & Sun), which was owned and occupied by one family and its descendants for almost 200 years. It's a delicate site, so bookings and guided tours are compulsory. Guntawong Rd is off Windsor Rd, south-east of Windsor.

Richmond

Richmond is 6km west of Windsor, at the end of the CityRail line and at the start of the Bells Line of Road across the Blue Mountains (see the Blue Mountains section later in this chapter). The town dates from 1811 and has some fine Georgian and Victorian buildings. These include the **courthouse** and **police station** on Windsor St, and, around the corner on Market St, **St Andrew's Church** (1845). A number of notable pioneers are buried in the cemetery at **St Peter's Church** (1841).

Putty Rd

On the Putty Rd about 20km north of Windsor there's a long descent to the lovely **Colo River**, a picturesque spot popular for swimming, canoeing and picnicking. It's a little village with a service station, shop and tourist information.

Colo Riverside Park (☎ 4575 5253, fax 4575 4000, ℮ coloriverside@hotmail.com, 1826 Singleton Rd, Colo) Tent/van site $8 per adult, powered tent/van site $10, onsite double vans $37-50 per night, double cabins $90. You can camp here, and also hire canoes for $13 an hour ($22 for two hours) for two to three persons.

Getting There & Away

Train CityRail trains run from Sydney to Windsor and Richmond, but getting to the other Macquarie Towns involves connecting with an infrequent local bus service (Westbus; ☎ 13 15 00).

Car & Motorcycle From Sydney the easiest routes heading to Windsor are on Windsor Rd (Route 40), the north-western continuation of Parramatta's Church St; and via Penrith, heading north from either the Western Motorway (M4) or the Great Western Hwy on Route 69 (Parker St and the Northern Rd).

The Putty Rd runs north from Windsor to Singleton, 160km north in the upper Hunter Valley. From Windsor take Bridge St across the river then turn right onto the Wilberforce Road (Route 69).

From Richmond, Bells Line of Road runs west up into the Blue Mountains (see the Blue Mountains later) and Lithgow. This is a more interesting (but considerably longer) route to Katoomba than the crowded Great Western Hwy.

THE BLUE MOUNTAINS

The Blue Mountains, part of the Great Dividing Range, have some truly fantastic scenery, excellent bushwalks and gorges, gum trees and cliffs galore. The foothills begin 65km inland from Sydney and rise up to 1100m, but the mountains are really a sandstone plateau riddled with spectacular gullies formed by erosion over millennia. The blue haze, which gave the mountains their name, is a result of the fine mist of oil given off by eucalyptus trees.

For more than a century the area has been a popular getaway for Sydneysiders seeking to escape the summer heat. Despite intensive tourist development, much of the area is so precipitous that it's still open only to bushwalkers.

Be prepared for the climatic difference between the Blue Mountains and the coast – you can swelter in Sydney but shiver in Katoomba. Autumn's mists and drizzle can make bushwalking a less attractive option. In winter the days are often clear, and in the valleys it can be almost warm. There is usually some snowfall some time between June and August, and the region has a Yulefest in July, when many restaurants and guesthouses have good deals on mid-year 'Christmas' dinners.

History

The first Europeans to explore the area found evidence of extensive Aboriginal occupation, but few Aborigines. It seems quite likely that catastrophic European-introduced diseases had spread from Sydney long before.

The colonists at Port Jackson attempted to cross the mountains within a year or so of arrival, driven not just by the usual lust for exploration but also by an urgent need to find agriculturally useful land for the new colony. However, the sheer cliffs and tough terrain defeated their attempts for nearly 25 years. Many convicts came to believe that China, and freedom, was just on the other side of the mountains.

The first crossing was made in 1813 by Gregory Blaxland, William C Wentworth and William Lawson. They followed the ridge-tops and their route was pretty much the same as today's Great Western Hwy. The first road across the mountains was built in just six months, and the great expansion into the western plains began.

After the railway across the mountains was completed in the 1860s, wealthy Sydney-siders began to build mansions here, as summer retreats from the heat and stench of Sydney Town. By the beginning of the 20th century, grand hotels and guesthouses had opened to cater for the increasing demand.

Orientation

The Great Western Hwy from Sydney follows a ridge from east to west through the Blue Mountains. Along this less-than-beautiful road, the Blue Mountains towns often merge into each other – Glenbrook, Springwood, Woodford, Lawson, Wentworth Falls, Leura, Katoomba (the main accommodation centre), Medlow Bath, Blackheath, Mt Victoria and Hartley. Just west of Mt Victoria township the road falls down the steep and winding Victoria Pass. On the western fringe of the mountains is the large town of Lithgow.

To the south and north of the highway's ridge the country drops away into precipitous valleys, including the Grose Valley to the north, and the Jamison Valley south of Katoomba. There is a succession of turn-offs to waterfalls, lookout points and scenic alternative routes along the highway.

The Bells Line of Road, much more scenic (and less congested) than the Great Western Hwy, is a more northerly approach

Getting Active in the Blue Mountains

Rugged terrain and superb scenery make the Blue Mountains ideal for bushwalking and other outdoor activities.

There are walks lasting from a few minutes to several days. The most popular areas, spectacular from the tops of the cliffs and the bottoms of the valleys, are the **Jamison Valley** immediately south of Katoomba and the **Grose Valley** area north-east of Katoomba, and Blackheath. South of Glenbrook is another good area.

Visit a National Parks & Wildlife Service (NPWS) visitors centre for information or, for shorter walks, ask at a tourist information centre. It's very rugged country and walkers sometimes get lost, so it's crucial that you get reliable information, go with other walkers and tell someone where you're going and when you expect to return. Most Blue Mountains watercourses are polluted, so you have to sterilise water or take your own. Be prepared for rapid weather changes.

There's free parking for bushwalkers' cars near the trailhead for the Grand Canyon Walk on Evans Lookout Rd.

There's a fairly easy three-day walk from Katoomba to Jenolan Caves along the **Six Foot Track** (see Jenolan Caves in the Katoomba section). On weekends and public holidays the NPWS runs a series of excellent guided walks, many of which have a historical or ecological theme; it also runs Aboriginal discovery tours (walks with an Indigenous focus). All these tours have to be booked. Call ☎ 4787 8877 for information.

The cliffs, gorges and valleys of the Blue Mountains offer outstanding abseiling, rock climbing and canyoning (exploring gorges by climbing, abseiling, swimming, walking etc). **Narrow Neck**, **Mt Victoria** and **Mt Peddington** are among the popular sites. Most outfits offering guided adventure activities and courses are based in Katoomba (see Activities in the Katoomba section).

Cycling is permitted on most national park trails and, except for the hassle of carrying your bike down to the valley floor and back up again, there's good riding. See Activities and Getting Around in the Katoomba section for information bike rentals and guided rides.

Several horse-riding outfits in the Megalong Valley have trail rides (see Megalong Valley in the Blue Mountains section).

from Sydney. From Richmond it runs north of the Grose Valley to emerge in Lithgow, although you can cut across from Bell to join the Great Western Hwy at Mt Victoria.

Information

There's a visitors centre (☎ 4739 6266) on the highway at Glenbrook and another centre (☎ 4782 0756) at Echo Point in Katoomba. (You can also call ☎ 1300 653 408 for either centre.) The excellent NPWS Blue Mountains Heritage Centre (☎ 4787 8877) is on Govetts Leap Rd near Blackheath, about 3km north of the highway. It's open 9am to 4.30pm daily.

Katoomba has its own tourist radio station (88 FM).

The Heritage Centre at Govetts Leap is the best place to ask about walks; it also sells maps and some books. Maps suitable for walkers are also sold at information centres. *Megalong Books (☎ 4784 1302, 183 The Mall, Leura)*, stocks books about the Blue Mountains, and is open 9am to 6pm daily.

The Blue Mountains on Foot, by Bruce Williams & Reece Scannell, is a useful book, and Lonely Planet's *Bushwalking in Australia* provides details of the Blue Gum Forest Walk.

Accommodation ranges from camp sites and hostels to guesthouses, B&Bs and resorts. Katoomba is the main accommodation centre. Most places charge more on weekends, and are often booked out on long weekends. Camping is banned in some parts of the national parks and in others you need a permit, so check with the NPWS first.

Information centres (including many in Sydney) stock brochures listing accommodation options in the Blue Mountains. Check prices before heading off – there are numerous packages available, and rates fluctuate seasonally.

National Parks

The **Blue Mountains National Park** protects large areas to the north and south of the Great Western Hwy. It's the most popular and accessible of the three national parks in the area, and offers great bushwalking, scenic lookouts, breathtaking waterfalls and Aboriginal stencils.

Wollemi National Park, north of Bells Line of Road, is the state's largest forested wilderness area (nearly 500,000 hectares). It stretches as far as Denman in the Hunter Valley, and has good rugged bushwalking and lots of wildlife. Access is limited and the park's centre is so isolated that a new species of tree, named the Wollemi pine, was discovered only in 1994.

Kanangra Boyd National Park is southwest of the southern section of the Blue Mountains National Park and 180km west of Sydney. It has bushwalking, limestone caves and grand scenery, including the spectacular **Kanangra Walls Plateau**, which is surrounded by sheer cliffs. The park can be reached on unsealed roads from Oberon or Jenolan Caves (see that section later).

Lookouts

Cliches have been used to describe the Blue Mountains' views for so long that it's a little surprising to find that the vistas *are* breathtaking. Don't miss the famous **Three Sisters** at **Echo Point** at Katoomba. **Cliff Drive**, running along the edge of the Jamison Valley between Leura and Katoomba, also offers some great views. **Govetts Leap** (near Blackheath, and the NPWS Heritage Centre) and **Evans Lookout** (north of the highway – turn off before Blackheath) afford spectacular vistas. Less famous but just as breathtaking are the viewpoints off Bells Line of Road, such as **Walls Lookout**. **Hawkesbury Heights**, between Springwood and Bells Line of Road, has views across the Nepean River to Sydney, sometimes muddied by a cloud of tan-coloured smog.

Further from the main centres there are more views from **McMahon's Lookout** on Kings Tableland, 22km from the Queen Victoria Memorial Hospital (south of Wentworth) – for the last 10km you'll need a 4WD (or a mountain bike).

Glenbrook to Katoomba

From **Marge's Lookout** and **Elizabeth's Lookout**, just north of Glenbrook, there are good views back to Sydney. The section of the Blue Mountains National Park south of Glenbrook contains **Red Hand Cave**, which is an old Aboriginal shelter with hand stencils on the walls. It's an easy 7km return walk south-west of the NPWS information centre.

Springwood The famous artist and author Norman Lindsay (1879–1969) lived in Springwood from 1912 until his death. His home is now the **Norman Lindsay Gallery & Museum** (☎ 4751 1067, 14 Norman Lindsay Cres, Faulconbridge via Springwood; adult/child $7.70/3.30; open 10am-4pm), and houses many of his paintings, cartoons, illustrations and sculptures. There's also a room dedicated to *The Magic Pudding*, and landscaped gardens.

Wentworth Falls South of town there are views of the Jamison Valley and of the lovely 300m Wentworth Falls from **Falls Reserve**, the starting point for a network of walking tracks.

Leura This quaint, tree-lined town is full of stores, galleries and cafes. **Leuralla** (☎ 4784 1169, 36 Olympian Pde; adult/child $8/2 to museum/house & garden, $5/1 garden only; open 10am-5pm) is an Art Deco mansion that has a fine collection of 19th-century Australian art, as well as a toy and model-railway museum. The historic house, set in five hectares of lovely gardens, is a memorial to HV 'Doc' Evatt, a former Labor Party leader and first president of the United Nations. There's also a nice lookout across the road, with two quaint statues and an amphitheatre.

South of Leura, **Sublime Point** is a great clifftop lookout. **Gordon Falls Reserve** is a popular picnic spot; from here you can follow the road back past Leuralla, then take the Cliff Drive or the more scenic Prince Henry Cliff Walk to Katoomba's Echo Point.

Places to Stay & Eat There are NPWS *camping areas* accessible by road at Euroka Clearing near Glenbrook, Murphys Glen near Woodford, Ingar near Wentworth Falls

and at Perrys Lookdown near Blackheath. To camp at Euroka Clearing, you need a permit (adult/child aged 5-15 $5/3 per day) from the Richmond NPWS (☎ 4588 5247). The tracks to Ingar and Murphys Glen may be closed after heavy rain.

Leura House (☎ 4784 2035, fax 4784 3329, 7 Britain St) Singles $121, doubles $76 per person midweek. This is a grand Victorian home (c. 1880) with the feel of a country retreat. Prices quoted here include breakfast; weekend prices are quite a bit higher, depending on demand, but there are sometimes specials in summer.

Hawkesbury Heights YHA (☎/fax 4754 5621, 836 Hawkesbury Rd, Hawkesbury Heights) Adult/child under 18 $14/7. This purpose-built place is surrounded by bush. It's an ecofriendly hostel with solar power, a 'green' toilet and a wood stove. Reservations are essential.

Peppers Fairmont Resort (☎ 4782 5222, 1 Sublime Point Rd) Doubles from $252/314 midweek/weekends. Leura's big, plush resort is right on the edge of the escarpment, overlooking the Jamison Valley.

Pins & Noodles (☎ 4784 1345, 121 The Mall) Dishes $7.70-11.70. This excellent small restaurant serves some of the best-tasting udon noodles you'll find outside Japan. The prices make it even more of a must.

Leura Gourmet (☎ 4784 1438, 159 The Mall) Breakfast $3.50-14.90. A deli and a cafe, the Leura Gourmet has lovely views towards Katoomba and is a nice place to unwind with coffee while you ogle a selection of foodstuffs for a picnic lunch.

Artisan Bakery (179 The Mall) Sandwiches $4.50-5.50. This bakery has *the* best bread in town, and a great range of tasty, affordable snacks too.

Katoomba (Map 13)

Katoomba and the adjacent centres of Wentworth Falls and Leura form the tourism centre of the Blue Mountains. Katoomba, with a population of 17,900, has long been a popular summer getaway spot for Sydney 'plains-dwellers'. But despite the number of tourists and its proximity to Sydney it remains a relaxed place, full of character and relatively devoid of touristy glitz, although the lookouts can be packed with vista-lovers. The town has the uncanny ambience of another time and place, its atmosphere accentuated by Art Deco and Art Nouveau guesthouses and cafes, its thick mists and occasional snowfalls.

Information The visitors centre (☎ 1300 653 408), at Echo Point, about 2km down Katoomba St from the train station, is open 9am to 5pm daily. The post office is tucked in behind the shopping centre, one street back from Katoomba St as you head downhill towards Waratah St.

Things to See The major scenic attraction is **Echo Point**, near the southern end of Katoomba St about 1km from the shopping centre. Here you'll find some of the best views of the Jamison Valley and the magnificent **Three Sisters** rock formation – floodlit at night, it's an awesome spectacle. A walking track follows the road. The story goes that the three sisters were turned to stone to protect them from the unwanted advances of three young men, but the sorcerer who helped them died before he could turn them back into women.

West of Echo Point, at the junction of Cliff Drive and Violet St, are the **Scenic Railway** (☎ *4782 2699, 1 Violet St; $10 return; open 9am-5pm)* and **Scenic Skyway** *(details as per railway; $8 return)*. The railway drops 200m to the bottom of the Jamison Valley where there's good bushwalking (see the Activities section). The railway was built in the 1880s to transport coal miners and its 45° incline is one of the steepest in the world. The Scenic Skyway cable car glides some 200m above the valley floor, traversing **Katoomba Falls gorge**. There's also the **Scenisender**, an enclosed cable car, which costs $10 return.

The **Explorers Marked Tree**, just west of Katoomba near the Great Western Hwy, was marked by Blaxland, Wentworth and Lawson, who, in 1813, were the first Europeans to find a way over the mountains. It's also the start of the Six Foot Track (see Walks under Jenolan Caves, later).

Activities The 12km-return **bushwalk** to the **Ruined Castle** rock formation on Narrow Neck Plateau, which divides the Jamison and Megalong Valleys another couple of kilometres west, is one of the best – watch out for leeches after rain. The **Golden Stairs** lead down from this plateau to more bushwalking tracks.

Several companies offer abseiling, rock climbing, canyoning and caving adventure activities. The competition keeps the deals fairly similar – expect to pay about $100 to $120 for a day's abseiling.

The Australian School of Mountaineering offers rock-climbing courses and abseiling days, plus many more activities, at **Paddy Pallin** *(☎ 4782 2014, 166b Katoomba St; abseiling from $89 per day for YHA, VIP & Australian Geographic members, $99 for nonmembers)*. We have received good feedback about this. The rescue course also sounds interesting!

Australian Outdoor Consulting at **Mountain Designs** *(☎ 4782 3877, 190 Katoomba St; activities from about $100 per day)* offers abseiling, rock climbing and canyoning. Mountain Designs stocks a good range of camping and outdoor paraphernalia (including maps).

Abseiling, canyoning, rock climbing, bushwalking and mountain biking can be arranged for the day, or for longer, with the **Blue Mountains Adventure Company** *(☎ 4782 1271, 84a Bathurst Rd; abseiling/ canyoning & rock climbing from $109/135)*.

A half-day's abseiling, rock climbing or canyoning is offered at **High 'n' Wild** *(☎ 4782 6224, 3/5 Katoomba St; abseiling $75-149)*; it can also help with mountain-biking, wilderness walking and bushcraft.

Places to Stay – Budget It is possible to stay comfortably in Katoomba on even a limited budget.

Katoomba Falls Caravan Park (☎ 4782 1835, Katoomba Falls Rd) Tent sites $12.10 per person, powered sites/cabins $26.40/ 81.40 for 2 people. This caravan park is about 2km south of the highway.

Blue Mountains YHA (☎ 4782 1416, fax 4782 6203, 207 Katoomba St) Dorm beds

$16.20, twins/doubles from $31 per person. In newly renovated premises, this hostel has modern facilities and incredibly helpful staff. There's parking, a BBQ, and bicycles.

Katoomba Mountain Lodge (☎ 4782 3933, 31 Lurline St) Dorm beds from $10, singles/doubles with share bathroom from $29 per person. This is an old brick guesthouse and hostel, with rather worn and sometimes cramped facilities. There are more-expensive rooms in the guesthouse section. Keep any valuables secure.

Blue Mountains Backpackers (☎ 4782 4226, 190 Bathurst Rd) Tent sites/dorm beds $12/17, twins & doubles $50 (VIP/YHA members pay $1/2 less). This backpackers' establishment, on Bathurst St, is in a worn but cosy old house near the train station. Dorms are large and other rooms are OK, and weekly rates are available. You need to book; this usually requires a money order or a credit card number.

Gearin Hotel (☎ 4782 4395, 273 Great Western Hwy) Dorm beds $16.50, singles & doubles $27.50 per person. The Art Deco Gearin is a good, friendly local pub with accommodation. Some of the rooms are much better than average pub rooms.

Katoomba Hotel (☎ 4782 1106, 15 Parke St) Dorm beds from $15, singles/doubles $35/55 Mon-Thur, $45/65 Fri-Sun. This old hotel, on the corner of Parke St and Bathurst Rd, is a smoky, boozy Aussie local. Rooms are decidedly unglamorous, but it's well heated.

Places to Stay – Mid-Range & Top End

There are numerous motels and guesthouses in the Katoomba area. Rates tend to rise on weekends and it's wise to book ahead, especially for long weekends and Yulefest (July).

Clarendon Guesthouse (☎ 4782 1322, fax 4782 2564, 68 Lurline St) Rooms with share/private bathroom $45/65 Mon-Thur, $65/88 Fri, Sat & Sun; weekend dinner & show packages from $142 per person. This guesthouse, on the corner of Lurline and Waratah Sts, has both old-fashioned and motel-style rooms and is quite atmospheric.

3 Sisters Motel (☎ 4782 2911, fax 4782 6263, 348 Katoomba St) Rooms from $110 weekends. Ten minutes' walk from town at the bottom end of Katoomba St and close to the Three Sisters, this motel is of average standard and fairly cheap.

The Cecil (☎ 4782 1411, 108 Katoomba St) Twins $37.50-70 per person Sun-Thur, 2-night weekend packages $110-165. The lovely Cecil is in the style of the grand guesthouses but with a lower tariff than many – some good packages are available at different times of the year. Access is also possible from Lurline St.

Hydro Majestic Hotel (☎ 4788 1002, fax 4788 1063, Great Western Hwy, Medlow Bath) Doubles $250-1200 midweek, $285-1350 weekends. At the top of the hotel scale is this lovingly restored hotel. A massive relic of an earlier era (complete with croquet lawn!), it's a few kilometres west of Katoomba at Medlow Bath. Buffet breakfast is included in the price, and the more expensive rooms have incredible views of the valley.

Carrington Hotel (☎ 4782 1111, fax 4782 1421, 15-47 Katoomba St) Rooms $100-185 Sun-Thur, $155-300 Fri & Sat, 2-night weekend package $410-700. The grand Carrington Hotel is another gorgeous old place that has been refurbished to within an inch of its life – very lavish. Breakfast is included in the prices. Check to see if specials are available.

Lilianfels Blue Mountains (☎ 4780 1200, free call 1800 024 452, Lilianfels Ave) Rooms $336/452 single/couple Sun-Thur, extra $55 for a valley view. The swish, well-appointed Lilianfels Blue Mountains is near Echo Point and boasts great views, English-style gardens and much luxury.

Places to Eat

Katoomba St, between Gang Gang and Waratah Sts, has plenty of good places to eat.

The Flapping Curtain Cafe (☎ 4782 1622, 10 Katoomba St) Dishes $2.60-9.30. The sign says 'helpful, friendly food served by simple, tasty people'. The Welsh Rarebit ($5.50) is indeed helpful and friendly.

Savoy (☎ 4782 5050, 26-8 Katoomba St) Mains $15-19. The pleasantly quirky Art Deco Savoy has an interesting menu with snacks and more substantial dishes.

Cafe Zuppa (☎ 4782 9247, 36 Katoomba St) Mains $10.50-17.50. This nice cafe has a good atmosphere and good prices.

Blues Cafe (☎ 4782 2347, 57 Katoomba St) Dishes $8-11. Open 9am-5pm daily. This cosy Art Deco cafe has healthy fare and a loyal following.

Paragon Cafe (☎ 4782 2928, 65 Katoomba St) Snacks $7.50-18.95. Paragon Cafe is Katoomba's undisputed Art Deco masterpiece, and a stroll or hike along Katoomba St demands that you pop in and at least have a coffee.

Go West Cafe (☎ 4782 6943, 181 Katoomba St) Dishes $5-8.50. A small place with outside seats, Go West Cafe serves good snacks with a smile and an easygoing charm. You can get fresh juices here, too.

Parakeet Cafe (☎ 4782 1815, 195b Katoomba St) Lunch $5.50-11.50. The sociable Parakeet Cafe has tables outside and serves vegie burgers and steak sandwiches. There's a discount for YHA cardholders.

Entertainment There are several entertainment options in town.

Carrington Bar (☎ 4782 6666, 15-47 Katoomba St) With its green-tiled facade, Carrington Bar often has live music on weekends.

Katoomba Hotel (☎ 4782 1106, 15 Parke St) This pub has local bands on weekends.

Gearin Hotel (☎ 4782 4395, 273 Great Western Hwy) There's a blues jam at the Gearin on Wednesday night and local bands on weekends.

Clarendon Guesthouse (☎ 4782 1322, 68 Lurline St) This is a theatre restaurant/cabaret with shows on Friday and Saturday nights – generally, big names passing through the area will play here.

Edge Cinema (☎ 4782 8900, 225-37 Great Western Hwy) The giant six-storey-high screen shows feature films and a stunning Blue Mountains documentary. See Mt Victoria, later, for information about the Mt Vic Flicks.

Getting Around Blue Mountains Bus Company (☎ 4782 4213) runs from opposite the Carrington Hotel to the Scenic Railway ($12), approximately hourly until about 4.30pm on weekdays and a few times on Saturday. Mountainlink (☎ 4782 3333) runs a service between Echo Point and Gordon Falls via Katoomba St and Leura Mall. There's roughly one service an hour midweek, fewer on weekends.

If you're driving, beware of the parking restrictions, because they're strictly enforced.

Cycletech (☎ 4782 2800), 182 Katoomba St, hires mountain bikes for $19/27.50 for a half/full day.

See also Getting Around at the end of the Blue Mountains section for information on the Blue Mountains Explorer bus.

Blackheath & Around

This town, 11km west of Katoomba on the Great Western Hwy, is a good base for visiting the Grose and Megalong Valleys. It has the closest train station to the NPWS **Blue Mountains Heritage Centre** (☎ 4787 8877, Govetts Leap Rd; open 9am-4.30pm), about 3km north-east along Govetts Leap Rd.

There are superb lookouts east of town, among them **Govetts Leap**, the adjacent **Bridal Veil Falls** (the highest in the Blue Mountains), and **Evans Lookout** (turn off the highway south of Blackheath). To the north-east, via Hat Hill Rd, are **Pulpit Rock**, **Perrys Lookdown** and **Anvil Rock**.

A long cliff-edge track leads from Govetts Leap to Pulpit Rock and there are walks down into the Grose Valley itself. Get details on walks from the NPWS Heritage Centre. Perrys Lookdown is at the beginning of the shortest route to the beautiful **Blue Gum Forest** in the bottom of the valley – about four hours return, but you'll want to linger longer.

To the west and south-west of Blackheath lie the Kanimbla and Megalong Valleys, with yet more spectacular views from places like **Hargreaves Lookout**.

Places to Stay The nearest NPWS *camp site* is Acacia Flat in the Grose Valley, near the Blue Gum Forest. It's a steep walk down from Govetts Leap or Perrys Lookdown. You can camp at Perrys Lookdown, which has a car park and is a convenient base for Grose Valley walks.

Blackheath Caravan Park (☎ *4787 8101, Prince Edward St)* Unpowered/powered tent sites from \$8.80/21.10, vans from \$41.80 for 2 people. This friendly caravan park is off Govetts Leap Rd, about 600m from the highway.

Lakeview Holiday Park (☎ *4787 8534, Prince Edward St)* Cabins with en suite from \$60 for 2 people, 4-bedroom house that sleeps 8 \$150. This simple place offers a range of well-priced accommodation (cabins and houses) and is close to the train station. Linen is not supplied.

Gardners Inn (☎ *4787 8347, 255 Great Western Hwy)* Singles/doubles \$38/65. This cosy and friendly inn is the oldest hotel (1832) in the Blue Mountains. Rooms are reasonable, the breakfasts (included in room rates) come with great jams and Denise's pies are justifiably famous.

Parklands (☎ *4787 7771, fax 4787 7211,* e *office@parklands-cgl.com.au,* w *www .parklands-cgl.com.au, Govetts Leap Rd)* Loft rooms from \$225/570 weeknights/ 2-night weekend package, garden suites from \$250/635. This luxurious small development is set in some of the nicest gardens in the Blue Mountains, dating from the 1880s.

Jemby-Rimbah Lodge (☎ *4787 7622, fax 4787 6230,* e *jembyrin@pnc.com.au, 336 Evans Lookout Rd)* Self-contained cabins \$135/180 for 2 people midweek/weekends. Set in secluded bushland, the self-contained cabins are good and organised activities with a local guide can be arranged from here.

Megalong Valley

The Megalong Valley feels like rural Australia, a refreshing change from the quasi-suburbs strung out along the ridges. It's largely cleared farmland, but it's still beautiful. The road down from Blackheath passes through pockets of rainforest; you can wander along the beautiful 600m **Coachwood Glen Nature Trail**, a couple of kilometres before the small settlement of Werriberri.

Megalong Australian Heritage Centre (☎ *4787 8188, Megalong Rd; open 9am-5pm)* has shearing, milking and other displays, as well as draught horses and native animals. Horse-riding trips are available

and there are hourly rides from \$22. There's also bunkhouse accommodation, with dorm beds for \$17 and comfy double rooms for \$99.50.

There are several **horse-riding** companies, such as **Werriberri Trail Rides** (☎ *4787 9171, Megalong Rd; \$24.20 1 hr)* near Megalong Valley Farm, and **Pack Saddlers** (☎ *4787 9150, Megalong Rd; \$25 1 hr)*, at the end of the valley in Green Gully. Both offer riding by the hour and longer treks, as well as accommodation.

Mt Victoria

Mt Victoria, the highest point in the mountains, is a small village with a semi-rural atmosphere 16km north-west of Katoomba on the Great Western Hwy.

Everything is an easy walk from the train station, where there's the **Mt Victoria Museum** (☎ *4787 1190, Mt Victoria Railway Station; open 2pm-5pm weekends, public & school holidays)*, which has an interesting collection of Australiana. Interesting buildings include the **Victoria & Albert Guesthouse** (1914), the **Tollkeeper's Cottage** (1849) and the 1870s **church**.

The charming **Mt Vic Flicks** (☎ *4787 1577, Harley Ave; adult/child & Thur \$8/6)* is a cinema of the old school, with a small candy bar, real cups of tea and the occasional piano player. Really good movies are shown from Thursday to Sunday.

Off the highway at **Mt York** there's a memorial to the explorers who first crossed the Blue Mountains.

Places to Stay & Eat There's some excellent food and accommodation on offer in Mt Victoria.

Hotel Imperial (☎ *4787 1878, fax 4787 1461, 1 Station St)* Dorm beds \$26, doubles \$81-197 Sun-Thur, \$99-222 Fri & Sat, packages available. This fine old hotel has arguably the best backpackers' rooms in the region, although there are only four beds in the dorm. The hotel faces the highway and quieter Station St, and the public bar is pretty good for a beer.

Victoria & Albert Guesthouse (☎ *4787 1241, fax 4787 1588, 19 Station St)* B&B

singles/doubles from $65/90 Sun-Thur, from $75/100 Fri & Sat. This lovely and comfortable guesthouse is in the grand old style. There's a cafe and a good restaurant.

Hartley Historic Site

The government established Hartley in the 1830s as a police post to protect travellers crossing the mountains from bushrangers (outlaws). The village became a popular place to break the journey, due to its safe atmosphere – and its welcoming pubs. Some fine sandstone buildings were constructed, notably the Greek Revival courthouse (1837). Many remain, although the village is now deserted.

The NPWS information centre (☎ 6355 2117) in the Farmer's Inn (1845) is open 10am to 1pm and 2pm to 4.30pm daily. You can wander around the village for free, but to enter the **Courthouse** *(tours 10am, 11am, noon, 2pm & 3pm; adult/concession $4.40/ 3.30)* you must book a tour.

The village is 10km west of Mt Victoria, off the Great Western Hwy on the way to Lithgow.

Jenolan Caves

South-west of Katoomba, on the western fringe of Kanangra Boyd National Park, the Jenolan Caves *(☎ 6359 3311; tours 10am-4.30pm weekdays, 9.30am-5pm weekends, 'ghost tour' 7.30pm Sat; from adult/child $14.50/10)* are the best-known limestone caves in Australia. One cave has been open to the public since 1867, although parts of the system are still unexplored. There are nine caves you can visit by guided tour. There are about 11 tours per day, and they last one to two hours. It's advisable to arrive early during holiday periods, as the best caves can be 'sold out' by 10am.

Walks There's a network of walking trails through the bush surrounding the Jenolan Caves.

The **Six Foot Track** from Katoomba to the Jenolan Caves is a fairly easy three-day walk. The Department of Conservation & Land Management (DCLM) has a detailed brochure, available from visitor information

centres in the Blue Mountains for around $1.50. Great Australian Walks (☎ 9555 7580) conducts guided walks along the track, with accommodation and food, for $400. The guides carry everything for you.

Organised Tours For information on the popular Wonderbus tour see Organised Tours at the end of the Blue Mountains section. Fantastic Aussie Tours (☎ 4782 1866, in Sydney ☎ 9938 5714) has day tours from Katoomba to the caves from adult/child $64/32 (including cave entry). Walkers can be dropped off at and collected from the Six Foot Track at Jenolan (from $44/22), but you have to book.

Places to Stay There are *camp sites* near Caves House for $11 per site.

Binda Bush Cabins (☎ 6359 3311, Jenolan Caves Rd) Cabins $75-90. These self-contained cabins, on the road from Hartley about 8km north of the caves, can accommodate six people in bunks.

Jenolan Caves Resort (☎ 6359 3322, fax 6359 3388, e *bookings@jenolancaves .com,* W *www.jenolancaves.com)* Gatehouse 4-person room low/high season $60.50/88, 6-person room $77/110; Binoomea Cottage $82.50/121; Caves House low season $110-231, high season $165-341; Mountain Lodge Units $132/209. There's a range of accommodation here – from the cheaper, 'bushwalker' rooms (shared facilities), to the lavish, old-fashioned Caves House. 'Low season' means weeknights, two-night weekends and three-night long weekends; 'high season' means Saturday night only and two-night public holiday weekends. Got it?

Jenolan Cabins (☎/fax 6335 6239, 42 Edith Rd) Cabins $98 Sun-Thur, from $105 weekends & school holidays. On the top on Porcupine Hill, these excellent 'green' cabins are cosy and tidy and also great value for groups. There's a cabin with disabled access. Bring food.

Jenolan Caravan Park (☎ 6336 0344, fax 6336 0044, Cunynghame St, Oberon) Unpowered/powered sites $11/15, on-site vans $35, en suite cabins $64. Half an hour from Jenolan Caves, this caravan park offers

Bowtell's Swing Bridge, Blue Mountains NP

Hartley historic site

Early morning mist in the Megalong Valley

The 300m-high Wentworth Falls

The 15,000 hectare Ku-Ring-Gai Chase National Park is a popular retreat for Sydney residents.

Three Sisters, Katoomba

Chardonnay grapes, Hunter Valley

Bridal Veil Falls, Govetts Leap

good rates in shady surrounds for those who don't mind a bit of hiking (or driving).

Bells Line of Road

The scenic Bells Line of Road was constructed in 1841 as an alternative route (to what is now the Great Western Hwy) across the mountains. It runs from near Richmond across the mountains to Lithgow, although you can cut across to join the Great Western Hwy near Mt Victoria. Bells Line of Road is much quieter than the highway, and is lined with bush, small farms and apple orchards. Fruit stalls are everywhere, and very cheap.

Mt Tomah Botanic Garden Midway between Bilpin and Bell, the delightful Mt Tomah Botanic Garden *(☎ 4567 2154; adult/ child $4.40/2.20; open 10am 4pm winter, 10am-5pm daylight saving time)* is a cool-climate annexe of Sydney's Royal Botanic Gardens. As well as native plants there are displays of exotic species, including some magnificent rhododendrons.

Mt Wilson Settled by people with a penchant for re-creating England, Mt Wilson is a tiny, beautiful village of hedgerows, large gardens and lines of European trees. It's 8km north of the Bells Line of Road; the turn-off is 7km east of Bell. Near the Post House there's an information board with details of public gardens and some short walks in the area. It's absolutely beautiful in autumn.

A kilometre or so from the village centre is a lovely remnant of rainforest thick with tree ferns, the **Cathedral of Ferns**.

Windyridge Garden *(☎ 4756 2019, Queens Ave)* is definitely worth a peek, featuring cool-climate plants (autumn and winter) and a sea of potted colour (spring and summer), all carefully planned and planted.

Tulip Tree Cafe (☎ 4756 2118, 31 The Avenue) Scones $4.95. On the road approaching Mt Wilson, this nice little cafe does world-class scones with jam and cream.

Blueberry Lodge & The Loft (☎/fax 4756 2022, Waterfall Rd) Doubles $154 Mon-Thur, $176 weekends, school holidays & public holidays. A charming place, offering

two-storey chalets in quiet surroundings. Recommended.

The *Post House (☎ 4756 2000, The Avenue)* serves tea and can help with B&B accommodation.

Zig Zag Railway The Zig Zag Railway *(☎ 6353 1795, Chifley Rd; adult/child/ family $15/7.50/45 return; open daily)* is at Clarence, about 11km east of Lithgow. It was built in 1869 and was quite an engineering wonder in its day. Trains descended from the Blue Mountains on this route until 1910. A section has been restored, and steam trains run the 12km trip daily. One-way tickets are available for hikers. Trains depart Clarence station at 11am, 1pm and 3pm. Special steam trains operate only on Wednesday, weekends and holidays.

Organised Tours

The major Sydney tour companies have day trips to the Blue Mountains for about $70.

Backpacker-friendly Wonderbus (☎ 9555 9800, 1800 669 800) runs day tours of the Blue Mountains ($70 to $100), and overnight trips ($290) that include the Jenolan Caves, dorm accommodation at the Blue Mountains YHA Hostel (you don't have to be a YHA member) and a bushwalk. Alternatively, book in person at the Sydney YHA Travel Centre or the YHA hostels in Sydney.

Another inexpensive tour operator that receives positive feedback is Oz-Trek (☎ 9360 3444), 263 Oxford St, East Sydney. See Getting Around at the end of the Blue Mountains section, later, for information on the Blue Mountains Explorer bus.

Getting There & Away

Katoomba, 109km from Sydney's city centre, is so close as to be a satellite suburb. CityRail trains run roughly hourly from Central station (adult/child $11/5.50, two hours). Make sure you sit on the left-hand side of the train coming from Sydney, as the views can be terrific. Countrylink buses meet trains at Mt Victoria on Tuesday, Friday and Sunday for the run to Oberon and Hartley. Call ☎ 13 22 32 or ☎ 6336 1664 for times.

To get there by car from Sydney, exit via Parramatta Rd and detour onto the Western Motorway (M4, $2.20) at Strathfield. West of Penrith the motorway becomes the Great Western Hwy. To reach the Bells Line of Road, exit the city on Parramatta Rd and from Parramatta head north-west on Windsor Rd to Windsor. Richmond Rd from Windsor becomes the Bells Line of Road west of Richmond.

See Organised Tours earlier in this section for tours that include transport from Sydney to the Blue Mountains.

Getting Around

Bus Mountainlink (☎ 4782 3333) runs between Leura, Katoomba, Medlow Bath, Blackheath and Mt Victoria, with some services along Hat Hill Rd and Govetts Leap Rd, which lead respectively to Perrys Lookdown and Govetts Leap. It'll take you to within about 1km of Govetts Leap, but for Perrys Lookdown you'll have to walk about 6km from the last stop. Services are less frequent on weekends. In Katoomba the bus leaves from the top of Katoomba St, outside the Carrington Hotel.

On weekends and public holidays the Blue Mountains Explorer bus offers all-day travel (adult/child $22/11). It departs regularly from the train station and visits the Scenic Railway, Skyway, Echo Point, Leura village and other places. The full circuit takes an hour, but you can get on or off where you like, and loiter at your leisure. Contact Fantastic Aussie Tours (☎ 4782 1866), 283 Main St, Katoomba.

Blue Mountains Bus Company (☎ 4782 4213) runs between Katoomba, Leura, Wentworth Falls, and east as far as Woodford. There's roughly one service every 45 minutes from Katoomba train station.

Train There are train stations in most Blue Mountains towns along the Great Western Hwy. Trains run roughly hourly between stations east of Katoomba and roughly two-hourly between stations to the west.

MACARTHUR COUNTRY

The Hume Hwy heads south-west from Sydney, flanked by the rugged Blue Mountains

The Mac's Magnificent Merinos

The Macarthur Country area was originally called Cow Pastures because a herd of escapee cattle from Sydney Cove thrived here, but it was John and Elizabeth Macarthur's sheep, arriving in 1805, that made the area famous. The couple's experiments with sheep-breeding led to the development of merino sheep suited to Australian conditions. These became the foundation of the Australian wool industry.

National Park to the west and the coastal escarpment to the east. This cleared and rolling sheep country has some of the state's oldest towns, although many have been swallowed by Sydney's ever-expanding suburban sprawl. For a more rural vista than the freeway allows, take the **Northern Rd** between Penrith and Narellan (just north of Camden).

Liverpool and, 20km further south, **Campbelltown**, are unattractive outer suburbs of Sydney, though both do have some interesting old buildings.

Camden & Around

This large country town is almost a dormitory suburb of Sydney. Camden retains some integrity, but the surrounding countryside is fast filling up with weekend attractions and housing developments for Sydneysiders. **John Oxley Cottage** *(☎ 4658 1370, Camden Valley Way, Elderslie; open 10am-3pm)* on the northern outskirts houses the Camden information centre. The **Camden Museum** *(☎ 4655 9210, 40 John St; adult/child $2.50/1; open 11am-4pm Thur-Sun)* can provide family history information and has displays about the district.

Built in 1835, the Macarthurs' home, **Camden Park House** *(☎ 4655 8466, Elizabeth Macarthur Ave)*, is only open to the public on the third weekend in September or by appointment for group tours. **Gledswood Homestead** *(☎ 9606 5111, Camden Valley Way; adult/child $6/4; open 9am-5pm)*, in Catherine Field close to Narellan, is an old homestead (1827) now housing a winery, gardens, farm activities and a restaurant. **Struggletown Fine Arts Complex** *(☎ 4648 2424, 4 Sharman Close, Narellan; open 10am-5pm Wed-Sun & public holidays)* is a collection of galleries in historic cottages.

Between Camden and Campbelltown is the **Mt Annan Botanic Garden** *(☎ 4648 2477, Mt Annan Dve; adult/child & concession/family $4/2/8; open 10am-6pm Oct-Mar, 10am-4pm Apr-Sept)*, which is an offshoot of Sydney's Royal Botanic Gardens and displays native flora on over 400 hectares. You can get here on Busways bus No 895 or 896, running approximately hourly from Campbelltown train station to Camden; call ☎ 4655 7501 for details. By car, take tourist drive 18, off the F5 Fwy.

Picton & Around
South of Camden and more rural, pretty Picton is an old village originally called Stonequarry. The Wollondilly Visitor Information Centre (☎ 4677 3962, Cnr Argyle & Menangle Sts) is in the old post office and has lots of brochures and fliers about things to see in the area and around NSW. It's open 10am-3pm.

A number of historic buildings still stand, including the train station and the 1839 *George IV Inn (☎ 4677 1415, 180 Old Hume Hwy/Argyle St)*, which brews great Bavarian-style beer in its own brewery and provides modest accommodation (doubles/triples/family rooms $49.50/55/66). **Menangle St West** is listed by the National Trust and worth a wander. On this street there's the sandstone **St Mark's Church and Pioneer Cemetery** (1850), with old graves for the town's early settlers.

Elizabeth Macarthur Agricultural Institute *(710 Morton Park Rd)* is a research station in Menangle, north-east of Picton. It takes in **Belgenny Farm** *(☎ 4655 9651, Elizabeth Macarthur Ave)*, the Macarthurs' first farm in the area and the oldest in Australia. It can be visited on organised tours that take place at 7pm on the first Friday and at 10am and 2pm on the last Sunday of each month; bookings are essential – call for details.

South of Picton in Thirlmere, the **Rail Transport Museum** *(☎ 4681 8001, Barbour Rd; adult/child $9/2.50; open 10am-3pm Mon-Fri, 9am-5pm Sat & Sun)* has a huge collection of carriages and locomotives (steam, diesel and electric). There are steam-train excursions (☎ 9744 9999) every Sunday, public holiday Monday and Wednesday during school holidays.

Getting There & Away
From Sydney take Parramatta Rd and turn south onto the Hume Hwy. The Narellan Rd exit on the Hume Hwy runs west to Camden and east to Campbelltown. Alternatively, take the Camden Valley Way (Route 89) as it forks off the Hume Hwy south of Liverpool.

To reach Picton, stay on the Hume Hwy past Campbelltown and turn off at the Picton exit. From Camden or Narellan, head south on Remembrance Dve.

CityRail trains stop at Liverpool, Campbelltown and Picton.

SOUTHERN HIGHLANDS
One hundred kilometres south of Sydney, the southern highlands was one of the first inland areas to be settled by white people. Many settlers still saw themselves as English landed gentry rather than Australian farmers, and promptly cleared the surrounding land of unruly native foliage in favour of English-style villages.

There was a second bout of nostalgia for the 'homeland' in the 1920s, which resulted in the building of lavish guesthouses catering to wealthy Sydneysiders.

The main source of information on the area is Tourism Southern Highlands (☎ 4871 2888), at 62-70 Main St, Mittagong; it's open 8am to 5.30pm daily. It also provides a free accommodation-booking service (☎ 1300 657 559). Craigie's *Visitors Map of the Southern Highlands* ($5.50) covers the area in detail.

Some of the towns in the highlands area include: **Mittagong**, the gateway to the highlands; **Bowral**, with the excellent **Bradman Museum** *(☎ 4862 1247, St Jude St; open 10am-5pm)* devoted to the town's most famous son and Australia's greatest cricketer, Sir Donald Bradman, as well as other cricketing greats; **Berrima**, a village with some wonderful old buildings and the good **Berrima Courthouse Museum** (*☎ 94877 1505, Cnr Argule & Wiltshire Sts; adult/child $5/3; open 10am-4pm)*; and **Bundanoon**, near the spectacular northern escarpments of **Morton National Park** (*☎ 4887 7270)*.

Getting There & Away

Bus Buses running along the Hume Hwy between Sydney and Melbourne call in at Mittagong, but most don't go on to Bowral or Moss Vale.

Berrima Coaches (*☎* 4871 3211) runs fairly frequent weekday services between Mittagong, Moss Vale and Bowral, with a few continuing on to Berrima, Sutton Forest, Exeter and Bundanoon. There are Saturday services between Mittagong, Moss Vale and Bowral. Buses also link Wollongong and Moss Vale, some via Bundanoon.

Train CityRail trains run to Mittagong, Bowral and Moss Vale. Some Countrylink trains on the Sydney-Canberra run stop at these stations and at Bundanoon. The XPT to/from Melbourne stops at one or more of them. Check with CityRail (*☎* 13 15 00) and Countrylink (*☎* 13 22 32, **w** www .countrylink.nsw.gov.au) for the most up-to-date schedules.

HAWKESBURY RIVER

The Hawkesbury River enters the sea 30km north of Sydney at Broken Bay. Dotted with coves, beaches, picnic spots and some fine riverside restaurants, it's one of Australia's most beautiful rivers and is a popular centre for boating. The last 20-odd kilometres of the river are fringed by inlets such as Berowra Creek, Cowan Water and Pittwater (to the south), and Brisbane Water (to the north).

The river flows between Marramarra and Ku-ring-gai Chase National Parks in the south; and Dharug, Brisbane Water and Bouddi National Parks to the north. Windsor and Richmond are about 120km further upstream from there.

Riverboat Postman

This mail boat (*☎ 9985 7566, Dangar Rd, Brooklyn wharf; adult/child $33/17)* is an excellent way to get a feel for the river. It does a 40km round trip weekdays, running upstream as far as Marlow, near Spencer. It leaves Brooklyn at 9.30am and returns at 1.15pm. There are also coffee cruises and all-day cruises, with booking recommended. See Getting There & Away later in this section for details on connecting with the *Riverboat Postman*.

Houseboats

You can hire houseboats in Brooklyn, Berowra Waters, Bobbin Head and Wisemans Ferry. Renting midweek during the low season can be affordable for a group.

Able Hawkesbury River Houseboats (*☎ 4566 4308, River Rd, Wisemans Ferry)* 4-berth houseboat 2-7 days $380-1120. The houseboats available here can accommodate four to 12 people. Rates vary according to the time of year and public holidays. Book ahead.

Other companies include *Holidays-A-Float* (*☎ 9985 7368, 60 Brooklyn Rd, Brooklyn)*, and *Ripples House Boats* (*☎ 9985 5530, e* info@ripples.com.au, **w** www.ripples .com.au, 87 Brooklyn Rd, Brooklyn)*.

See the Places to Stay entry for Ku-ring-gai Chase National Park, earlier, for details on hiring a houseboat in that area.

Brooklyn & Berowra Waters

The settlements along the river have their own distinct character. Life in Brooklyn revolves totally around boats and the river. The town is on the Sydney-Newcastle railway line, just east of the Pacific Hwy.

The small town of Berowra Waters, further upstream on a narrow, forested waterway, is clustered around a free 24-hour winch-ferry that crosses Berowra Creek. It's a pretty location, with boat hire and walking tracks through the bush, plus some lovely *restaurants and cafes* overlooking the water.

Berowra Waters is 5km west of the Pacific Hwy. There is a train station at Berowra, but from there it's a 6km hike down to the ferry.

Wisemans Ferry & St Albans

The tranquil settlement of Wisemans Ferry is a popular spot on the Hawkesbury River, roughly equidistant from Windsor and the mouth of the river. Free 24-hour winch-ferries are the only means of crossing the river here. The NPWS shop (☎ 4566 4382) has information on the area.

Wisemans Ferry Inn (☎ 4566 4301, Old Northern Rd) Doubles, triples & family rooms $60-88. This historic inn has decent (if a little cramped) rooms. There's often a lot going on in the pub, from singers to lingerie waitresses, if that's your thang.

Del Rio Riverside Resort (☎ 4566 4330, e *visit@delrioresort.com.au,* w *www.del rioresort.com.au, Chaseling Rd, Webbs Creek, Wisemans Ferry)* Unpowered/powered sites $20.90/23.10 a double in peak season. This is one of several caravan parks in the area. It's 3km south-west of the village centre and standards are high.

Unsealed road sections run north along both sides of the river from Wisemans Ferry to the tiny hamlet of St Albans. It's a pretty drive, with bush on one side, river flats on the other, and the occasional old house or horse.

Settlers Arms Inn (1836; ☎ 4568 2111, e *settlersarms@hotmail.com, 1 Wharf St, St Albans)* Doubles $110. This charming inn dates from 1836, and the public bar is worth having a beer in. It has a few pleasant rooms and there's good food available.

Dharug National Park (14,834 hectares), across the river, is a wilderness noted for its Aboriginal rock carvings, which date back nearly 10,000 years, and for the convict-built Old Great North Rd. There's *camping* at Mill Creek and Ten Mile Hollow (walk-in only track). Contact the NPWS shop (☎ 4566 4382) for information.

Yengo National Park (139,861 hectares), a rugged sandstone area covering the foothills of the Blue Mountains, stretches from Wisemans Ferry to the Hunter Valley. It's a wilderness area with no facilities and limited road access.

Marramarra National Park (11,759 hectares) south of the Hawkesbury, has vehicle access from the Old Northern Rd

south of Wisemans Ferry. *Camping* is allowed here. Contact the NPWS Central Coast District Office (☎ 4324 4911), in suites 36–8, at 207 Albany St, Gosford.

Getting There & Away

Train Trains run from Central station to Brooklyn's Hawkesbury River train station. The 8.16am train from Central station ($5.60 one way) gets you to Brooklyn's Hawkesbury River station in time to meet the morning *Riverboat Postman*.

Car & Motorcycle To reach Berowra Waters, turn off Pacific Hwy at Berowra, or take the longer scenic road through the Galston Gorge, north of Hornsby in Sydney's north-east.

A road leads to Wisemans Ferry from Pitt Town, near Windsor. You can also get there from Sydney on Old Northern Rd, which branches off Windsor Rd north of Parramatta.

Both of these routes culminate in a choice of two car ferries: the ferry in the west of town (at the bottom of the steep hill) takes you to St Albans Rd, which runs to St Albans; the ferry on the north-eastern side (just out of town, near the park) takes you to Settlers Rd, which also leads to St Albans; in the other direction it leads to Central Mangrove and, eventually, the central coast or the Sydney-Newcastle Fwy.

An unsealed road runs north-east from St Albans to Bucketty, from where you can travel on to Wollombi and Cessnock in the Hunter Valley.

To reach Brooklyn by car, take the Sydney-Newcastle Fwy or follow the old Pacific Hwy.

Ferry The *Riverboat Postman* (☎ 9985 7566) runs a ferry service from Brooklyn to Patonga Beach six times a week (except Friday) for adult/child $16/8 return. Bookings are necessary.

There's also a daily ferry between Palm Beach, Patonga and Bobbin Head in Ku-ring-gai Chase National Park; see the Getting There & Away entry for Ku-ring-gai Chase National Park, earlier, for details. From

Patonga, Busways Peninsula (☎ 4368 2277) has infrequent buses to Gosford, where you can catch a northbound bus or train.

THE CENTRAL COAST

The central coast has superb surf beaches, lakes and national parks, but rampant suburban housing.

Its beautiful waterways include **Broken Bay** and **Brisbane Water** in the south and three contiguous lakes in the north. The northern lakes are Tuggerah Lake; **Lake Budgewoi**, near Toukley; and **Lake Munmorah**. A few kilometres north of Lake Munmorah is **Lake Macquarie**, which stretches north to Newcastle.

West of the lakes, in the modest Watagan Mountains, are 13 **state forests** that run north to the Hunter Valley. The forests have walking trails; camping is permitted, except in picnic areas. The old village of **Cooranbong** is the main access point to the mountains. Further west again, you come to the vast national parks of the Blue Mountains.

Gosford is the main town in the area. Larger beachside centres include Terrigal and The Entrance.

Gosford Visitors Centre (☎ 4385 4430, 1300 659 285), 200 Mann St, is near the train station and is open 9am to 5pm weekdays, to 3pm on weekends. There are also visitors centres at Terrigal and The Entrance (for information call same telephone numbers as for Gosford). There is an NPWS office (☎ 4324 4911) in Gosford.

Accommodation is scarce during school holidays.

Gosford & Around

Gosford, the largest town in the area, is 12km inland on the shores of Brisbane Water, about 85km north of Sydney. Gosford has good transport links with Sydney, and is an ideal base from which to explore the region, including Brisbane Water National Park.

Brisbane Water National Park On the northern side of the Hawkesbury River, across from Ku-ring-gai Chase National Park, Brisbane Water National Park is 9km south-west of Gosford. It extends from the Pacific Hwy in the west to Brisbane Water in the east but, despite its name, this national park has only a short frontage onto this body of water.

In rugged sandstone country, the park is known for its **wildflowers** in early spring, and there are many walking trails. South of the township of Kariong is the turn-off for the **Bulgandry Aboriginal Engraving Site**, where there are interesting rock carvings.

The main road access is at Girrakool; travel west from Gosford or exit the Sydney-Newcastle Fwy at the Calga interchange. Wondabyne train station, on the Sydney-Newcastle line, is inside the park near several walking trails (including part of the Great North Walk). You must tell the guard that you want to get off at Wondabyne, and travel in the rear carriage. Ferries from Palm Beach run to Patonga; ferries from Brooklyn run to Wobby Beach, on a peninsula south of the park near some walking trails.

For more information contact the Gosford NPWS (☎ 4324 4911).

Old Sydney Town Off the freeway 9km south-west of Gosford, Old Sydney Town (☎ 4340 1104, Pacific Hwy, Somersby; adult/child/family $22/13/60; open 10am-4pm) is a major reconstruction of early Sydney with street theatre retelling events from the colony's early history (complete with historically accurate overacting during the 'convict punishment' displays). Busways Peninsula (☎ 4655 7501) runs here from Gosford and AAT Kings (☎ 1800 334 009) runs tours from Sydney.

Other Things to See & Do West of Gosford on the Pacific Hwy in Somersby, the **Australian Reptile Park** (☎ 4340 1146, Pacific Hwy; adult/child $15.50/8; open 9am-5pm) has native animals and birds as well as reptiles. Off Brisbane Water Dve in West Gosford is **Henry Kendall Cottage** (☎ 4325 2270, 27 Henry Kendall St; adult/concession $3/1.50; open 10am-4pm Wed, Sat & Sun, daily during school holidays), a small museum in the home of an early poet. Another attraction is the **Forest of Tranquillity**

Wildlife Sanctuary (☎ 4362 1855, Ourimbah Creek Rd; adult/child $9/4.50; open 10am-5pm Wed-Sun), a private forest reserve and bird sanctuary west off the freeway at Ourimbah.

South of the national park is **Patonga**, a small fishing village on Broken Bay, with camping available at *Patonga Beach Caravanning & Camping Area (☎ 4379 1287)* for $27.50 per night during peak periods. Off the road to Patonga is the worthwhile **Warrah Lookout**.

Not far away, but screened from the housing estates of Umina and Woy Woy by a steep road over Mt Ettalong, **Pearl Beach** is a lovely National Trust hamlet on the eastern edge of the national park. The only way to stay here is to rent a holiday house or apartment, and they're scarce.

Terrigal & Around

Terrigal, on the ocean about 12km east of Gosford, is probably the most upmarket of the central coast's beachside towns. You can contact the visitors centre on ☎ 4385 4430 or ☎ 1300 659 285.

Holiday Inn Crowne Plaza (☎ 4384 9111, Pine Trees Lane) Rooms from $230, weekend packages over $500. This big Holiday Inn dominates the foreshore, and caters to couples looking for a flashy weekend break.

Terrigal Beach Lodge YHA (☎/fax 4385 3330, e rockwall@enterprise.net.au, 12 Campbell Cres) Dorm beds/doubles $19/23.50 per person. This is a good, quiet hostel with tidy facilities, about a block from the beach.

South of Terrigal is the tiny beachside town of **Copacabana**. North of Terrigal, **Bateau Bay** meets the southern section of the small Wyrrabalong National Park. It's popular for surfing and the beach is patrolled by life-savers.

Bouddi National Park, 19km south-east of Gosford, extends south from MacMasters beach to the north head of Broken Bay. It also extends out to sea as a marine reserve. There's *camping* in the park, but you have to book through the Gosford NPWS (☎ 4324 4911).

The Entrance & Tuggerah Lake

The Entrance, on the sea inlet of Tuggerah Lake, 15km north of Terrigal, is a suburban sprawl of relentlessly cheerful cream brick, palm trees and plastic chairs, set beside a beautiful lake and superb surf beach. You can reach The Entrance either by driving north from Terrigal or by taking the Tuggerah exit off the Sydney-Newcastle Fwy.

The **pelicans** are fed at 3.30pm daily on the beachfront near the visitors centre (☎ 4385 4430, 1300 659 285).

On the peninsula north of The Entrance is the northern section of the small **Wyrrabalong National Park**, which has walking trails and diverse flora habitats. North of the park are the towns of **Toukley** and **Budgewoi**, popular bases for boating and fishing.

Running up the coast for 12km is **Munmorah State Recreation Area**. State recreation areas (SRAs) are similar to national parks but have less-strict conservation rules. There are three *camping areas* – at Freemans, Frazer and Geebung Beaches – but they're usually full at peak times; book at the office (☎ 4358 0400), off the road south of Elizabeth Bay.

Getting There & Away CityRail trains running between Sydney and the Hunter Valley stop at central coast destinations including Gosford and Wyong.

The central coast is easily accessible from Sydney via the Sydney-Newcastle Fwy.

A ferry (☎ 9918 2747) runs from Palm Beach, a northern beachside suburb of Sydney, to Patonga in Broken Bay (adult/child/family $24/15/30). From Patonga, Busways Peninsula (☎ 4368 2277) has infrequent buses to Gosford. The 11am ferry continues on to Bobbin Head in Kuring-gai Chase National Park.

From Brooklyn you can get to Patonga on a cruise boat (☎ 9985 7566) for about $16 return, or to Wobby Beach for $6.80 return with the Dangar Island Ferry Service (☎ 9985 7605), near the trailhead for a walking track through Brisbane Water National Park. Hawkesbury River train station in Brooklyn is near the ferry wharf.

Getting Around The two local bus services covering the main centres in the area are The Entrance Red Bus Services (☎ 4332 8655), and Busways Peninsula (☎ 4368 2277).

HUNTER VALLEY WINERIES (MAP 14)

Only a two-hour drive north of Sydney, the Hunter Valley is a superb scenic area liberally sprinkled with vineyards. The lower Hunter is the largest wine-growing area, but there are also wineries in the less-visited upper Hunter, especially around the village of **Denman**.

The lower Hunter has more than 50 vineyards concentrated in a small, pretty area around tiny **Pokolbin village**, north-west of Cessnock. It's a popular weekend destination, so visit midweek if possible.

The main towns in the wilder upper Hunter Valley are **Scone** and **Muswellbrook**.

The lower Hunter's information centre (☎ 4990 4477), at Turner Park, Aberdare Rd in Cessnock, is open daily (but closes at 3.30pm on Sunday). Drop in for brochures and maps (Broadbent's is a handy one) before setting out for the wineries.

If you need to get to an ATM to pay for all that wine you want to buy, you can get cash from the machine outside the general store in Pokolbin, at 188 Broke Rd.

Things to See & Do

Most wineries encourage casual visits, but several also have tours. They include: **McWilliams** (☎ 4998 7505, Marrowbone Rd, Pokolbin; tours 11am; $2 per person); **Draytons Family Wines** (☎ 4998 7513, Oakley Creek Rd, Pokolbin; tours 11am weekdays); **McGuigans** (☎ 4998 7402, MacDonalds Rd, Pokolbin); **Tyrrells** (☎ 4993 7000, Broke Rd, Pokolbin; tours 1.30pm) and **Rothbury Estate** (☎ 4998 7363, Broke Rd, Pokolbin).

Balloon Aloft (☎ 4938 1955, 1800 028 568, ⓔ balloons@balloonaloft.com, ⓦ www .balloonaloft.com, Lot 1, Main Rd, North Rothbury) has flights over the valley from $180 for a last-minute booking to $250 on weekends and public holidays.

You can hire bicycles from **Grapemobile** (☎ 4998 7639, Cnr McDonalds & Gillards Rds, Pokolbin; $15/25 half/full day).

The **Hunter Vintage Festival**, held during harvest period (January to March), attracts hordes of wine buffs for tasting, and grape-picking and treading contests. Accommodation can be scarce, but with some planning you can find good package deals. In September there's the **Wine & Food Affair**.

Organised Tours

Hunter Vineyard Tours (☎ 4991 1659) has daily departures from Newcastle and other Hunter Valley centres and charges adult/pensioner $55/52 ($38/35 without lunch).

Grapemobile (☎ 4991 2339) offers one-day bike rides through the wineries, with a support bus, overnight accommodation and all meals for $189 per person. It also has day tours ($98).

Places to Stay & Eat

Accommodation prices rise on weekends, and beds can be scarce – it's wise to book ahead. There's a multitude of accommodation options in the area, and the Cessnock information centre (☎ 4990 4477) can arrange bookings and special deals. There are a couple of caravan parks fairly close to town.

Big 4 Valley Vineyard Tourist Park (☎/fax 4990 2573, ⓔ valleyvineyard@hunter link.net.au, Mount View Rd) Mid-week camp sites/vans $20/40, budget cabins from $60.50. Only 1km from town, and close to wineries, this good, comfortable place has a pool and air-conditioned cottages.

Cessnock's pubs offer good accommodation at reasonable prices.

Black Opal Hotel (☎ 4990 1070, 220 Vincent St) Rooms $30/35 per person midweek/weekends. At the southern end of the main street, this place has much better rooms than the exterior or the main bar may suggest, and the staff are friendly.

Cessnock Hotel (☎ 4990 1002, fax 4991 4021, 234 Wollombi Rd) Singles & doubles $35/45 per person midweek/weekends. This good-value pub near Vincent St has been renovated and offers nice rooms with friendly management. Another bonus is the *Kurrajong restaurant* (☎ 4991 4414) and cafe next door. Prices quoted here include breakfast; packages including meals and bicycle rental are also available.

Wentworth Hotel (☎ 4990 1364, fax 4990 7254, 36 Vincent St) Singles/doubles $50/70. This friendly hotel has refurbished rooms, although the Irish theme and memorabilia gets a bit much after the first Guinness in the bar downstairs. Room rates include breakfast.

Aussie Rest Motel (☎ 4991 4197, 43 Shedden St) Rooms from $110. Off Wollombi Rd, this spotless, well-maintained four-star motel has good facilities, although friendliness was lacking when we visited.

Many vineyards offer accommodation. Most charge well over $140 a night on weekends, but midweek a few charge between $70 and $100 a double.

Peppers Convent (☎ 4998 7764, fax 4998 7323, [e] tcpres@peppers.com.au, [w] www .peppers.com.au, Halls Rd, Pokolbin) Deluxe/superior doubles $338/424 Sun-Thur, $724/837 weekends (2 night stay). Once a Brigidine convent, this place has been restored and redecorated and looks very romantic and inviting, especially after some strenuous wine tasting at Pepper Tree.

Hunter Country Lodge (☎ 4938 1744, Branxton Rd) Doubles $120 midweek. The Hunter Country Lodge is about 12km north of Cessnock and is a delightful place to stay, surrounded by peace and quiet. Weekend prices rise sharply.

Cafe Vincents (☎ 4990 9233, 60 Vincent St) Meals $4-7. This place offers good snacks and meals at reasonable prices.

The Cellar Restaurant (☎ 4998 7584, Broke Rd, Pokolbin) Entrees $9.90-15, mains $29-29.50. If you're after a slap-up lunch or dinner, you can't go past the wonderful cooking at The Cellar. Using local produce and armed with a great wine list, this place is probably the best in the area. Try the smoked lamb rump ($29.50) on warm beets, sweet potato with spinach salad, prosciutto and citrus aioli. Heaven.

Getting There & Away

Bus Rover Motors (☎ 4990 1699) runs between Newcastle and Cessnock ($9.80) six times daily weekdays and four times on Saturday. The last bus from Newcastle to Cessnock departs at 5.15pm on weekdays, at 4.45pm on Saturday. There are also services between Cessnock and Maitland. Rover's office is at 231-3 Vincent St in Cessnock.

Kean's (☎ 1800 625 587) stops at Cessnock ($27) daily on the run from Sydney to Scone. In Sydney, book at the Sydney Coach Terminal (☎ 9281 9366) on Eddy Ave.

Train CityRail runs from Sydney to Newcastle about 25 times daily, taking nearly three hours. The one-way fare is $16.60; an off-peak return is $19.40. Some trains connect with Rover Motors buses to Cessnock.

Car & Motorcycle There are several routes into the Hunter Valley from Sydney. The quickest is the Sydney-Newcastle Fwy.

The Putty Rd between Windsor and Singleton is longer, but more interesting (see the Macquarie Towns section earlier in this chapter). There's also an interesting but bumpy route from Wisemans Ferry, passing through Wollombi.

From Newcastle, follow the New England Hwy and turn off to Kurri Kurri and Cessnock about 4km west of Hexham Bridge.

Thanks

Many thanks to the travellers who used the last edition and wrote to us with helpful hints, useful advice and interesting anecdotes:

Christa Achermann, Amir Aharon, Coral Anderson, Jim Antisdel, Maureen Ball, Howard Barker, Brett Baxter, Marie Boisvert-Smithers, Terri Bromley, Hayley Cameron, Guy Carrier, Helen Chalmers, Nigel Chent, Jim & Elayne Coakes, Ciara Coughlan, D W Davis, Virginie Delannoy, Clare Dingle, Lucy Dougans, John Michael Dovey, Andrew Dwyer, Lynn Edwards, Sarina Eliyakim, Adri en Wim, Isabella Enimsajo, Ceri & Matt Evans, Linda Feutz Smith, Mary Forret, Bridget Fox, Jason Garman, Doug Gatrell, Stephen Gilligan, Don Grunbaum, Liz Hardy, Anna Hardwick, Shane Harvey, Russell Hayse, Paul Hobbs, Vicki Horne, Pia Hotstad, Simon Issacs, Mike Jacobs, Kaja Karlsen, Kristel & Filip Kennis-Verbeek, Anthony Keogh, Silke Kerwick, M Kirchner, Tom Kleijwegt, Tony Lammens, John Lam-Po-Tang, Oeghan Lewis, Derrick Little, Julie Macklin, Norm & Mary Mainland, Peter Mansell, Valerie Marx, Susi Mattis, Jim McNaughton, Pat Metharom, Jo Mulholland, Thomas Munday, Sue & Steve Neilson, James Norman, Jim O'Hagan, Nikki O'Sullivan, James Parry, Cathe Pedersen, Chris Pickles, J Place, Paul Prowting, David Pruet, Geoff Rhys, Nicole Rickards, Libbie Ripper, August Rusli Lie, Andrew & Pippa Sargent, Peter Saundry, Joanne Shalders, Ed Schenk, Jonas Schwartz, Claudine Senn, Hans P Shomsaus, Cameron Smith, Chris Smith, Gary Spinks, Silvia Spoel, Ximena Tapia, Mikael Torma, Tim Turner, Richard Ure, Rob van der Heijden, Peter Paul van Reenen, Odeke Schade van Westrum, Shane Vuletich, John Wakefield, Edwin Wan, Torsten Weickert, Annabel Westney, Lorna & Ken Williamson, Paul Williamson, Andy Wilson, Maartje Wolff, Trebor & Doris Yensen.

LONELY PLANET

You already know that Lonely Planet produces more than this one guidebook, but you might not be aware of the other products we have on this region. Here is a selection of titles that you may want to check out as well:

Aboriginal Australia & the Torres Strait Islands
ISBN 1 86450 114 6
US$19.99 • UK£12.99

New South Wales
ISBN 0 86442 706 9
US$19.99 • UK£12.99

Australian phrasebook
ISBN 0 86442 576 7
US$5.95 • UK£3.99

Sydney Condensed
ISBN 1 86450 045 X
US$9.95 • UK£5.99

Walking in Australia
ISBN 0 86442 669 0
US$21.99 • UK£13.99

Australia
ISBN 1 86450 068 9
US$24.95 • UK£14.99

Out to Eat Sydney
ISBN 1 74059 311 1
US$14.99 • UK£9.99

Cycling Australia
ISBN 1 86450 166 9
US$21.99 • UK£13.99

Watching Wildlife Australia
ISBN 1 86450 032 8
US$19.99 • UK£12.99

Sydney City Map
ISBN 1 86450 051 8
US$5.95 • UK£3.99

Australia Road Atlas
ISBN 1 86450 065 4
US$14.99 • UK£8.99

Healthy Travel Australia, NZ & the Pacific
ISBN 1 86450 052 2
US$5.95 • UK£3.99

Available wherever books are sold

ON THE ROAD

Travel Guides explore cities, regions and countries, and supply information on transport, restaurants and accommodation, covering all budgets. They come with reliable, easy-to-use maps, practical advice, cultural and historical facts and a rundown on attractions both on and off the beaten track. There are over 200 titles in this classic series, covering nearly every country in the world.

 Lonely Planet Upgrades extend the shelf life of existing travel guides by detailing any changes that may affect travel in a region since a book has been published. Upgrades can be downloaded for free from **www.lonelyplanet.com/upgrades**

For travellers with more time than money, **Shoestring** guides offer dependable, first-hand information with hundreds of detailed maps, plus insider tips for stretching money as far as possible. Covering entire continents in most cases, the six-volume shoestring guides are known around the world as 'backpackers bibles'.

For the discerning short-term visitor, **Condensed** guides highlight the best a destination has to offer in a full-colour, pocket-sized format designed for quick access. They include everything from top sights and walking tours to opinionated reviews of where to eat, stay, shop and have fun.

CitySync lets travellers use their Palm™ or Visor™ hand-held computers to guide them through a city with handy tips on transport, history, cultural life, major sights, and shopping and entertainment options. It can also quickly search and sort hundreds of reviews of hotels, restaurants and attractions, and pinpoint their location on scrollable street maps. CitySync can be downloaded from **www.citysync.com**

MAPS & ATLASES

Lonely Planet's **City Maps** feature downtown and metropolitan maps, as well as transit routes and walking tours. The maps come complete with an index of streets, a listing of sights and a plastic coat for extra durability.

Road Atlases are an essential navigation tool for serious travellers. Cross-referenced with the guidebooks, they also feature distance and climate charts and a complete site index.

ESSENTIALS

Read This First books help new travellers to hit the road with confidence. These invaluable predeparture guides give step-by-step advice on preparing for a trip, budgeting, arranging a visa, planning an itinerary and staying safe while still getting off the beaten track.

Healthy Travel pocket guides offer a regional rundown on disease hot spots and practical advice on predeparture health measures, staying well on the road and what to do in emergencies. The guides come with a user-friendly design and helpful diagrams and tables.

Lonely Planet's **Phrasebooks** cover the essential words and phrases travellers need when they're strangers in a strange land. They come in a pocket-sized format with colour tabs for quick reference, extensive vocabulary lists, easy-to-follow pronunciation keys and two-way dictionaries.

Miffed by blurry photos of the Taj Mahal? Tired of the classic 'top of the head cut off' shot? **Travel Photography: A Guide to Taking Better Pictures** will help you turn ordinary holiday snaps into striking images and give you the know-how to capture every scene, from frenetic festivals to peaceful beach sunrises.

Lonely Planet's **Travel Journal** is a lightweight but sturdy travel diary for jotting down all those on-the-road observations and significant travel moments. It comes with a handy time-zone wheel, a world map and useful travel information.

Lonely Planet's **eKno** is an all-in-one communication service developed especially for travellers. It offers low-cost international calls and free email and voicemail so that you can keep in touch while on the road. Check it out on **www.ekno.lonelyplanet.com**

FOOD & RESTAURANT GUIDES

Lonely Planet's **Out to Eat** guides recommend the brightest and best places to eat and drink in top international cities. These gourmet companions are arranged by neighbourhood, packed with dependable maps, garnished with scene-setting photos and served with quirky features.

For people who live to eat, drink and travel, **World Food** guides explore the culinary culture of each country. Entertaining and adventurous, each guide is packed with detail on staples and specialities, regional cuisine and local markets, as well as sumptuous recipes, comprehensive culinary dictionaries and lavish photos good enough to eat.

OUTDOOR GUIDES

For those who believe the best way to see the world is on foot, Lonely Planet's **Walking Guides** detail everything from family strolls to difficult treks, with 'when to go and how to do it' advice supplemented by reliable maps and essential travel information.

Cycling Guides map a destination's best bike tours, long and short, in day-by-day detail. They contain all the information a cyclist needs, including advice on bike maintenance, places to eat and stay, innovative maps with detailed cues to the rides, and elevation charts.

The **Watching Wildlife** series is perfect for travellers who want authoritative information but don't want to tote a heavy field guide. Packed with advice on where, when and how to view a region's wildlife, each title features photos of over 300 species and contains engaging comments on the local flora and fauna.

With underwater colour photos throughout, **Pisces Books** explore the world's best diving and snorkelling areas. Each book contains listings of diving services and dive resorts, detailed information on depth, visibility and difficulty of dives, and a roundup of the marine life you're likely to see through your mask.

OFF THE ROAD

Journeys, the travel literature series written by renowned travel authors, capture the spirit of a place or illuminate a culture with a journalist's attention to detail and a novelist's flair for words. These are tales to soak up while you're actually on the road or dip into as an at-home armchair indulgence.

The range of lavishly illustrated **Pictorial** books is just the ticket for both travellers and dreamers. Off-beat tales and vivid photographs bring the adventure of travel to your doorstep long before the journey begins and long after it is over.

Lonely Planet **Videos** encourage the same independent, tough-minded approach as the guidebooks. Currently airing throughout the world, this award-winning series features innovative footage and an original soundtrack.

Yes, we know, work is tough, so do a little bit of deskside dreaming with the spiral-bound Lonely Planet **Diary** or a Lonely Planet **Wall Calendar**, filled with great photos from around the world.

Chasing Rickshaws

TRAVELLERS NETWORK

Lonely Planet Online. Lonely Planet's award-winning Web site has insider information on hundreds of destinations, from Amsterdam to Zimbabwe, complete with interactive maps and relevant links. The site also offers the latest travel news, recent reports from travellers on the road, guidebook upgrades, a travel links site, an online book-buying option and a lively travellers bulletin board. It can be viewed at **www.lonelyplanet.com** or AOL keyword. lp.

Planet Talk is a quarterly print newsletter, full of gossip, advice, anecdotes and author articles. It provides an antidote to the being-at-home blues and lets you plan and dream for the next trip. Contact the nearest Lonely Planet office for your free copy.

Comet, the free Lonely Planet newsletter, comes via email once a month. It's loaded with travel news, advice, dispatches from authors, travel competitions and letters from readers. To subscribe, click on the Comet subscription link on the front page of the Web site.

Lonely Planet Guides by Region

Lonely Planet is known worldwide for publishing practical, reliable and no-nonsense travel information in our guides and on our Web site. The Lonely Planet list covers just about every accessible part of the world. Currently there are 16 series: Travel guides, Shoestring guides, Condensed guides, Phrasebooks, Read This First, Healthy Travel, Walking guides, Cycling guides, Watching Wildlife guides, Pisces Diving & Snorkeling guides, City Maps, Road Atlases, Out to Eat, World Food, Journeys travel literature and Pictorials.

AFRICA Africa on a shoestring • Botswana • Cairo • Cairo City Map • Cape Town • Cape Town City Map • East Africa • Egypt • Egyptian Arabic phrasebook • Ethiopia, Eritrea & Djibouti • Ethiopian Amharic phrasebook • The Gambia & Senegal • Healthy Travel Africa • Kenya • Malawi • Morocco • Moroccan Arabic phrasebook • Mozambique • Namibia • Read This First: Africa • South Africa, Lesotho & Swaziland • Southern Africa • Southern Africa Road Atlas • Swahili phrasebook • Tanzania, Zanzibar & Pemba • Trekking in East Africa • Tunisia • Watching Wildlife East Africa • Watching Wildlife Southern Africa • West Africa • World Food Morocco • Zambia • Zimbabwe, Botswana & Namibia
Travel Literature: Mali Blues: Traveling to an African Beat • The Rainbird: A Central African Journey • Songs to an African Sunset: A Zimbabwean Story

AUSTRALIA & THE PACIFIC Aboriginal Australia & the Torres Strait Islands •Auckland • Australia • Australian phrasebook • Australia Road Atlas • Cycling Australia • Cycling New Zealand • Fiji • Fijian phrasebook • Healthy Travel Australia, NZ & the Pacific • Islands of Australia's Great Barrier Reef • Melbourne • Melbourne City Map • Micronesia • New Caledonia • New South Wales • New Zealand • Northern Territory • Outback Australia • Out to Eat – Melbourne • Out to Eat – Sydney • Papua New Guinea • Pidgin phrasebook • Queensland • Rarotonga & the Cook Islands • Samoa • Solomon Islands • South Australia • South Pacific • South Pacific phrasebook • Sydney • Sydney City Map • Sydney Condensed • Tahiti & French Polynesia • Tasmania • Tonga • Tramping in New Zealand • Vanuatu • Victoria • Walking in Australia • Watching Wildlife Australia • Western Australia
Travel Literature: Islands in the Clouds: Travels in the Highlands of New Guinea • Kiwi Tracks: A New Zealand Journey • Sean & David's Long Drive

CENTRAL AMERICA & THE CARIBBEAN Bahamas, Turks & Caicos • Baja California • Belize, Guatemala & Yucatán • Bermuda • Central America on a shoestring • Costa Rica • Costa Rica Spanish phrasebook • Cuba • Cycling Cuba • Dominican Republic & Haiti • Eastern Caribbean • Guatemala • Havana • Healthy Travel Central & South America • Jamaica • Mexico • Mexico City • Panama • Puerto Rico • Read This First: Central & South America • Virgin Islands • World Food Caribbean • World Food Mexico • Yucatán
Travel Literature: Green Dreams: Travels in Central America

EUROPE Amsterdam • Amsterdam City Map • Amsterdam Condensed • Andalucía • Athens • Austria • Baltic States phrasebook • Barcelona • Barcelona City Map • Belgium & Luxembourg • Berlin • Berlin City Map • Britain • British phrasebook • Brussels, Bruges & Antwerp • Brussels City Map • Budapest • Budapest City Map • Canary Islands • Catalunya & the Costa Brava • Central Europe • Central Europe phrasebook • Copenhagen • Corfu & the Ionians • Corsica • Crete • Crete Condensed • Croatia • Cycling Britain • Cycling France • Cyprus • Czech & Slovak Republics • Czech phrasebook • Denmark • Dublin • Dublin City Map • Dublin Condensed • Eastern Europe • Eastern Europe phrasebook • Edinburgh • Edinburgh City Map • England • Estonia, Latvia & Lithuania • Europe on a shoestring • Europe phrasebook • Finland • Florence • Florence City Map • France • Frankfurt City Map • Frankfurt Condensed • French phrasebook • Georgia, Armenia & Azerbaijan • Germany • German phrasebook • Greece • Greek Islands • Greek phrasebook • Hungary • Iceland, Greenland & the Faroe Islands • Ireland • Italian phrasebook • Italy • Kraków • Lisbon • The Loire • London • London City Map • London Condensed • Madrid • Madrid City Map • Malta • Mediterranean Europe • Milan, Turin & Genoa • Moscow • Munich • Netherlands • Normandy • Norway • Out to Eat – London • Out to Eat – Paris • Paris • Paris City Map • Paris Condensed • Poland • Polish phrasebook • Portugal • Portuguese phrasebook • Prague • Prague City Map • Provence & the Côte d'Azur • Read This First: Europe • Rhodes & the Dodecanese • Romania & Moldova • Rome • Rome City Map • Rome Condensed • Russia, Ukraine & Belarus • Russian phrasebook • Scandinavian & Baltic Europe • Scandinavian phrasebook • Scotland • Sicily • Slovenia • South-West France • Spain • Spanish phrasebook • Stockholm • St Petersburg • St Petersburg City Map • Sweden • Switzerland • Tuscany • Ukrainian phrasebook • Venice • Vienna • Wales • Walking in Britain • Walking in France • Walking in Ireland • Walking in Italy • Walking in Scotland • Walking in Spain • Walking in Switzerland • Western Europe • World Food France • World Food Greece • World Food Ireland • World Food Italy • World Food Spain **Travel Literature:** After Yugoslavia • Love and War in the Apennines • The Olive Grove: Travels in Greece • On the Shores of the Mediterranean • Round Ireland in Low Gear • A Small Place in Italy

Lonely Planet Mail Order

Lonely Planet products are distributed worldwide. They are also available by mail order from Lonely Planet, so if you have difficulty finding a title please write to us. North and South American residents should write to 150 Linden St, Oakland, CA 94607, USA; European and African residents should write to 10a Spring Place, London NW5 3BH, UK; and residents of other countries to Locked Bag 1, Footscray, Victoria 3011, Australia.

INDIAN SUBCONTINENT & THE INDIAN OCEAN Bangladesh • Bengali phrasebook • Bhutan • Delhi • Goa • Healthy Travel Asia & India • Hindi & Urdu phrasebook • India • India & Bangladesh City Map • Indian Himalaya • Karakoram Highway • Kathmandu City Map • Kerala • Madagascar • Maldives • Mauritius, Réunion & Seychelles • Mumbai (Bombay) • Nepal • Nepali phrasebook • North India • Pakistan • Rajasthan • Read This First: Asia & India • South India • Sri Lanka • Sri Lanka phrasebook • Tibet • Tibetan phrasebook • Trekking in the Indian Himalaya • Trekking in the Karakoram & Hindukush • Trekking in the Nepal Himalaya • World Food India **Travel Literature:** The Age of Kali: Indian Travels and Encounters • Hello Goodnight: A Life of Goa • In Rajasthan • Maverick in Madagascar • A Season in Heaven: True Tales from the Road to Kathmandu • Shopping for Buddhas • A Short Walk in the Hindu Kush • Slowly Down the Ganges

MIDDLE EAST & CENTRAL ASIA Bahrain, Kuwait & Qatar • Central Asia • Central Asia phrasebook • Dubai • Farsi (Persian) phrasebook • Hebrew phrasebook • Iran • Israel & the Palestinian Territories • Istanbul • Istanbul City Map • Istanbul to Cairo • Istanbul to Kathmandu • Jerusalem • Jerusalem City Map • Jordan • Lebanon • Middle East • Oman & the United Arab Emirates • Syria • Turkey • Turkish phrasebook • World Food Turkey • Yemen **Travel Literature:** Black on Black: Iran Revisited • Breaking Ranks: Turbulent Travels in the Promised Land • The Gates of Damascus • Kingdom of the Film Stars: Journey into Jordan

NORTH AMERICA Alaska • Boston • Boston City Map • Boston Condensed • British Columbia • California & Nevada • California Condensed • Canada • Chicago • Chicago City Map • Chicago Condensed • Florida • Georgia & the Carolinas • Great Lakes • Hawaii • Hiking in Alaska • Hiking in the USA • Honolulu & Oahu City Map • Las Vegas • Los Angeles • Los Angeles City Map • Louisiana & the Deep South • Miami • Miami City Map • Montreal • New England • New Orleans • New Orleans City Map • New York City • New York City City Map • New York City Condensed • New York, New Jersey & Pennsylvania • Oahu • Out to Eat – San Francisco • Pacific Northwest • Rocky Mountains • San Diego & Tijuana • San Francisco • San Francisco City Map • Seattle • Seattle City Map • Southwest • Texas • Toronto • USA • USA phrasebook • Vancouver • Vancouver City Map • Virginia & the Capital Region • Washington, DC • Washington, DC City Map • World Food New Orleans **Travel Literature**: Caught Inside: A Surfer's Year on the California Coast • Drive Thru America

NORTH-EAST ASIA Beijing • Beijing City Map • Cantonese phrasebook • China • Hiking in Japan • Hong Kong & Macau • Hong Kong City Map • Hong Kong Condensed • Japan • Japanese phrasebook • Korea • Korean phrasebook • Kyoto • Mandarin phrasebook • Mongolia • Mongolian phrasebook • Seoul • Shanghai • South-West China • Taiwan • Tokyo • Tokyo Condensed • World Food Hong Kong • World Food Japan **Travel Literature:** In Xanadu: A Quest • Lost Japan

SOUTH AMERICA Argentina, Uruguay & Paraguay • Bolivia • Brazil • Brazilian phrasebook • Buenos Aires • Buenos Aires City Map • Chile & Easter Island • Colombia • Ecuador & the Galapagos Islands • Healthy Travel Central & South America • Latin American Spanish phrasebook • Peru • Quechua phrasebook • Read This First: Central & South America • Rio de Janeiro • Rio de Janeiro City Map • Santiago de Chile • South America on a shoestring • Trekking in the Patagonian Andes • Venezuela **Travel Literature**: Full Circle: A South American Journey

SOUTH-EAST ASIA Bali & Lombok • Bangkok • Bangkok City Map • Burmese phrasebook • Cambodia • Cycling Vietnam, Laos & Cambodia • East Timor phrasebook • Hanoi • Healthy Travel Asia & India • Hill Tribes phrasebook • Ho Chi Minh City (Saigon) • Indonesia • Indonesian phrasebook • Indonesia's Eastern Islands • Java • Lao phrasebook • Laos • Malay phrasebook • Malaysia, Singapore & Brunei • Myanmar (Burma) • Philippines • Pilipino (Tagalog) phrasebook • Read This First: Asia & India • Singapore • Singapore City Map • South-East Asia on a shoestring • South-East Asia phrasebook • Thailand • Thailand's Islands & Beaches • Thailand, Vietnam, Laos & Cambodia Road Atlas • Thai phrasebook • Vietnam • Vietnamese phrasebook • World Food Thailand • World Food Vietnam

ALSO AVAILABLE: Antarctica • The Arctic • The Blue Man: Tales of Travel, Love and Coffee • Brief Encounters: Stories of Love, Sex & Travel • Buddhist Stupas in Asia: The Shape of Perfection • Chasing Rickshaws • The Last Grain Race • Lonely Planet ... On the Edge: Adventurous Escapades from Around the World • Lonely Planet Unpacked • Lonely Planet Unpacked Again • Not the Only Planet: Science Fiction Travel Stories • Ports of Call: A Journey by Sea • Sacred India • Travel Photography: A Guide to Taking Better Pictures • Travel with Children • Tuvalu: Portrait of an Island Nation

Index

Text

Places to Stay

Places to Eat

Boxed Text

Sydney Maps

MAP 1 – AROUND SYDNEY

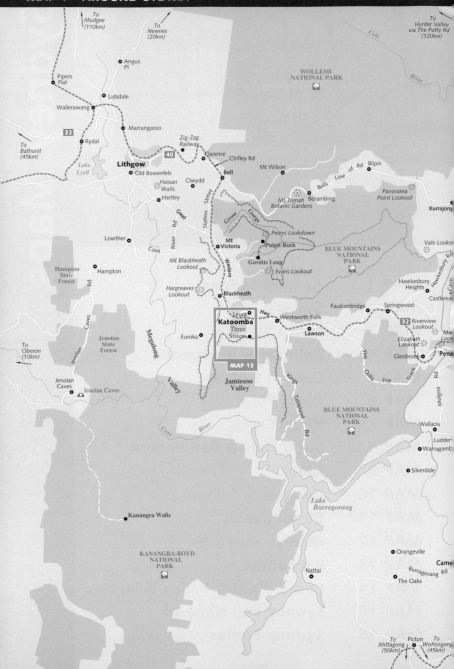

To Mudgee (110km)

To Newnes (20km)

To Hunter Valley via The Putty Rd (120km)

Cox

Colo River

Angus Pl

Pipers Flat

Lidsdale

Wallerawang

WOLLEMI NATIONAL PARK

Marrangaroo

32

Rydal

Zig-Zag Railway

Clarence

Chifley Rd

Mt Wilson

Bilpin

To Bathurst (45km)

40

Lithgow

Old Bowenfels

Lake Lyell

Clwydd

Bell

Bells Line of Rd

Berambing

Panorama Point Lookout

Kurrajong

Hassan Walls

Hartley

Mt Tomah Botanic Gardens

Great River Rd

Station Street

Grose

Gorge

Perrys Lookdown

Pulpit Rock

Vale Lookout

Lowther

Coxs

Mt Victoria

Govetts Leap

BLUE MOUNTAINS NATIONAL PARK

Evans Lookout

Hawkesbury Rd

Hampton State Forest

Hampton

Caves Rd

Mt Blackheath Lookout

Western

Hawkesbury Heights

Castlerea

Hargreaves Lookout

Blackheath

Faulconbridge

Springwood

Jenolan State Forest

Jenolan Rd

Megalong

Leura

Wentworth Falls

32

Riverview Lookout

Ma Loo

Katoomba

Three Sisters

Lawson

Elizabeth Lookout

To Oberon (10km)

Euroka

MAP 13

The Oaks

Glenbrook

Pen

Mulgoa Rd

Jenolan Caves

Jenolan Caves

Valley

Jamieson Valley

Kings

Fire

Track

Wallacia

Coxs River

Tableland Rd

BLUE MOUNTAINS NATIONAL PARK

Ludder

Warragamb

Silverdale

Lake Burragorang

Kanangra Walls

Orangeville

Cam

Burragorang Rd

KANANGRA-BOYD NATIONAL PARK

Nattai

The Oaks

To Mittagong (50km)

Picton

To Wollongong (45km)

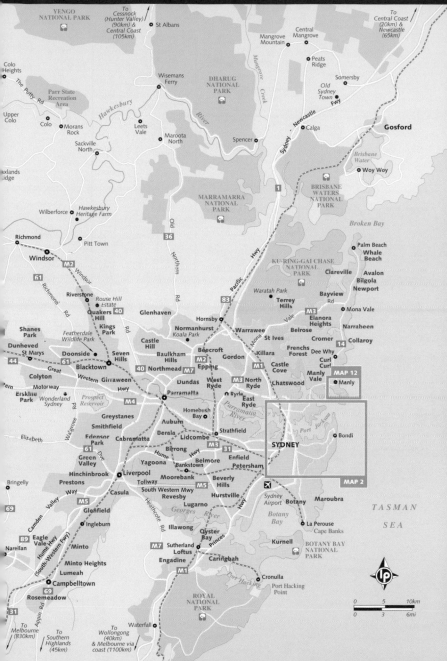

MAP 2 – SYDNEY

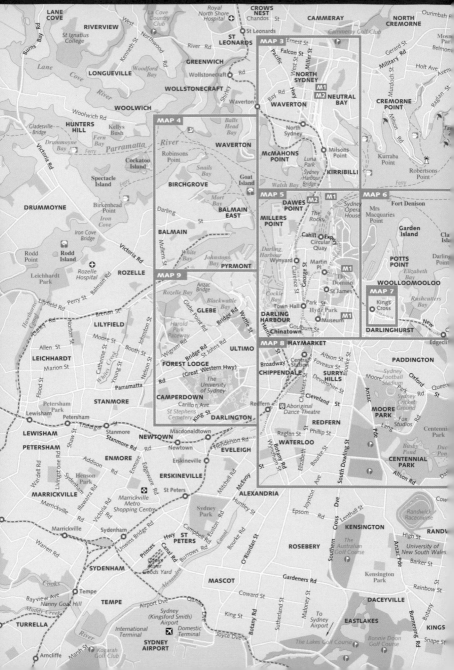

LMORAL

Hunters
Bay

Middle Harbour

SYDNEY
HARBOUR
NATIONAL PARK

North
Head

Balmoral
Beach

Middle
Head

Middle Head

GEORGES
HEIGHTS

South
Head

Lady
Bay

Hornby
Lighthouse

Middle Head Rd

Lady Beach

Military Reserve

Clifton Gardens

Georges
Head

Camp
Cove

Inner
South Head

Chowder
Bay

Laings Point

Gap Bluff

Chowder
Head

Watsons
Bay

The
Gap

Gap Park

Taylors
Bay

Vaucluse
Point

Shark
Bay

Parsley
Bay

WATSONS
BAY

SYDNEY HARBOUR
NATIONAL PARK

Shark
Beach

Vaucluse
Bay

Dunbar Head

Steel
Point

Outer
South Head

Bradleys Head

VAUCLUSE

Macquarie
Lighthouse

HMAS Sydney
Mast

Shark
Island

Hermit
Point

Port Jackson
(Sydney Harbour)

Diamond
Bay

TASMAN

Woollahra
Point

SEA

Felix
Bay

Rose Bay

Rd

DOVER
HEIGHTS

POINT PIPER

Rd

Rose Bay Rd

Dover

South Head Rd

Rd

Rodney
Reserve

Double
Bay

BELLEVUE
HILL

ROSE BAY

South Head Rd

Military Rd

Hardy St

DOUBLE
BAY

Victoria Rd

O'Sullivan Rd

Royal
Sydney
Golf
Course

Old South Head Rd

NORTH
BONDI

Bellevue Rd

Murriverie St

Cooper Park

Blair St

Edgecliff Rd

Linfield Dve

Bondi
Junction

BONDI

MAP 11

Hall St

Bondi
Golf
Club

Wellington

BONDI
BEACH

Campbell Pde

Bondi
Beach

Ben Buckler

Waverley
Park

Bondi Rd

Bondi
Bay

QUEENS
PARK

Birrell St

TAMARAMA

Bondi Baths

WAVERLEY

Tamarama Bay

Queens Park
Rd

Bronte Rd

Bronte
Beach

Nelson
Bay

Tamarama Beach

Clovelly

BRONTE

Waverley
Cemetery

CLOVELLY

Rd

Burrows Park
Shark Point

MAP 10

Gordons
Bay

Clovelly
Bay

COOGEE

Arden St

Coogee Bay Rd

Coogee
Beach

Mount St

Trenerry
Reserve

Latham
Park

0   1   2km

0   0.5   1mi

MAP 3 – NORTH SYDNEY

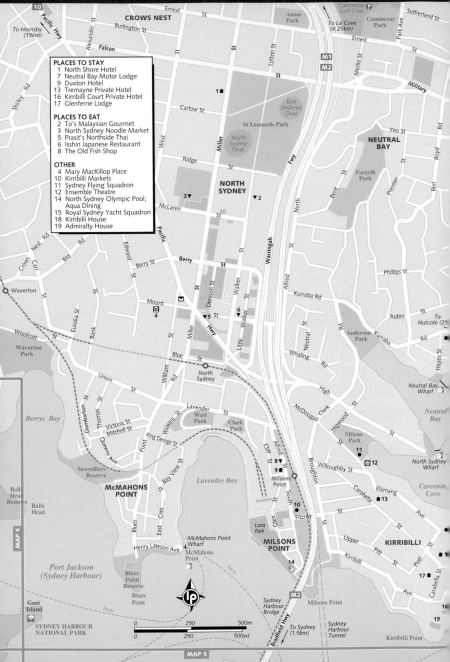

PLACES TO STAY
1 North Shore Hotel
7 Neutral Bay Motor Lodge
9 Duxton Hotel
13 Tremayne Private Hotel
16 Kirribilli Court Private Hotel
17 Glenferrie Lodge

PLACES TO EAT
2 To's Malaysian Gourmet
3 North Sydney Noodle Market
5 Prasit's Northside Thai
6 Isshin Japanese Restaurant
8 The Old Fish Shop

OTHER
4 Mary MacKillop Place
10 Kirribilli Markets
11 Sydney Flying Squadron
12 Ensemble Theatre
14 North Sydney Olympic Pool;
   Aqua Dining
15 Royal Sydney Yacht Squadron
18 Kirribilli House
19 Admiralty House

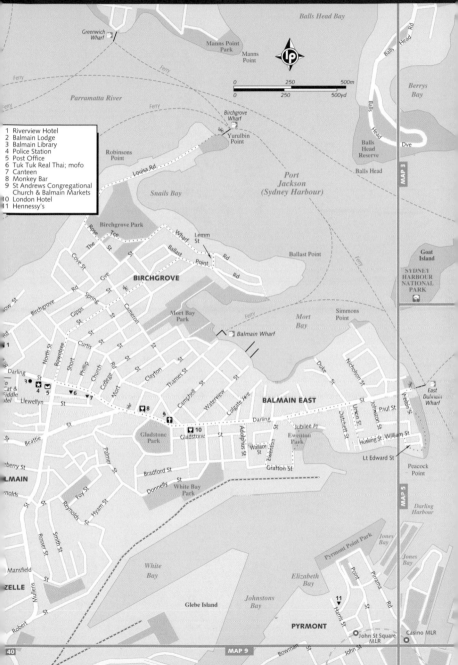

Balls Head Bay

Greenwich Wharf

Manns Point Park

Manns Point

Ferry

Ferry

Parramatta River

Ferry

Ferry

0   250   500m
0   250   500yd

Berrys Bay

Balls Head Rd

Balls Head Rd

Birchgrove Wharf

Yurulbin Point

Robinsons Point

Louisa Rd

Port Jackson (Sydney Harbour)

Balls Head Reserve

Dve

Balls Head

Balls Head

MAP 3

Snails Bay

Birchgrove Park

Rose Tce

The

Cove St

Gve

Spring St

Birchgrove Rd

Gipps St

Rowntree St

North St

Short St

Cameron

Curtis St

Church St

Cottage Rd

Mort St

Wharf Rd

Ballast Point Rd

Lemm St

Rd

Ballast Point

BIRCHGROVE

Mort Bay Park

Balmain Wharf

Ferry

Mort Bay

Simmons Point

Ferry

Goat Island

SYDNEY HARBOUR NATIONAL PARK

Ferry

Darling St

Llewellyn St

Beattie St

Clayton St

Thames St

Campbell St

Waterview St

Colgate Ave

Duke St

Nicholson St

Uren St

Johnston St

Paul St

Datchett St

Trenton St

BALMAIN EAST

Darling St

Jubilee Pl

Ewenton Park

Hunking St

William St

Lt Edward St

East Balmain Wharf

Peacock Point

MAP 5

Cat & Fiddle Hotel

Gladstone Park

Gladstone St

Adolphus St

Wallace St

Ewenton St

Grafton St

Darling Harbour

Berry St

Reynolds St

Bradford St

Donnelly St

White Bay Park

Palmer St

Foy St

Hyam St

Smith St

Rosser St

Mullens St

Robert St

Mansfield St

LMAIN

ZELLE

White Bay

Glebe Island

Johnstons Bay

Elizabeth Bay

Point

Pirrama Rd

Pyrmont Point Park

Jones Bay

Jones Bay

11

Harris St

John St Square MLR

PYRMONT

Bowman St

John St

Casino MLR

40

MAP 9

MAP 5 – CENTRAL SYDNEY

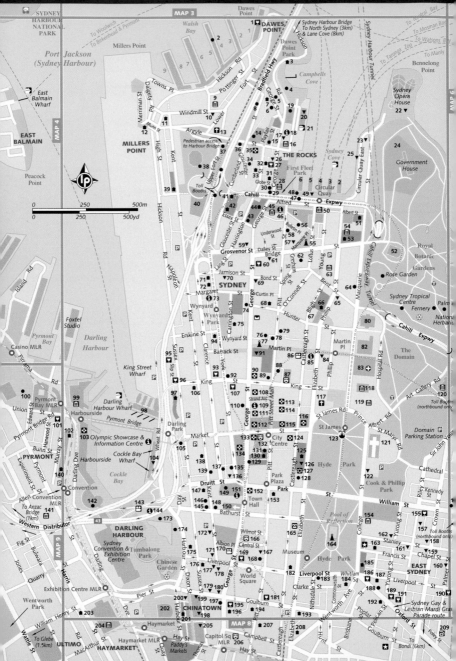

MAP 3

MAP 4

MAP 6

MAP 9

MAP 8

MAP 5 – CENTRAL SYDNEY

PLACES TO STAY
3 Park Hyatt Sydney
7 Mercantile Hotel
11 Lord Nelson Brewery Hotel
12 Palisade Hotel
31 The Russell
32 Harbour Rocks Hotel
33 The Stafford
39 Observatory Hotel
41 ANA Hotel Sydney
42 Quay West Sydney
44 Regent
51 Sir Stamford at Circular Quay
53 Hotel Inter-Continental
66 Wentworth Hotel
68 Grand Hotel
71 The York
72 Sydney Vista Hotel
75 Menzies Hotel
94 The Carrington Apartments
97 Four Points Hotel Sheraton
102 Hotel Ibis
106 Savoy Apartments
125 Sheraton on the Park
130 Sydney Hilton; Marble Bar
138 Pacific International
140 Novotel Sydney on Darling Harbour
147 Wanderers on Kent
153 Criterion Hotel
163 Sydney Park Inn
175 Southern Cross Executive Suites
176 The Waldorf
182 Hyde Park Inn & Serviced Apartments
184 Y on the Park
185 Hyde Park Plaza; Sydney Marriot
187 Parkridge Corporate Apartments
192 Oxford Koala Hotel
193 Southern Cross Hotel
194 Hotel Bakpak CB
196 The George Street Private Hotel
201 Furama
203 Glasgow Arms Hotel
207 Hotel Bakpak Westend
208 Sydney Central Private Hotel

PLACES TO EAT
10 The Hero of Waterloo
17 Sailors Thai
20 Doyle's at the Quay
22 Bennelong; Harbour; Concourse
23 Aria; Dendy Cinema
25 Sydney Cove Oyster Bar; Portobello Caffe
26 Rockpool
49 Rossini
57 Obelisk Cafe
59 The Brooklyn Hotel
61 VII

65 Chifley Tower; Forty One
69 The Summit
70 Volnay; Le Meridien
84 Banc; Wine Banc; Mint Bar
91 Sosumi
104 Cockle Bay Wharf; Blackbird; Chinta Ria...The Temple of Love; Home Nightclub
122 Bodhi; Cook & Phillip Park
126 Bambini Trust Cafe
136 Zenergy
157 The Edge
158 Bill & Toni's; Divino; Palati Fini
159 No Names; Arch Coffee Lounge
160 bonne femme
161 Two Chefs
162 Beppi's
167 Mother Chu's Vegetarian Kitchen
171 Don Quixote
172 Tetsuya's
177 Capitan Torres
178 Casa Asturiana
179 BBQ King
180 Lam's Seafood Restaurant
198 Sussex Centre
199 Golden Century Seafood Restaurant
200 Harbour Plaza Food Court
205 Dixon House Food Court

BARS & CLUBS
1 Harbourside Brasserie
27 Fortune of War
60 Establishment; Sushi e; Est
93 Hotel CBD
95 Bristol Arms Retro Hotel
96 Slip Inn; Dundee Arms Tavern
101 Pyrmont Bridge Hotel
107 Forbes Hotel
155 Club 77
169 Century Tavern
181 Civic Hotel
186 Burdekin Hotel
189 Exchange Hotel
190 East Village
191 Q Bar
195 Scuffy Murphy's

OTHER
2 Pier 4; Sydney Dance Company; Sydney Theatre Company; Wharf Theatre; Bangarra Dance Theatre; Australian Theatre for Young People
4 Campbell's Storehouse
5 Metcalfe Arcade
6 Australian Conservation Foundation Shop
8 Naisda Studios (Indigenous Dance); Bridgeclimb
9 Colonial House Museum
13 Garrison Church
14 Argyle Stores; Antibar
15 Rocks Centre
16 Cadman's Cottage
18 Sydney Visitors Centre
19 Ken Done Gallery
21 Overseas Passenger Terminal
24 Government House
28 Museum of Contemporary Art; MCA Cafe
29 DFS Galleria
30 Aboriginal & Tribal Art Centre
34 Susannah Place
35 Clocktower Square Shopping Centre
36 Argyle Cut
37 Pedestrian Access to Harbour Bridge
38 Sydney Observatory
40 National Trust of Australia
43 Site of Public Gallows; Sydney's First Gaol
45 Goldfields House; Australian Wine Centre
46 City Host Visitor Information Booth
47 CityRail Booth
48 Australian Travel Specialists (CQ)
50 Customs House; Cafe Sydney
52 Conservatorium of Music
54 Justice & Police Museum
55 Obelisk
56 The Basement
58 Downtown Duty Free
62 Lands Department Building
63 Museum of Sydney; MoS Cafe
64 Historic House
67 Qantas Centre
73 Countrylink Travel Centre
74 Paxton's
76 City Recital Hall
77 Cenotaph
78 Thomas Cook Boot & Clothing Company
79 City International Duty Free
80 State Library
81 Gardens Shop
82 Parliament House
83 Sydney Hospital
85 City Host Visitor Information Booth
86 Dendy Cinema; Dendy Bar & Bistro
87 Theatre Royal
88 American Express
89 Thomas Cook

MAP 5 – CENTRAL SYDNEY

PAUL BEINSSEN

Highrise architecture: tall glass towers in the city centre

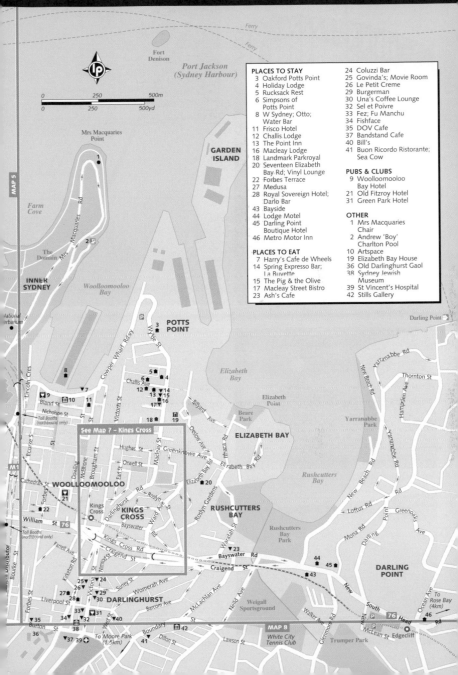

PLACES TO STAY
3 Oakford Potts Point
4 Holiday Lodge
5 Rucksack Rest
6 Simpsons of
  Potts Point
8 W Sydney; Otto;
  Water Bar
11 Frisco Hotel
12 Challis Lodge
13 The Point Inn
16 Macleay Lodge
18 Landmark Parkroyal
20 Seventeen Elizabeth
  Bay Rd; Vinyl Lounge
22 Forbes Terrace
27 Medusa
28 Royal Sovereign Hotel;
  Darlo Bar
43 Bayside
44 Lodge Motel
45 Darling Point
  Boutique Hotel
46 Metro Motor Inn

PLACES TO EAT
7 Harry's Cafe de Wheels
14 Spring Expresso Bar;
  La Buvette
15 The Pig & the Olive
17 Macleay Street Bistro
23 Ash's Cafe

24 Coluzzi Bar
25 Govinda's; Movie Room
26 Le Petit Creme
29 Burgerman
30 Una's Coffee Lounge
32 Sel et Poivre
33 Fez; Fu Manchu
34 Fishface
35 DOV Cafe
37 Bandstand Cafe
40 Bill's
41 Buon Ricordo Ristorante;
  Sea Cow

PUBS & CLUBS
9 Woolloomooloo
  Bay Hotel
21 Old Fitzroy Hotel
31 Green Park Hotel

OTHER
1 Mrs Macquaries
  Chair
2 Andrew 'Boy'
  Charlton Pool
10 Artspace
19 Elizabeth Bay House
36 Old Darlinghurst Gaol
38 Sydney Jewish
  Museum
39 St Vincent's Hospital
42 Stills Gallery

Great weather, coffee and views

Sydney Opera House detail

Sophisticated outfits – Queen Victoria Building

Swimmers at the Bronte Baths

Tanning at Bondi Beach

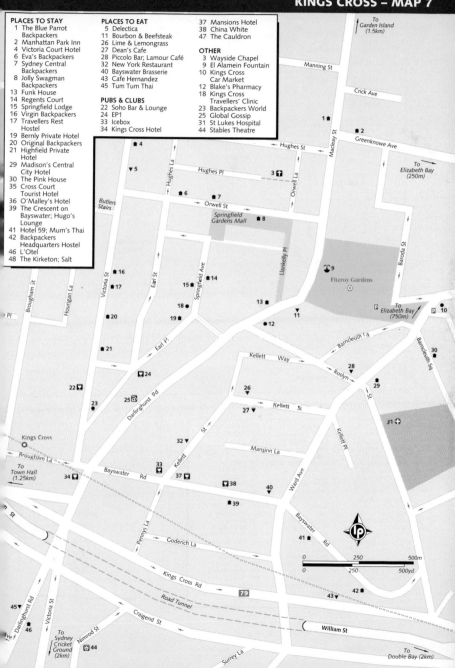

PLACES TO STAY
1 The Blue Parrot Backpackers
2 Manhattan Park Inn
4 Victoria Court Hotel
6 Eva's Backpackers
7 Sydney Central Backpackers
8 Jolly Swagman Backpackers
13 Funk House
14 Regents Court
15 Springfield Lodge
16 Virgin Backpackers
17 Travellers Rest Hostel
19 Bernly Private Hotel
20 Original Backpackers
21 Highfield Private Hotel
29 Madison's Central City Hotel
30 The Pink House
35 Cross Court Tourist Hotel
36 O'Malley's Hotel
39 The Crescent on Bayswater; Hugo's Lounge
41 Hotel 59; Mum's Thai
42 Backpackers Headquarters Hostel
46 L'Otel
48 The Kirketon; Salt

PLACES TO EAT
5 Delectica
11 Bourbon & Beefsteak
26 Lime & Lemongrass
27 Dean's Cafe
28 Piccolo Bar; Lamour Café
32 New York Restaurant
40 Bayswater Brasserie
43 Cafe Hernandez
45 Tum Tum Thai

PUBS & CLUBS
22 Soho Bar & Lounge
24 EP1
33 Icebox
34 Kings Cross Hotel

37 Mansions Hotel
38 China White
47 The Cauldron

OTHER
3 Wayside Chapel
9 El Alamein Fountain
10 Kings Cross Car Market
12 Blake's Pharmacy
18 Kings Cross Travellers' Clinic
23 Backpackers World
25 Global Gossip
31 St Lukes Hospital
44 Stables Theatre

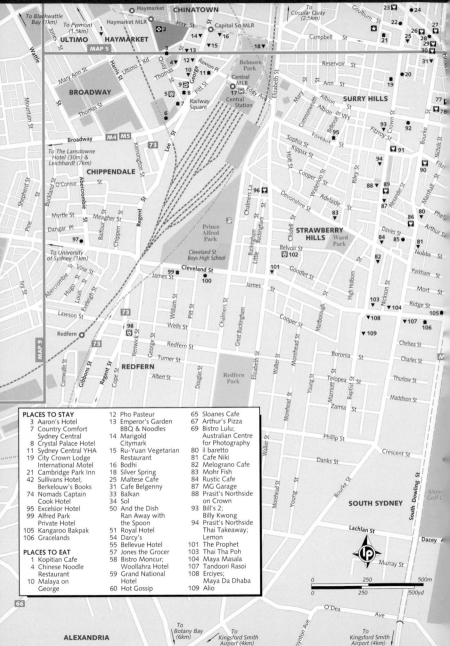

MAP 8 – SURRY HILLS & PADDINGTON

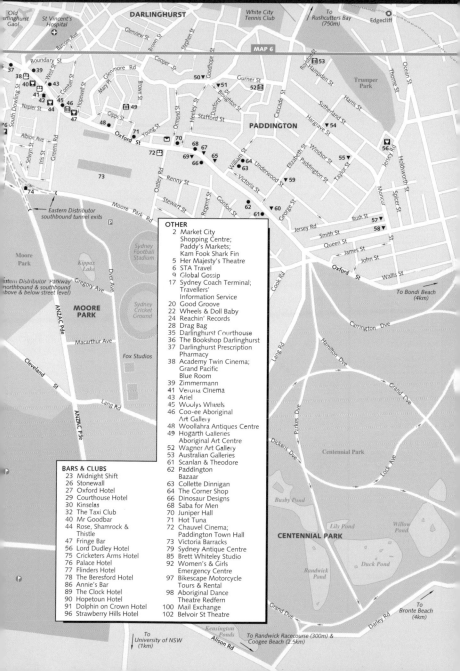

DARLINGHURST

Old Darlinghurst Gaol

St Vincent's Hospital

White City Tennis Club

To Rushcutters Bay (750m)

Edgecliff

MAP 6

PADDINGTON

Trumper Park

Eastern Distributor southbound tunnel exits

Eastern Distributor Parkway (northbound & southbound above & below street level)

Moore Park

Kippax Lake

MOORE PARK

Sydney Football Stadium

Sydney Cricket Ground

Fox Studios

To Bondi Beach (4km)

Centennial Park

CENTENNIAL PARK

Busby Pond

Lily Pond

Willow Pond

Duck Pond

Randwick Pond

To Bronte Beach (4km)

Kensington Ponds

To University of NSW (1km)

To Randwick Racecourse (300m) & Coogee Beach (2.5km)

OTHER
2 Market City
    Shopping Centre;
    Paddy's Markets;
    Kam Fook Shark Fin
5 Her Majesty's Theatre
9 STA Travel
9 Global Gossip
17 Sydney Coach Terminal;
    Travellers'
    Information Service
20 Good Groove
22 Wheels & Doll Baby
24 Reachin' Records
28 Drag Bag
35 Darlinghurst Courthouse
36 The Bookshop Darlinghurst
37 Darlinghurst Prescription
    Pharmacy
38 Academy Twin Cinema;
    Grand Pacific
    Blue Room
39 Zimmermann
41 Verona Cinema
43 Ariel
45 Woolys Wheels
46 Coo-ee Aboriginal
    Art Gallery
48 Woollahra Antiques Centre
49 Hogarth Galleries
    Aboriginal Art Centre
52 Wagner Art Gallery
53 Australian Galleries
61 Scanlan & Theodore
62 Paddington
    Bazaar
63 Collette Dinnigan
64 The Corner Shop
66 Dinosaur Designs
68 Saba for Men
70 Juniper Hall
71 Hot Tuna
72 Chauvel Cinema;
    Paddington Town Hall
73 Victoria Barracks
79 Sydney Antique Centre
85 Brett Whiteley Studio
92 Women's & Girls
    Emergency Centre
97 Bikescape Motorcycle
    Tours & Rental
98 Aboriginal Dance
    Theatre Redfern
100 Mail Exchange
102 Belvoir St Theatre

BARS & CLUBS
23 Midnight Shift
26 Stonewall
27 Oxford Hotel
29 Courthouse Hotel
30 Kinselas
32 The Taxi Club
40 Mr Goodbar
44 Rose, Shamrock &
    Thistle
47 Fringe Bar
75 Lord Dudley Hotel
75 Cricketers Arms Hotel
76 Palace Hotel
77 Flinders Hotel
78 The Beresford Hotel
86 Annie's Bar
89 The Clock Hotel
90 Hopetoun Hotel
91 Dolphin on Crown Hotel
96 Strawberry Hills Hotel

MAP 9 – GLEBE

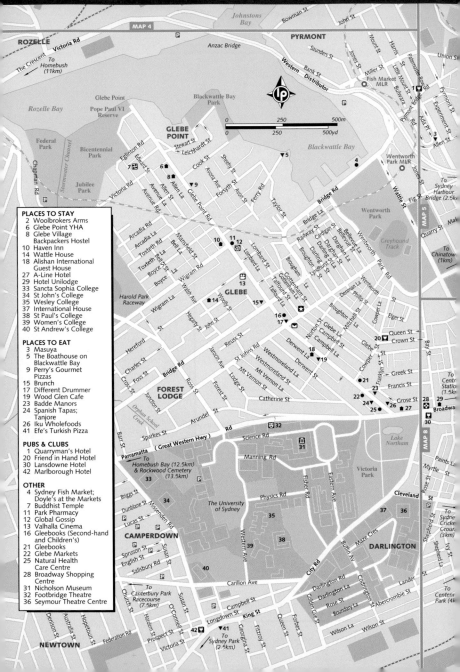

ROZELLE

PYRMONT

GLEBE POINT

GLEBE

FOREST LODGE

CAMPERDOWN

DARLINGTON

NEWTOWN

PLACES TO STAY
2 Woolbrokers Arms
6 Glebe Point YHA
8 Glebe Village Backpackers Hostel
10 Haven Inn
14 Wattle House
18 Alishan International Guest House
27 A-Line Hotel
29 Hotel Unilodge
33 Sancta Sophia College
34 St John's College
35 Wesley College
37 International House
38 St Paul's College
39 Women's College
40 St Andrew's College

PLACES TO EAT
3 Masuya
5 The Boathouse on Blackwattle Bay
9 Perry's Gourmet Pizzas
15 Brunch
17 Different Drummer
19 Wood Glen Cafe
23 Badde Manors
24 Spanish Tapas; Tanjore
26 Iku Wholefoods
41 Efe's Turkish Pizza

PUBS & CLUBS
1 Quarryman's Hotel
20 Friend in Hand Hotel
30 Lansdowne Hotel
42 Marlborough Hotel

OTHER
4 Sydney Fish Market; Doyle's at the Markets
7 Buddhist Temple
11 Park Pharmacy
12 Global Gossip
13 Valhalla Cinema
16 Gleebooks (Second-hand and Children's)
21 Gleebooks
22 Glebe Markets
25 Natural Health Care Centre
28 Broadway Shopping Centre
31 Nicholson Museum
32 Footbridge Theatre
36 Seymour Theatre Centre

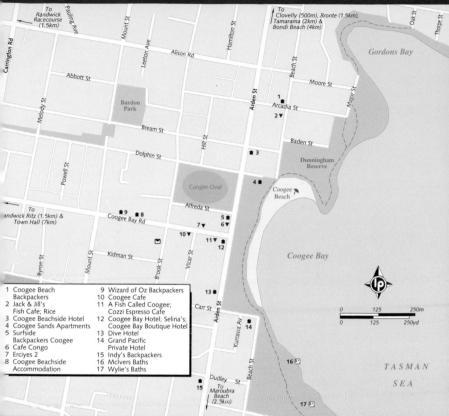

To Randwick Racecourse (1.5km)

To Clovelly (500m), Bronte (1.5km), Tamarama (2km) & Bondi Beach (4km)

Gordons Bay

Pauling Ave

Carrington Rd

Mount St

Leeton Ave

Alison Rd

Hamilton St

Beach St

Moore St

Major St

Sackville St

Oak St

Abbott St

Melody St

Bardon Park

Bream St

Hill St

Arden St

Arcadia St

1 ■
2 ▼

Baden St

Dolphin St

Powell St

Coogee Oval

■ 3

■ 4

Dunningham Reserve

Coogee Beach

Alfreda St

To Randwick Ritz (1.5km) & Town Hall (7km)

Coogee Bay Rd

■ 9 ■ 8

5 ■
6 ▼
7 ▼

Coogee Bay

Byron St

Mount St

Kidman St

Brook St

Vicar St

10 ▼

11 ▼
12

▣

13 ■

Carr St

Arden St

Kurrawa Ave

14

15

Dudley St

Beach St

To Maroubra Beach (2.5km)

16 ⚑

17 ⚑

TASMAN SEA

0 ___ 125 ___ 250m
0 ___ 125 ___ 250yd

1 Coogee Beach Backpackers
2 Jack & Jill's Fish Cafe; Rice
3 Coogee Beachside Hotel
4 Coogee Sands Apartments
5 Surfside Backpackers Coogee
6 Cafe Congo
7 Erciyes 2
8 Coogee Beachside Accommodation
9 Wizard of Oz Backpackers
10 Coogee Cafe
11 A Fish Called Coogee; Cozzi Espresso Cafe
12 Coogee Bay Hotel; Selina's; Coogee Bay Boutique Hotel
13 Dive Hotel
14 Grand Pacific Private Hotel
15 Indy's Backpackers
16 McIvers Baths
17 Wylie's Baths

Pounding the surf: Sydney's famous surf lifesavers in action

DENNIS JONES

MAP 11 – BONDI BEACH

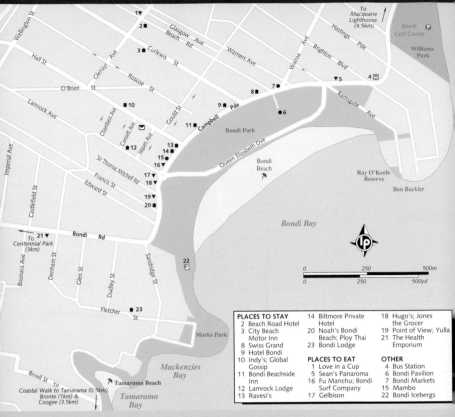

PLACES TO STAY
2 Beach Road Hotel
3 City Beach Motor Inn
8 Swiss Grand
9 Hotel Bondi
10 Indy's; Global Gossip
11 Bondi Beachside Inn
12 Lamrock Lodge
13 Ravesi's
14 Biltmore Private Hotel
20 Noah's Bondi Beach; Ploy Thai
23 Bondi Lodge

PLACES TO EAT
1 Love in a Cup
5 Sean's Panorama
16 Fu Manchu; Bondi Surf Company
17 Gelbison

18 Hugo's; Jones the Grocer
19 Point of View; Yulla
21 The Health Emporium

OTHER
4 Bus Station
6 Bondi Pavilion
7 Bondi Markets
15 Mambo
22 Bondi Icebergs

Swim between the flags – and stay safe

PAUL BEINSSEN

PLACES TO STAY
1 Manly Beach Hut
2 Manly Beach Resort Backpackers
3 Manly Astra Backpackers
6 Manly Backpackers Beachside
7 Manly Pacific Parkroyal
10 Manly Paradise Motel
13 Steyne Hotel
17 Grande Esplanade; Alhambra Cafe & Tapas Bar
25 Manly Lodge
26 Radisson Kestrel
32 Periwinkle Guest House

PLACES TO EAT
9 Fresh
11 Barking Frog
12 Wi Marn Thai
14 Blue Water Cafe
15 Malacca Straits
21 Armstrong's Bar & Restaurant
28 The Bower Restaurant
30 Le Kiosk

OTHER
4 Aloha Surf
5 Manly Cycles
8 Manly Blades
16 Dive Centre Manly
18 Manly Art Gallery & Museum
19 Oceanworld
20 Netted Swimming Area
22 Bus Interchange
23 Manly Visitors Information Bureau
24 Manly Twin Cinemas
27 Manly Surf Lifesaving Club
29 Saltwater Swimming Pool
31 St Patrick's College

MICHAEL LAANELA

A guided tour of the Sydney Opera House can offer some fascinating insights into the building's history.

MAP 13 – KATOOMBA

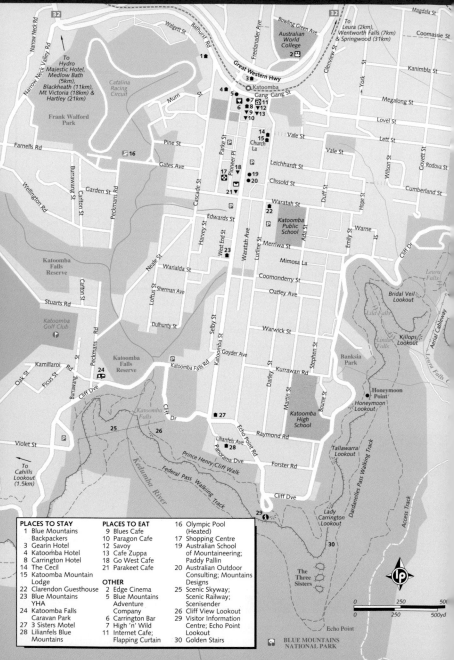

LOWER HUNTER VALLEY WINERIES – MAP 14

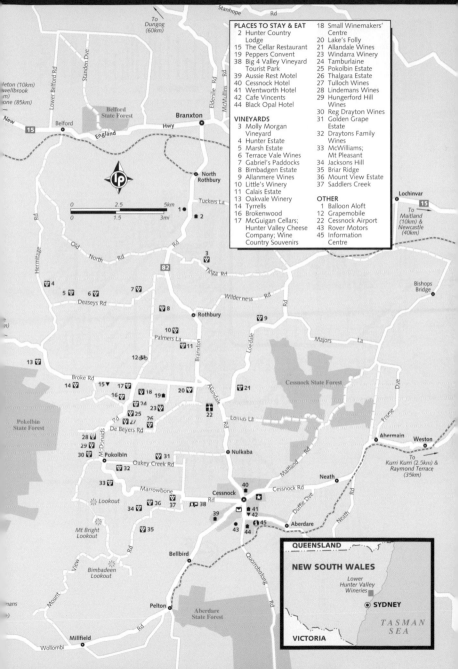

PLACES TO STAY & EAT
2 Hunter Country Lodge
15 The Cellar Restaurant
19 Peppers Convent
38 Big 4 Valley Vineyard Tourist Park
39 Aussie Rest Motel
40 Cessnock Hotel
41 Wentworth Hotel
42 Cafe Vincents
44 Black Opal Hotel

VINEYARDS
3 Molly Morgan Vineyard
4 Hunter Estate
5 Marsh Estate
6 Terrace Vale Wines
7 Gabriel's Paddocks
8 Bimbadgen Estate
9 Allanmere Wines
10 Little's Winery
11 Calais Estate
13 Oakvale Winery
14 Tyrrells
16 Brokenwood
17 McGuigan Cellars; Hunter Valley Cheese Company; Wine Country Souvenirs
18 Small Winemakers' Centre
20 Lake's Folly
21 Allandale Wines
23 Windarra Winery
24 Tamburlaine
25 Pokolbin Estate
26 Thalgara Estate
27 Tulloch Wines
28 Lindemans Wines
29 Hungerford Hill Wines
30 Reg Drayton Wines
31 Golden Grape Estate
32 Draytons Family Wines
33 McWilliams; Mt Pleasant
34 Jacksons Hill
35 Briar Ridge
36 Mount View Estate
37 Saddlers Creek

OTHER
1 Balloon Aloft
12 Grapemobile
22 Cessnock Airport
43 Rover Motors
45 Information Centre

MAP 15 – SYDNEY RAIL NETWORK

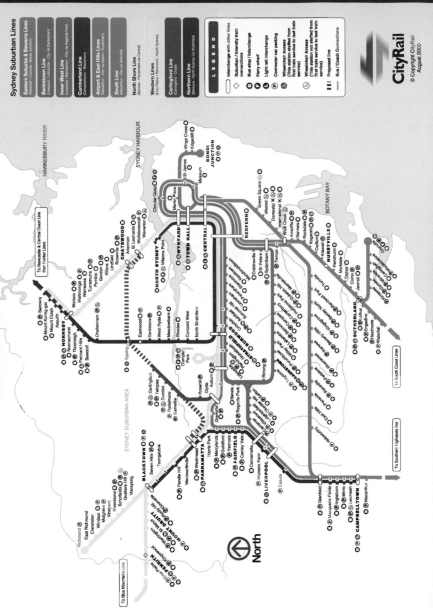

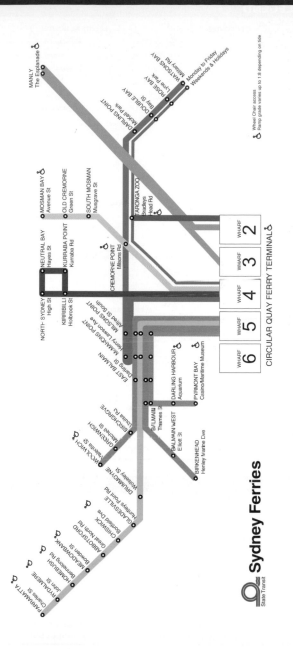

Sydney Ferries
State Transit

CIRCULAR QUAY FERRY TERMINAL

WHARF 2
WHARF 3
WHARF 4
WHARF 5
WHARF 6

MANLY
The Esplanade

MOSMAN BAY
Avenue St

OLD CREMORNE
Green St

SOUTH MOSMAN
Musgrave St

NEUTRAL BAY
Hayes St

KURRABA POINT
Kurraba Rd

CREMORNE POINT
Milsons Rd

TARONGA ZOO
Bradleys
Head Rd

DARLING POINT
McKell Park

DOUBLE BAY
Bay St

ROSE BAY
Lyne Park

WATSONS BAY
Military Rd

Monday to Friday
Weekends & Holidays

NORTH SYDNEY
High St

KIRRIBILLI
Holbrook St

MILSONS POINT
Alfred St South

McMAHONS POINT
Henry Lawson Ave

EAST BALMAIN
Darling St

DARLING HARBOUR
Aquarium

PYRMONT BAY
Casino/Maritime Museum

BALMAIN
Thames St

GREENWICH
Mitchell St

BIRCHGROVE
Louisa Rd

BALMAIN WEST
Elliott St

BIRKENHEAD
Henley Marine Dve

WOOLWICH
Valentia St

DRUMMOYNE
Wolseley St

GLADESVILLE
Punt Rd

CHISWICK
Bortfield Dve

ABBOTSFORD
Great North Rd

MEADOWBANK
Bowden St

HOMEBUSH
Bennelong Rd

RYDALMERE
John St

PARRAMATTA
Charles St

Wheel Chair access
Ramp grade varies up to 1:8 depending on tide

MAP LEGEND

CITY ROUTES

Freeway .... Freeway	————— Unsealed Road
Highway .... Primary Road	——→ One Way Street
Road .... Secondary Road	Pedestrian Street
Street .... Street	▪▪▪▪▪▪▪▪▪▪ Stepped Street
Lane .... Lane	⌐= = = Tunnel
On/Off Ramp	Footbridge

HYDROGRAPHY

River, Creek	Dry Lake; Salt Lake
Canal	Spring; Rapids
Lake	Waterfalls

REGIONAL ROUTES

Tollway, Freeway	
Primary Road	
Secondary Road	
Minor Road	

BOUNDARIES

—▪—▪— International	
—▪—▪— State	
— — — Disputed	
▪▪▪▪▪▪ Fortified Wall	

TRANSPORT ROUTES & STATIONS

▪▪▪▪▪O▪▪ Train	———— Ferry
▪▪▪▪▪▪▪▪▪▪ Underground Train	——↗ Walking Trail
—▪—Ⓜ— Metro	▪▪▪▪▪▪↗ Walking Tour
▪▪▪▪▪▪▪▪▪▪▪▪ Tramway	Path
Cable Car, Chairlift	———— Pier or Jetty

AREA FEATURES

Building	Market	Beach	Campus
Park, Gardens	Sports Ground	+ + + Cemetery	Plaza

POPULATION SYMBOLS

○ **CAPITAL** .... National Capital	● **CITY** .... City	● Village .... Village
◎ **CAPITAL** .... State Capital	● **Town** .... Town	Urban Area

MAP SYMBOLS

▪ .... Place to Stay	▼ .... Place to Eat	● .... Point of Interest

✈	.... Airport	⯃	.... Cycling	⬚	.... Museum	⬚	...... Swimming Pool
⊛	.... Bank	⚲	...... Golf Course	⬚	...... National Park	⬚	.... Synagogue
⬚	..... Bus Terminal	⊕	.... Hospital	⬚	..... Police Station	⬚	.... Telephone
⚏	..... Caravan Park	⬚	...... Internet Cafe	⬚	.... Post Office	⬚	.. Temple (Buddhist)
⌂	.... Cave	⁂	.... Lookout	⬚	.... Pub or Bar	❶	.. Tourist Information
✚ ⬚	.... Church	⬧	.... Monument	⬚	... Shopping Centre	⬚	.... Winery
⬚ ⬚	... Cinema/Theatre	⬢	.... Mosque	⬚	...... Stately Home	⬚	.... Zoo

Note: not all symbols displayed above appear in this book

LONELY PLANET OFFICES

Australia
Locked Bag 1, Footscray, Victoria 3011
☎ 03 8379 8000 fax 03 8379 8111
email: talk2us@lonelyplanet.com.au

USA
150 Linden St, Oakland, CA 94607
☎ 510 893 8555 TOLL FREE: 800 275 8555
fax 510 893 8572
email: info@lonelyplanet.com

UK
10a Spring Place, London NW5 3BH
☎ 020 7428 4800 fax 020 7428 4828
email: go@lonelyplanet.co.uk

France
1 rue du Dahomey, 75011 Paris
☎ 01 55 25 33 00 fax 01 55 25 33 01
email: bip@lonelyplanet.fr
www.lonelyplanet.fr

World Wide Web: www.lonelyplanet.com *or* AOL keyword: lp
Lonely Planet Images: lpi@lonelyplanet.com.au